SELECTED LETTERS OF
DYLAN THOMAS

SELECTED LETTERS OF
DYLAN
THOMAS

Edited and with commentary by
CONSTANTINE
FITZGIBBON

A NEW DIRECTIONS BOOK

Manufactured in the United States of America.

New Directions Books are published for James Laughlin by
New Directions Publishing Corporation,
333 Sixth Avenue, New York 10014.

SECOND PRINTING

For
Pamela Hansford Johnson
with gratitude

Introduction

IN SELECTING these letters of Dylan Thomas's for publication, I have been guided by certain principles of which the reader should be aware. The first of these is that Dylan Thomas's primary claim on the attention of posterity lies in the fact that he was a poet of great brilliance, whose apparent obscurity is rapidly being dissolved in the river of time to reveal poems of a style and content that are both unique and highly personal. In order to help this process of elucidation, I have therefore included almost all his letters that bear directly on his methods of composing poems, on his views concerning poetry in general and on his own poetic ambition. In three cases, however, I have departed from this principle. He was a stern and at times a harsh critic of other men's poems, as is perhaps to be expected of a poet who was so severe and exacting a taskmaster to himself. Some of his comments on poets still alive are cruel and on occasion unfair, and these I have omitted, where I could not simply leave out the name of the poet condemned. Many years hence, when *The Collected Letters of Dylan Thomas* can at last be published, these pungent comments will be of interest to another generation and will not inflict pain upon the living. Secondly, in his long 1933–4 correspondence with Pamela Hansford Johnson he comments, in almost every letter and often at very great length, on the many poems of hers that she was sending him. These poems when published are long out of print, when not published are lost. His comments are often repetitive. I have therefore cut these, save where they throw light on his view of poetry as a whole: what remains will, I believe, convey quite adequately his critical attitude at the age of twenty or twenty-one. Thirdly his long correspondence, almost entirely about his own poems, with Vernon Watkins has already been published under the title *Dylan Thomas: Letters to Vernon Watkins,* and is therefore readily available to scholars interested in the minutiae of his methods of composition. I have, as a result, reprinted here only those letters that seemed to me the most interesting in a correspondence that deserves to be read as a unit.

The second guiding principle has been that Dylan Thomas was also a most brilliant writer of prose, though he regarded this as very much a secondary activity except perhaps for a brief period between 1936 and 1938. He seldom theorizes about his prose, as he did so often about his verse, but when he does so, I include what he has to say. However, many of his letters are in themselves works of art, in particular some that he wrote towards the end of his life, written and rewritten half a dozen times or more. Thus John Davenport has told me that after a visit from Dylan he found innumerable drafts of a letter to Princess Caetani asking for financial help. This is probably the letter on pages 330–2, and for those interested in Dylan's prose style it repays careful study. Whenever a letter seems to me to be written with such close attention to style and form, I have included it, for it belongs with the rest of his prose work. In any event, in almost all such cases the content is of interest. It may well be that future critics will think that with Dylan, as with Byron, whom in some ways he so closely resembled, the poet's letters are his finest prose.

My third principle of selection, which should perhaps rank first, has been that these letters should give, so far as possible, the flavour of the man, of his complex, enchanting, maddening and ultimately tragic personality. I have not made this choice as a biographical, but rather as a psychological, document. My connecting notes and my comments on individual letters will, I trust, enable the reader to read them in the context of his life, but for further detail I must, without pretence of modesty, refer him to my *Life of Dylan Thomas*. The brief chronology that follows this introduction will enable him to see where Dylan was and perhaps what he was doing when each letter was written.

In some cases, and with some of his best letters, comment is almost irrelevant. Many of them are the written equivalent of conversation. Dylan Thomas's conversation was remarkable: it could be witty, it could be bawdy, it could be profound—particularly when poems were discussed—but it was almost never about abstractions. And it was always directed to the person with whom Dylan was talking: it was communication, not display. That is why he had so many friends, and made friends of all sorts so very quickly. He would give his undivided attention, if he liked the man, to a postman in a Welsh pub as easily as to a Nobel prize-winner in a New York restaurant, and would do his equal best to entertain them both. He would fit into their moods and their worlds. That is why so many of his almost countless friends had and have such differing views of him. It would be wrong to say that he was all things to all men: he was always and unmistakably Dylan. But in his social intercourse, at least until he had had too much to drink, he strove for human contact, for communication, and he knew that this requires a certain compromise on either side. Thus his conversation could not be preserved, as Oscar Wilde's has been, in an anthology of anecdotes and epigrams. Dylan could and did tell very funny stories of his own creation, he could be and was highly epigrammatic in certain circles, but the essence of his outward personality was the ease that hides shyness and the adaptability that conceals the fear of rejection. This becomes apparent in the very different tones visible in letters to different people. Perhaps we all do this to some extent. But Dylan, to a higher degree than most of us, had the exquisite courtesy never to forget whom it was that he was addressing, nor what was likely to interest or please him.

Such then are the principles on which these letters have been selected: to cast light, with his own pen, upon his poems: to present his unpublished prose: and to show the man, as his friends knew him.

The reasons why more than half of his letters are omitted are, perhaps, obvious though sometimes regrettable. Some letters are trivial, some mere duplicates of others (this is particularly true of his many begging letters), some are damaging to men or women still alive. But I hope that this selection will at least serve as an echo.

Meanwhile I must express my thanks and acknowledgments to Pamela Hansford Johnson and Vernon Watkins whose advice and help have once again proved invaluable; to Wyn Henderson, Keidrych Rhys, Randall Swingler and many others who have cleared up knotty problems for me; to Davina Cole, Wyn Henderson, Shelagh Macklin and Mrs Rietman, who typed, often from very difficult manuscripts; and finally to all those persons who let me see the letters here reproduced. I have done my best to acknowledge the source of each letter, or its location when first I saw it; if some are unacknowledged, it is because I do not know where the originals are, or, in the case of one collection, because the owner did not allow me to see the originals and I have had to rely on copies. With two exceptions almost everyone, both librarians and private persons, has been most helpful. I express my heartfelt thanks.

Chronology

22 Oct. 1914. Born in Swansea.

Sept. 1925–July 1931. At Swansea Grammar School.

Aug. 1931–? Nov. 1932. Reporter on *South Wales Evening Post.*

Mar. 1933. First poem published in London.

? Aug. 1933. First visit to London.

Sept. 1933. First appears in 'Poets' Corner' of the *Sunday Referee.*
Correspondence with Pamela Hansford Johnson begins.

Mar. 1934–Nov. 1934. Frequent visits to London.

10 Nov. 1934. Moves to London.

Dec. 1934. *18 Poems* published.

Apr. 1936. Meets Caitlin Macnamara.

10 Sept. 1936. *Twenty-five Poems* published.

11 July 1937. Marries Caitlin Macnamara.

Jan. 1939. Llewelyn Thomas born.

24 Aug. 1939. *The Map of Love* published.

20 Dec. 1939. *The World I Breathe* (his first book to appear in the United
States) published.

4 Apr. 1940. *Portrait of the Artist as a Young Dog* published.

? July 1940. Leaves Laugharne.

Sept. 1940. Begins to work in films.

1940–1942. Living between London and Wales.

Late 1942. Brings Caitlin to London, Chelsea.

Mar. 1943. Aeronwy born.

1943. Begins to broadcast extensively.

Summer 1944–summer 1945. At New Quay, Cardiganshire.

Summer 1945–spring 1946. In London.

7 Feb. 1946. *Deaths and Entrances* published.

Mar. 1946–May 1949. In or near Oxford.

Spring 1947. Visits Italy.

Mar. 1949. Visits Prague.

May 1949. Moves into the Boat House, Laugharne.

July 1949. Colm born.

Feb.–June 1950. First American tour.

Jan.–May 1952. Second American tour.

10 Nov. 1952. *Collected Poems* published.

Apr.–June 1953. Third American tour.

Oct. 1953. Final departure for America.

9 Nov. 1953. Dies in New York City.

The first letter of Dylan Thomas's that has been preserved is dated 10th June 1931, when he was a little over sixteen and a half years old. He was then in his last term at the Swansea Grammar School, where he edited the school magazine—most of which he wrote himself—but was for the rest uninterested in school activities, scholarly or otherwise. He was about to get a job on a local newspaper, the *Swansea Daily Post*, and he was living in his parents' home. He hoped, however, to continue to be an editor and he planned to start a literary periodical to be called *Prose and Verse*. He therefore advertised both for contributions and for subscriptions. One of the first contributions that he received was from Trevor Hughes, a young Swansea writer only a few years older than himself. They were to become and remain fast friends for several years. Trevor Hughes indeed was perhaps the first grown man to recognize Dylan's literary talents.

TO TREVOR HUGHES

10th June 1931
5 Cwmdonkin Drive,
Swansea

Dear Mr. Hughes,

Thank you very much for your short story, 'Freedom'. It is one of the few contributions I have received so far which does really suit the requirements of the type of periodical I wish to produce. Needless to say your story is accepted without reservation. But, unless I can foster interest in the notoriously stony bosoms of the local public, neither 'Freedom', nor any of the other material at my disposal, will ever see the light in the form of Prose & Verse. For it is subscribers more than contributors I need now—I am not speaking of your type of contribution which is as gratefully received as it is rarely sent—for out of the two hundred subscribers at two shillings each needed to cover the cost of publication (£20) I have amassed just over twenty. More will

1

be coming this week, but that is all I have been absolutely guaranteed so far. Admittedly, I have not written to any of the people who are supposed to be interested in literary matters; I put the particulars and my address in the local paper, and trusted to the depth of their interest, which, I am beginning to believe is almost legendary. I shall wait a few days before I knock at the houses of the nouveaux riches and the Swansea bohemians, asking, in a hopeless voice, for donations, or at any rate, subscriptions.

I wonder whether you could help me in a business way as much as you have helped me in a literary way. If you could gather the names of as many subscribers as possible towards Prose & Verse, and then give them in to me, you would be doing a great deal towards furthering my project.

I am,

Yours faithfully
D. M. Thomas

MSS.: Lockwood Memorial Library, Buffalo

Throughout that summer and autumn of 1931 Dylan saw a great deal of Trevor Hughes. They made excursions into the countryside, discussed literature at length and drank beer together. Dylan was now working on the newspaper—Job was one of the senior reporters—and also acting with the amateur company at the Little Theatre. That winter Trevor Hughes went up to London and found work there.

TO TREVOR HUGHES

14th February 1932
5 Cwmdonkin Drive, Swansea

Dear Trevor,

Your letter was late, but mine is later, and the trouble is I have no real excuse except the chronic and self-condemnatory one of innate laziness to offer you. You will, I know, brush aside my faltering cry of 'Work'. You have been one of the World's Workers long enough to realise there is always time enough to complete one's correspondence. So, humbly, and with a forced smile upon my lips, I tender—what a curious word that is—apologies as sincere as they are lame. I have such little time. My right hand is injured from a colliery accident. I have no ink.

Now that the bridge of reticence is spanned (God, what style! The man's a Burke!) and the waves of consciousness met (The man's a Lawrence!) writing becomes distinctly easier. A phrase is a phrase again an image an image now.

The purple of your dreams is untroubled—unstirred as you say. I am glad to hear that. What I shall be gladder to hear is that you are still writing. You may not know it, but you could, with practice and time, become a very considerable prose-writer. You've got something to say and a new way to say it.

My purple is turning, I think, into a dull grey. I am at the most transitional period now. Whatever talents I possess may suddenly diminish or may suddenly increase. I can, with great ease, become an ordinary fool. I may be one now. But it doesn't do to upset one's own vanity, and this letter is gradually becoming a cry from the depths.

I am playing in Noel Coward's Hay Fever at the Little Theatre this season. Much of my time is taken up with rehearsals. Much is taken up with concerts, deaths, meetings and dinners. It's odd, but between all these I manage to become drunk at least four nights of the week. Muse or Mermaid? That's the transition I spoke about. M or M? I'd prefer M any day, so that clears the air a lot.

Job is a very curious man, isn't he? I agree he has no sense of humour and a dislike of alcohol, but I have heard him laugh, and he told me, quite jocularly, that my voice, inexplicably enough, was always thicker at three o'clock than it was at 12.30—you see I dine in town. (Dine? You compliment yourself sir.)

When you write next, and I hope you write soon, enclose either a story you have written or the particulars of one you are writing. Otherwise, my insane annoyance will know no bounds.

I can't concentrate. My mind leaps from thought to thought like a wombat. I'll have to stop. Beside, the ink is getting low.

Dont forget to write soon.

Is your Ma any better?

How is London treating you, if at all?

Mermaid?

Are you writing much?

Am I writing much?

Are we writing much?

Can you write? can I write, can we write?

Clear up this lot in your next epistle. Pardon mine. It's a Sunday morning; I've got a head like a wind-mill.

Dylan

MSS.: Lockwood Memorial Library, Buffalo

The letter that follows is probably the next in the correspondence. Dan Jones, now Dr Daniel Jones the composer and author, was Dylan's closest childhood friend. More than this it was he, more than any other single person, who introduced Dylan to modern, and what was then ultra-modern, literature. He was slightly older than Dylan, and had won a scholarship to Oxford.

The Mermaid is a public house in that part of Swansea called the Mumbles. Paul de Kock was a French nineteenth-century writer whose novels were considered pornographic. 'Domdaniel' was a story, never completed, on which Dylan was then working.

Trevor Hughes had recently been afflicted with great and repeated domestic tragedy, and was subject to bouts of severe pessimism and melancholia. This letter is perhaps an early example of Dylan reflecting the recipient's mood: it also shows the strong influence of Trevor Hughes's prose style upon his own. Who Anna may have been, I do not know.

TO TREVOR HUGHES

1932 ?

5 Cwmdonkin Drive, Swansea

Dear Trevor,

I have the villain of a headache, my eyes are two piss-holes in the sand, my tongue is fish-and-chip paper. Dan Jones is staying here for a few days, and last night and the night before we wasted our substances and distended our bellies with low company. It's difficult to write, because the bending of the head hurts like fury. And my hand 'ain't what she was. Oh, woe, woe, woe, unto Mumbles and the oystered beer.

Dan is playing very weak music. I wish I loved the human race; but ghouls, vampires, women-rippers, deflowerers of weeny infants, warted soaks, pimps and financiers pass by the window, going God knows where or why, in a dream up and down the hill. It isn't a silly face, it's a purposeful face, with a big vein of rottenness, an almighty canker growing under the nose. The horrid moustaches of the human face; dripping with last twelvemonth's tears and beer, stained with egg, cows' kisses, udder-rubbings and night custard. The teeth, the werewolf's teeth, big as gob-stoppers, windy teeth, full of holes, just like Ramsay MacDonald, crunching on the paste and putty of our hearts—what utter snobs we are to imagine that the card-shapes under our waistcoats hold more of beauty and sensitivity than the little cupid abortions of gelatine beating under a whore's shirt. Look at the notices

4

in tram-cars: Spitting on Christ prohibited. In the parks; Do not walk on God. What shall it be? Jew's mucus or gentile's praise? Ripeness is all—all balls. We're over-ripe, we night-walkers, cunt-stalkers, wall-chalkers. The women of the world, perpetually out of perspective, cry Focus, Focus. Is it our fault that we misinterpret them? Perhaps we've got to be superstitious, natural, supernatural, all one huge satanic process. Our words—'Give me a half-pint, a Hovis, a book by Paul de Kock, and thou, thou old lavatory chain'— are spells to drag up the personified Domdaniel pleasure. Everything we do drags up a devil.

Last night, Dan and I, none too brightly, for the womb of the Mermaid was empty and the radiogram blaring, discovered we had too little feeling. We almost lost our tempers proving how unfeeling we were. The petty emotions, hates, loves and spites, we said grandly, were nothing to us. We were artistic Ishmaels, and we scorned with a ha and a ho the lusts that shot up bushes, burning like cantharides, all over the waterless places. Sex was an instrument to annoy women with and the anachronistic loyalties, faithfulnesses, holy desires, gratitudes, mercies and charities were no more than words to cover over the evil intentions of our inferiors. (Because they are inferior these blubbery-eyed old men, stiff-dickied, these shop assistants with their ingrown virginities priced at $1/11\frac{3}{4}$, these friggin boys, these wailing mothers, and disappointed communists, and God help our godheads if we can't play Christ, and Christ was always the white sheep among the black, the superior, the natty gent in a tramps' ward.) We started to remember old cruelties, the purposeful raising of desire in girls we knew and the purposeful unsatisfying of them, the tongue-outs, the embarrassments, the ungrateful things we had done, the muck we'd uttered with our tongues in our cheeks. Our lowest feelings when we sit drunk, maudlin, holding a whore's hand, are the highest feelings of the maggoty men around us. Artists don't have to die etc. They crucify themselves etc. All the old bullshit.

Why am I writing this? Is it to show the futility of effort? Are you playing Freud to me as I tell you that, like Havelock Ellis, I bore holes in the floor to piss through, or cut a pigeon's throat as I copulate? I don't know why or what, but last night we, who had no feelings, spoke passionately, waving our arms in the air, saying Desire is nothing, as we stroked her buttocks, saying Hunger is vanity, as we swilled and wallowed, damning the conventions as we took a bus home and lied when we got there. Why I am writing this is uselessness. Stop it. I can't shout like Lawrence, of the red sea of the living blood. Why can't I put a message in a parcel? There's muck in the soul of man, and a devil in his loins. God was deposed years ago, before the loin-cloth in the garden. Now the Old Boy reigns, with a red-hot pincers for a penis. Here's to him.

But the sun's shining, there's a froth on the park trees, mother has made Welshcakes, I've got a large Players, and my shoes are off. Take now content, no longer posturing as raped and reaped, the final emblem. Very contented I promise to write again soon. And soon I'll be seeing you, sadder than ever before with a cough and a headache, I say, Goodbye Trevor, mind Anna and the blue trees. Like a devil too, I wave my pincers at the stars.

Dylan

MSS.: Lockwood Memorial Library, Buffalo

In late 1932 Dylan was dismissed from the newspaper, but in friendly fashion. As this letter shows, he continued to write for the *Post*, as well as for its weekly stable companion, the *Herald of Wales*. The B.O.P. is the *Boy's Own Paper*, which is precisely what its name implies. The poem in *Everyman* has not been traced. The story called 'The Diarists' was not published in the *London Mercury*, nor was any other story by Dylan Thomas. It is possible that both were published pseudonymously, the story under another title, though this seems unlikely.

TO TREVOR HUGHES

December 1932 ?

5 Cwmdonkin Drive, Swansea

Dear Trevor,

In my more melancholy moods, when the brightest things can be made to appear the most drab, and when life—you probably detest such a sententious opening to a letter as much as I do—offers little more than the preferably sharp razor and the necessarily painless drug, I turn over, with a certain perverse pleasure, all my ill-fortunate experiences which amount as nearly to heartbreak as one, like myself who has never felt the desire to fall in love, can realise. And among those experiences I count that of losing, apparently for ever, my friendship with you. It is easier to write than to talk about it. I have a horrid fear, when talking, of plunging into a hot bath of sentimentality; but on paper the most girlish thoughts can be expressed without much fear of a sudden immersion into those wicked waters.

I realise I am writing the most utter nonsense. This is what I mean to say: When you left Swansea I thought that the end had come of a friendship, quite short, that I, at any rate, will always think of happily. We wrote letters for a time. Then they stopped for God knows what reason. Laziness on both our parts probably. I didn't hear from you for six months. My sister stayed the night in Torrington Square and asked where you were. Nobody appeared to know. And then the day before Christmas, a much over-rated holiday, I received a letter. Thanks for it, but don't let it be in the way of a conscience-reliever. Dont lie back, a smug smile on your face, and hands folded over a pious belly, thinking, 'Well, well everything is alright now. I've let the cat out, done my day's accounts, and written to that little fellow in Swansea—what's his name, now? Thomas I think, No, No, Williams,' and after the strain of such concentration is over, warming your hooves before the fire, letting a contented mind dwell on the beauties of the world-to-come, where suburban gentlemen, small as agates on an alderman's thumb, hymn the Eternal Bowler.

I am writing you a long letter, and I want to hear regularly from you. Let the mind run. If you haven't any facts I won't mind—I rarely have any of my own. Spin a lot of sentences out of your guts. If nothing else, it's practise for that polished prose of yours, which one day, and I don't mean maybe, is going to earn you a respectable living and the plaudits of sound literary people. You have a solidity in your writing—for once I use that word in a complimentary, not derogatory sense—which is bound to get you somewhere one day. It's that solidity and perception of detail, sense of values, if you like, an at-the-root indestructibility of matter, which I haven't got. All I may eventually do is to

Astound the salons and the cliques
Of half-wits, publicists and freaks.

I was out for little else. The majority of literature is the outcome of ill men, and, though you might not know it, I am always ill.

Logically that means I am producing, or am going to produce, literature. But I have given up believing in logic long ago. Which is a very logical thing to do. Please believe me when I do throw a little bouquet now and then. You'll have enough buckets thrown in your direction because of your literary sincerity. So treasure, like a squirrel, every complimentary bunch of flowers, for though the scent's bound to wither and the stalks drop, and, of course, he who gave the flowers utterly forgotten, the memory—bring out your tracts! How everyone nowadays is so terribly frightened of becoming maudlin!—will last for a long time. That kind of memory, and the hope that that kind of memory fosters, are among the few things that keep a man alive. Faith, he said, smoothing his tired brow with buffalo's milk, keeps a man breathing,

7

When the moon sinks behind the lawn
With an old smell of camphor and collected roses
Will you and I wait for the certain sign,
And wait for ever one supposes,
Watching, our hands cupped holding matches,
Sun after moon, and then again
The same celestial repetition.

What you want to keep out is morbidity, even though everything
is despondent. Not a forced cheerfulness, nor a preoccupation with
the pleasant instead of the dirty side. But there's a fountain of cleanness
in every one, Bach found it, Mozart, D. H. Lawrence, W. B. Yeats
and probably Jesus Christ. Have a shot at finding it. You may
succeed, I never will. And, for God's sake don't take to writing
poetry in my style. Try Longfellow, not me. This sounds awfully
conceited. Try your own style. But then, of course, that's what you
really are doing.

To answer a question of yours, I have left the Post. They offered
me a five years' contract in Swansea. I refused. The sixteen months or
less I was on the staff were already showing signs of a reporter's
decadence. Another ten years and I'd have been done for. Not that I
was afraid of the Mermaid's grip. I still sedulously pluck the flower
of alcohol, and, occasionally, but not as often as I wish am pricked
by the drunken thorn (an atrocious image!) No, what I feared was
the slow but sure stamping out of individuality, the gradual content-
ment with life as it was, so much per week, so much for this, for that,
and so much left over for drink and cigarettes. That be no loife for
such as Oi!

I am attempting to earn a living now—attempting is the correct
word—by free-lance journalism, and contribute, fairly regularly,
humorous articles to the Post, less regularly literary articles to the
Herald, now and then funny verses to the B.O.P. (what a come-down
was that O men of Israel!) seasonable and snappy titbits for the Northcliffe Distributive Press. I had a bad poem in the Everyman, and a
story is accepted by Squire in the Mercury—that's where you want to
plant your stuff. When the story 'The Diarists' is published, I'll
send you a copy. It isn't particularly good. I still write poems, of
course. It's an incurable disease. I write prose too, and am thinking
of tackling a short novel. THINKING I said.

The purple of your dreams is, I hope, still purple. I am glad to hear
official responsibilities are not preventing you from writing fiction,
as they have, in the past, prevented you from writing letters.

Dylan

8

Remember me quite sincerely, and not as a matter of form, to your sister and mother, and don't on any account, save the imperative dictates of the angels, fail to write soon, again, and again soon.

MSS.: Lockwood Memorial Library, Buffalo

The next letter to Trevor Hughes, whose much-loved brother had died of tuberculosis and whose mother was seriously ill, again reveals Dylan's reflection of mood. The reference to Roman Catholicism should be understood in relationship to Trevor Hughes's interest in spiritual matters.

The dying aunt is Ann Jones, and the 'insanitary farm' Fern Hill.

TO TREVOR HUGHES

January 1933

5 Cwmdonkin Drive,

Swansea

Dear Trevor,

Thank you for your letter, and excuse mine, written in pencil on the world's worst paper. The only thing I hope is that it is legible. You certainly did let the mind run, scorning even the mechanical medium of the typewriter, and penning your thoughts—they were of course sunk in a deeper melancholy than mine could ever be—in immaculate caligraphy. Your letter was beautifully sincere. In my little ivory temple, immune from the winds and whips of the world, shut, if you like, Proustlike in my conservatory, I find it hard to think in any but a cynical and theoretical manner of the blood and withering diseases you have such first-hand knowledge of. Beauty, you say, comes out of suffering. For we are born in others' pain and perish in our own. That, to those who have suffered, and in spite of it are still capable of appreciating and, sometimes, creating beauty, must appear perfectly true. I can't appreciate it, firstly because I have known very little physical suffering and no actual hardships or heartbreaks, and secondly because, at the root of it all, I can't reconcile life and art. Obviously one is born before one can be an artist, but after that it doesn't matter what happens. The artistic consciousness is there or it isn't. Suffering is not going to touch it. Consciousness of beauty—and what that elusive thing is I haven't the remotest idea; woman isn't, because she dies. Nothing that dies is truly beautiful—is born with you or not at all. Suffering is not going to create that consciousness, nor happiness, nor anything else you may experience. True beauty,

9

I shall always believe, lies in that which is undestroyable, and logically therefore is very little. But it is there. Not that what you have suffered does not influence you deeply and terribly. It is bound to upset and disillusion, carry you, unless you are careful, to the margins of madness. But it is not going to touch in any way at all that which really makes you an artist; knowledge of the actual world's deplorable sordidness, and of the invisible world's splendour (not heaven with God clothed like a deacon, sitting on a golden cloud, but the unseen places clouding above the brain). Suffer as much as you like, that world remains. It is only the complexion of the outer, and absurd, world that changes.

Words are so misleading. I don't urge a monastic seclusion, and preoccupation with the invisible places (you see, even my facile flow of self-conscious images fails, and I am left with the word 'places', which is quite unsatisfactory). That is Roman Catholicism. (One day I may turn Catholic, but not yet.) You must live in the outer world, suffer in it and with it, enjoy its changes, despair at them, carry on ordinarily with money-making routines, fall in love, mate, and die. You have to do that. Where the true artist differs from his fellows is that that, for him, is not the only world. He has the inner splendour (which sounds like a piece of D. H. Lawrence or a fribble of Dean Inge). The outer and inner worlds are not, I admit, entirely separate. Suffering colours the inner places, and probably adds beauty to them. So does happiness.

You may think this philosophy—only, in fact, a very slight adaptation of the Roman Catholic religion—strange for me to believe in. I have always believed in it. My poems rarely contain any of it. That is why they are not satisfactory to me. Most of them are the outer poems. Three quarters of the world's literature deals with the outer world. Most modern fiction does. Some of it, of course, is purely reporting of outer incidents. Not that that need condemn it. Perhaps the greatest works of art are those that reconcile, perfectly, inner and outer.

There is nothing new in what I have been saying. But it sprang to my mind when I read your reply to my sincere advice—shun morbidity (as I haven't). You say, or at least imply, that you couldn't because of your terrible misfortunes. And I say that you can. Morbidity is sickness, unhealthiness. That need play no great part in your stories. They might be very fine stories anyway. But they will be finer without. This is not a stirring plea to be British, only to let the inner conscious-ness—you've got it because you are an artist from the little I have read of yours—develop. 'Raise up thine eyes to the hills.'

And now, when I look back over what I have written, I feel conscious that there is a terrible lot of priggery in it—intellectual and emotional priggery. It reads like a chunk of adulterated Chesterton revised by Sir Edward Elgar. Looking over it again I doubt its sincerity, such is the horribly argumentative, contradictory nature of my mind. Give me a sheet of paper and I can't help filling it in. The result, more often than not, is good and bad, serious and comic, sincere and insincere, lucid or nonsensical by the turns of my whirligig mentality, started from the wrong end, a mentality that ran before it walked, and perhaps will never walk, that wanted to fly before it had the right even to think of wings. Tomorrow, the next moment, I may believe in my beastly inner and outer. I may be believing in it now. It may be facile, immature humbug. Again it may be the expression of a real belief. The prince of darkness is a gentleman. But his satanic convolutions and contradictions abide by no gentlemanly conditions.

As I am writing, a telegram arrives. Mother's sister, who is in the Carmarthen Infirmary suffering from cancer of the womb, is dying. There is much lamentation in the family and Mother leaves. The old aunt will be dead by the time she arrives. This is a well-worn incident in fiction, and one that has happened time after time in real life. The odour of death stinks through a thousand books and a thousand homes. I have rarely encountered it (apart from journalistic enquiries), and find it rather pleasant. It lends a little welcome melodrama to the drawing-room tragi-comedy of my most uneventful life. After Mother's departure I am left alone in the house, feeling slightly theatrical. Telegrams, dying aunts, cancer, especially of such a private part as the womb, distraught mothers and unpremeditated train journeys, come rarely. They must be savoured properly and relished in the right spirit. Many summer weeks I spent happily with the cancered aunt on her insanitary farm. She loved me quite inordinately, gave me sweets and money, though she could little afford it, petted, patted, and spoiled me. She writes—is it, I wonder, a past tense yet— regularly. Her postscripts are endearing. She still loves—or loved— me, though I don't know why. And now she is dying, or dead, and you will pardon the theatrical writing. Allow me my moment of drama.

But the foul thing is I feel utterly unmoved, apart, as I said, from the pleasant death-reek at my negroid nostrils. I haven't really the faintest interest in her or her womb. She is dying. She is dead. She is alive. It is all the same thing. I shall miss her bi-annual postal orders. And yet I like—liked her. She loves—loved—me. Am I, he said with the diarist's unctuous, egotistic preoccupation with his own blasted psychological reactions to his own trivial affairs, callous and nasty? Should I weep? Should I pity the old thing? For a moment I feel I should. There must be something lacking in me. I don't feel worried, or hardly ever, about other people. It's self, self, all the time. I'm rarely interested in other people's emotions, except those of my paste-board characters. I prefer (this is one of the thousand contradictory devils speaking) style to life, my own reactions to emotions rather than the emotions themselves. Is this, he pondered, a lack of soul?

There was a certain theatrical quality about your letter, too, a little of the purple dreams of the yellow nineties, the red roses of the wine, and the final falling of the final curtain. And now I wish I hadn't said that. The histrionic quality was sincere. Your answer to my DO NOT BE MORBID statement was enough to shove me under the table. Go on writing future letters just as theatrically. Tons of good stuff comes out of the theatre. This, again, may sound facetious. I am not deriding what you spoke of. That goes too deep for the playhouse. The self-conscious can escape, momentarily, by dressing their soul-cries in ermine and astrakhan, and letting them stand before the footlights before the footlights fade out.

I am interested in what you say about your story-writing—the quick, quiet, dream-come idea, the lifting of the pen, and then the faces of past miseries and horrors obliterating everything. I can realise why your output is so small. In your letter you say it will be something if we can help each other towards, I forget your exact image, the planting of seeds in the forest of literature or something like that. From my seat among the ancients, may I, for one moment, shake a few stalactites off my frosty beard, and give you a little advice? I asked you, in a letter, to write from your guts. You did. And of course you do in your short stories. But why not, just for a few times, put a sheet of paper in front of you, and without thinking twice, write half, or a quarter, or all of a short story. Don't begin with a polished idea in which every incident is fixed in your mind. Just shove a girl on a sea-shore on a summer day and let her make her own story. Write, write, regardless of everything. Your present method of story writing —the draft after draft, the interminable going-over-again—can be compared to the method of the marksman who spends weeks and weeks polishing his rifle, weeks and weeks cleaning it, weeks and weeks getting the exact ammunition for it, weeks and weeks deciding on a target, weeks and weeks weighing his rifle in his hand, weeks and weeks weighing it in a different way, and, at the end of the year, having a pop at the bull's-eye. Why not, for a change, fire off round after round of ammunition from any old gun you can get hold of. You'll miss hundreds of times, but you're bound to get the bull's-eye a lot of times too. You'll find the hit-or-miss, the writing with no plot, technique will help you considerably in loosening your mind and in getting rid of those old stifling memories, which may, unless you are careful, get in the way of your literary progress. I now rest my beard upon my knees again, and the crows return to their nests.

Swansea still stands where it did. No one has blown up the churches. The Watch Committee still stands on its one leg and hands its glass eye round from member to member. There are the taverns and cafés. There is the hospital and the mortuary. Job—I have seen him several times since I left him—still drones around the edges of the local news like a Cornish bee. My friend Dan still tears his fearsome chord from the entrails of a much-abused piano. I continue writing in the most futile manner, looking at the gas-oven at periodic intervals, with a wistful glimmer in my eye. My sister is soon to be married. She will live in London. I shall stay occasionally with her. The London Mercury has not yet printed my story. Neither have I received a cheque for it. I have just evaded a libel action through some pot-boiling article of mine for the Northcliffe Press. A lone tea beckons on the table.

I have been a long time replying to your last long letter. Please forgive me and let your next be longer.

Dylan

MSS.: Lockwood Memorial Library, Buffalo

This letter, ostensibly tendered as advice to Trevor Hughes, can also be read as Dylan's affirmation of his own poetic purpose, as he understood this to be a few months before he first left Swansea.

TO TREVOR HUGHES

9th May 1933
5 Cwmdonkin Drive,
Swansea

Dear Trevor,

Many months have passed between the posting of my letter, which as you say, you found provocative of thought, and the written result. I have a very good mind indeed to send you a shallow letter. You would probably send an answer to it by return of post, for the more lengthy and profound (?) my letter, the longer do you seem to take in replying. This little reprimand over, and never, I hope, to be repeated, I can now tackle your correspondence in as serious a manner as I am able.

You ask me for criticism of your story, but I would rather, if it is the same to you, and even if it isn't, criticize the attitude of mind behind its writing and not so much the result of such an attitude. Again I was struck by the brilliance of your letter, a subterranean brilliance, if you will, and too near the rim to be pleasant. But brilliance nevertheless, of a high imaginative order as they say in textbooks. But how much do I prefer the passionate wordiness of your letter to the unnecessary wordiness of your story! I am not going to, even if I could, destroy your story in a couple of cheap sentences. It is a bad story, but that doesn't matter. You are, and you know it despite your self-termed apologia, capable of a much better story than that. It must be as unsatisfactory to you as it is to me.

This is my main contention: Why, when you can, as you show in your letter, struggle with the fundamentals of belief, and the rock-bottom ideas of artistic bewilderment, morbidity and disillusionment, when you can write with a pen dipped in fire and vinegar, when you have something to say, however terrible it may be, and the vocabulary to say it with, do you waste time on the machinations of a Stacy Aumonier plot and on the unreal emotions of a paste-board character whose replica one could find in a hundred novelettes of the 'nineties'? Why go to the cafés and French cafés at that, for your plots? You are not really interested in people. I doubt whether you are a fiction writer at all. Why go to the cafés for worn plots when the only things you are interested in are the antagonistic interplay of emotions and ideas, the rubbing together of sensibilities, brain chords and nerve chords, convolutions of style, tortuities of new expressions?

My contention boils down to the fact that the short story is not your medium. What your medium is I can do nothing but suggest. It is prose, undoubtedly, but an utterly non-commercial prose, a prose of passionate ideas, a metaphysical prose. I repeat my last letter's advice to you: Write, write, write, out of your guts, out of the sweat on your forehead and the blood in your veins. Do not think about Mr Potter's guide to the salesmanship of short stories, produced, apparently, on the lines of the Ford works. Do not bother your head about the length of the stuff you are writing. Don't descend, that is the main point. You descended badly in the story I have at my elbow as I write. You tagged on, under some misapprehension as to the quality of the intellect of your audience, that magazine little bit about the inquest. You see that sort of ending in the Windsor and the Pall Mall periodicals, and even in the London Mercury on an off month. (Please don't think that anything I say resembles a sneer at your work. I am honestly doing my best to help you.) You descended from the Stygian heights —a very true paradox—of your real style, which I have only seen in

14

your letters, when you make your pseudo-French characters say, 'It is very difficult—difficile,' or words to that effect. Whether the addition of the foreign word is to add atmosphere, or merely to instruct junior readers, I don't know. In either case it is a ghastly thing to do. What you want to do is to sit down and write, regardless of plot or characters, just as you write a letter to me. You know Middleton Murry's prose, and Lawrence's non-fiction prose. Murry is not interested in plots or characters. He is interested in the symbols of the world, in the mystery and meaning of the world, in the fundamentals of the soul. And these things he writes about. These things you are interested in. Write about them. You have a style as individual as Murry's. Murry writes with a sober, contemplative pen, and you with an inebriate pen. But it doesn't matter a bit. Write a story (if you must write stories) about yourself searching for your soul amid the horrors of corruption and disease, about your passionate strivings after something you don't know and can't express. (This is one of the few ways of knowing it and expressing it.)

In one letter I remember telling you to steer clear as quickly as you could from morbidity and morbid introspection. Now I am telling you to delve, deep, deep, into yourself until you find your soul, and until you know yourself. These two bits of advice aren't contradictory. The true search for the soul lies so far within the last circle of intro-spection that it is out of it. You will, of course, have to revolve on every circle first. But until you reach that little red hot core, you are not alive. The number of dead men who walk, breathe, and talk is amazing. (I am not taking any trouble over the phrasing of this letter. You, from your peak of sultry glory where the gods of clauses and of commas walk under the exclamatory moon, might be annoyed with my rough way with words and grammar. But the faster I write the more sincere I am in what I write.)

It is not Utopian advice that I am attempting to ladle out to you. It is terribly practical. Forget the 'annihilative reverse' of the rejection slip, and the 'intellectual catarrh'. Plunge, rather, head first and boldly into Charon's ferry. And who knows? Charon's ferry may turn at last into the river Jordan and purge you of ills.

You speak of a world in which the effort of thought will be un-necessary. Write of it. You speak of your 'curious surprising of beauty' and its metamorphosis into ugliness, your 'charred crucifix'. Write, write, write. You are one of the dark-eyed company of Poe and Thompson, Nerval and Baudelaire, Rilke and Verlaine. Be a Thompson in prose. You complain that you haven't his genius. Of course you haven't, but you have your own red sparks of genius.

And you must not allow the old stagnant waters to put them out. You say you have the honey. You say you have nothing but honey and greyness. You have honey and senna. Mix them together, dip your pen into them and write.

Don't forget: To hell with all the preconceived notions of short story writing, to the world of dyspeptic editors and rejection slips, to the cardboard men and women. Into the sea of yourself like a young dog and bring out a pearl.

Remember: you are not another Aumonier, another Manhood, another Bullett. You are one of the white-faced company whose tears wash the world.

To hell with everything except the inner necessity for expression and the medium of expression, everything except the great need of forever striving after this mystery and meaning I moan about. There is only one object: the removing of veils from your soul and scabs from your body. Reaching a self freedom is the only object. You will get nearer to it by writing as I have suggested—make your own variations—than by all the writing of clever and eminently saleable short stories. And, lastly, it doesn't matter a damn whether your stuff is printed or not. Better a bundle of pages on which you have strived after something worth striving after, than a story in every magazine and an international reputation.

Come back to Wales in the Neath of adversity. Leave London and come to Neath. That is particularly bad advice I'm sure, but it is written from purely selfish motives—from a desire to see you and talk to you again, to hear you speak, to read your mad prose, and to read you my mad poems. Three months are all too long.

Dylan

MSS.: Lockwood Memorial Library, Buffalo

This one needs no comment, save that Coney Hill is probably a mistake for Colney Hatch, a well-known lunatic asylum.

This forthcoming visit to London was probably, though not certainly, his first. He was now eighteen and a half years old.

TO TREVOR HUGHES

July 1933
5 Cwmdonkin Drive,
Swansea

I looked through a pile of old papers the other day, and found your last letter to me. Reading it again, I realised how very good it was. I

16

know of nothing, in any literature I have read, to compare with it. Among the cribbed and cabined, the bored and strangled destructivism of so much modern writing, it stands out supremely, a vast wind of pessimism (though that is not the right word) among the despondent farts of the little men. Poe has nothing on you. He had his ravens, you have a flock of monstrous carrion-pickers. Forget the Hound of Heaven and bay down your own hell hounds. I am looking forward to your sequel to Burton-Hughes' Guts of Melancholia. If I can but make you write always as well as you can write in the letter by my side, then I shall be doing, for once in my life, something worthwhile.

I am writing this near a two-foot statue of Echo, who cocks her marble ear at me, listening to me mouth these words aloud. Do you want your story back? I have lost it, and one of my own in which there were four characters—a dead man and three hawks. It was very pretty. I am writing this in an odd mood, smoking, toasting my toes. I have such a bad headache that it is hard to write connected sentences. When a new thought comes I want to put it down, slipshod, in probably a most inapt place. My pen started to write 'ebony'.

Oh, to be a critic! 'Mr X shows promise. This week's masterpiece. Mr Y is bad.' So simple, no bother, no bleeding of writing. I think you bleed more than I do, God help you. Remember the Worm, read a meaning into it's symbol—a serpent's head rising out of the clean sea.

Think this self-conscious. A pal o' mine's mad, in Coney Hill, saying all the time, so his aunt says, 'Keep a straight bat, sir'. We have a new asylum. It leers down the valley like a fool, or like a snail with the two turrets of its water towers two snail's horns.

How good it is to feel that I can write anything to you. Your last letter shows me that you understand, though understand what I shall never know more than I shall know the answer to the looking-glass question, 'Why is this me?' Remember—'Don't be morbid'. Sometimes only a worm is companion, its grey voice at your ear the only voice. (This, too, you might laugh off. 'Juvenilia'. A shrug. A slight condecension. Boys will be old men.)

I will be in London for a fortnight, from Bank holiday on, staying on the Thames with Nancy, my sister, who married some months ago. Write and tell me when I can come to see you, or where I can meet you sometime. We might go to the ballet together. Or we might sit and talk. Or sit. Beachcomber would love this.

Dylan

MSS.: Lockwood Memorial Library, Buffalo

Back from London he found life in Swansea even more constricting than before. In the spring of 1933 Geoffrey Grigson had published the first number of *New Verse*, which is perhaps the most outstanding magazine of its kind to have appeared in England in this century. Dylan Thomas had so far had only one poem published in London, 'And Death shall have no dominion', which had appeared in the *New English Weekly* in May of that year, and no serious writing elsewhere. It is curious that he appears to have then seen no actual copy of *New Verse*. The poems he sent to Grigson were returned: it is not known which ones they were, but it is probable that they were published later in the *Sunday Referee* and elsewhere.

TO GEOFFREY GRIGSON

August 1933

5 Cwmdonkin Drive,
Swansea

Dear Sir,

I am sending you some poems to be considered for publication in New Verse, about which I read in John O'London's Weekly, a month or two ago. Out of a large number of poems I found it extremely difficult to choose six to send you. As a matter of fact, the enclosed poems were picked almost entirely at random. If you think the poems unsuitable for publication, and if, of course, you are sufficiently interested, I could let you see some more. I probably have far better ones in some of my innumerable exercise books.

A considerable period lies between the writing of some of the enclosed poems, as perhaps you will be able to see. Whether time has shown any improvement I find it hard to say, as I have developed, intellectually at least, in the smug darkness of a provincial town, and have only on rare occasions shown any of my work to any critics, generally uninterested or incompetent. If you could see your way clear to publish any of these poems, or find in them sufficient merit to warrant the reading of some more, you would be doing me a very great favour. Grinding out poetry, whether good or bad, in such an atmosphere as surrounds me, is depressing and disheartening.

Yours sincerely,
Dylan Thomas

MSS.: Lockwood Memorial Library, Buffalo

During his visit to London in August he had offered his poems to Sir Richard Rees, who had taken over the editorship of the *Adelphi* from Middleton Murry in 1930; one poem, 'No man believes', appeared in the September issue of that periodical. But more important both to his career as a poet and to his life as a man was the publication of 'That sanity be kept' in the *Sunday Referee* on 3rd September 1933.

That newspaper, now long defunct, had a feature called 'Poet's Corner', ater corrected at Dylan's suggestion to 'Poets' Corner', which awarded prizes each week to the poets there published. These ranged from half a guinea (about $2.50 in American currency in 1933) for the best, to small objects such as penknives for those judged less successful. The editor of 'Poets' Corner' was a most eccentric person called Victor Neuberg, nick-named 'The Vickybird', who was anxious to create a coterie and who therefore sought the company of young poets of both sexes. The best poet he had published before Dylan's first poem appeared was Pamela Hansford Johnson, who was to achieve fame as a novelist. She was two years older than Dylan.

When his poem appeared, she wrote from her London home to congratulate him on it. His reply must have been written a few days after 10th September. It is characteristic that he should have added two years to his age: at that time he was shy about his extreme youth.

'Blaen-Cwm' was the home of his mother's brother, Tom Williams, a small cottage between Fern Hill and Llanstephan.

TO PAMELA HANSFORD JOHNSON

Mid September 1933

Blaen-Cwm,
Llangain,
nr. Carmarthen

Beginning this letter in the way I do, removes the necessity of using the formal, 'madam', the stiff, 'Miss Johnson' (rather ambiguous but entirely unmeant), and the impudent, 'Pamela' (also ambiguous, also unmeant). It removes a similar obstacle in your case.

If it is 'gruesome' to reply to letters, then I am as much of a ghoul as you are. I return frequently, in the characterless scrawl God and a demure education gave me.

Incidentally, when you reply to this—and let it be long and soon—don't write to the above address. It is merely a highly poetical cottage where I sometimes spend week-ends. Reply to my nasty, provincial address.

Thank you for the poems. Mr. Neuberg has payed you a large and almost merited compliment. 'One of the few exquisite word-artists of our day', needs little praise or abuse from me. But, still, I must compliment you upon 'The Nightingale', by far the best of the three poems. Comparing that with the, 'Sea Poem for G', one of the most perfect examples of bloody verse I have ever seen, and with other Referee poems, is like comparing Milton with Stilton. I like the other two poems, you sent me, but not as much, and the first stanza of 'Prothalamium', I don't like at all. Too many adjectives, too much sugar. And the fifth and sixth lines are pure cliché. 'I write from the heart', said a character in some novel I've forgotten. 'You write', was the reply, 'From the bowels as after a strong emetic.' Not that I apply that rude remark to Prothalamium; I'm quoting not because of it but for the sake of it.

Of course you are not an aged virgin. But many of the contributions to the Poet's Corner are, and woo the moon for want of a better bedfellow. I can't agree with you that the majority of the Referee poems are good. With a few exceptions they are nauseatingly bad. Your's are among the exceptions, of course. Do you remember a poem called '1914' printed a couple of weeks ago? Do you remember the 'Sea Poem'? Do you remember those few diabetic lines about an Abyssinian cat? What did you think of last week's 'Blue Gum Tree'? That is a real test of taste. Like that, you like anything. It would be hard to realise the number of people bluffed into believing 'Blue Gum Tree' to be a good poem. Its sprawling formlessness they would call 'modern', its diction 'harsh but effective', and some of its single lines, such as, 'The cloth of silver over a white balustrade', would send them into some sort of colourful rapture. In reality, the formlessness is the outcome of entire prosodaical incompetence, the diction is not even tailor-made but ready-to-wear, and the 'colourful' lines are like cheap, vermilion splotches on a tenth-rate music-hall backcloth. In the very interesting copy you sent me of the first Poet's Corner it is explained that when, during any week, no poetry is received, the best verse would be printed. That would be perfectly all right if it did happen. But the pretensious palming off of doggerel (not even verse) as 'arty' poetry is too much.

It was on the same grounds that I objected to 'Poet's Corner' as a title. There was a time when only poets were called poets. Now anyone with an insufficient knowledge of the English language, a Marie Corelli sentiment, and a couple of 'bright' images to sprinkle over the lines, is called a poet. He can't even leave his excretion in a private spot. They give him a public 'Corner' to leave it in (a vulgar metaphor! I hope you don't object).

This is in no way a biased or personal attack. It's the general principles of the thing I like to use as Aunt Sallies. Pray God, I, too, am not 'arty'. A physical pacifist and a mental militarist, I can't resist having a knock—or even a blow at a dead horse—when all I put my faith in is utterly contradicted. I put my faith in poetry, and too many poets deny it.

To return to your poetry (you must excuse my slight soap-box attitude): It shows a tremendous passion for words, and a real knowledge of them. Your grasp of form and your handling of metre is among the best I know to-day. And—the main thing—your thoughts are worth expressing. Have you written a great deal? when do you write? I'm interested to know all sorts of things like that, and to see some more.

What I like about your poems is that they state not contradict, that they create, not destroy. Poem after poem, recording, in sickening detail, the wrinkles on the author's navel, fill the contemporary journals, poem after poem recording, none too clearly, the chaos of to-day. Out of chaos they make nothing, but, themselves part of the post-war carnage, fade away like dead soldiers. So much new verse (do you know 'New Verse'?) can be summarised into, 'Well, there's been a hell of a war, it's left us in a mess, what the hell are we going to do about it?' The answer is fairly obvious. But is it worth writing about? No, you answer in a loud voice, or at least I hope you do. You are not like that, and your 'not-ness' alone is worth all the superlatives at my command.

So you are the same age as myself. You say one has enough time ahead, too, to regret one's immodesty. The more I think of my Referee poem the less I like it. The idea of myself, sitting in the open window, in my shirt, and imagining myself as some Jehovah of the West, is really odd. If I were some Apollo it would be different. As a matter of fact, I am a little person with much untidy hair.

With this letter you will find two poems of mine. I am sending them to show you, or to hope to show you, that I can do much better than you think from what you have seen of mine. Incidentally, I'd better mention that the poem starting, 'No food suffices' is, though complete in itself, the woman's lament from an unfortunately unfinished play. I think this needs mention; references in the poem would otherwise cast aspersions on the nature of my sex. The second poem you may not like at all, it is distinctly unfashionable.

After my violent outburst against the Referee poets, you'll probably read my two poems with a stern & predujiced eye. I hope you don't, and I hope you like them. Whether you do or not, tell me.

Can I keep your poems for a little longer?

Dylan Thomas

PS. The Woman poem is to be printed in the Adelphi. I can't resist adding that, because I like the magazine so much. The Jesus poem is probably to be printed in T. S. Eliot's Criterion, though, as a rule, the Criterion doesn't print any metaphysic verse at all. I mention the 'C' for the same reason that I mention the 'A'.

PPS. I am staying, as you see, in Carmarthenshire & have forgotten to bring your address with me. I am trusting to luck that 12 is the right number. If it is, you will read this explanation, if it isn't, you won't. So there was no point at all in writing it. D.T.

MSS.: Lockwood Memorial Library, Buffalo

In the remarkable correspondence that follows—and went on for more than a year—few of his letters are dated and all of hers are lost. Even though Lady Snow, as she now is, has done me the great kindness of going through them with me most carefully, it is possible that the tentative dates may be wrong. It seems, however, probable that this is his second letter to her.

David Gascoyne was a surrealist poet of Dylan's age, the rival *Wunderkind* in those days. *Cold Comfort Farm* by Stella Gibbons was an immensely successful parody of the rustic novel—in particular those of Mary Webb. Runia Tharp was Neuberg's principal assistant on 'Poet's Corner', and Steyning was where he lived.

Henceforth I have corrected small spelling mistakes, since these serve only to distract the reader.

TO PAMELA HANSFORD JOHNSON

Undated, probably September 1933
5 Cwmdonkin Drive,
Uplands,
Swansea

Thank you. I should have been very sorry hadn't I posted the card. The mutual outpourings of a crank and a romantic (there is little doubt as to which is which) would have been lost to posterity; creeds and beliefs, that will change as the years change us, but are nevertheless sincere, would have remained unexpressed, insults and compliments, hasty judgments, wisdoms and nonsenses, would have been unsaid; and a considerably nice friendship would have been broken up almost before it began. Even now twelve heartfelt pages are titivating the senses of a Dead Letter superintendent, and three heartfelt poems are lying beneath the pillow of some postmaster's boy in the depths of Llangyfellach or Pwllddu. (I, too, know not a word of Welsh and these names are as fearsome to me as they are to you.)

What have I missed in your letter? Three poems, twelve passionate pages of affirmation and denial, a thought on Shakespeare and a sob for Siegfried! Dear God, and all for three-halfpence.

There is so much to talk about in your last letter, to agree with and to argue with most violently, that I must light my cigarette, and then, with a steady hand and a more-or-less contented mind, tackle the points in order from the very beginning to the last curve on the last letter of the totally unnecessary 'Johnson'.

1. I'm glad you're not as riddled with silliness as I am. I should have carried on for months, never writing your name, consciously avoiding such an ordinary gesture of friendliness as calling you Pamela, or Pam, or whatever I am to call you. My unusual name— for some mad reason it comes from the Mabinogion and means the 'prince of darkness'—rhymes with 'Chillun', as you suggest. I don't know what Pamela rhymes with, unless the very cultured way of saying 'family', and therefore cannot reply with a little couplet.

2. The Vicky-Bird, undoubtedly of the parrot variety, doesn't appear to like what we sent him last week. But then I always said his taste was abysmal. I sent him a very short and obscure poem with one indecent line. What did you send him to be so ignominiously placed among the spavined horses? A very short and obscure poem with two indecent lines? No I hardly think so. He doesn't want to give too many prizes to the same people, on principle. He must print the work of others sometimes, and spread the vomit evenly and impartially over his pages. Miss Gertrude Pitt must show her mettle, rusty tin to me; and Mr. Martineau must patch his broken heart with a sentimental song.

3. I am in the path of Blake, but so far behind him that only the wings of his heels are in sight. I have been writing since I was a very little boy, and have always been struggling with the same things, with the idea of poetry as a thing entirely removed from such accomplishments as 'word-painting', and the setting down of delicate but usual emotions in a few, well-chosen words. There must be no compromise;

there is always the one right word: use it, despite its foul or merely ludicrous associations; I used 'double-crossed' because it was what I meant. It is part of a poet's job to take a debauched and prostituted word, like the beautiful word, 'blond', and to smooth away the lines of its dissipation, and to put it on the market again, fresh and virgin. Neuburg blabs of some unsectarian region in the clouds where poetry reaches its highest level. He ruins the truth of that by saying that the artist must, of necessity, preach socialism. There is no necessity for the artist to do anything. There is no necessity. He is a law unto himself, and his greatness or smallness rises or falls by that. He has only one limitation, and that is the widest of all: the limitation of form. Poetry finds its own form; form should never be superimposed; the structure should rise out of the words and the expression of them. I do not want to express only what other people have felt; I want to rip something away and show what they have never seen. Because of the twist in myself I will never be a very good poet: only treading the first waves, putting my hands in deeper and then taking them out again.

But even that, to me, is better than the building of perfectly ornate structures in the sand. To change the image, one is a brief adventure in the wilderness, and the other a little gallop on an ordered plot of land.

4. I apologise for, No Man Believes, but I really didn't think it was obscure. I understood it so perfectly myself, but I was probably the only one who did. And even that's ungrammatical.

5. But why Wordsworth? Why quote that decay? Shelley I can stand, but old Father William was a human nannygoat with a pantheistic obsession. He hadn't a spark of mysticism in him. How could he be a metaphysicist? Metaphysics is merely the structure of logic, intellect, and supposition on a mystical basis. And mysticism is illogical, unintellectual, and dogmatic. Quote Shelley, yes. But Wordsworth was a tea-time bore, the great Frost of literature, the verbose, the humourless, the platitudinary reporter of Nature in her dullest moods. Open him at any page: and there lies the English language not, as George Moore said of Pater, in a glass coffin, but in a large, sultry, and unhygienic box. Degutted and desouled. Catch him in his cry moods, walking the hills with a daffodil pressed to his lips, and his winter woollies tickling his chest. Catch him in his pompous mood his Virginity and Victoria mood, his heavy-footed humourlessness pursuing a wanton dogma down a blind alley full of broken bones of words. I admit the Immortality Ode is better than anything he ever did (with the exception of the pantheistic creed expressed in Tintern Abbey); among the mediocrity and rank badness it stands out like a masterpiece; but judged from a proper perspective,

along the lines of Shakespeare, Dante, Goethe, Blake, John Donne, Verlaine & Yeats, it is no more than moderately good. All it says has been said before and better, and all it was incapable of saying. Try to rub away its halo of fame and the mist of veneration that has grown up around it; try to forget the drummed in fact that he is an English mystic—: and you will see it chockful of clichés, ridiculous inversions of speech and thought, all the tricks-of-trade of the unoriginal verse-writer whose bluff has not yet been called. I put by its side the poems of Matthew Arnold, and think what a delightfully loud splash the two would make if I dropped them into the river.

Perhaps you gather that I don't like Wordsworth. I'm sorry, but he's one of the few 'accepted' whom I refuse in any way to accept at all. This is my important point about him in summary: He writes about mysticism but he is not a mystic; he describes what mystics have been known to feel, but he himself doesn't feel anything, not even a pain in the neck. He could well have written his Ode in the form of a treatise: 'Mysticism and its Relations to the Juvenile Mind.' Just as an experiment, read him again with my adverse opinions at the back of your mind. I changed from loving to loathing Swinburne in a day. Enough. You shall have your own back.

6. I, too, should like to meet you. This possibly can be arranged, but not before the beginning of September when I am going to see my sister near Chertsey.

Don't expect too much of me (it's conceit to suppose that you would); I'm an odd little person. Don't imagine the great jawed writer brooding over his latest masterpiece in the oak study, but a thin, curly little person, smoking too many cigarettes, with a crocked lung, and writing his vague verses in the back room of a provincial villa.

.   .   .   .

8. I've heard such a lot about 'Cold Comfort Farm' that I'll have to get hold of it. It sounds incredible. Isn't there a Grandma Doom in it who once saw something frightful in the woodshed?

9. The Steyning incidents are almost too good to be true. Mrs. Runia Tharp! I've been muttering the magic names all day. It's enough to Runia, and I hope you'll excuse that. Don't take any notice of what the intellectual bullies told you. Tell 'em you've got more in your little finger than they have in the whole of their fact-crammed brains.

10. But for God's sake don't defend the Sunday Referee literary whippets any more. I'm repeating myself, I know, but I regard the verses printed (with very few exceptions—you, notably) as schoolgirl posies plucked from a virgin garden, and the saccharine wallowings of near-schoolboys in the bowels of a castrated muse. Even the Bentley

25

bodies covering the Ford engines are badly battered. I'd like to carry the image further and say that the chassis is made from a scrapheap of dis-used spare parts. Neuburg indulges in a horrid compromise: between the outlooks of the romanticist and the theorist, the mincing tread of the 'one-line and memorable passage taster and memoriser', and the galumphing of the dogmatic theorist. In fact the compromise between Beer and No Beer. The result is partial inebriation—his muse is never drunk enough to be really emotional and never sober enough to be really intellectual.

11. Please don't type again; the warmest words look cold.

And now I, too, must finish, not because of any business appointment, but because I think I've written plenty. Now it is your turn. There are many things I want to write about, but they'll do next time. I'll expect a letter very, very soon—and as long as mine.

Dylan

PS. Three poems for you. Tell me if you like them or not. And why. I'll do the same if you'll send me some. The 'conversation' poem is very violent, as you will see, the 'Moise' poem very romantic, and the other in my more usual style. Take your choice, mum.

MSS.: Lockwood Memorial Library, Buffalo

I have dated the next letter October 1933, but only on the slenderest evidence. 'Night and Day' is clearly a reference to the Cole Porter song which was the hit of the year. What 'Chestnut Saturday' means, I have no idea.

TO PAMELA HANSFORD JOHNSON

October? 1933
Swansea

Night and Day: A Provincial Rhythm

At half past nine there is a slight stirring in the Thomas body, an eyelid quivers, a limb trembles. At a quarter to ten, or thereabouts, breakfast, consisting of an apple, an orange, and a banana, is brought to the side of the bed and left there along with the Daily Telegraph. Some five minutes later the body raises itself, looks blindly around it, and, stretching out a weak arm, lifts the apple to its mouth. Waking is achieved between bites, and, over the now more-or-less clear scrutiny of the fruit, the webs of the past night's dreams are remembered and disentangled. Then, still weakly but with increasing certainty of touch, the banana is peeled and the newspaper opened. At the last bite I have taken complete possession of the Thomas body, and read the criminal courtcases on page three with great concentration. The orange, incidentally, is never touched until I get downstairs, the process of peeling and pipping being too cold and lengthy for such an hour of the morning. When the reports of rapes, frauds, and murders have been thoroughly digested, I light a cigarette, very slowly lay my head back on the pillow, and then, without any warning, leap suddenly out of bed, tear off my pyjamas, scramble into a vest and trousers, and run, as if the fiends of winter were at my heels, into the bathroom. There, holding the cigarette, I scrape the beard from my face and dab about with a futile sponge. And then downstairs where, after another cigarette, I seat myself in front of the fire and commence to read, to read anything that is near, poetry or prose, translations out of the Greek or the Film Pictorial, a new novel from Smith's, a new book of criticism, or an old favourite like Grimm or George Herbert, anything in the world so long as it is printed. I read on until twelve or thereabouts, when perhaps I have read a quarter of a novel, a couple of poems, a short story, an article on the keeping of bees in Upper Silesia, and a review by somebody I have never heard of on a play I never want to see. Then down the hill into the Uplands—a lowland collection of crossroads and shops, for one (or perhaps two) pints of beer in the Uplands Hotel. Then home for lunch. After lunch, I retire again to the fire where perhaps I shall read all the afternoon— and read a great deal of everything, or continue on a poem or a story I have left unfinished, or to start another or to start drafting another, or to add a note to a letter to you, or to type something already completed, or merely to write—to write anything, just to let the words and ideas, the half-remembered half forgotten images, tumble on the sheets of paper. Or perhaps I go out, spend the afternoon in walking alone over the very desolate Gower cliffs, communing with the cold and the quietness. I call this taking my devils for an airing. This takes me to tea-time. After tea I read or write again, as haphazardly as before, until six-o'-clock. I then go to Mumbles (remember the woman of Mumbles Head), a rather nice village, despite its name, right on the edge of the sea. First I call at the Marine, then the Antelope, and then the Mermaid. If there is a rehearsal I leave there at eight o'clock and find my way to the Little Theatre, conveniently situated between the Mermaid and the Antelope. If there is no rehearsal, I continue to commune with these two legendary creatures, and, more often than not, to conduct metaphysical arguments with a Chestertonian toper, (last night it was 'Existence or Being'.), who apparently makes a good living out of designing scanty and dirty costumes for provincial revues. Then a three mile walk home to supper and perhaps more reading, to bed and certainly more writing. Thus drifts an average day. Not a very British day. Too much thinkin', too much talkin', too much alcohol.

We are both slaves to habit. I do not think that either of us are wide, and can never expect to be wide poets (though doubtlessly, you are a little wider physically than I am). We both have to concentrate on depth. Another average day, recorded above, has passed. I am sitting up in bed, none too sober, with a blank sheet of paper on the eiderdown in front of me. But no words will come. The paper is covered with a divinity of thoughts, but it is as naked as the hand that holds it. The smoke of my cigarette reminds me of a lot of things.

I am going to put out the light, and think vain and absurd and never-to-be things until I fall to sleep.

Chestnut Saturday

Very unfortunately your mirth-provoking story of the mental Don Juan was familiar to me (and why my English doesn't permit me to say, 'I know the story about the man in the pub', I can't imagine). My best story is a very long one, spoken in the broadest of Welsh accents, about Marged Ann and the Vicar, but it's very vulgar and I'm afraid it loses nearly all the little point it has if its written down. I'll keep that as a special treat to tell you, though again I can't imagine why it should be a special treat for you to hear a bawdy story told by a small Welshman in Anglo-Welsh.

Just a Thought

Every thinking man—that is, every man who builds up, on a structure of tradition, the seeds of his own revolution—and every artist—that is, every man who expresses this revolution through an artistic medium—gradually forms a series of laws for living, which he may or may not adhere to. These laws are brought about slowly in the individual mind, are fostered by mental and physical experience. They do not enter the brain as laws but as the raw matter for thought; it is the brain that explores them, finds what is worthy in them, and then dogmatises them. And this is only right. I have theories on the art of poetry, and these theories—as you know, my poor sufferer of so much of my theoretical nonsense—are obviously dogmatic. Those theories entered the brain as impressions. On reading Wordsworth, I was given the impression that, although he talked of mysticism he was not a mystic but only a moraliser. Later I stabilised this impression as a dogma, or rather as two dogmas: Morals are the imposed trimmings around inherent doubt, and: a mystic is a man who takes things literally. All theories are made in that way. And that, too, is only right, for by this method alone can the individual have any hand in the shaping of his own spiritual & mental life. I dislike meat, I dislike killing, therefore I make my own law: It is wrong to eat meat. Thus all the laws in the world have been made. The words Jesus said were only his impressions erected into laws. Rémy de Gourmont has called such an erection the principle of criticism, and, here again, I am in agreement, for Jesus was himself a critic more than anything else; he was given God to read, he read God, understood Him, appreciated Him, and then, stern in his duty as a critic, decided it was his mission in life to explain the meaning of God to his fellows.

God is the country of the spirit, and each of us is given a little holding of ground in that country, it is our duty to explore that holding to gain certain impressions by such exploring, to stabilise as laws the most valuable of these impressions, and, as far as we can, to abide by them. It is our duty to criticise, for criticism is the personal explanation of appreciation. Though a man may hate the world he still appreciates it, and his hate is as valuable as my love; he may hate it for its madness, as I love it for that; he may hate the whole of humanity as I hate the social system that is pulling it to buggery; he may hate pain, as I believe in pain. But we are both critics of life, however misguided. The man who hates & the man who loves are all right, but there is no room in the country of the spirit for the man who accepts, or does not accept, without hate or love.

Hate and love, after all, are nearly one; a blow can be a kiss out of heaven, and a kiss a blow out of hell.

I am writing this at the window. Outside in the cold I see the structure of the sky. Yes, the structure of the sky, the vast grey erection from the edge of here to the edge of nowhere. Yes, the erection of the sky, for the sky is more than a godly dogma made out of a heavenly impression.

'And if thou wilt, remember,
And if thou wilt, forget.'

Your latest poem has made one thing certain to me: your alliance with the Pre-Raphaelite school of poets and with Christina Rossetti, the best Pre-Raphaelite of the whole bunch, in particular. But perhaps you will take the word 'alliance' uncomplimentarily, so let me suggest —and this is most certainly a compliment—that you are the only writer I know to-day who can be said to be in the true Pre-Raphaelite descent. Again, this is not to say that anything in your work is not your own, for above all it is a personal expression; but the merits of that particular, unfashionable, and mis-judged school are shown very clearly in your poems. And, added to these merits, is your own undeniable gusto (a word I hope you won't take exception to), your joy in living and in expressing, and your continual fecundity of natural emotions. Your verse is narrow, but it seems to be a deliberate narrowness, and does not destroy any of its intensity. It is, I am sure, in increased subtlety and elusiveness that you are certain to develop. Christina Rossetti is too little known, except by some of her moralistic verses; she had a most delicate command of rhythm, as you have when you take the trouble, a delicate sense of the sounds of words, and a highly competent technical ability which never appeared laboured because of its simplicity; you have all these, too. But it is her perspective of life that interests me most: sweet, small & narrow, delicate to the point of elusion. Those are four of your qualities, but whereas she was so often caught in semi-theological arguments, was probably too virginal to look at herself in the mirror, and was, on her own admission, disgusted by the sound of laughter, you have a startling sense of humour (I'm not piling on compliments, please, I'm trying to make some sort of a valuation), and a vitality which that other very charming lady never possessed. Walter de la Mare owes much to Christina, and, if there is any labelling to be done, I would put you & de la Mare, that questioning poet, in the same compartment & mark it 'Subtlety and Sensitivity. Perishable. With Care.' You are young, young enough to become subtler and more sensitive, to trust your own sense of harmony much farther, and to produce poetry that will stand out far above the singing of even the best lyricists of to-day.

I do not think 'The King Dies' is a good poem, but it is a promising poem; it is not subtle enough, either in rhythm or in the play of vowels; but it is a poem in what I consider to be the right direction for you; it points towards the progress that you are bound to make. I prefer you when you are more personal than this, when you have no guiding thought behind you, but rather when you are in the process of selection—selecting your images to suit your particular moods, selecting your thoughts to fit those images. The substance of your poetry is always slight, and in 'The King Dies' the slightness is too little redeemed by subtlety of expression. I don't think there is any necessity for me to go into it in detail; all I have to say I've said in this note, and I may appear to have said nothing. That is why I very modestly prefaced the note with a quotation from the Rossetti itself.

Leave the lambkins alone, or never, at least, use them unless you can then take them literally, that is rid of all their associations, or unless you can build new & worth-while associations around 'em. But don't worry about that at the moment; go on writing but more carefully still; submit every syllable to a thorough test; never be afraid of subtlety, even though it may lead you to obscurity (dangerous advice to some, but not to you).

And show me all you write.

A Complaint

This method of letter writing, this selection of odd notes, is very satisfying, but it's a swine in some ways. I write the notes for my letters to you at odd times & in pencil on bits of paper. It takes me a hell of a time to copy them all out on these mammoth sheets.

Put this in your Pipe—and if you haven't got one, I'll lend you mine;
it reeks.

Ha, child, I was as crafty as you. I confess that my reference to your love of Kipling was no more than a highly titivating bait. Of course you don't like his flagflapping, for you know as well as I do that patriotism is a publicity ramp organised by holders of excess armament shares; you know that the Union Jack is only a national loin-cloth to hide the decaying organs of a diseased social system; you know that the Great War was purposely protracted in order for financiers to make more money; that had it not been for the shares in the armament firms the War would have ended in three weeks; that at one period of the War French and German were shelling each other with ammunition provided by the same firm, a firm in which English clergymen and politicians, French ambassadors and German business men all had a great deal of money invested; that Kipling, rejected by the army because of weak physique, is nevertheless a 'I gave my son' militarist; that the country which he lauds and eulogises is a country that supports a system by which men are starved, and fish, wheat and coffee are burnt by the hundreds of tons; a system by which men are not allowed to work, to marry, to have children; by which they are driven mad daily; by which children are brought into the world scrofulous; by which the church is allowed to prevent the prevention of sexual diseases; a system so just that a man is arrested on Christmas

Day for arrears of rates, when his wife is expecting a baby & his children are dying of typhoid fever caused through the eating of bad fish supplied by a profiteering tradesman. Woah! England, my England. And Kipling still flaps his belly for it, and it is easier to bribe a politician than it is to bribe a costermonger.

And what's all this about the 'delicacy of a silver-point drawing' in the five weak lines you quoted from 'The Way through the Wood'.

A Story for the Very Young

Once upon a time there was a little girl. And this little girl, odd to say, was a po-et-ess. She was very ro-man-tic in her out-look, and wrote many nice ro-man-tic poems, using such words as, 'wings' 'melody', & 'breast', all of which was very nice. But she grew older, and vis-it-ors and rel-at-ives said, Oh yes, she is a very nice girl, but what is she going to do? It was ob-vi-ous that she would be a po-et-ess always, or even something more im-moral. So she went on being a po-et-ess, and a kind man put her poems in a litt-le book. But one day she became ac-quaint-ed with a little poet, who was the funniest little poet you could imagine. And he wrote vul-gar poems about wombs and things. Well, dears, the po-et-ess and the little poet went on being ac-quaint-ed, and at last, the po-et-ess took the Wrong Turning. She, too, wrote vul-gar poems, and it was nothing for her to use the horrible word 'cancer' twice in one stan-za. And the little poet went all flower-faced, and wrote a lot of verses about the sun coming up and the moon going down. But the po-et-ess grew tired of her tu-ber-cular muse, and returned to her babb-ling brooks etc. And the little po-et burnt all his so-nice poems, and returned to his vomit and vul-gar-it-y. And they both lived happy ever after.
Moral   Let Cancer Be.

This seems rather a nasty and un-true story, and I don't know why I wrote it. But, then, this letter is such a terrible hotchpotch, written in odd places and at odd times, that the story fits in with the chaotic atmosphere.

Only half an hour ago I picked up the new Referee, & read Mr. Vicky Bird's glowing article of praise. How it warms the cockles of my heart. Let me very boastfully say this: Take all his praise with a barrel of salt; take mine with none at all. I mean all I have said about you & your poems; in his pretty little cage, God knows what the editing parrot means or does not mean.

And his infantile remark about 'never faltering in metre' or whatever he said. It's as if a man said of Wiley Post, 'What a marvellous flyer; one of the greatest things about his success is the skilful way in which he keeps up in the air!' Oh God, oh Montreal! Oh Neuberg! Oh Jesus!

I agree with a lot he says, and I'll say a lot more in my next letter.

Dylan

Pardon all irrelevancies & inconsistencies, the bad grammar & the worse spelling. And take to heart, O Battersea Stich (remark the tonal value of the words) all I have said from the depths of a tidal, though slightly corrupted, heart.

MSS.: Lockwood Memorial Library, Buffalo

In fact *Prose and Verse* never came to anything, though Keidrych Rhys's publication *Wales*, of which Dylan helped edit the first number in 1937, might be described as its successor.

TO TREVOR HUGHES

Postmark: 10th October 1933

(Postcard)

5 Cwmdonkin Drive
[Swansea]

Dear Trevor,

First let me apologise for not having written before this, and secondly for writing such a little now. I have, really, the most concrete excuses, too complicated to put on a postcard. The only thing of importance is this: Prose and Verse, that stillborn child, is to be resurrected. Grocer Trick is to do the financial and business part of it, and I, as it was arranged before, am to edit it. The high standards, formerly set, will be strictly adhered to; but there is one important, new condition. P & V will print only the work of Welshmen and women—this includes those of dim Welsh ancestry and those born in Wales—who write in English. This condition necessarily restricts, but it is that which will make, I hope and trust, the journal a unique affair. Another highbrow periodical, especially produced from a blowsy town such as this—on the furthest peaks of the literary world —is doomed to hell from the beginning. But a new highclass periodical for Welshmen? Up Cymru! I don't see why it shouldn't be a great success. Already Trick is corresponding with universities, libraries, museums, and other intellectual morgues, with spinsters, knights, and philanthropists. Do you know any Welshmen who might be interested in the project? If so, tell me when you write. And when you can, send me along all your original prose still existing. I'd like to go through it carefully and critically, picking out what is suitable for publication. You've got four or five printed pages at your disposal. I'm not going to write any more now. Write and tell me your views.

Dylan

MSS.: Lockwood Memorial Library, Buffalo

Again, the date of this letter is uncertain. The reference at the end to Laugharne is also confusing, but then Laugharne is only across the estuary from Llanstephan, and in those days the town and the village were linked by a ferry.

His reference to 'his disease' is obscure. He thought, or pretended he thought, that he had tuberculosis, a 'poetic' illness in those days with its echoes of Keats.

I omit his criticism of her poems, since it has little interest for most readers. Scholars are referred to the Lockwood Memorial Library, where this correspondence is entombed. The version of this letter here printed resumes when he returns from the specific to the general.

'Laleham arrangement' refers to an intention to meet her—they had not yet met—which came to nothing.

TO PAMELA HANSFORD JOHNSON

Late October 1933

Blaen-Cwm,
Llangain,
near Carmarthen

One day a very tired and bewildered young man will haunt the steps of the General Post Office, crying aloud, in broken Welsh, this one sad sentence: 'Why, in the name of God and the angelic clerks, cannot my letter be delivered to me?' He will be shooed away, but he will always return, crying his same question to a deaf Post Master and a malicious deity.

The trouble is that, for the last fortnight, I have been leading a very nomad existence, a few days in a rat-infested cottage in the heart of Wales, a few days with an eccentric friend, and a few days at home.

34

Consequently, my letters are delivered to all three addresses, redelivered, and delivered again. Your last letter reached me on Saturday. I am replying with the greatest speed and at the greatest length.

When I came down here there were two letters of yours waiting for me—the proverbial twelve pages, and three typewritten sheets, to say nothing of the three last poems. Now I reply to your collected correspondence.

I am staying, as you see, in a country cottage, eight miles from a town and a hundred miles from anyone to whom I can speak to on any subjects but the prospect of rain and the quickest way to snare rabbits. It is raining as I write, a thin purposeless rain hiding the long miles of desolate fields and scattered farmhouses. I can smell the river, and hear the beastly little brook that goes gingle-gingle past this room. I am facing an uncomfortable fire, a row of china dogs, and a bureau bearing the photograph of myself aged seven—thick-lipped, Fauntleroy-haired, wide-eyed, and empty as the bureau itself. There are a few books on the floor beside me—an anthology of poetry from Johnson to Dryden, the prose of Donne, a Psychology of Insanity. There are a few books in the case behind me—a Bible, from Jest to Earnest, a History of Welsh Castles. Some hours ago a man came into the kitchen, opened the bag he was carrying, and dropped the riddled bodies of eight rabbits on to the floor. He said it was a good sport, showed me their torn bellies and opened heads, brought out the ferret from his pocket for me to see. The ferret might have been his own child, he fondled it so. His own eyes were as close-set as the eyes of the terrible thing he held in his hand. He called it 'Billy Fach.'

Later, when I have finished this letter, I'll walk down the lane. It will be dark then; lamps will be lit in the farmhouses, and the farmers will be sitting at their fires, looking into the blazing wood and thinking of God knows what littlenesses, or thinking of nothing at all but their own animal warmth.

But even this, grey as it is and full of the noise of sanitating water, and full of the sight of miserably wet fields, is better than the industrial small towns. I passed them in the bus coming down here, each town a festering sore on the body of a dead country, half a mile of main street with its Prudential, its Co-op, the Star, its cinema and pub. On the pavements I saw nothing but hideously pretty young girls with cheap berets on their heads and paint smudged over their cheeks; thin youths with caps and stained fingers holding their cigarettes; women, all breast and bottom, hugging their purses to them and staring in at the shop windows; little colliers, diseased in mind and body as only the Welsh can be, standing in groups outside the Welfare Hall. I

35

passed the rows of colliers' houses, hundreds of them, each with a pot of ferns in the window, a hundred jerry-built huts built by a charitable corporation for the men of the town to breed and eat in.

All Wales is like this. I have a friend who writes long and entirely unprintable verses beginning, 'What are you, Wales, but a tired old bitch?' and, 'Wales my country, Wales my sow.'

It's impossible for me to tell you how much I want to get out of it all, out of narrowness and dirtiness, out of the eternal ugliness of the Welsh people, and all that belongs to them, out of the pettiness of a mother I don't care for and the giggling batch of relatives. What are you doing? I'm writing. Writing? You're always writing. What do you know? You're too young to write. (I admit that I very often look even younger than I am.) And I will get out. In some months I will be living in London. You shall call every day then and show me the poetry of cooking. I shall have to get out soon or there will be no need. I'm sick, and this bloody country's killing me.

All of which may sound very melodramatic. I don't want to make this letter sound like a third-rate play in which the 'artistic' hero boasts of his superiority over his fellows and moans of his highly poetical disease, or into a mere agony column. I hope you will excuse even the little bit of ranting and self pity I have indulged in.

I did like your illustrations, but the drawing of the oysters was far too good for the poem. I've given up tearing my hair at the products of the Neuberg Academy for the Production of Inferior Verse. I read them, put them aside, and try my hardest to forget. 'To The Hen', is the best thing I have seen in the Referee recently, but it is compensated for by the 'Cornflowers' of Miss Arlett. And now, to complete it all, the Sea Poem woman is assistant editor. Ah well. No more will my vague efforts adorn the Neuburg altar. Now even closer will I hug them to me.

But what's this about form? Are you misreading my cryptic comments? Or have I subconsciously (that word has gone sour since Lawrence flung it at his own addled head, and the Vicky Bird roosted on it) written what I did not intend. Rhyme, certainly, but with qualifications. I've been under the impression that I have defended form in my recent letters and spat me of the sprawling formlessness of Ezra Pound's performing Yanks and others. But, for all I know, I may have reiterated Geoffrey Grigson's vast maxim, 'Modern Art does not need logic or balance', or Herbert Read's statement to the effect that modern art need have no meaning at all.

Now to your twelve pages. Twelve pages, after all, is very little if you have a lot to say. Your flattering description of yourself, aided by the drawing in your last letter, must have given you great amusement. But don't say the drawing's true. And why the desire to look like everybody else? If you were the usual gutless, unimaginative, slang-flinging flapper, your adherence to a conventional style of looks would be excusable. But you aren't. As an individual you should look individual, apart from the mass members of society. For commercial, and sanitary, reasons it is better to dress cleanly. But I do like colour. I don't look a bit like anybody else—I couldn't if I wanted to, and I'm damned if I do want to. I like conversational (your word) shirts. And I see no reason why I shouldn't. Man's dress is unhygienic and hideous. Silk scarlet shirts would be a vast improvement. This isn't the statement of an artistic poseur; I haven't got the tact to pose as anything. Oh to look, if nothing else, different from the striped trouser lads with their cancer-festering stiff collars and their tight little bowlers.

I was surprised to hear that you had written only 30 poems; a bus-going life explains it. May the Kiddies' Kompleat Poetry Set be put to severe work in the future, and may I, humbly and yet critically, cast my eyes upon the virgin words.

And now I have eight poems of yours to do what I like with. And I am going to do what I like with them—criticise each in turn, not very minutely, for nothing short of fifty pages would allow it, but at least in some detail. Remember, that nothing I say, Pamela, is for the sake of being smart, or to relieve any acid emotions I may have bottled up within me. I mean what I say and I mean it to help. Tell me if it is worth my while and your attention. If it is, then I will willingly, more than willingly, criticize in the same way every and any poem you have written.

· · · · · · ·

But let me get off the point for a moment, and make what will probably be quite a futile attack upon your creed of simplicity. I admit that everything should be said as simply as possible, that meaning should never be smothered by conscious obscurity, that the most prized ornamentations of style and phrase have to go under when the meaning dictates it. But that all good poetry is necessarily simple seems to me very absurd. Because I can understand the English of Mrs. Beeton, there is no earthly reason why I should understand the English of Manley Hopkins—or W. H. Davies & W. H. Auden. I see no necessity why the greatest truths of the world, and the greatest variations of these truths, should be so simple that the most naive mind can understand them. There are things, and valuable things, so complicated that even he who writes of them does not comprehend what he is writing.

37

I admire the simplicity of Shakespeare, the easy language of Twelfth Night and the hard language of Coriolanus. I admire the simplicity of Mozart and the bewildering obscurity of the later Scriabin. Both had a great thing to say, and why the message of Mozart, because of its easiness to understand, is rated above the message of Scriabin, which is a separate message and the devil to follow, I shall never know. It is the simplicity of the human mind that believes the universal mind to be as simple.

Thank you for all you have said about the poems I've sent you. I profit by all criticism; yours is far from peurile, and though I am bound to disagree with much you say I agree heartily with most. With this letter I am enclosing two more poems. They are not typed, I'm afraid, but I hope that won't prevent you from reading and criticising them carefully. There is a sort of finality about the type-written word which the written word lacks. Spare no compliment—I don't go all girlish; spare no condemnation—I am used to it and profit by it.

One day I want to send you ten thousand words of prose, 'Uncommon Genesis', a story set in no time or place, with only two characters, a man & a woman. And the woman, of course, is not human. She wouldn't be. If you want it, I'll send it to you. If you don't, I won't.

Whatever you do to letters, story or poems, don't give them the answer that so shocked the pundits of Steyning. If anyone said 'Sez You' after I had shown him or her a poem I think I should wither up. So, please, be genteel even if you must be condemnatory.

Laleham arrangement, though in the air, is oke by me, and if there is any one expression worse than 'sez you' this is it. You are right, of course. December it is. Yes, I do paint, but very little, and the results are extraordinary.

I should have loved to reply to your hideous drawing with an equally hideous one of myself, but no ordinary pencil can do me justice. If I can find a photograph of myself when in the very far distance I will send it to you.

Dylan

PS. Important. I shall be here (Laugharne) until Saturday of this week. If you reply before I leave, and I hope you do, send the letter straight here. It can't go wrong.

MSS.: Lockwood Memorial Library, Buffalo

Yet another undated letter, ascribed to October 1933.

Victor Neuburg had decided that the young men and women of his coterie were interested in the Creative Life.

TO PAMELA HANSFORD JOHNSON　　Late October 1933

In the Bath

The water is lapping upon my abdominal shore, and a cigarette-end, slowly disintegrating, is being carried along by the steaming stream that runs, like a stream from the springs of hell, over my feet. No, this is not an abstraction; I am laying in the bath, smoking Woodbines, and staring, through hot mists, on to the paper that lies on my front. I cover the waterfront. The click click of the geyser sounds like the distant champing of a lady tenor. All is very wet and white, giving rise to thoughts on life and love, on the impermanence of human emotions, the futility of personal effort, the dirty doings of Creative doctors and the sudden alarming thought of Cinderella. Now it is hot and still. Peace, like an old hat, sits on me.

This is nonsense of course, but it is a good opening to a letter; it tears down all formalities; it does away with many of the layers of bluff, double bluff, and self-doubt that so often prevent me from saying what I want to say; it is as intimate as the legs of the Pope's pyjamas.

But it is difficult, in this blasted bath, to know what to write about. In the ebullience of my youth and the limitless depths of my greenaged immodesty, I confess to having opinions on everything under the sun. The opinions are often immoderate, generally impetuous, and always verbose. But that matters very little. The great thing is to think, however wrongly.

What shall I regale you with: an attack on George Too Shaw To Be Good? a defence of Lesbia? a belief in vegetarianism? But no— George is clever but visionless; Lesbia is an aestiaboginous (I can't spell it) island; and vegetarianism is inevitable.

Let me, instead, scrub the marks of the roads from my little feet, cough, spit, and whistle, pull up the plug, and retire, like an emaciated Cupid with pen for arrow, to a bleak, unmaidened bed.

In The Bed

Now that the drunkeness of a too-hot bath is wearing off a little, and the water of the bath has got into the ink, I shall write in pencil a few straightforward (oh yeah?) facts.

Thomas: HIS IDEAS

I am looking forward to what you've written—or are still writing—

of the 'Woman Arisen'; I should love to add my few stanzas, or the ideas for the few stanzas (whichever you like), though my experience of waking with a woman at my side has been necessarily limited.

The medieval laws of this corrupted hemisphere have dictated a more or less compulsory virginity during the period of life when virginity should be regarded as a crime against the dictates of the body. During the period of adolescence, when the blood and seed of the growing flesh need, for the first time and more than ever again, communion and contact with the blood and seed of another flesh, sexual relationships are looked upon as being unnecessary and unclean. The body must be kept intact for marriage, which is rarely possible before the age of twenty; the physical expression of sex must be aaged up for six or more years until for the price of a ring, a licence, cnd a few hampering words, opportunity is presented with all the ceremony of a phallic religion. But so often the opportunity comes too late, the seed has soured, love has turned to lust, and lust to sadism; the mind has become covered and choked by the weeds of inhibition; and the union of two starved creatures suddenly allowed the latitude of their sexes, is doomed from the start. The woman carries her marriage licence about with her as a bitch might carry the testimony of its liberated heat.

Such things may not be pleasant to talk about, but they do exist, and they are evil.

From the first months of puberty, girls & boys should be allowed to know their bodies (I am not trying to twist phrases, nor am I wishing to write down the bare words in all their ugliness). More than that, their sexual expression should be encouraged. It would be very nearly impossible for a young girl to live, permanently, with a young boy, especially if both were in school; they would not live together peaceably; they would have no money, and it would be difficult for them to earn. But the family of the girl should, for a certain time—the time of the mutual devotion of boy and girl—keep the boy in their house. And vice-versa. The lives of the boy and girl would continue individually—there would be school and school associations for both of them—but their domestic closeness and their sleeping together would blend the two individual lives in one & would keep both brains and bodies perpetually clean. And both would grow up physically and mentally uncontaminated and refreshened.

Don't think I'm regaling you with some crank-ridden, pornographic notion. I really believe in what I say, and no argument has ever shifted my belief. It is not a theory, but an adjustment of the present corrupted facts to uncorrupted ideals. The issues of such an adjustment are, of course, tremendous; they attack the basis of established morals and the foundations of society. But are they wrong?*

To expand the argument, let me point out that some sort of attraction or devotion would have to be the prelude of the association of the boy and girl. The two sexes, on reaching puberty, would not be lumped inconsiderately together; the honest friendship of boy & girl would be allowed entire freedom and culmination, that is all. There would be no binding agreements between the two families, and boy and girl could have as many lovers as they wished, until, eventually, they find a lover with whom they could be for a longer time, or for ever.

After that—and pray God it didn't sound like Mr. Mybug in an inspired moment—let me return to the beginning. Send the 'Woman Arises' with your next letter, and, conjuring up the emotions of husbandly love, I shall attempt to send it back with additions—in my next.

But real collaboration has to be more than this. The poem has to be born in the presence of the two authors. And I hope that it won't be very long before that is possible.

Just a Word

You were very stern about the fragments of poems I sent you. They were written when I was fourteen, remember, and they damned well had to be bad.

Uncommon

Tomorrow, when this is posted, I shall send you my 'Uncommon Genesis', that much-promised story. I'm afraid it's rather long, and will take up a lot of your time. Do read it, though, won't you, and tell me exactly what you think of it. It was written just under a year ago, written straight off and never revised. When I was typing it, I saw all sort of sentences that, had I been more careful, I should not have hesitated to correct or cut out altogether. Not being careful, I typed out good and bad. And here it is.

The passages in red type should really be in italics. You'll have to excuse the typing all along: in some places it's abominable. But I'm not very nimble-fingered at the best of times, and my machine, as you've notice from the poems I've sent you, is moody and antique. It possesses all the French accents, but, unfortunately, I write in English.

* This is a question to you.

41

'Uncommon Genesis' is an uncommon story (I'm sorry to preface it with so many absurd remarks), and you'll either like it, or dislike it very strongly. I'm hoping you'll like it. It has to be read with an unbiased mind, for it is written in a high and wordily romantic style that could, if the attention was shifted only momentarily off its meaning, be turned to bathos. But if you do really read it carefully & without prejudice, I don't think you will laugh. But you tell me all about it, if you will. It's just struck me: Since we've been writing to one another I've loaded you with an immense quantity of my stuff; crowds of my poems accompany every letter; and now here comes over 20 closely typed sheets to add to the pile. Perhaps it would be better if I gave you a little rest—not from letter-writing, I'll be damned if I'll stop that—but from the inclusion of so much of my stuff. I know you honestly like it—just as I honestly like so much of the little I have seen of yours—but you can have too much of a good thing.

More about Luv

Thank you for telling me about your lost, but not forgotten, lovers, and if the pages did occasionally remind me of Ella M. Ruck, that composite novelist and poet, they were none the less sincere for that.

And that was a horribly patronising remark, the remark of an introvertive crank on the extrovertism (what a word!) of a far superior person. I'm very sorry. It probably took a great deal of courage for you to tell me about the frigid reader of newspapers upon whom you wasted such a lot of your affection. And who, by the navel of St. Francis, am I to comment on it? You paid me a compliment by telling me about him, & the G.N.L., & the British boy (your taste doesn't seem to lie in the direction of the arty & poetical young men) & the emotional part of me thanks you very much. Never mind the intellectual part: that is nothing.

But why, if you fall in love again—& you are bound to at some time or another—will you not give again all that you gave before, not necessarily That Which Is Dearer etc. but all the energy of your youngness (youth, here is the wrong word), your sweetness etc. (I evade saying everything, you know), your brightness & sulkiness and every other bloody mood and feeling you possess. I said your failing was the failing of loving too much. It is, and it always will be. So fasten your affections on some immaculately profiled young man, and love the swine to death. Love among the angels is a perpetual distemper.

(It didn't remind me of Ella M., really, I loved it, only I'm too xxxx selfconscious to say so, damn my rabbit's eyes!)

Gower is a very beautiful peninsula, some miles from this blowsy
town, and so far the Tea-Shop philistines have not spoilt the more
beautiful of its bays. Gower, as a matter of fact, is one of the loveliest
sea-coast stretches in the whole of Britain, and some of its tiny villages
are as obscure, as little inhabited, and as lovely as they were a hundred
years ago.*

I often go down in the mornings to the furthest point of Gower—
the village of Rhossilli—and stay there until evening. The bay is the
wildest, bleakest, and barrenest I know—four or five miles of yellow
coldness going away into the distance of the sea. And the Worm**,
a seaworm of rock pointing into the channel, is the very promontory
of depression. Nothing lives on it but gulls and rats, the millionth
generation of the winged and tailed families that screamed in the air
and ran through the grass when the first sea thudded on the Rhossilli
beach. There is one table of rock on the Worm's back that is covered
with long yellow grass, and, walking on it, one feeling like something
out of the Tales of Mystery & Imagination treading, for a terrible
eternity, on the long hairs of rats. Going over that grass is one of the
strangest experiences; it gives under one's feet; it makes little sucking
noises, & smells—and this to me is the most grisly smell in the world—
like the fur of rabbits after rain.

When the tide comes in, the reef of needle rocks that leads to the
base of the Worm is covered under water. I was trapped on the
Worm once. I had gone on it early in the afternoon with a book & a
bag of food, and, going to the very, very end, had slept in the sun,
with the gulls crying like mad over me. And when I woke the sun
was going down. I ran over the rocks, over the abominable grass,
and on to the ridge overlooking the little reef. The tide had come in.
I stayed on that Worm from dusk till midnight, sitting on the top
grass, frightened to go further in because of the rats and because of
the things I am ashamed to be frightened of. Then the tips of the reef
began to poke out of the water, &, perilously, I climbed along them
on to the shore, with an 18 mile walk in front of me. It was a dark,
entirely silent, entirely empty road. I saw everything on that walk—
from snails, lizards, glow-worms & hares to diaphanous young ladies
in white who vanished as I approached them.

One day, when I know you even better than I do now, you must
come & stay with me, sometime in the summer. Swansea is a dingy

* This sounds like a passage from a Tourist's Guide.
** Perhaps this accounts for my Complex.

hell, and my mother is a vulgar humbug; but I'm not so bad, and Gower is as beautiful as anywhere.

There is one bay almost too lovely to look at. You shall come & see it with me; we shall both utter words of maudlin wonder, and swoon away on the blasted heath.

My father was a master in the Swansea Grammar School, and still would be, for he is not yet old enough to retire. But the last three months he has spent in the London University Hospital, undergoing treatment for cancer of the throat. He is home now, partially cured and exceedingly despondent. His time limit is even shorter than mine (!). Ours is a nice 'ouse*. There is one unintelligent dog, too, with the highly original name of Spot.

I will write more—not, fortunately for you, more of this depressing serial autobiography—tomorrow. Now I am going to wash and shave, preparatory to travelling to Gwaen-cae-Gurwen (I love introducing names like these), where a spirited melodrama will be rendered by a talented cast. Thank you.

Coplans Comment

Why didn't someone kick that perverted doctor in the bottom? Aren't any of the Creative Lifers men of action? Here in barbaric Wales, where men are men, he would have been stoned to death by members of Y Gobaith Cymru Wrdd.

There's a charming incident in some novel—I can't remember which where a very narsty young man lies at the feet of a very nice young girl, &, looking into her eyes, says, 'You remind me of cabbages and big brown messes—I adore you'. It's much the same type of incident, with the exception that I am sure you do not remind anybody of such things. But, really, the astonishing part of that astonishing party—and it must be pleasant to have a literary party held in one's own little honour**—was the way in which the narsty doctor was tolerated for so long. Creative Lifer or not, I should have bitten him severely in the calf.

Your aversion to him he most certainly will put down to inhibitions on your part; perverted & unsuccessful lechers of his variety never believe that their love-making (far too good a word) could appeal only to the base of the stomach.

Interlude for Refreshments

No, I don't really spit in the piano, so there'll be no need to nail the top down. And I certainly indulge in the singing of lewd

* All this doesn't sound very nice after an invitation, does it? I mean it, though.
** Bah, envy!

44

roundelays. I shall probably turn shy, & hide myself away in the lavatory all day (up the stairs to the right) first.

My only real domestic vice is my indiscriminate sprinkling of cigarette ash over everything and everybody. Apart from this, I am not a particular nuisance, and I smell quite nice. I look about fourteen, and I have a large, round nose; nature gave it to me, but fate, and a weak banister, broke it; in cold weather it is sufficiently glossy to light up any room. When I am about on winter nights there is no need for the gas.

Cough! cough! cough! my death is marching on; the Venus in front of me cocks a marble eye in my direction, & the calendar, with a watercolour view of Lake Como, sways in the incredibly cold wind.

First Epilogue

I was sorry after sending those three sheets of socialism; they were nothing but facts, and facts, unvarnished, are always boring or bewildering. I am not going to indulge in any more propaganda in this letter; I shall keep two or three red hot notes—along with a note on W. H. Auden, the Poet of Revolution—& send them to you next time.

So the Tharp ranks oratory as one of the Fine Arts? I don't know about that, but the speaking of poetry is certainly one of them. You shall read some 'tweety' poems to me one day, &, rolling my Cymric r's, I shall reply.

Second Epilogue

This letter isn't as long as most of the letters I send you, but the long enclosed story does more than compensate. I'll write a very long letter next week; it will probably need a special postman to deliver it all by itself.

And if you don't reply very quickly & at great length, I shall turn myself, with considerable magic, into a winter fly, & come and die in your hair. This is the most terrible threat I know. Let it close the letter, also with an expression of bonhomie, and Old School affection.

Dylan

[*On the back of the sheet—a drawing of himself.*]

I'm sorry about this. It was on the back, & I didn't see it. I don't always draw like that, thank God.

MSS.: Lockwood Memorial Library, Buffalo

On 29th October 1933 Pamela Hansford Johnson was awarded the major 'Poets' Corner' prize, which was to have a book of poems published at the newspaper's expense. This book came out in the spring of the following year with title *Symphony for Full Orchestra*. On 30th October Dylan sent her a postcard of congratulation, and promised that a long letter would follow. Yet this is a comparatively short letter.

He was still pretending to be her own age, and the rigmarole in the first paragraph is almost certainly untrue.

TO PAMELA HANSFORD JOHNSON

First week November 1933

5 Cwmdonkin Drive,
Uplands,
Swansea

Excuses

I've taken a terribly long time to reply, I know, but, during the last week, I have been so utterly and suicidally morbid that my letter would have read like an excerpt from the Undertakers' Gazette. I hope, in the long week that has passed, you haven't forgotten my existence. And please don't be long in replying because I was. I look forward to a letter soon.

On receiving your photograph I went immediately to have my own likeness taken, there being no existent photograph of myself at this stage of decline. Either I proved too much for the delicate photographic plates, or else the photographer has gone moaning away, for I have had nothing from him. I don't want to hold the correspondence up any longer, so here is a very bad and uncomplimentary passport photograph taken two years ago. It's a poor return, but I shall send you a better and more recent photograph when, or if, it arrives. I do look something like the enclosed snap. Imagine the same face two years older, a bit thinner & more lined. The black shirt (strictly non-political) is the same. I am rarely as tidy or as well-groomed as that, and, pray God, I rarely have that cherub's expression. Still, it has its resemblance. Add a few shadows, draw in a cigarette & ruffle the hair: there I am, in my full glory.

Kind Action

I give you full authorisation to use this new letter form. You'll find it very useful. All you have to do is to write odd notes at different

46

times—on whatever subject, & in whatever mood—and then bung them together under terse little headings. Go ahead, girl!

Congratulatory Hand and Helping Hand

Congratulations. Neuberg, for once, has not gone wrong. It is hardly possible to imagine that he could, for the choice was inevitable. I take as much interest in the publication of your poems as I do in the publication of my own. And if they were my own, I could not be more delighted to hear that your poems are to be published.

You will, I suppose, publish all you have written, but I do advise you to be careful in your editing of the earlier poems. There is no necessity at all why one of the printed poems should be bad, providing you use a blue pencil and a scissors with discrimination. If I can help you, in any way, to polish up the final drafts, or to do anything to help your book towards the success it is bound to be, let me know. I'll do my best, too, to advertise the book among those who do not believe Browning to be something to do with gravy. I'll want to buy a copy, too, and to receive a neatly autographed first edition. But don't forget it: if there is anything, anything at all, you would like me to do, I should have the greatest possible pleasure in doing it.

MSS.: Lockwood Memorial Library, Buffalo

The reference to the half-rhymes in 'The force that through the green fuse drives the flower' which was published 'last Sunday' shows that this fragmentary letter was written in the first week of November 1933. It is possible that it is a continuation of the previous letter, thus making together the 'long letter' promised on his postcard. His poem 'The Eye of Sleep' is unknown to me, nor can I trace these half-rhymes in any other poem.

TO PAMELA HANSFORD JOHNSON

Early November 1933

5. Defence of Poesie

What you call ugly in my poetry is, in reality, nothing but the strong stressing of the physical. Nearly all my images, coming, as they do, from my solid and fluid world of flesh and blood, are set out in terms of their progenitors. To contrast a superficial beauty with a superficial ugliness, I do not contrast a tree with a pylon, or a bird with a weazel, but rather the human limbs with the human tripes. Deeply, of course, all these contrasting things are equally beautiful and equally ugly. Only by association is the refuse of the body more to be abhorred than the body itself. Standards have been set for us. What is little realised is that it was only chance that dictated these standards. It is polite to be seen at one's dining table, and impolite to be seen in one's lavatory. It might well have been decided, when the tumour of civilisation was first fostered, that celebrations should be held in the w.c., and that the mere mention of 'eating and drinking' would be the height of impropriety. It was decided by Adam and Eve, the first society lawmakers, that certain parts of the body should be hidden and certain be left uncovered. Again, it was chance that decided them to hide their genital organs, and not, say, their armpits or throats. While life is based upon such chance conventions and standards as these, it is little wonder that any poetry dealing impartially with the parts of the anatomy (not quite impartially, perhaps, for the belly emphasises an abstruse point better than the Atlas-bone), and with the functions of the body, should be considered as something rather hideous, unnecessary, and, to say the least, indelicate. But I fail to see how the emphasizing of the body can, in any way, be regarded as hideous. The body, its appearance, death, and disease, is a fact, sure as the fact of a tree. It has its roots in the same earth as the tree. The greatest description I know of our own 'earthiness' is to be found in John Donne's Devotions, where he describes man as earth of the earth, his body earth, his hair a wild shrub growing out of the land. All thoughts and actions emanate from the body. Therefore the description of a thought or action—however abstruse it may be—can be beaten home by bringing it onto a physical level. Every idea, intuitive or intellectual, can be imaged and translated in terms of the body, its flesh, skin, blood, sinews, veins, glands, organs, cells, or senses.

Through my small, bonebound island I have learnt all I know, experienced all, and sensed all. All I write is inseperable from the island. As much as possible, therefore, I employ the scenery of the island to describe the scenery of my thoughts, the earthquake of the body to describe the earthquake of the heart.

Fatal selfconsciousness prevents me from carrying on in the same noble vein. (How about the idiom to help my argument?) It is typical of the physically weak to emphasise the strength of life (Nietzsche); of the apprehensive and complex-ridden to emphasise its naiveté and dark wholesomeness (D. H. Lawrence); of the naked-nerved and blood-timid to emphasise its brutality and horror (Me!).

There's some truth, too.

48

6. Refutation and Explanation

The 'dream' poem that you like is not the best I have sent you. Only superficially is it the most visionary. There is more in the poem, 'Before I Knocked', more of what I consider to be of importance in my poetry. Please, this isn't boasting. I'm incurably pessimistic and eternally dissatisfied.

So the poor old snail has wound his horn before. It is a long time since I read the Ode to Evening, so long that my memory refuses all responsibility.

But surely you haven't missed one of the biggest warps in my poetry. My melting-pot is all sour. In two out of three of all the poems I have sent you, there has been a steady scheme of consonantal rhyming. The Eye of Sleep is rhymed throughout. I never use a full rhyme, but nearly always a half rhyme.

Take the poem published in the Referee last Sunday (did you like it?)

a weather	a earth	a sings	a flower	rocks
b stars	b head	b land	b trees	streams
xa other	a mouth	a gangs and so on	a destroyer	wax
b trees	a death	a wings	b rose	veins
xa feather	b replied	b fads	a fever	sucks,
				and so on.

I do not always keep to my rhyming schemes with complete faithfulness. As a rule, yes. But perhaps this elaborate explanation has been a waste of time. You may have noticed it all before, for it has a strange effect.

7. Patronising Remark

Certainly let friend Mednikoff read my poems, but don't show him the 'Eye of Sleep' alone. Show him the others, and tell me what he says, won't you, even if, with a sardonic Russian leer, he spits him of all the batch. From your meagre description of him he sounds most interesting, and I'm glad he waxed romantic over your Symphony. But what 'circle' does he move in? The squared circle of the Geometrists? The fleshy circle of the Academicians?

8. Stop Press

The typewriter is still labouring over its Uncommon Genesis. The story was written a year ago, but I have never typed it. The first—and

49

probably the last,—typed copy is for you. It will be ready when I write to you next. I will keep my explanatory comments until then.

9. Forward the Verse Brigade!

I do not think that I have misunderstood your Creed of Simplicity. Perhaps I attacked it from the wrong angle. You were careful in your wording when you contrasted the beauty of simplicity and the beauty of obscurity, of light and dark, for if I think you a Wilhelmina (and I protest I don't; I think you a Pamela), you think of me as some Stygian cesshound forever plumbing the intestinal emotions. You may be right, damn you, but all the words you use, 'beauty', 'simplicity', 'obscurity', mean different things to different people, are based upon individual preconceptions. 'Simplicity' to me is the best way of expressing a thing, and the ultimate expression may still be obscure as D. H. Lawrence's Heaven. 'Obscurity' is the worst way. I thought of a definition of beauty, but, like all such definitions, it is too limited. One of the greatest aspects of it is 'acquaintance plus wonder', but the expansion of this would lead me, through many vague pages, to the point where I started. Beauty, too, is the sense of unity in diversity. This needs no expansion.

And poetry need not appeal to the intelligent mind more than to the unintelligent. It is appreciated to the greatest extent by the unbiased mind. Each genuine poet has his own standards, his own codes of appreciation, his own aura. Reading a poet for the first time, one cannot be acquainted with him, & therefore, judging him by preconceived standards, however elastic these standards may be—one cannot fully appreciate him. One should take first an empty brain and a full heart to every poem one reads: an impossible task. The only possible way lies in the reading & re-reading, preferably aloud, of any new poem that strikes one as holding some and however little value.

The speaking of poetry should certainly be encouraged. I do hope you read aloud. I myself chant aloud in a sonorous voice every poem I read. The neighbours must know your poems by heart; they certainly know my own, and are bound to be acquainted with many passages of Macbeth, Death's Jester, and the Prophetic Books. I often think that baths were built especially for drowsy poets to lie in and there intone aloud amid the steam and boiling ripples.

10. A Potpourri of Original and Unoriginal Satire

> The Tharp that once through Neuburg's Halls
> The soul of humbug shed,
> Now hangs as mute upon your scrawls
> As if that soul had fled.

So sleeps the vice of former days,
So humbug's thrill is o'er,
And hearts that once gave Tupper praise
Now praise you all the more.

I don't know quite what this means, but, apart from 'scrawls',
which was brought in because it rhymed, it appears to be vaguely
complimentary.

God help the Creative Arts Circle. I hope you won't. It would
probably be something like this:

'I will now call on Alberic Morphine to give a reading.
The rows of young women look up; their eyes glisten;
                                        they shiver
With the kind of emotion that's very misleading.
All have fine eyes, yellow faces, vile clothes &
                                        a liver.
They smoke a great deal, bath little, and wear no stays.'

Or like this:

'You would meet Iris, she who lives serene
In the intense confusion of the obscene,
And drags her tea-time sex affair all fresh
To the dinner table, like a cat with flesh;
Lesbia, whose outward form proclaims at least
Some variation as the normal beast;
Onan, recalling complexes before I speak,
His childhood roles of cad and sneak,
Youth's coprolytic loves and grosser fancies
Derived from reading Ernest Jones' romances.'

'You would melt Mrs. Murgatroud Martin:
She tells you of Pater and Pankhurst, of Tagore and
                                        Wilde,
Of man-made laws and the virtues of proteid peas,
Of Folk Song and Art and of sterilized milk for
                                        the child,
Of the joys of the Morris Dance and of Poetry Teas.'

You would hear a lot of nice things about Art, and lots of nice people
would read your poems and say the nicest things, and you would go
home and get sick on the mat.

But, as Ruskin once remarked to Carlyle, Please don't go all stiff-
shirted on me. 'Doesn't any man or woman know exactly what sex

means before life brings that great experience to them?' Yes, you wrote that, and it will need some explaining away at the gates of heaven where the phallus is taken as a fact and not as a peg upon which to hang one's little platitudes.

11. LOVE and HATE

> Scoff at this enchanted Wood,
> Ye who dare.

I wouldn't jibe at the old war-horse. His hooves have beaten out time to nearly all the great orchestral pieces of the world. He introduced Schönberg to England. He arranged these stirring Sea Tunes that quicken the blood of every true-veined Englishman. What feet have not thumped to his conducting of the marches from Pomp & Circumcision. And I like his beard.

There are only two men in England whom I hate with all my heart. Sir Edward Elgar and Mr. Geoffrey Grigson. One has inflicted more pedantic wind & blather upon a supine public than any man who has ever lived. The other edits New Verse. His place is already reserved in the lower regions where, for all eternity, he shall read the cantos of Ezra Pound to a company of red-hot devils.

12. My life. A Touching Autobiography In One Paragraph

I first saw the light of day in a Glamorgan villa, and, amid the terrors of the Welsh accent and the smoke of the tinplate stacks, grew up to be a sweet baby, a precocious child, a rebellious boy, and a morbid youth. My father was a schoolmaster: a broader-minded man I have never known. My mother came from the agricultural depths of Carmarthenshire: a pettier woman I have never known. My only sister passed through the stages of long-legged schoolgirlishness, shortfrocked flappery and social snobbery into a comfortable married life. I was first introduced to Tobacco (the Boy Scout's Enemy) when a small boy in a preparatory school, to alcohol (the Demon King) when a senior member of a secondary school. Poetry (the Spinster's Friend) first unveiled herself to me when I was six or seven years old; she still remains, though sometimes her face is cracked across like an old saucer. For two years I was a newspaper reporter, making my daily call at the mortuaries, the houses of suicides—there's a lot of suicide in Wales—and Calvinistic 'capels'. Two years was enough. Now I do nothing but write, and occasionally make a few guineas out of my dramatic expositions of How Not To Act. A misanthropic doctor, who apparently did not like the way I did my eyebrows, has given me four years to live. May I borrow that foul expression of yours—it isn't yours, really—and whisper Sez You into his ear.

13. A Touching Experience.

After my last letter to you, written from the despondency of a Welsh hill cottage, I ran out of cigarettes and walked three miles to the nearest village, Llanstephan, to buy some.

It was a fool of a night. The clouds were asses' ears. The moon was ploughing up the Towy river as if he expected it to yield a crop of stars. And the stars themselves:—hundreds of bright-eyed urchins nudging each other over a celestial joke. It is a long road to Llanstephan, bounded by trees and farmers' boys pressed amorously upon the udders of their dairymaids. But the further I walked the more lonely it became. I found the madness of the night to be a false madness, and the vast horseplay of the sky to be a vaster symbol. It was as if the night were crying, crying out the terrible explanation of itself. On all sides of me, under my feet, above my head, the symbols moved, all waiting in vain to be translated. The trees that night were like prophet's fingers. What had been a fool in the sky was the wisest cloud of all—a huge, musical ghost thumping out one, coded tune. It was a sage of a night, and made me forgive even my own foolishness.

There was, of course, no cigarette machine in Llanstephan.

14. A Rude Poem

Let me explain first that this was written in a violent mood when there seemed little to do but to insult someone. After reading his comments in the last Referee, I picked on Neuburg to be that someone. Its HARDLY CRICKET, I know, & I'm RATHER A CAD considering he is going to publish all your poems & has published a couple of mine, one very recently—but here it is:

A Sunday paper did its best
To build a Sunday singing nest
Where poets from their shells could burst
With trembling rhymes and do their worst
To break the laws of man and metre
By publishing their young excreta.

A highfalutin little bloke
Conducted (with an artichoke)
The choir of birds who weekly piped
From pages very neatly typed.

53

Hail to the Referee all plastered
With products of the pimp and bastard.

With each prophetic phrase or clause
Dropped from their educated jaws,
The guts of Logic turn about,
The swine of Bathos shows his snout.
With every — verse they print
Their Muse develops a worse squint.

Not all rejoice that Victor N
Is far above the run of men.
A new Messiah of the Muse
Would that we could, like these old Jews
Place on thy head an ink-filled crown
And crucify thee upside down.

15. A Piece of Sentiment

How long have I known you? I seem to have been writing these nonsensical letters of mine for ever, and for ever to have been receiving these letters of yours. But it can't have been for more than a few months. Yet I know you as well as I have ever known anybody in my life. Much of what I write to you is, I know, very silly, and much of it I've regretted as soon as I've posted the letters. But I have written what I wanted to write, I've got all sorts of things off my mind, and I have tried to be honest. I've found a poetess, and one, moreover, who likes my poems. I've found a very good friend. No, I refuse to become maudlin, but I'm glad that I've found you or, rather, that you've found me. I write to several people, but to none with the freedom that I adopt in my letters to you. You don't take offence when I become vulgar, as I so often do, or when I say unpleasant things about the poems of yours I don't like; you don't mind if I attack all the windmills in the world with a rusty pen; and, though you say you find much to laugh at in my letters, you don't, I know, laugh at what I am sincere, really sincere, in expressing. You like my letters. I hope our meeting, when it does take place, will not disappoint you. I won't run myself down any more; by this time you know as many of my faults and shortcomings as I do myself.

This is the first time, I think, that I've written like this, and it will be the last. I only wanted to tell you how much I appreciate you & your letters. Enough. Enough. Let the correspondence now continue as of yore, and still the postman bear into thy house and mine the brilliant products of the Battersea & Swansea Muse, and the dazzling correspondence of two diverse but well-attuned imaginations.

Dylan

This is not a modernist design but an afterthought on a particular glowing sentence. May it stir your curiosity.

[There are some thick black lines crossing out something he had written.]

MSS.: Lockwood Memorial Library, Buffalo

The teasing parodies that follow are hard to date, but the reference to her poem 'Béguinage' in the last paragraph makes Pamela Hansford Johnson believe that it too dates from November 1933, as does the reference to the photographs. Does one detect in this letter a slight tinge of jealousy that she should have won the prize?

TO PAMELA HANSFORD JOHNSON

? November 1933

My dear Pamela (I may call you that, mayn't I?)

So glad to have your letter. What a nice hand you have. You must write to me again some time. I do so love receiving intellectual letters, don't you? It gives you a sort of—how shall I put it—a sort of stimulus, don't you find? And when one is plucking one's own little flowers from the Garden of Poesy (such a lovely phrase, don't you think. It was told to me by a Mr. Wheeble), it helps, nay invigorates one to fresh horticultural efforts, to know that far away from one is yet another soul searching for Beauty ('Truth is Beauty', you know, as Keats so aptly put it) in those Evergreen Haunts.

And my dear, how can I tell you in words—words! ah, frail words! such gossamer cups they be!—the emotions your prose poems inspired in my bosom. (I have often thought, haven't you, that whereas the Upper Classes have bosoms the Working Classes almost invariably have breasts). Those dainty pieces smacked—ah, false pen! See how you play your gay little tricks with me!—of a loveliness which even I, humble in my devotion to the Great God Pan (Elisabeth Browning, you remember) have sought after through many sunny hours. So sweetly indeed did they fall upon my ears (Shakespeare, I think, but if Sir Walter Scott I stand corrected) that I have arranged with Mrs. Grimmfluf that you address our next weekly meeting of the Ladies Culture Guild on 'Inspirations I Have Received'. Is this too personal a title? Perhaps I could arrange for you to speak on, 'The Sexual Habits of Moths.' Our Guild is so entranced with Natural History. Do write to me again. Who knows, maybe I shall let you see my little volume of verse. I call it, 'Thru' Hull with the Muses'.

Yours,
Sinfonietta Bradshaw (Miss).

Kind Lady,

Hearin yew ar a poitess and travel on the tramz I hav beene wonderin if you would care to spare me a 2/6. I have a mutual perculeirity with yew, kind lady: I, too, travel on the tramz, though, being a bachelor of sum 57 years I am no poitess. By perfession I am a Female Impersonator, and I were silk nex to my skin.
Thankin yew for the 2/6, I hope,

I am,
Lesley Pough.

Dar Sir,

We are sorry but we must return your poem. You are, we assume, under a misapprehension. Our offices are the offices of the London Mercury-Manufacturers Association, & not of the Mercury Periodical edited, we believe, by Sir John Sitwell.

Yours faithfully,
Rod, Pole, & Perch Ltd.

Dear Madam,

Will you do us the honour of accepting this small Rhyming Dictionary, a tribute of our sincerest admiration. (Move up the car, please!)

From,
The L.C.C. Tramway Workers Union.

Physiognomical Comment

You do look formidable, my Wilhelmina. I did not expect you to be so full and bright and strong, with such a British chin. What a dominant personality! Tut, girl, what a zest for life! And here I am, small, chinless, and like an emasculate Eton boy. Ah, the waves of self pity that engulf me as I gaze first upon your features and then

56

upon mine. (Even though mine is two and a bit years old, and yours as recent as this morning's dew!) But, to pass from Jest to Earnest, let me thank you for sending your photograph. You are very, very pleasant to look at. There is meaning and strength in your face. I shall hang you in my room. This is certainly one of the things that could have been expressed better. All I have said is probably in the worst taste (don't think I have sent an—untidier letter. Excuse it.)

So now, if I look long upon your photograph, and you, looking upon mine, exercise your imagination in the details of age and cleanliness, we shan't be strangers to each other. From your photograph I know the lines of your face, from your poetry the lines of your mind. I'm not a physiognamist—I can't even spell the damned word—but I see how you bristle (images of a herd of porcupine) with individuality. Look like everybody else? No, no. But then I am biased.

Attack on Bats and Defence of Vermin

Believe me or not, the first two lines of Béguinage are as bad as anything you've written. The image is smart and cheap; it falls too easily on the paper. And the attitude behind it is wrong, relying too much on a quick, admittedly vivid, visual, impression, instead of upon a mentally digested experience. It is written from the mind's eye, not even from the mind's ear, for the sounds are unintentionally ugly. You have seized on a glimpse of what you wanted to express, and not on the still, slow scrutiny.

Your remark about the end of my Feverish poem is entirely justified. I plead guilty to bathos, but offer in excuse the fact that I copied out the poem as soon as I had written it, wanting to get it off to you and too hurried to worry about its conclusion. In the ordinary way I would never have passed it.

Leave me my 'hatching of the hair'. It's verminous, I know, but isn't it lovely? And what is more refreshing than the smell of vermin? Hardy loved to sit beside a rotten sheep and see the flies make a banquet of it. A dark thought, but good and lively. One of the hardest and most beneficial kicks of life comes from the decaying foot of death. Uncover her face, she died young.

MSS: Lockwood Memorial Library, Buffalo

The whole question of Dylan Thomas's health when young is one that I have not been able to solve to my complete satisfaction. On the one hand, his friends in Swansea all believed him to be very healthy: on the other, he himself had already started spreading stories in London that he was dying of tuberculosis. He certainly had weak lungs and a consequent tendency towards bronchitis, and he was certainly asthmatic, which was aggravated by chain-smoking, but it is most unlikely that he ever had tuberculosis. He was, of course, intensely sensitive, to the extent that at this period of his life he seems to have been afraid lest he were going mad. This nervous condition was later both alleviated and exacerbated by drink, but in 1933 he could not afford more than a little beer. However, the image of himself as the damned and dying boy-poet of romantic tradition appealed to him greatly, and he made the most of it to impress others. The letter that follows is an early example of this.

Eliot Crawshay-Williams, a soldier, politician and most prolific author, had produced two volumes of Grand Guignol plays.

'Dayspring' was Pamela Hansford Johnson's original choice of title for her book of poems.

The 'communist grocer' was his friend A. E. (Bert) Trick, of whom more later.

I have cut some two thousand words of detailed criticism of half a dozen poems she had sent him. These add little if anything to remarks already made.

TO PAMELA HANSFORD JOHNSON

11th November 1933

Excuse the worse than usually
terrible writing!

Preface

In my untidy bedroom, surrounded with books and papers, full of the unhealthy smell of very bad tobacco, I sit and write. There is a beautiful winter sun outside, and by my side the oil-stove shines like a parhelion. On the wall immediately in front of me hangs my pastel drawing of the Two Brothers of Death; one is a syphilitic Christ, and the other a green-bearded Moses. Both have skin the colour of figs, and walk, for want of a better place, on a horizontal ladder of moons. The hot water pipes are swearing at me, and, despite the nearness of the stove, my tiny hands are frozen.

Last night I slept for the first time this month; today I am writing a poem in praise of sleep and veronal that stained the ravelled sleeve. These twelve November nights have been twelve long centuries to me. Minute by minute through the eight hours of the dark I lay and looked up into the empty corners of this room. First I would seize upon some tiny thought, hug it close to me, turn it over and over in my brain, hoping, by such concentration, to find my senses dropping away into oblivion. But soon my lips would speak sentences aloud, and I listen to them.

'The man of substance never walks.' Then my lips say 'He only wheels a truck', and, a thousand years later, I understand what I have spoken. Then I would repeat all the poetry I knew, but if I forgot a word I could never think of another to put in its place, unless it was a mad word and had no meaning. Then I would hear my heart beat, and count its beats, and hear their regularity.

And now, thanks to the God who looked with benevolent eye upon the antics of Lot's daughters, I have slept. Now I can reply to your letter and do my dance around your poems.

Some of the enclosed notes—I think this newspaper style we have adopted in our last letters suits our particular kinds of mentalities very well indeed—have been written during the last and letterless week. If half your notes are composed during the period between the sending of your letter and the receiving of mine, then much valuable time (the adjective depends on you, of course) would not be lost. This, for me, is a statement of great common-sense, and having delivered myself of such a commonsensible idea, I shall probably be half-witted for the rest of the week.

The moods of the notes I leave to you. One, again, was written in the bath—a striking condemnation of those of my acquaintances who do not believe I ever take one—one in the bus from Swansea to Trecynon (you have never heard of it, but it boasts a Little Theatre where I occasionally perform); and the rest in the privacy of my pensive and worm-ridden room.

Personal Accomplishment and Failing

What a terribly accomplished person you are! I can't sing, can't play any musical instrument, and can't draw. I paint a good deal, but quite untechnically, and the startling effects I sometimes do produce are owing to a diseased mentality and an entire lack of skill. O Wilhelmina Bernhardt! I apologise at once. I'm glad you're an actress, and I'm sure you're a good one. I've been acting on and off—mostly off—both as an amateur and as a vague professional since I was the size of your thumb. But I can't say I'm improved much, since that time. My speciality is the playing of madmen, neurotics, nasty 'modern' young men and low comedians—quite straight acting. At the present time I—and the Little Theatre of Wales (it sounds good) are rehearsing 'Strange Orchestra'. Do you know it? I'm playing Val, if you do, and if you don't I'll explain that Val is a nervous, unhappy writer of unpopular books, in love and yet frightened to be, full of bathetic and half-digested notions on life with a Capital letter. What sort of things do you play? Tell me you play hysterical young women with tumours, or erotic young things with Notions, and we'll go round together on the provincial music-halls playing Grand Guignol.

Talking of Grand Guignol, I met Eliot Crawshay Williams last week.

Barter

For one 'jasmine' I will give you one 'belly'
    "   " 'daffodil' " "   "   "   " 'senna'

But I'm damned if I'll swap my warmy wombs for all the fairy bubbles this side of St. Pauls. We're extremists, girl, one upstairs in our lady's chamber and the other downstairs in our lady's chamber-pot. Still, I will do my best to comb out the superfluous horrors in my beard on the one condition that you let Spring pass out next year without bestowing one single lavish spate upon its tomb.

The Publication of a Book

I said that your book was bound to be successful, successful, that is, compared with any book of poetry recently published, and I repeat it, what harm can it do you? An unbiased reader does not expect a first book to be perfect. All he looks for are parts of promise and fragments of achievement. There have probably been no first poems ever published that have had more to offer than that. And there is certainly promise in all you've written. In two or three instances, there has been undeniable and individual achievement. You are young, and can't expect any more than that. Even if you were withered and corsetted into shape, there would be no need for you to expect more. Great reputations have been built upon much promise and small achievement.

You are, I know, capable of achieving perfection in a certain type of poetry, a poetry born out of Christina Rossetti and the Georgian and Poetry Bookshop Gang. And you have failed, I know, in attempting a far higher thing—the creation of personal poetry, born out of Battersea, Mrs. Johnson and wide and haphazard reading. Really, your future as a poetess is capable of developing in one of two ways: along the hedgerows, littered with the Pre-Raphaelite and Georgian corpses, to a narrow but popular perfection, or in the middle of the road, scorning hedges and the Referee ruts, towards a wide, unpopular and very splendid failure.

You yourself have to decide which way to go, but the literary people you will associate with will certainly help you to make up your mind. I know which way Neuburg wishes, and I hope to God that my sprawling letters will help you to take the other way. Fear Neuburg and all the Creative Lifers as you would fear the Boojum.

So speaks the Snark.

Pawky (Your Word) Remarks

Why do you call your book Dayspring? It isn't as if the poems in it had sprung out of natural associations. You don't snoop around the country lanes, looking for a ragwort to pour a bellyful of words on, or pimp in the recesses of the gasworks at the amours of stale and repetitive lovers, hoping to hear some words of love that you might jot down upon your pad of paper. Yours is a selfspring; everything comes out of yourself, and darkness, despite what you say, has infinitely more possibilities than day. There is too much doing in life, and not enough being. Proof of life lies in the answer to one question, and that question is not troubled with the mechanics of living, with the function of living, or with the appearances of living—but with the vast verb, To Be. Age is not a matter of years, but of Action. 'Dayspring'! I may have missed the point of the title, and, anyway, God knows why I am so suddenly vehement.

Comment upon the Comments upon the Nastiness of the Present Writer. You ikkle bitch!

But seriously, it was the attitude behind what you said, rather than what you said, that called forth my singular nastiness. To call Sex the Great Experience is to call Birth the Great Adventure, and a prostitute the Lady of Dubious Morals. It is the escape of the coward-worded and the last resort of the prig-moralled journalist (neither of which applies to you). Do you remember Rampion in Point-Counter-Point? He painted a wild picture of a naked man and woman. 'What do you call it?' he was asked. 'Some people call it love', he replied, 'And others call it —.'

It was not that you made your remarks—with which I thoroughly agree—for 'pretty'; I'm not corrupted enough to ask for the language of the gutter on every possible occasion. But there are only three vocabularies at your disposal when you talk of sex;: the vocabulary of the clinic, of the gutter, & of the moralist. Of the three the last is by far the worst; it is compromise and the jargon of the prude. The clinic, at least, talks from knowledge of its subject, and the gutter talks from acquaintance. The moralist, with his half learnt knowledge

61

and his frustrated or perverted acquaintance, cloaks everything in words & symbols. The naked man & woman remain.

Pathos (and forgive the pencil, for I've mislaid the ink)

Four years, my sweet. 1340 days & nights. And thank you for the optimistic remarks. I don't believe it either, but then it would be very odd if I did. You should hear me cough, though—a most pleasing sound, exactly like a sea-lion peeved.

No I don't think consumption has very much effect on what I write (oh my bravery with that not-quite-polite word). I can't help what I write. It is part of me, however unpleasant a part it may be, and however necessary it should be to cauterize and castrate that part. Your belief in my power to write is one of the few things that makes me deny that twice-damned, diabetic doctor. I have another believer— a communist grocer with a passion for obscurity & the Powys family. Both of you shall have a seat in heaven, or in my comfortable, but slightly wormy, hell.

Just after writing this, I received a rather disquieting note from Richard Rees of the Adelphi, who, last week, asked me to send him some recent poems. He compliments me upon the high standard & the great originality exhibited & said my technique was amazing (One Up for Formal Me), but accused me—not in quite so many words—of being in the grip of devils. 'The poems have an unsubstantiality, a dream-like quality', he writes, 'which non-plussed me.' He then goes on to say that the poems, as a whole, reminded him of automatic or trance-writing.

Automatic writing is worthless as literature, however interesting it may be to the psychologist & pathologist. So perhaps, after all I am nothing but a literary oddity, a little freak of nature whose madness runs into print rather than into ravings and illusions. It may be, too, an illusion that keeps me writing, the illusion of myself as some misunderstood poet of talent. The note has depressed me more than the usual adverse criticism. It shows not dislike, or mere incomprehension, but confession of bewilderment, & almost fear, at the method by which I write my poetry.

But he is wrong, I swear it. My facility, as he calls it, is, in reality, tremendously hard work. I write at the speed of two lines an hour. I have written hundreds of poems, & each one has taken me a great many painful, brain-racking and sweaty hours.

If you like, pay little attention to the following criticisms of your poems, for they are based, as what I write is based on my own peculiar standards, which may be the standards of a theorising failure & a bilious little crank.

I now stop turning over the dirty pages of my soul, lick my pencil, wipe my cold-filled nose, light a cigarette, & write.

. . . .

Hymn of Despair and Hope

This is written on Armistice Day, 1933, when the war is no more than a memory of privations and the cutting down of the young. There were women who had 'lost' their sons, though where they had lost them and why they could not find them, we, who were children born out of blood into blood, could never tell. The state was a murderer, and every country in this rumour-ridden world, peopled by the unsuccessful suicides left over by the four mad years, is branded like Cain across the forehead. What was Christ in us was stuck with a bayonet to the sky, and what was Judas we fed and sheltered, rewarding, at the end, with thirty hanks of flesh. Civilisation is a murderer. We, with the cross of a castrated Saviour cut on our brows, sink deeper and deeper with the days into the pit of the West. The head of Christ is to be inspected in the museum, dry as a mole's hand in its glass case. And all the dominions of heaven have their calculated limits; the stars move to man's arithmetic; and the sun, leering like a fool over the valleys of Europe, sinks as the drops in a test-tube dry and are gone.

This is a lament on the death of the West. Your bones and mine shall manure an empty island set in a waste sea. The stars shall shine over England, but the darkness of England and the sarcophagos of a spoonfed nation, and the pitch in the slain souls of our children, will never be lit.

'And the earth was without form and void; and darkness was upon the face of the deep.' The old buffers of this world still cling to chaos, believing it to be Order. The day will come when the old Dis-Order changeth, yielding to a new Order. Genius is being strangled every day by the legion of old Buffers, by the last long line of the Edwardians, clinging, for God and capital, to an outgrown and decaying system. Light is being turned to darkness by the capitalists and industrialists. There is only one thing you and I, who are of this generation, must look forward to, must work for and pray for, and, because, as we fondly hope, we are poets and voicers not only of our personal selves but of our social selves, we must pray for it all the more vehemently. It is the Revolution. There is no need for it to be a revolution of blood. We do not ask that. All that we ask is that the present Dis-Order, this medieval machine which is grinding into powder the bones and guts of the postwar generation, shall be broken in two, and that all that is in us of godliness and strength, of happiness and genius, shall be allowed to exult in the sun. We are said to be faithless, because our God is not a capitalist God, to be unpatriotic because we do not believe in the Tory Government. We are said to be immoral because we know that marriage is a dead institution, that the old rigid mono-gamous lifelong union of male and female—the exceptions are the exceptions of beauty—is a corrupted thought.

The hope of Revolution, even though all of us will not admit it, is uppermost in all our minds. If there were not that revolutionary spark within us, that faith in a new faith, and that belief in our power to squash the chaos surrounding us like a belt of weeds, we would turn on the tap of war and drown ourselves in its gasses.

Everything is wrong that forbids the freedom of the individual. The governments are wrong, because they are the committees of prohibitors; the presses are wrong, because they feed us what they desire to feed us, and not what we desire to eat; the churches are wrong, because they standardize our gods, because they label our morals, because they laud the death of a vanished Christ, and fear the crying of the new Christ in the wilderness; the poets are wrong, because their vision is not a vision but a squint; they look at our world, and yet their eyes are staring back along the roads of the past centuries, never into the huge, electric promise of the future.

There is injustice, muddleheadedness, criminal ignorance, corrupted and inverted virtue, hypocrisy and stone blindness, in every sphere of life. If only for one moment the Western world could drop the veils that, ever since the Reformation, have clung around it like the films of a disease, and look, with lightened eyes, upon the cess it has created, on the greatness it has split & strangled, on the starvation it has fostered, on the perversions and ignorances it has taught, then it would die for shame. And we, who have not been long enough alive to be corrupted utterly, could build out of its manuring bones the base of an equal and sensible civilisation.

I will not bore you with any more propaganda, though why it should bore you God knows, for it is near to you as it is to me. Later, in another letter, I will give you a more reasoned outline of Revolu-tion, the hard facts of communism—which is above communism for it holds the individual above everything else—and hope that you, too, may don your scarlet tie, and, striding into the Hampstead dens, scorch the Creative Lifers with an invective their poor bloody brains could never fathom.

But only if it does not bore you. The precious seeds of revolution must not be wasted, though I do not think they will be in you.

The Arty Party

The type of party you describe—and you describe it very well indeed—is a menace to art, much as I dislike the phrase. Wyndham (Tarr) Lewis has struck them hard in 'Apes of God'; Roy Campbell, in his 'Georgiad', has trampled them down under the feet of his eighteenth-century charger, but still they flourish. Still do seedy things in their mother's pyjamas enthuse over some soon-to-be-forgotten lyrist, or some never-to-be-heard-of painter of nature in the raw and angular. Neuter men and lady tenors rub shoulders with 'the shams and shamans, the amateur hobo and homo of Bloomsbury W.C.1.', while their hostess, clad in scarlet corduroy, drinks to their health in methylated spirits.

With a smattering, often incorrectly memorised, of encyclopedia learning, with the names of the transient stars of their decade on the tips of their tongues, with their men's breasts shaped with the aid of wadding, the young women speak on. Sodomhipped young men, with the inevitable side-whiskers and cigarettes, the faulty livers and the stained teeth, reading Lawrence as an aphrodisiac and Marie Corelli in their infrequent baths, spew onto paper and canvas their ignorance and perversions, wetting the bed of their brains with discharges of fungoid verse. This is the art of to-day; posturing, shamming, cribbing, and all the artifice of a damned generation.

In the corner stands an emaciated female chanting that sentimental ballad 'Proust A Song at Twilight'. From behind a divan rises a grisly laugh. Someone has made a joke about André Gide.

Seedy Young Thing: Do you like Ibsen? P.H.J. No, I prefer Glauber.

Oversight

Thank you for the detailed criticism of the '16 Poems'—a hell of a lot, really, to inflict on you in one dose—but as I haven't kept a copy of the little book I don't know which poems you are criticizing. Its terrible: I read 'This is a ghastly line', or 'this is very wormy', and I immediately want to look up the particular poem and agree with you. But I can't. In the next letter send me all the first lines with the numbers above them, will you? Don't forget.

On Skeletons

I was neither surprised or revolted at the sight of your little grinning skeleton. When you do sink you sink deep enough into the sugary pits to please all the Womens' Friends in England. Don't you dare do it again.

I, too, have a wicked secret. I used to write articles for the Northcliffe

Press on 'Do Novelists make Good Husbands?' and 'Are Poets Mad?'
etc.—very literary, very James Douglas, very bloody. I don't do that
any more now: I ran the Northcliffe Press into a libel suit by calling
Miss Nina Hamnet (who wrote the book called 'Laughing Torso', I
don't know whether you remember it) insane. Apparently she wasn't,
that was the trouble.

Epilogue

I've neglected to touch on several of the points I intended to, and
I've left many of your comments unanswered. But five of these huge,
tinily written sheets are enough to give you at a time. Write very soon,
not in a week but in a few days; I'm giving you a whole week-end to
compose your notes. Make them as long as these 'ere. I'm enclosing
one poem, just finished. It's quite my usual stuff, I'm afraid, & quite
probably you won't like it. But, honestly, the one 'cancer' mentioned
is necessary. And I will try to be good in future.

Dylan

Looking back over these notes I see many of them to be unusually
aggressive & particularly humourless. Sorry!

And another thing before I forget it: If this letter is illegible—you
haven't complained of my ugly writing once yet— tell me, & my next
letter shall be done on the typewriter.

About the Chertsey trip I'm terribly dubious at the moment about
when I am coming up. I want a really good excuse first. I might be
able to arrange a meeting with Middleton Murry—I met him this
August in Chelsea. Or even with T. S. Eliot. (God 'elp me.) More
about this, & other things, again.

MSS.: Lockwood Memorial Library, Buffalo

In this letter I have again cut his detailed criticism of three poems she had sent him.

By Robeyism, Dylan is referring to George Robey, a comedian famous, among other reasons, for his coarseness.

The story of Dylan and Dan Jones staring at each other in a darkening room until terrified by the apparent distortion of each other's heads has also been told by Dr Jones, and is reprinted in Prof. Tedlock's *Dylan Thomas: The Legend and the Poet.*

TO PAMELA HANSFORD JOHNSON

Late 1933

Unwilling Reply

Nothing I can think of—including the personal delivery of Miss Garbo in a tin box—would please me so much as to spend Christmas with you, and to talk to you (though, really, I don't talk as much as all that) until Boxing Day. The towel and the jar of holly, especially the jar of holly, are terribly big temptations. But I must stand like a little martyr, denying the calls of the flesh (no, I don't mean that at all; it sounds as though you'd invited me to a pyjama party) and obeying, instead, the requests of a benighted family. My sister, brother-in-law and uncle will be down here for the holiday, and great fun will be had by all. Will it, hell! We'll all eat too much, I suppose, read the newspapers, sleep, and crack nuts. There will be no Yuletide festivity about it, and I, in an extra-black shirt, will brood over the fire, contemplating, in the coals, the shapes of past Miseries and Follies.

I'm flattered to receive a Christmas invitation from you, from you who have known me for such a little time and in such unusual ways— more flattered (and terribly pleased) than I can tell you.

(By the way, I've discovered a new way of getting ill. You buy an ounce of Sailors' Plug Tobacco, a little machine for making cigarettes, and a packet of cigarette papers. Put a layer of plug in the machine, put in the paper, turn round, draw out, and smoke the result, It's the worst taste I've ever known. I'm smoking one now.)

Your mother, I suppose, is in the charming invitation, too. Give her my Christmas greetings, and tell her to write separately and give me the low-down on her daughter (how the daughter is a champion ice-skater or steeple-chaser or Derby winner, how she likes Berta Ruck so much more than James Joyce, how she writes novels in her spare time and contributes to the, say to the 'Ladies' Chat' and 'Miriam's Weekly').

By the way, again, have you written any prose? If so, let me see it, won't you? I remember you told me something in a very longago letter about some stories you'd put on the fire. But aren't there any stories not used so harshly and, I'm sure, so needlessly? I think you should be able to write very good prose. But then, as I said before somewhere, I'm very biased.

I'd love to spend Christmas with you. Circumstances say otherwise, and my father is going up to Hospital in London in the first few days of January to have, as far as I know, several very necessary glands removed.

. . . .

Hints for Recognition

The gradual shrinking you complain of is chiefly mental, for the more despondent I become the littler and weaker I feel.

Height—five foot six (about).

Weight—eight stone ten (about).

Hair—some sort of rat-coloured brown.

Eyes—big, brown and green (this sounds as though one were brown & the other green; the colours are mixed).

Distinguishing Marks—Three moles on right cheek, scar on arm and ankle, though as I generally wear socks you won't see the little mark there.

Sex—male, I think.

Voice—I suppose it would be called baritone, though sometimes it sweeps towards tenor and sometimes droops towards bass. Except in moments of hilarity, I believe I speak without an accent.

Size of Feet—five (this is not number).

Cigarettes—Players, forty a day stuck in centre of mouth.

Food—Hay.

This is neither very funny nor very illuminating, I admit, but I must, by any method possible, steer clear of the soulful outpouring that ended my last letter. I apologise, incidentally, for apologising for the overflow of feeling. I should have known how interesting such overflowing is, because little, pulsating bits in your letters—when you defend your theism before a pack of negative-brained scoffers, or dwell, unhappily but brokenly, upon the passing of juvenile loves—are of immense interest to me, who am also pleased by the fact that I have your confidence. My little Welsh ear is open for all secrets.

But the prospect of being comforted—unsubstantially, it is true, but then the substance of life is and always will be to me less than the unreality—by a nice and slant-eyed shade, tempts me to indulge in even more abysmal desolations of the spirit.

Then sport an open skirt and blouse,
For every arty thing allows
Her wretched bosom to be loosed
For men to see who talk of Proust.
Remember this at every table
Talk as rudely as you're able,
And never pass the peas with less
Than one remark on sexiness.

Your wardrobe done (forget the rest,
The little things like drawers and vest),
You next must learn the tricks of speech
sorry! (Here nothing rhymes but 'Chelsea Reach').
Learn to begin with words like these:
'Chiaroscuro', 'Bright's Disease',
'Timbre', 'soul', 'essential cheese',
'The social art', 'the rhomboid quip',
'The rhythmic works of Stink and Drip',
'The Joyce of Love', 'the D. H. 'Ell',
'The formal spheres of Little Nell'.
With such fine phrases on your tongue,
A knowledge of the old and Jung,
You can converse in any party
And keep the conversation arty.

From a letter to my Aunt, Discussing the Correct Approach to Modern
Poetry.

To you, my aunt, who would explore
The literary Chankley Bore,
The paths are hard for you are not
A literary Hotentot
But just a kind and cultured dame
Who knows not Eliot (to her shame).
Fie on you, aunt, that you should see
No genius in David G.,
No elemental form and sound
In T. S. E. and Ezra Pound.
Fie on you, aunt! I'll show you how
To elevate your middle brow,
And how to scale and see the sights,
From modernist Parnassian heights.

First buy a hat, no Paris model
what a line! But one the Swiss wear when they yodel,

A bowler thing with one or two
Feathers to conceal the view.
And then in sandals walk the street
(All modern painters use their feet
For painting, on their canvas strips,
Their wives or mothers minus hips.)

Perhaps it would be best if you
Created something very new,
A dirty novel done in Erse
Or written backwards in Welsh verse,
Or paintings on the backs of vests,
Or Sanskrit psalms on lepers' chests.
But if this proved imposs-i-ble
Perhaps it would be just as well,
For you could then write what you please,
And modern verse is done with ease.

Do not forget that 'limpet' rhymes
With 'strumpet' in these troubled times,
And commas are the worst of crimes;
Few understand the works of Cummings,
And few James Joyce's mental slummings,
And few young Auden's coded chatter;
But then it is the few that matter.
Never be lucid, never state,
If you would be regarded great,
The simplest thought or sentiment,
(For thought, we know, is decadent);
Never omit such vital words
As belly, genitals, and — ,
For these are things that play a part
(And what a part) in all good art.
Remember this: each rose is wormy.
And every lovely woman's germy;
Remember this: that love depends
On how the Gallic letter bends;
Remember, too, that life is hell
And even heaven has a smell
Of putrefying angels who
Make deadly whoopee in the blue.
These things remembered, what can stop
A poet going to the top?

A final word: before you start
The convulsions of your art,
Remove your brains, take out your heart;
Minus these curses, you can be
A genius like David G.

Take courage, aunt, and send your stuff
To Geoffrey Grigson with my luff,
And may I yet live to admire
How well your poems light the fire.

More Theorising

Only today, after reading for the hundredth time out of the 'Plumed Serpent', have I come to make a valuation of Lawrence. And as nearly everyone today has some sort of set ideas upon that almost legendary figure, it may interest you to know what conclusions I— on the outskirts of the literary world, if any such world exists—have reached. I don't know whether you'll follow all of this note; anyway it isn't worth burrowing into the syntactical tunnels I so often lose myself in.

Lawrence was a moralist, a preacher, but his morals & his sermons were not progressive. He preached a doctrine of paganism and, to the best of his tubercular ability, attempted to live a pagan life. But the more paganistic, sun-and-sex loving, one becomes, the less one feels the desire to write. A born writer is born scrofulous; his career is an accident dictated by physical or circumstantial disabilities. Lawrence preached paganism, and paganism, as the life by the body in the body for the body, is a doctrine that contents man with his lot. It defies the brain, and it is only through the brain that man can realise the chaos of civilisation and attempt to better it. Aldous Huxley, as his direct protagonist, preaches the sermon of the intellect; his god is cellular, and his heaven a socialist Towards. He would, as someone brighter than myself has said, condense the generative principle into a test-tube; Lawrence, on the other hand, would condense the world into the generative principle, and make his apostles decline not cogitare but copulare.

The young writer, if he would wish to label himself at all, must class himself under one of two headings: under the philosophy (for want of a better word) which declares the body to be all and the intellect nothing, and which would limit the desires of life, the perceptions and the creation of life, within the walls of the flesh; or under the philosophy which, declaring the intellect and reason and the intelligence to be all, denies the warmth of the blood and the body's promise. You have to class yourself under one heading—the labels might overlap a little—for the equilibrium between flesh and non-flesh can never be reached by an individual. While the life of the body is, perhaps, more directly pleasant, it is terribly limited, and the life of the non-body, while physically unsatisfying, is capable of developing, of realising infinity, of getting somewhere, and of creating an artistic progeny.

Lawrence and his disease grew parallel and one was nothing without the other. If he had had no disease, he would have been a pagan liver, and would never have written at all. As it was, weak and diseased, he wrote of the struggle of the ideas of the pagan strong. And his literature, therefore, however valuable, is a lie from start to finish.

Perhaps I haven't developed the argument sufficiently, and perhaps, o uncomplaining receiver of so many half-baked theories, I may be entirely wrong.

You get a rather beastly angle on Lawrence if you read 'Lorenzo in Taos'. And unless you want to regard the man as a vain, weak-skinned, egocentric, domineering little charlatan, don't borrow the book.

Us Girls

How is 'Cinderella' going on? This is a really interested question, although it leads up to another personal statement. I've just started rehearsals for the 'Way of the World', a play to be carted around the Welsh valleys where they won't understand one bawdy word from the beginning to the end. Do you know the play? (Of course you do.) I'm playing Witwoud, the second consecutive effeminate part. Much more of this type of playing and I shall be becoming decidedly girlish.

Have you remarked upon the terrible young men of this generation, the willing-buttocked, celluloid-trousered degenerates who are gradually taking the place of the bright young things of even five years ago. Or is the degeneracy, the almost unbelievable effeminacy, the product of the Welsh slums alone? In an hotel last night a boy, wearing a light green hat, white shirt, red tie, light green trousers and tightly fitting fawn overcoat, went up to the bar and said 'a whate port and a smale Ardathe, girlie'. I heard him. He was the most perfect example I've ever seen, the sort of thing one hears of in coarse stories but rarely encounters in the flesh (God deliver me from the flesh; the outer trappings are enough). I see more and more of them every day. They always existed, but in recent months—it seems months to me—they are coming, unashamedly, out into the open. I saw one with a drunken nigger last night.

It is the only vice, I think, that revolts me and makes me misanthropic. I can—theoretically—tolerate even incest (Tell me, have you read Leonhard Frank's 'Brother & Sister'; if not, get hold of it by some method and do read it; it's brilliant) and other domestic sins. But the sin of the boy with the nigger goes up like a rocketed scab to Heaven.

I'm trying to borrow that historical novel. Do you still keep up a correspondence with the author, or am I your only deliverer of long and literary—not always literary, either—letters?

Devils

Today I am starting on a new short story which will in a few weeks, I hope, be finished and good enough to send you. The theme of the story I dreamed in a nightmare. If successful, if the words fit to the thoughts, it will be one of the most ghastly short stories ever written. The action in it will be grisly enough, but—if it will come to pass—the tone of it will be so quiet that the horror should rise up like a clot of blood in the throat. 'I brought the broom for her to brush it into the wall', is the opening sentence which, standing alone, is quite meaningless. But even alone it is horrible to me.

This is no despondency to-day. I feel like a dead man exulting in the company of his beetles, incarnadining the monstrous earth—words, words, words—with the blood of the worms (yes, worms again, my dear) that he breaks—as a housemaid crushes a flea—between the tips of his nails.

Sometimes I am very nice, but to-day I'm awful; I'm caught in my complexes, and they're giving me immense, if unholy, joy.

Do you know the experience of sitting in a corner of a darkened room, a little light coming in through the window, and staring, fixedly and unmovably, at the face of another in an opposite corner, never taking the eyes off the lines of the other's face? Slowly the face changes, the jaw drops, the brow slips into the cheeks, and the face is one strange white circle, utter darkness around it. Then new features form on the face, a goat's mouth slides across the circle, eyes shine in the pits of the cheeks. Then there is nothing but the circle again, and from the darkness around it rises, perhaps, the antlers of a deer, or a cloven foot, or the fingers of a hand, or a thing no words can ever describe, a shape, not beautiful or horrible, but as deep as hell and as quiet as heaven.

If you don't know the experience, try it. It's all optical illusion, I suppose, but I always call it the invoking of devils. And, mark my grisly words, invoke the devils too much, and by God they will come.

I've got the devils to-day; little blue ones they are, with spats and bowlers and dentists' tweezers. So I'd better not write any more to you until tomorrow. This will delay the letter, I'm afraid, and it's been delayed, for various reasons, long enough already. But I don't want to write you—you of all people—a panegyric on the eye-sockets of skeletons.

Words

A new poem accompanies this. I suppose it's my usual stuff again, and even a little more death-struck. But don't be put off by my anatomical imagery, which I explained months ago. Because I so often write in terms of the body, of the death, disease, and breaking of the body, it doesn't necessarily mean that my Muse (not one of my favourite words) is a sadist. For the time at least, I believe in the writing of poetry from the flesh, and, generally, from the dead flesh. So many modern poets take the living flesh as their object, and, by their clever dissecting, turn it into a carcase. I prefer to take the dead flesh, and, by any positivity of faith and belief that is in me, build up a living flesh from it.

Talking of 'Muse', I read in an old John O'London (blast the tit-bitty paper) several individual lists of favourite words, and was surprised to see that the choice depended almost entirely upon the associations of the words. 'Chime', 'melody', 'golden', 'silver', 'alive', etc. appeared in almost every list; 'chime', is to me, the only word of that lot that can, intrinsically and minus its associations, be called beautiful. The greatest single word I know is 'drome' which, for some reason, nearly opens the doors of heaven for me. Say it yourself, out aloud, and see if you hear the golden gates swing backward as the last, long sound of the 'm' fades away.

'Drome', 'bone', 'dome', 'doom', 'province', 'dwell', 'prove', 'dolomite'—these are only a few of my favourite words, which are insufferably beautiful to me. The first four words are visionary; God moves in a long 'o'. Have you any especial favourite? If so, now's your time, lidy.

Robeyism

Thank you for giving a selection of my poems that might please the mighty Neuburg, but I don't know about the love poem; such a thing is so entirely out of my sphere that I'm frightened to think how bad it might be; I'll send it to the Referee next week, anyway. And thank you for taking all the callous things I said about 'May Day' without being at all annoyed, and for heeding my dogmatic tub-thumpery. Let me see, at the first opportunity, any new poems passed by the acid tests. I love the verses you put in your letters; they have many of the qualities I should like to see exhibited in your more serious work.

You must, you know, be an awfully entertaining little girl. Anyone who can be intelligently artistic, artistically intelligent, and downright vulgar must be nice. So your Resolution will be one you can't help fulfilling. It's remarkable how few of the moreorless cultivated young women one meets can be honestly vulgar. They talk, possibly, of matters which, a 100 years ago, were not supposed to exist, but they talk in a sly, subtle, sophisticated way, and their jokes—when they tell any—depend upon innuendoes. Now you, to your shame and credit, have a decidely coarse wit, and your naughty verses about Gascoyne and his morbid preoccupations are little masterpieces in their way. I hope these compliments won't make your Correspondence Muse (a broad creature, not, on any account, to be confused with the slim, doe-eyed apparition of your green book) selfconscious. More power to her, and to you, sweet Rabelaisian Pamela.

Dylan

Write soon; I should like to have a letter for Christmas; and write as long a letter as this. Don't complain of lack of material—these notes should be able to provide enough of that.

MSS.: Lockwood Memorial Library, Buffalo

This Christmas Day letter makes a curious contrast with his broadcast script, written over a dozen years later about 'A Child's Christmas in Wales', and is perhaps an interesting comment on how, in his maturity, he romanticized his memories of long ago.

She had sent him a volume of Robert Graves's poems for Christmas, and a box of Player's cigarettes.

TO PAMELA HANSFORD JOHNSON

25th December 1933

Another Aftermath: Christmas Day.

Thank you for the cigarettes. The Christmas dinner over, and the memories of it—so far at least—more in the mouth than in the belly. I have been sprawling in an armchair (yes, we possess one), smoking the first of your so very kind and unexpected presents. While the family is collected around the wireless, listening to the voice of His Majesty, let me write a note to you to tell you glad I was to read your last letter, and how horrified to think that you thought Robert Graves necessarily indicated the return of John Player. The reference to my diabolical machine was not a hint to your generosity: I must assure you on that point, even though I have no doubt that the reading of my many letters has established this invisible personality of mine as one too honourable and Balliolic (not to say bucolic) for such an unmannerly action to be possible on my part. Play the game, you cads! And my style this gray December evening (a reference to robins will appear now any moment) is as heavy as the brandied pudding now rising in revolt, deep in the chambers of the intestines, against too much four-and-sixpenny port and vegetables.

Child: Mother, how many pips in a tangerine?

Mother: Shut up, you little bastard.

My gifts are arrayed in front of me: a startlingly yellow tie and a peculiar pair of string gloves from my sister; a cigarette case from my brother-in-law; ten cigars from my father; 50 cigarettes from an uncle; 50 cigarettes from a young woman in Battersea, a knitted thing from the manageress of the hotel near my Little Theatre; the complete Blake from another uncle; a new edition of the Koran from a friend who writes music (I'll tell you something very interesting about him one day); Mrs. Munro's 1923—1933 Anthology (including three poems by the Gascoyne), from a friend who writes communism; two James Joyce pamphlets from myself; while outside hangs a neat, but tight, black hat from my mother, who has despaired for some time of the curves and angles of a decrepit trilby. That is all; and though your gift will vanish far more quickly than some of the others, it will last far longer in my memory than any of them.

Now I could be more explicit than that.

I have been reading Blake's letters for the first time, and find, among other things, that his headings include: 'Dear leader of my angels', 'Dear sculptor of eternity', 'Dear friend of my angels', 'Dear friend of religion and order'—all of which, in this mellow mood, and with the possible exception of the last, I might apply to you.

Over dinner I told, with no remarkable effect, the following story which I hope may benefit and amuse those of your friends to whom vulgarity, or at least the trimmings of it, is as amusing as it is to you.

A. My sister has just returned from a week's holiday in Paris, and, do you know, she didn't go to the Louvre once.

B. Good lord, change of food, I expect.

I hear the roofs of the ancentral house quake with your laughter. Do I? The story reads badly but speaks well. A story which reads better than it speaks is the story of the two goldfish swimming around in a bowl, one singing to the other that old song, 'No roes in all the world until you came'.

I have, as a rule, been averse to including such obvious rudery in my letters to you, but the sight of your crazy supplement (thank you for it), has quelled my aversion. If I could think of another funny story I'd tell you it, but the arms of Morpheus, (along with the none-too-nimble fingers of Orpheus (damn that next door Chopin-er), are closing around me. Goodbye until to-morrow, when I hope that the heavy, academic idioms of this note will leave me lucid enough to write more and at more considerable length. The wireless is continually re-iterating the fact that Christmas is here, but Christmas, for me, is nearly over. How many more Christmases will these old eyes be blessed to see approach and vanish? Who knows: one far-off day I may gather my children (though a resolution denies it) around my spavined knee, tickle their chops, and tell them of the miracle of Christ and the devastating effect of too many nuts upon a young stomach.

A Tragic Conversation

A. Pity the philosophers, the specialists, and the careerists, for, being too acquainted with the fundaments of life or with a very small part of the mechanism of life, they have no time to look upon the vast panorama of social idiocy, of political wise-cracking and literary slapstick. Let us for once be superficial, pull a cracker and blow a whistle before the maggots play naughts and crosses on the delicate structure of our forms.

B. No, let us rather seize upon an aspect of this human tragedy, and pull it to bits, making it even more tragic. Let us walk in the lanes of an English county, remarking upon the futile stirrings of life in the hedges, and, taking out our inevitable notebooks, be vain enough to imagine that the words and rhymes we pen upon the pages are a sufficient excuse for the absurdity of our lives.

C. Pity the cynic and the man of letters, the two creatures in one of all God's creatures furthest removed from God.

Very Serious Question?

Am I mad?

Librarian's Corner

An ancient and immovable bias against Mr. Kipling, who stands for everything in this cankered world which I would wish were otherwise; an inexplicable dislike of Washington Irving, fostered by a clergical uncle whose favourite book, as he so often insists, is his Life of Mahomet; a hatred of Latin, fostered by a ridiculously inept education; an appreciation of what s's (long 's') can do in the place of s's (look at Graves's poem), a total ignorance of Lady Guff Gordon and Lady Longford; and a theoretical hatred of Byron, Keats, Shelley, and Wordsworth, do not assist me in admiring the Battersea shelves. Stella Gibbons I allow, though Cold Comfort Farm is not half as successful as it should be, owing to some carelessness in the development of the plot and the totally incredible and farcical climax; Gerfalcon I should allow if I knew it; and the Scarlet Letter is splendid. But where are yer moderns? (By the way, I have read, and don't like, most of Dreiser, what he writes of is good and valuable, but he should learn how to write. After all, if a writer of English can only express himself awkwardly in that language, he should have a shot at German; as a matter of fact Dreiser's style is thoroughly Teutonic. And, by the way again, I read 'Look Homeward, Angel' a few years ago, and I thought it particularly good.)

Our books are divided into two sections, Dad's and mine. Dad has a room full of all the accepted stuff, from Chaucer to Henry James, all the encyclopedias and books of reference, all Saintsbury, and innumerable books on the theory of literature. His library contains nearly everything that a respectable highbrow library should contain. My books, on the other hand, are nearly all poetry, and mostly modern at that. I have the collected poems of Manley Hopkins, Stephen Crane, Yeats, de la Mare, Osbert Sitwell, Wilfred Owen, W. H. Auden, & T. S. Eliot, volumes of poetry by Aldous Huxley, Sacheverell & Edith Sitwell, Edna St. Vincent Millay, D. H. Lawrence, Humbert Wolfe, Sassoon, and Harold Monro; most of the ghastly Best Poems of the Year; two of the Georgian Anthologies, one of the Imagist Anthologies, 'Whips & Scorpions' (modern satiric verse), the London Mercury Anthology, the Nineties Anthology (what Dowsonery!); a volume of Cambridge Poetry & Oxford Undergraduate Poetry; most of Lawrence, most of Joyce, with the exception of Ulysses, all Gilbert Murray's Greek translations, some Shaw, a little Virginia Woolf, & some E. M. Forster. This is inadequate, really, but added to Dad's, it makes a really comprehensive selection of literature. If any of the modern poets I've mentioned are not very well known to you I should truly, truly like to lend you them. All the ones I mentioned are worth knowing well. If you feel like reading, tell me which of the above you'd like to have & I'll lend them to you one by one, will you?

Legend

What beautiful words are 'legend' & 'island'; they shall certainly go on my list. But Ruth is the loveliest name.

Enclosed is a note to your very kind mother. If you are a good girl you can read it. It doesn't say anything at all. But then what does? And which as well?

Up Nero!

The last poem I sent you, the one you didn't like, is not very good, and I'm glad you attacked it; thank you, too, for expressing—in your remarks about the hiding of light and the running around in the same weary and minor track—much that I myself have felt and have never been able to express. On one point I disagree; the images are not mixed; they are severely physical all through; what gave you the impression of 'mixedness' was the conscious rapidity with which I changed the angles of the images. Yes, the 'iris' is a little bit too facile. But the poem (if you'll still allow me to call it that) is certainly not mixed in any way at all; it is on one level and one note, with one idea and one image, changed and transfigured as that image may be. But any bettering in my poetry won't come at one leap; it's going to be, (or it's not going to be, according to the depths of my moods), a very slow and ugly business; the 'hangman' has still a lot of work to do, and the anatomical imagery is not yet exhausted. But one day I hope to write something altogether out of the hangman's sphere, something larger, wider, more comprehensible, and less selfcentred; one day I may even come up to your expectations. And if I do, if ever I do, much of the credit will belong to a delightful (I will say it) young woman I have never seen.

Your 'poem' is, at least, serious and simple, with many nice words and rhymes and a lovely little hop-skip-and-jump rhythm. The sentiment is agreeable, a straightforward expression of pantheism; and one or two lines almost transcend pantheistic thought (Jesus!) and hover about on the edges of mysticism. With two such words as 'mysticism' & 'pantheism' on my tongue I could go on for hours, but I'll spare you that.

A thing I have always noticed and always admired in your verses and poems is the directness of the opening lines; there is never any beating about; you say what you have to say as quickly and as simply as possible. And you have never—as you said of me—put anything in to make it more difficult. The 'Poem' is so simple in thought and structure that it loses rather than gains by the repetition of the statement of your alliance of things as diverse as a swallow and a sod.

'Sod' when it rhymes with 'god' is, in itself, a most horrible cliché; whenever I see 'God' in line two of a bad poem I will inevitably look down to line four to see how the poor old sod is dragged in there. And although this is not altogether a bad poem the too-close proximity of 'God', 'sod', 'heifer' & 'zephyr' must lead one to believe that the thought in which these words appear was dictated by the rhymes, and is therefore false. You started off with a very simple thought (I, for one, will never believe that the most valuable thoughts are, of necessity, simple); you confessed that you were one with the 'sparrow', and then, as a natural conclusion, went on to say that you were one with the 'arrow', too. If it comes to that you can say you are one with the barrow as well. For you are, my dear, you certainly are. I'm not trying to be flippant; I'm merely trying to show you, by any method, how essentially false such writing is.

> I am one with the wind and one with the breezes,
> And one with the torrent that drowns the plain,
> I am one with the streams and one with the seas-es,
> And one with the maggot that snores in the grain.

A rhyming dictionary, a little selection of natural objects, and a halfpenny gift for stringing pretty words together, and one can write like this all day. 'My blood is drawn from the veins of the roses' is on an altogether different plane; here you have added to the by-now meaningless repetition of associations, and have contributed something quite lovely both to yourself and to the rose. Is this clear? It's something I'm always hammering at. The man who said, for the first time, 'I see the rose', said nothing, but the man who said for the first time 'The rose sees me' uttered a very wonderful truth. There's little value in going on indefinitely saying,

> 'I am one with the steamship & one with the trolley,
> And one with the airdale & one with the collie';

there's too much 'Uncle Tom Collie & all' about that. Primarily, you see, the reader refuses to believe that you believe you are one with all these things; you have to prove it to him, and you most certainly won't be cataloguing a number of other things to which you say you are related.

By the magic of words and images you must make it clear to him that the relationships are real. And only in, 'My blood is drawn from the veins of the roses', do you provide any proof. You gave the rose a human vein, and you gave your own vein the blood of the rose; now that is relationship. 'I am his son' means little compared with 'I am his flesh and blood.'

This is a final compression of what I want to say about the 'Poem', and what I do want you to read. As it is, the 16 lines are all separate, too separate; you could have written one, gone to sleep, woken up, and written the next. Though you talk all through of the relationship of yourself to other things, there is no relationship at all in the poem between the things you example. If you are one with the swallow & one with the rose, then the rose is one with the swallow. Link together these things you talk of, show, in your words & images, how your flesh covers the tree & the tree's flesh covers you. I see what you have done, of course—'I am one with the opposites', you say. You are, I know, but you must prove it to me by linking yourself to the opposites and by linking the opposites together. Only in the 'rose' line did you do it.

Is this all clear, or am I talking through my new black hat?

The Green Idyll of the Little Yellow God

Wagner moves me, too, but much in the same way as the final spectacular scene in a pantomime. I won't deny, for a moment, that he's a great composer, but his greatness lies in girth rather than in depth; it lacks humour and subtlety; he creates everything for you in a vast Cecil de Mille way; his orchestration is a perpetual 'close-up'; there is altogether too much showmanship and exhibitionism about him. His Valhalla is a very large and a very splendid place, but built in the style of a German baronial castle; the tapestries are too voluminous & highly coloured, there is too great a display of gold; while the gods that held dominion over it are florid deities, puffed out with self-importance, wearing gaudy garments and angelic watch-chains.

You know the experience of walking through the palatial chambers at Windsor, admiring the wealth and the magnificence with an open mouth, and longing to sneak away into a small and quiet room where you can eat chips and drink mild beer in comfort. That is the experience which Wagner gives me; he reminds me of a huge and overblown profiteer, wallowing in fineries, over-exhibiting his monstrous paunch and purse, and drowning his ten-ton wife in a great orgy of jewels. Compare him with an aristocrat like Bach!

Still I admire the way in which you admire him, and realise that it is only natural that Wagner should be one of your high gods. Whatever I can say about him, he is a big man, an overpowering man, a man with a vast personality and an overpowering voice, a dominant, arrogant, gestureful man forever in passion and turmoil over the turbulent, passionate universe. He's all that, I admit; part of Tristan and Isolde are exquisite; and my sneers are the sneers of a pygmy at a dwarf, not even a David at a Goliath. Yes, he was bound to be the composer you admire, for the qualities (enumerated above) are the qualities that, artistically at any rate, seem to count most with you. You like the raucous, billowy, bawdy historical novel, the 'up-&-at 'em! kick-em-in-the-belly, God's an Englishman' shoutings of Mr. Kipling (though I do not, on any account, call you a hearty), the cloudy brawlings of Shelley, the virility of Washington Irving. If you like all these, how on earth do you like me—if you do? I'm little with no health at all, curled up in an old copy of the 'Funeral Gazette', sneering at the worm.

Neuburg

He didn't appear to like the poem I sent him last week; it was not very inspired, I admit, but it was so wonderfully comprehensible that I felt sure it would appeal to him. However, this week I'll send him that love poem. So your book is to be published in the spring now? who by? And don't say you're going to call yourself Pamela Hansford Johnson; the three-name method is utterly American. If you do I shall call myself Dylan Marlais Thomas. So there!

Some Resolutions etc.

As this is the season of the year to make resolutions, I shall devote some of my time and, let it be hoped, some of yours, to the propounding of much idealistic nonsense to which it is my intention to adhere. This is such an ugly sentence that the brain naturally turns to the question of ugliness. Now there is nothing on God's earth that is, in itself, an ugly thing; it is the sickness of the mind that turns a thing sick and the dirtiness of the mind that turns a thing dirty. I do not speak of parliaments and committees, eternally ugly things, for they are composed of a collection of ugly minds; I speak of the pig and the popular conception of death. The pig is a particular animal and will eat only what is good for him; because what he eats is not good for us it does not follow that it is a messy food. The pig lies down in dung to sleep, because dung is warm and soft; he would probably think it a very dirty thing indeed to sleep on a sheet. Death is said to be ugly only because we entertain an ugly conception of the body. A live body is a building around the soul, and a dead body a building without it; without the soul a body breaks, but broken pieces are beautiful and meaningful because the soul has made them so and has left its marks. Just as a live body has its rhythms and its pattern and its promise (promise is perhaps the greatest thing in the world), so has a dead body; and not only an abstract pattern but a physical one. A dead body promises the earth as a live body promises its mate; and the earth is our mate. Looking on one dead, we should say, there lies beauty, for it has housed beauty, the soul being beautiful; just as, on looking on an empty house, we should say, there stands strength (or anything else) for it has housed strength, strength being beautiful. What has this to do with a resolution? It leads me to resolve that I shall never take things for granted, but that I shall attempt to take them as they are, that nothing is ugly except what I make ugly, and that the lowest and the highest are level to the eyes of the air.

I resolve not to label the brain into separate compartments, that is, not to differentiate between what is in me that writes poetry and what is in me that says, here comes one-o'clock; at this time I lunch. That is, again, a resolution not to differentiate between what is called rational and what is called irrational, but to attempt to create, or to let be created, one rationalism. It is said to be mad to write poetry and sane to lunch at one o'clock; but it is the other way about: Art is praise and it is sane to praise, for, praising, we praise the godliness that gives us sanity; the clock is a symbol of the limitations of time, and time is limitless; therefore it is wrong to obey the clock and right to eat not when hands of the clock, but the fingers of hunger, dictate. I resolve firstly to make poetry and secondly, to write it; there is poetry in the hands of the clock if only I can realise that the clock is a limitation, and can express, in my poetry, the knowledge of that limitation and the knowledge of illimitability. I can learn, by such resolving, to say that nothing in this world is uninteresting. How can a thing have no interest that is in this world, that has the world around it, that has the associations of a million million minds engrained in it. A chunk of stone is as interesting as a cathedral, or even more interesting, for it is the cathedral in essence; it gave substance to the building of the cathedral and meaning to the meaning of the cathedral, for stones are sermons, as are all things. And if I can bring myself to know, not to think, that nothing is uninteresting, I can broaden my own outlook and believe once more, as I so passionately believed and so passionately want to believe, in the magic of this burning and bewildering universe, in the meaning and the power of symbols, in the miracle of myself & of all mortals, in the divinity that is so near us and so longing to be nearer, in the staggering, bloody, starry wonder of the sky I can see above and the sky I can think of below. When I learn that the stars I see may be but the backs of the stars I see there, I am filled with the terror which is the beginning of love. They tell me space is endless and space curves. And I understand.

And now that I am started I can't stop; I've saddled a bright horse, and his brightness, not his body, keeps me bouncing up and down like a rubber star on his back. I have never raved to you before for as long as this have I? But it really is natural raving. Before one gets to a truth in one's own mind one has to cut through so many crusts of self-hypocrisy and doubt, self bluff and hypnotism; the polishing of phrases rubs off the sharp madness of the words and leaves only their blunt sanity. Here I am writing naturally; take it or leave it; this stream is yours, if you want it, and can go on for as long as the teeth hold in the gums, for as long as (any image will do) the hairs of your head are as sweet as the ropes that hang down from the hands of the sky, hanging down to be pulled at—if one had the strength.

And to begin, I want to believe in dragons, not the windy, tank-like creature who quarrelled with St. George, but the vast and fiery legend, bearing half a planet on its shoulders, with hell in its nostrils and heaven in its scales, with a comet in the steaming socket of its eye, with a couple of dragon-lets at its side, with a grandmother at home knitting unbelievably large socks and finding counties in her hair.

I want to imagine a new colour, so much whiter than white that white is black.

I want to forget all that I have ever written and start again, informed with a new wonder, empty of all my old dreariness, and rid of the sophistication which is disease. How can I ever lie on my belly on the floor, turning a narrow thought over and over again on the tip of my tongue, crying in my wordy wilderness, mean of spirit, brooding over the death of my finger which lies straight in front of me? How can I, when I have news to scream up to heaven, and when heaven has news to scream down to me? I want to read the headlines in the sky: birth of a star, death of a comet. I want to believe, to believe for ever, that heaven is being, a state of being, and the only hell is the hell of myself. I want to burn hell with its own flames.

No, but my wants are not all cloudy as that; I want to live and love & be loved; I want to praise and be praised; I want to sleep and wake, and look upon my sleeping as only another waking; I want to live and die.

We don't worship nature; nature is what we wish it and worships us; we stop the sun, we tell the sun to go on.

'The universe is wild and full of marvels.' In the shape of a boy, and a funny boy at that, I have only a very short time to learn how mad and marvellous it is; I think in cells; one day I may think in rains. All round us, now and forever, a spirit is bearing and killing and resurrecting a body; I care not a damn for Christ, but only for his symbol, the symbol of death. But suicide is wrong; a man who commits suicide is like a man who longs for a gate to be opened and who cuts his throat before he reaches the gate.

There is an imp in your room, looking with my eyes at you.

Finale: The Hate talks

There is a foghorn crying out to the ships in the Bristol Channel as an albatross might have cried to the ancient mariner, over Shakespeare's multitudinous ocean on a deep, dark night. I should like to be somewhere very wet, preferably under the sea, green as a merman, with cyclamine crabs on my shoulders, and the skeleton of a commercial magnate floating, Desdemona-wise, past me; but I should like to be very much alive under the sea, so that the moon, shining through the crests of the waves, would be a beautiful pea-green.

I am very often—especially in such fantastic frames of mind as have entertained me during the last few days—convinced that the angle of man is necessarily inconducive to the higher thoughts. Walking, as we do, at right angles with the earth, we are prevented from looking, as much as we should, at the legendary sky above us and the only-a-little-bit-more-possible ground under us. We can only (without effort) look in front of us and around us; we can look only at things that are between the earth and sky, and are much in the position of a reader of books who can look only at the middles of pages and never (without effort) at the tops and bottoms. We see what we imagine to be a tree, but we see only a part of the tree; what the insects under the earth see when they look upwards at the tree, & what the stars see when they look downwards at the tree, is left to our imagination. And perhaps the materialist can be called the man who believes only in the part of the tree he sees, & the spiritualist a man who believes in a lot more of the tree than is within his sight. Think how much wiser we would be if it were possible for us to change our angles of perspective as regularly as we change our vests: a certain period would be spent in propelling ourselves along on our backs, in order to see the sky properly and all the time; and another period in drifting belly-downwards through the air in order to see the earth. As it is, this perpetual right-angle of ours leads to a prejudiced vision. Probably this was the divine plan, anyway, but I certainly intend to spend more time lying on my back, and will even, if circumstances permit, follow Mr. Chesterton's admirable advice and spend as much time as possible standing on my head.

And so, for the present, I leave you, a short, ambiguous person in a runcible hat, feeling very lost in a big and magic universe, wishing you love and a healthy new year.

Dylan

MSS.: Lockwood Memorial Library, Buffalo

Rayner's Lane, near Harrow, is the London suburb where Trevor Hughes lived with his sick mother.

The Fitzroy Tavern is a public house in Charlotte Street, Soho, much frequented in those days by painters and writers.

TO TREVOR HUGHES

12th January 1934

Swansea

Ever since I left you alone on the deserted railway platform, waving a last, forlorn handkerchief as the train rushed me onwards to Chelsea and Sir Richard Rees, I have been meaning to write you a long letter. Sometimes the monstrous shape of the Rayner's Lane illuminated sign has risen up in my dreams like the advertisement of my conscience, and I have sworn to jump out of bed the next morning, grab pencil and paper, and write until darkness fell again upon the emptiness of Wales with an accustomed clatter. But the mornings have been cold, the pencil has not been near enough, the paper has been too virgin to deflower, and my own incorrigible laziness has made me postpone, time upon time, the pleasure of continuing our correspondence. Once I can start, then everything's all right; the words, God knows, come easily enough, too easily for some, as I will tell you later. But the inspiration to begin has not knocked in the blood nor fingered the fingers. Now—with divine help—this letter can go on for some time.

I was with you in September; now Christmas has gone, and the only letters between us during that period have been short and almost businesslike in tone. Did I thank you for sending my story? I know I never sent the new poems as I promised. Let this be my repentance, and may I join you, if only for a little while, in your single wilderness?

You seem no cheerier than when I last saw you, and indeed I would be surprised if you were. Living in Metroland with a crippled mother—and please don't imagine for a moment that these words are flippant in any way—is not conducive to the Higher Optimism, nor, in the midst of such respectability and subservience to the office clock, to the unrespectable creation of literature. I remember advising you to climb out of your morbidity, little realising then, perhaps, that you were not the Jonah swallowed by your own whale, but the whale—I have faith in your ability to write—swallowed by the Jonah of circumstance. And either this is a deeper tortuity than it appears, or it has no meaning at all.

Now I understand a little, but only a little, of the circumstance

86

that has played so hard with you, and if it has not swallowed me it is because of my self-centredness, my islandic egoism which allows few of the day's waves to touch it. Soon after I left you, my father went to the University College Hospital to be operated upon for cancer of the throat; today he went back to school, weak and uncured. And only a little while ago I learnt the truth of my own health. But the statement of Dad's disease and the warning of mine have left me horribly unmoved; I become a greater introvert day by day, though, day by day again, I am conscious of more external wonders in the world. It is my aim as an artist—that, too, has been denied, but not by the pontifical Eliot—to bring these wonders into myself, to prove beyond doubt to myself that the flesh that covers me is the flesh that covers the sun, that the blood in my lungs is the blood that goes up and down in a tree. It is the simplicity of religion. Artists, as far as I can gather, have set out, however unconsciously, to prove one of two things: either that they are mad in a sane world, or that they are sane in a mad world. It has been given to few to make a perfect fusion of madness and sanity, and all is sane except what we make mad, and all is mad except what we make sane.

No, the great Eliot has not damned me, but he has been cautious. Rees, on the other hand, though printing two poems of mine and taking a peculiar interest in all I write, has made one very startling accusation: that much of what I write is not written consciously, that any talent I may have is clairvoyant, and my fecundity is accounted for by 'automatic writing'. Charles Williams of the Oxford University Press, and author, as you know, of several mystic books, has read many of my poems but confesses that he does not understand them; they cannot be 'pooh-poohed' but he could not say that he liked them. And so we go on, meeting nothing but courtesy and interest, and nothing but a rather bewildered refusal to print.

I am sending you a few recent poems to criticize, not in the pedantic way of the professors but by your own and far more valuable methods. Be as honest as I am with you. They are, I admit, unpretty things, with their imagery almost totally anatomical. But I defend the diction, the perhaps wearisome succession of blood and bones, the never-ending similes of the streams in the veins and the lights in the eyes, by saying that, for the time at least, I realise that it is impossible for me to raise myself to the altitude of the stars, and that I am forced, therefore, to bring down the stars to my own level and to incorporate them in my own physical universe.

Prose and Verse is a sad story, and postponed as often as my letter. Only a little while ago it was budding into light, creeping up even through my lethargy; now it has sunk down again, and is no more than a legend for old men to tell their children: Once upon a time there was a boy who had Literary Pretensions, not only for himself but also for those friends who, too, burdened the editors of England with their sad expostulations. And the boy decided to produce a periodical in which he himself and the other unfortunate young men might express the vicissitudes of their spirits in great detail; he advertised it and interested in it many of the leading Intellectuals of his Philistine town. But something happened; one friend went to London, and another to a University, both very big and bewildering places, while the boy was left with a few equally bewildering contributions upon his hands. Time passed, and a new Intellectual arose who, hearing of the boy's frustrated plans, resolved to see that, at long last, those plans should come to fruition. Again something happened, or, to tell the truth, two things happened, and one was the fault of the boy and the other was the fault of the Intellectual. The boy, very suddenly, became disgusted with the mental disease of his country, the warped apathy of his countrymen, and of the essentially freakish nature of himself. And the Intellectual became lazy. So again the periodical was buried under the mists of the mind, and again were the boy's friends done dirt on. But one day Prose and Verse will arise in all its splendour, and be published not out of the bowels of dirty Wales but from the heart of the metropolis. And he and his friends will be older and wiser, and their contributions may even be better than they were before. Yes, Prose and Verse is buried but not forgotten. It shall be published, that I promise. And that some of it, at least, shall be good, you yourself shall see to.

It may be a day or two before this letter is completed, for, intent as I am upon writing it, I seem to become busier with every new idle day. In the mornings and afternoons I find I have more and more to write, and the fact that what I write may be valueless does not alter the fact of the time it takes; my evenings are given to rehearsals and performances at the Little Theatre, or to the steady but increasingly copious sinking of drink. Remember, too, that the scrappiness of this letter is owing entirely to the odd minutes I am devoting to it, and not, as it might appear, to such a startlingly untidy brain.

This new year has brought back to my mind the sense of magic that was lost—irretrievably, I thought—so long ago. I am conscious, if not of the probability of the impossible, at least of its possibility, and the paradox has clothed itself like a fairy. It needed courage to say that 'like a fairy', for the young pantomime ladies, gallivanting in gossamer nudity, have robbed the fairy of all but her woman's body.

A fairy is not supernatural; she is the most natural thing in the world. How much easier it is to believe in her, in her magnificent transformations, in her wings and wonder, than it is to believe in the invulnerability of the Pope, the genius of Bernard Shaw, and the Loch Ness monster. Not that I doubt the existence of the latter, but those who see him look upon him wrongly. A man who perceives a particularly unbelievable sunrise or sunset does not phone the news to the papers; if he sees—as all of us have seen—a fire-breathing centaur in the shapes of the clouds, he does not take a photograph of it so that his friends might be impressed with its reality. He says, Very wonderful, and he goes on his way. So it should be with the monster in the Loch; the villagers should see it, if it is to be seen, remark upon the legendary curves of its trunk and the horns on its head, then go home quietly to their beds. 'I saw the monster,' they would say to their wives. 'Go on, do you believe that?' 'I don't know about believing it,' would be the reply, 'but I saw it all right, and very unbelievable it was.' There the matter would drop.

Superstition is a moral vice, but a man who believes in the supernatural is a man who takes things literally. It is the aim of the church—that embodiment of medieval moral—to do away with man's sense of the literal. How much better to say that God is big than that he is 'all-pervading'.

There is no vice (a deliberate contradiction); what we know as vices are social crimes; it is the fault of society that it will not adjust itself so as to make those crimes either uncriminal or unthinkable. But society to adjust itself has to break itself. Society should accommodate man, not hinder him; but it has grown up rotten with its capitalist child, and only revolutionary socialism can clean it up. Capitalism is a system made for a time of scarcity, and the truth of today is the truth of fertility. All that renounces fertility is a lie.

The trouble, of course, with preoccupation with the roots and the substance of magic is the frequency with which the devil and his forked apprentices inhabit the mind of the believer. Despondency can so easily be put down, not to an organic disturbance or to self-insufficiency or to a misanthropic philosophy, but to the bedevilled paradoxes of the brain; the faults in oneself can be too easily blamed on the things that go squawk in the night; Satanism is too easy a synonym for sadism. The most terrifying figure in history is, to me, the French abbé who became, through some sexual stringency or latitude, a connoisseur of the grave and a worshipper of his sister Worm. He would not lie with a woman unless she dressed herself in a shroud, painted her face as the face of a corpse, and lay as stiff and unbreathing as though she were in the clasp of her last lover. The abbé was probably a gentleman and kind to dogs, but his view on the living was through the lenses of the dead—there is a delightful image somewhere which pictures each blade of grass as the periscope of a dead man—and this, despite my own morbid system of aesthetics, strikes me as an unpardonable fault. The most beautiful thing in the world to Poe was a woman dead. Poe is not to be challenged on the grounds of taste but on those of accuracy, for a woman dead is not a woman at all, the spirit that made her a woman being fled and already metamorphised. To love a dead woman does not appear to me to be necessarily unhealthy, but it is a love too onesided to be pure. Love is onesided, I admit, for it lies more in what you put into a woman—and for once I am not speaking anatomically—than in what you take out of her. The cynic would say that it is the other way about; but then the cynic is a dead man, and despite the fact that I consider paganism to be the most evil of doctrines, the body was given to live as much as the stars were given to live up to.

You said once in one of your valuable letters that still, incidentally, have a prominent place on my desk, that your troubles at my age encompassed the whole of womanhood, while mine—little toper that I am bound to become—could be circled by the limits of a half pint measure. While disagreeing thoroughly that my adolescent troubles could be confined to a short and bewildered acquaintance with drink, I confess that woman as a generalisation, even as a physical generalisation, has never worried me at all. The actual leaping in my blood has always been caused through the memory of, or the contact with, some particular and actual person. It is also my pleasure or misfortune to confess to a lean and suspicious creator of pathological literature that I am in love. What is more, it is not an unnaturally onesided love. Laugh as much as you like, though I don't think you will. Will you?

Have you been reading as much as usual, or has that hindered inspiration of yours at last burst out of the womb of the pen? I am looking forward to the reading of your promised story, and am hoping, too, that you are satisfied with it. You know your own faults as well as I know my own, and while I am spending more and more time on the shapes of paragraphs, the slow formation of sentences, and the deletion of commas, it would still be probably advisable for you to spend less and less time on remodelling and more on the redhot creation of your prose. Much is against you, I know, but I find it hard to say whether adverse circumstances are a hindrance or not. The best in a man comes out in suffering; there is a prophet in pain, and an oracle in the agony of the mind. Such things are easy to say; it is easier to recognize the prophet than to heed him; if only I could say with Blake, Death to me is no more than going into another room. How easy, too, it is to say that; there is as much charlatanism in a poet as there is in an astrologer, and it may be that the genuineness and the value of the one is the genuineness and the value of the other; both have a love and an awe of the miraculous world, and both are conscious of horizons.

Does one need 'New styles of architecture, a change of heart'? Does one not need a new consciousness of the old universal architecture and a tearing away from the old heart of the things that have clogged it? Still our minds are hovering too much about our testicles, complaining

> . . . In delicate and exhausted metres
> That the twitching of three abdominal nerves
> Is incapable of producing a lasting Nirvana.

We look upon a thing a thousand times; perhaps we shall have to look upon it a million times before we see it for the first time. Centuries of problematical progress have blinded us to the literal world; each bright and naked object is shrouded around with a thick peasoup mist of associations; no single word in all our poetical vocabulary is a virgin word, ready for our first love, willing to be what we make it. Each word has been wooed and gotten by a vast procession of dead litterateurs who put their coins in the plate of a procuring Muse, entered at the brothel doors of a divine language, and whored the syllables of Milton and the Bible.

But consciousness of such prostitution need not lead us, as it has led James Joyce, into the inventing of new words; it need not make us, as it has made Gertrude Stein, repeat our simplicities over and over again in intricate and abstract patterns so that the meaning shall be lost and only the bare and beautiful shells of the words remain. All we need do is to rid our minds of the humbug of words, to scorn the prearranged leaping together of words, to make by our own judicious and, let it be prayed for, artistic selection, new associations for each word. Each word should be a basin for us to cough our individual diseases into, and not a vessel full already of others' and past diseases for us to play about with as a juggler plays with puddings.

> Stands Harrow steeple where it did
> When Horace Vachell was a kid?
> And does the Sign stand like a sinner?
> And is there still too much for dinner?
> Lie my old poems unremoved?
> And is your mother's health improved?

91

And other questions I've no time
Or inclination, too, to rhyme,
And questions better left unsaid
Till next I sleep in Trevor's bed.

Now the sooner you write the sooner I shall reply—and I certainly
want to; and the more of your work you send me the more shall I be
pleased. Write as much as you like, or even more, and I promise
that my next letter will be longer than this one and will have much
more to say. I hope to be coming up to stay with my sister in the next
three or four weeks. No definite date is arranged yet, but I'll let you
know as soon as it is; and, if nothing else, we can spend a few hours
together in the Fitzroy Tavern. But I hope I'll be able to see you
longer than that. Goodbye and God bless you.

Dylan

MSS.: Lockwood Memorial Library, Buffalo

This letter to the *Swansea and West Wales Guardian* is, so far as I know,
the only one he ever wrote to a newspaper. His political incoherence, even
its undertones of Fascism, show how little he had profited from the Marxist
instruction he had received from his left-wing friend, A. E. Trick.

TO THE EDITOR OF THE 'SWANSEA AND WEST
WALES GUARDIAN'   14th January 1934

TELLING THE TRUTH TO THE PUBLIC
EXPOSURE HUMBUG AND SMUG RESPECTABILITY

Sir—In this overpeopled breeding box of ours, this ugly contradiction of a town for ever compromised between the stacks and the littered
bays, the Philistines exercise an inevitable dictatorship and regard the
first glimmerings of a social intelligence and the first signs of a godly
abhorrence of the parochial diseases much as the black man must have
first regarded the features of his lily-faced brother.

You have most worthily demonstrated the fact that a local newspaper need not exclusively confine itself to the printing of photographs
of our more bovine notabilities; the detailed reports of crimes which,
in a less criminal state of society, would be unnecessary; insipid
gossipings on the topographical positions of vanished streets and the
references in bad novels to our God-chosen town; the retelling of old

jokes; running commentaries on the gradual break down of the parish pump, and the useless quibblings between Christ-denying Christians, irrational Rationalists, and the white-spatted representatives of a social system that has, for too many years, used its bowler hat for the one purpose of keeping its ears apart.

But the colour of a shirt counts little to the man who has no shirt on his back, and the musical heaven after death harped on by the gentleman with the harmonium is a poor substitute for the man whose heaven on earth—warmth, clothes, food, a woman, and may be, children—is denied him on all sides. You can do more than merely allow the amateur and professional politicians of the town to display their bad manners in public. It is within your power to force, up to the very limits of censorship, upon all your readers some little consciousness of the immoral restrictions placed upon them, of the humbug and smug respectability that works behind them all their handcuffed days, and to do this, not from any political bias, but from the undeniable conviction that the divinity of man is not to be trifled with, that the manna of God is not the lukewarm soup and starch of the chapels, but the redhot grains of love and life distributed equally and impartially among us all, and that at our roots of being lies not the greed for property or money, but the desire, large as a universe, to express ourselves freely and to the utmost limits of our individual capabilities.

Fascism would sprout to life like a flower through a coffin's cracks, watered by the excreta of the dead, the droppings of the political dead, the spittle of the Anti-Christs who have crucified Him and His children since the kiss of a man who wanted thirty pieces of silver in order, perhaps, to bribe one of the councillors of Jerusalem with a sack of coal or a cask of wine, or, as a member of the Jerusalem Road Improvement Committee, to buy a row of houses that the committee had decided to knock down for extension purposes. It would still stink of the weeds of this decomposing system of society, and all the tails of all the black shirts in the world would not wipe away the mud and the black and blue bruises from the well kicked bottom of the British public.

That we know. The shirts are changed, but the masks remain, hiding the riddle faces of those to whom the beauty of the tangible world approximates to the individual leisure for observing it. To them there is no world that is not to be touched and felt or sensed by the ambiguous senses of the maltreated body. To them the individual is a factor towards a state, and still an intricate machine for work that sells its sweat and muscle or else starves and is broken down. To them the individual is not a world, a structure of bone, blood, nerves and flesh, all made miraculous by the miracle of the mind, but a creature that works for the profit of its fellow creatures so that it may drag out its days and eat what is provided it and be buried at its own expense.

Fascism would clear the working man's house of bugs and attempt to provide him with a little more of what he should never have deprived of; the divine right to live, regardless of his own working capacity.

Fascism would do this and more, so that he might work the harder and be dragged deeper into a false state of security and a blasphemous content, with his position at the very bottom of an anti-religious world of class.

That we know. It is within your power to force the consciousness of that, and the hate of that, upon a thousand brains, and to show, through the medium of that consciousness that the beautiful world has been made foul by the men who have worked against men, by the devil in man which has worked against the God in man.

Teach to hate, and then to believe in the antithesis of what is hated.

Yours etc.

Swansea   DYLAN THOMAS

In March he had received a letter from Glyn Jones, the poet, who was to become a friend, and in the same month he also received a congratulatory letter from Stephen Spender who was already well known in London. Dylan was beginning to achieve a reputation, at least among other poets.

TO STEPHEN SPENDER

March 1934

5 Cwmdonkin Drive,
Uplands,
Swansea

Dear Mr. Spender,

I'm very glad you wrote and very pleased that you like the poems of mine which you have seen. I'm glad in more ways than one that you wrote to me, for I have been trying during the last few weeks to write to you and tell you how much I liked your last poem in New Verse. Your poems in New Verse, and the last one especially, seem to me to be by far the most valuable things that have been printed there. I hope you won't think I am saying this merely because you have been so kind about my own poems.

Here, in this worst of provincial towns, I am so utterly removed from any intellectual life at all, that it is a great pleasure for me to receive even the shortest congratulatory letter. The fact that I am unemployed helps, too, to add to my natural hatred of Wales.

Mr. Grigson has asked me, through the Listener, to send him a few poems with a view to having them printed in New Verse. But I don't think he'll like what I sent him. What periodicals are there that publish the sort of verse I am trying to write? I have been printed in the Adelphi, the New English Weekly, the Listener, & the Referee. Do you know of any other papers—or rather, would it be too much trouble for you to write and tell me—which might publish my poems? This is asking rather a lot, I'm afraid. If you're too busy to write, perhaps I could see you in London when I come up next—just after Easter.

Thank you again.

Yours sincerely,

Dylan Thomas

MSS.: Harvard

At about the same time he attempted to define his poetical attitude in a letter to Glyn Jones.

TO GLYN JONES

Just after 16th March 1934

5, Cwmdonkin Drive,

Uplands, Swansea

If you are not coming to Swansea for some time, why not send me a few of your poems—poems, preferably, that have not been published? If possible, I want only unpublished material for my anthology which, with the grace of God may be brought out sometime this year. You needn't worry about the poems that I shall accept; W. H. Davies, and all his little money parasites are banned. I don't care so much about the 'hardness and the stiffness' of the poems, so long as they are in the best sense modern, and so long as there has been a genuine necessity for writing them. As a matter of fact I hope that some good 'fluid' verse will find its way to me. There seems to be an aversion today to poems which flow quite evenly along the pages; readers are always looking for knobbly, gristly bits of conflict in modern poems, apparently not realising that a poem can express the most complex of conflicts and yet show none of the actual conflicting gristle. I would really like to see some of the things you write. You are, I suppose, a good Socialist. As a Socialist myself, though a very unconventional one, I like to read good propaganda, but the most recent poems of Auden and Day-Lewis seem to me to be neither good poetry nor propaganda. A good propagandist needs little intellectual appeal; and the emotional appeal in Auden wouldn't raise a corresponding emotion in a tick. Are you obscure? But yes, all good modern poetry is bound to be obscure. Remember Eliot: 'The chief use of the "meaning" of a poem, in the ordinary sense, may be to satisfy one habit of the reader, to keep his mind diverted and quiet, while the poem does its work upon him.' And again: 'Some poets, assuming that there are other minds like their own, become impatient of this "meaning" which seems superfluous, and perceive possibilities of intensity through its elimination.' (If you know these quotations, I am sorry.) The fact that a good poem is obscure does mean that it is obscure to most people, and its author is therefore—contrary to his own ideas, for every poet thinks that he writes for an universal audience—appealing to a limited public. None of us today want to read poems which we can understand as easily as the front page of the Express, but we all want to get out of the poems twice as much as we ourselves put into them. It would be possible to catalogue most of the reasons for modern obscurity. Some poets, like Gertrude Stein, and the French-American Transitionists of Eugene Jolas, have evolved a mathematically precise method of removing the associations from words, and giving language, or attempting to give language, its literal sound, so that the word 'cat' becomes no more than a one-syllabled word with a hard consonantal ending; others, like Joyce, have magnified words, lengthened and animated them with contrary inferences, and built around them a vast structure of unexpected and often inexplicable associations; others, like Auden, have taken their public too much for granted, and have cut out all words that seem to themselves unnecessary, leaving their poems at the end written in an imaginative shorthand; others, again like Rimbaud, have introduced exclusively personal symbols and associations so that reading him and his satellites, we feel as though we were intruding into a private party in which nearly every sentence has a family meaning that escapes us; others, like Eliot, have become so aware of the huge mechanism of the past that their poems read like scholarly conglomerations of a century's wisdom, and are difficult to follow unless we have an intimate knowledge of Dante, the Golden Bough, and the weather-reports in Sanskrit; others, like Graves and Riding, have something intellectually new to inform us and indulge in a logical game of acrostics. Then there are the Cummings, so very often short, who obsessed by the idea of form, chop up their poems into little strips and pin them horizontally, diagonally & upside-down on the pages.

My own obscurity is quite an unfashionable one, based, as it is, on a preconceived symbolism derived (I'm afraid all this sounds very woolly and pretentious) from the cosmic significance of the human anatomy. And I think that is about enough of that.

If this letter sounds too annoyingly dogmatic, send me a picture postcard of the National Museum, will you? (I shall know what to do with it.) No, but I should like to see your work ver, much, not for the sake of pinning it down and labelling it like a butte fly, as I appear to have done above, but merely to enjoy, or not to en, v, it.

Now to answer a few questions. I am in the very early twentie. I was self-educated at the local Grammar School where I did no work at all and failed all examinations. I did not go to a university. I am not unemployed for the reason that I have never been employed. I have done nothing but write, though it is only recently that I have tried to have some things published. I have had two poems in the Adelphi, several in the Sunday Referee (a paper you should take), some stories & poems (there is one story in this week's issue) in the New English Weekly, some poems in the Listener (I have a very obscure one in this week's, too), many things in the 'Herald of Wales', a poem in John O'London's, while the Adelphi, the New English Weekly & other papers including, I hope, the Criterion, are going to print some things in the fairly near future. And that's about all. Not a very formidable list. Oh, I forgot, a poem of mine was read over the wireless from London last year. I believe I am going to live in London soon, but as, so far at least, no-one has offered me suitable employment, living is rather an ambiguous word. I will probably manage to exist, and possibly to starve. Until quite recently there has been no need for me to do anything but sit, read and write (I have written a great deal, by the way), but now it is essential that I go out into the bleak and inhospitable world with my erotic manuscripts thrown over my shoulder in a sack. If you know any kind people who want a clean young man with a fairly extensive knowledge of morbid literature, a ready pen, and no responsibilities, do let me know. Oh, would the days of literary Patronage were back again!

Write me a letter, and send along some poems. Tell me about yourself. I'm too lazy to ask questions. And if you do really want an obscure poem, invest threepence on a copy of this week's Listener. Even if you don't like my poem there's a good Latin crossword.

Dylan Thomas

Geoffrey Grigson accepted 'Our eunuch dreams' and another poem for publication in *New Verse*, and promptly ceased to be one of the two men Dylan hated most in Britain.

TO GEOFFREY GRIGSON

27th March 1934
5 Cwmdonkin Drive,
Swansea

De . Mr. Grigson,

Thank you very much. I am glad you are going to print the two poems I sent you. I am enclosing a new poem, just completed which may be some good to you. I shall send you some more poems later if I may.

I shall be up in London from Easter Saturday until the end of the following week, and am visiting Hampstead during that time to see some friends. Could I call and see you?

Yours sincerely,
Dylan Thomas

P.S. I have been reading over again my poem starting 'Our eunuch dreams', and am struck more forcibly than before by what might seem to be the jarring optimism of the first six lines of the fourth part. I suggest that this revised stanza sounds far less false:

> This is the world: the lying likeness of
> Our strips of stuff that tatter as we move
> Loving from rag to bone;
> The dream that kicks the buried from their sack
> And lets their trash be honoured as the quick.
> Suffer this world to spin.

But, of course, it's entirely in your hands. If you think this revised version to be better in any way, I do hope you'll use it.

Dylan Thomas

MSS.: Lockwood Memorial Library, Buffalo

Early in 1934 he sent Pamela Hansford Johnson a letter in the form of a play. The two characters are called Spajma Oh-no-Nell and Saldany Moth, anagrams of her name and his. It is largely nonsense and belongs, if anywhere, in a volume of his juvenilia rather than among his letters. I have therefore omitted it.

The next to be preserved can be dated, approximately, 28th March 1934. The two earlier letters to which he refers have been lost.

I have cut three pages of detailed criticism.

The tone of this letter is different and for a good reason. They had now met. He had been in London, staying with her and her mother in Battersea, from 23rd February to 5th March, with a few days away visiting his sister. Pamela and Dylan had become close friends during this visit, going to the theatre together, visiting Neuburg's establishment, drinking beer in the Chelsea pubs. Indeed her diary shows that she was poised to fall in love with him, as was he with her, for as soon as he returned to Wales he wrote and told her he loved her. She rebuffed him as nice young women were supposed to do in those days, to begin with, and he wrote a reply which she described as 'acrid'. But as the letter which follows reveals, this lovers' quarrel was only an April shower. He was coming to London, again to stay with her, in a few days' time.

TO PAMELA HANSFORD JOHNSON

About 28th March 1934

5, Cwmdonkin Drive,
Uplands,
Swansea

Apology & regret

I apologise for having delayed this letter so long; usually I write my letters very quickly & then forget to post them, but this time it's quite different. I've been too ill to write, to do anything but sit fatalistically by the fire, sip Turkish tobacco out of a most exotic pipe, and scribble small conceits on the backs of postcards. Which shows you how very ill I must have been. Now I am regaining vitality, and will have to write at a hell of a speed in order that you may receive my honeyed words before the end of the week. I shall also endeavour to keep clear of the emotional element. I still regret that now famous letter with all the conviction of my murky conscience. And I do regret having hurt you, as you said, in my last outpouring. I do regret that letter. It gives me pain where I eat and where I sit down. And the pathos of the second folio is equally regrettable. Of course I know that nothing has, or even can be, spoilt. Of course . . . I . . . know . . . of course . . . I . . . know! The Sub-editor can go out of business and the woolly reporter of the soul regain his position.

Health

The nicest thing that has ever been said to me you put at the foot of the first page of your letter. You won't remember what it was, and I'm not going to tell you. But I shall fight the Spectre of Disease with all my puny powers and grow as pinguid as your melancholy satyr himself, if only to live up to those so many words. And when at last the Great Cricketer disturbs my bails, I shall go serenely back into the Heavenly Pavilion, talking of you & Alma Mater to the enthusiastic crowd, & conscious that my Innings had not let down the prestige you so beneficially granted. This sounds like Mr. Baldwin's humour, but it's deadly true. You alone know how True-Blue I really am, & what a collection of old school ties my vest conceals.

Beyond the Agates

I'm so glad your pantomime was a success; it deserved to be; I, from my prophetic couch, willed that it would be so. Mind, I allow you a little congratulation for the success; you wrote it and acted it, I admit: but I had an awful lot to do with it, too. But why say it didn't amuse me? It struck me as being very good. It's not the sort of humour that makes me laugh uproariously & bite my neighbour's ears, but that's my fault & not yours. Wit is something entirely out of my comprehension. I can understand slap-stick, rude stories, lunacy and modern verse. And that's about all. Oscar and his little epigrams would have left me as cold as an Eskimo during the breeding season.

This is the sort of humour I like & understand (I hope you haven't heard it, you can't stop me anyhow.)

A man attended a large Society banquet, & was placed in the next seat to his hostess. When the spinach was brought on to the table, he immediately put his hands into the bowl & rubbed a great deal of spinach into his hair. Sensation. 'Do you always rub spinach into your hair at dinner?' enquired his hostess in an icy tone. The man looked flabbergasted. 'What a terrible mistake', he said, 'I thought it was cabbage.'

I find that that story is very rarely successful. But—if it has not already done so—Battersea Rise should roll & retch with its prodigious laughter.

Yes, when we quarrel, your solid Ted shall come & watch us; it should be a very good lesson for him. Do you fling things? When I used to quarrel with friend Jones, we used to take it in turns to sit on each other's heads. We might adopt that slightly eccentric method. Had enough? says one. Yes, says the other in an agonised voice. Then the positions are changed. And eventually, tired and hurt, the two arguers sit hiccuping on the floor & wonder what the argument was about.

Your poems are changing, and for the better. The change, not the fulfilment, is quite evident in the poem you sent me. 'Pinguid' is a lovely word, but it is also an affected word. It means fat, doesn't it, & is an obvious Latinization. Your first line would be vastly improved if you changed it to its English equivalent. Or even said 'A gray, old satyr, lying in the shade.' Anything like that, the more naive the better. I see that the females who now adorn your poems are a very athletic lot. One woman would keep leaping on to vines (probably an alcoholic complex), & now you have a girl who leaps about so indiscriminately that she is called the 'leaping' girl and left at that. I'm not laughing at this sudden introduction of the sporting element. Far from it. I'm just writing a lot of nonsense while I try to define my reaction to the 'Poem' as a whole. The motif—let me have my jargon—is good, and 'Curling' into the womb is just the sort of juicy anatomical conceit I love.

.   .   .   .

I've had a few poems in the papers lately (New English Weekly—Listener, & John O'London), but I've been frightfully lucky in other ways. After my poem was printed in 'The Listener', Stephen Spender wrote me a letter, saying that he liked it, & offering me some review work on a few good periodicals. I'm going to meet him & have dinner with him when I come up. He might be able to do something for me. Geoffrey Grigson, too, wrote a letter, asking me if I'd like to have some poems printed in New Verse. And, best of all, T. S. Eliot wants me to call & see him. He was, for him, quite complimentary. From a literary point of view this has been a very good week. From every point it's been terrible. I've been feeling ill, and I've wanted to have you to talk to. Now I'm better, and I'm coming up to town next Thursday. I will come to your place on Saturday. Don't say you have visitors or anything like that will you? (anyway you asked me, & I know you want me to come).

I'm not going to write any more. This is probably the worst letter I've ever sent you. But I want you to get it before the weekend. Write to me before Thursday, & reassure me.

Love,
Dylan

I'm sending you two poems—one very simple—& a bad short story. The story is included only because it will give you an opportunity to give me the bird as ferociously (what a curious idiom, especially with that adjective) as I gave it to you over the Prose Things. I'm almost frightened that it's whimsy, God deliver me.

Love again,

Dylan

I couldn't—just couldn't—finish the poem I told you about. Very caddishly I used the dolphins in another poem which I'm enclosing.

MSS.: Lockwood Memorial Library, Buffalo

On 9th April 1934 he returned to Swansea from Battersea and by now there was no doubt but that he and Pamela Hansford Johnson were in love with each other. From now on his one overriding ambition was to get to London.

TO PAMELA HANSFORD JOHNSON

15th April 1934

5, Cwmdonkin Drive,

Uplands,

Swansea

Soliloquy. Morning

The worms are doing very nicely today. Sunday in Wales. The Sunday-walkers have slunk out of the warrens in which they sleep and breed all the unholy week, have put on their black suits, reddest eyes, & meanest expressions, and are now marching up the hill past my window. Fathers are pointing out the view to their stiff-collared whelps. I'd like a big green stick with spikes on the end. Mothers are resting their bellies on pram-handles; little girls are telling each other their harmless stories of affectionate Sunday School mistresses; boys with pomaded scalps are thinking of picture shows and lingerie; and all the starch, the thin, pink blood, the hot salty longings, and the respectable cream on the top of the surburban scum, run down the stones, like a river end up in the sabbath well where the corpses of strangled preachers, promising all their days a heaven they don't believe in to people who won't go there, float and hide truth. Life passes the windows, and I hate it more minute by minute. I see the rehearsed gestures, the correct smiles, the grey cells revolving around nothing under the godly bowlers. I see the unborn children struggling up the hill in their mothers, beating on the jailing slab of the womb, little realising what a smugger prison they wish to leap into, how the eyes of men are abused by the town light, how the gasoline has crept under their nostrils like the smell of a new mechanical flower, how the stars have been counted for us, how the smiles of Moon, the seventh planetary god, have been translated to the shapes of hills & shores on which, from the first marking of time, the atomed tides of light break and make no sound, how the God of our image, gloved, hatted, & white, sits no longer playing with his stars but curving his Infinite length to the limits of a Jew's theory, and how, each Easter dawn, the sun moves back a finger's length into the East, riding, to satisfy the Christian convictions of the astrologers, in the sign of Aries, the sign of the lamb.

I wish I could see these passing men and women as ghosts only, and look on their cheap shapes and substances as the own cheapness of my mind clothing itself, for a minute's maggot, in all these diversities. But I see them solid and brutal; if there are ghosts, I am turnip and sawdust, and you are the longest shadow that ever fell under the sun. I wish I could see them as the pagan houses of flesh and blood, as creature-boned and sky-sexed, as the beings that have grown like a bug out of the garden of Eden, as the fleshes that need no brains but only the conscience of their fleshes and the consciousness of their fleshes and the freedom and the Mexican splendour. If I, incorrigibly romantic, could see them as a Yucatan people, call them to a cat-drinking ceremony, and know their names as childish Nazul, Tilim, & Yum-Chas, my Sunday worm would disappear like a Japanese mouse in a flash of green light—you remember the story—and my letter would be as loving as I wish it. Loving it is now, but recondite and scaly as the Zodiacal Scorpion.

I wish I could see these passing men and women in the sun as the motes of virtues, this little fellow as a sunny Fidelity, this corsetted hank as Mother-Love, this abusing lout as the Spirit of Youth, & this eminently beatable child in what was once a party frock as the walking embodiment of Innocence. But I can't. The passers are dreadful. I see all their little horrors.

I wish I could see them as the pitiable products of a capitalist system, wage-slaves, economic eunuchs, mass-systemized, the capitally lettered Workers that Sir Richard Rees, & men who need do no work, are so intent upon making the martyrs of their own intellectual Inquisition. Again I can't. What are these Workers to me? Isn't every thought, every lift of the lids, every smile, every kiss, a Work that no creature but this divine, this rational meat-eating man can accomplish? Man himself is a work. Today he is a dirty piece of work. But tomorrow he may sprout wings under his serge shoulders, be faced and sided like Aquarius, who is the first sign of the vital year. He may be a bluff, white Tsar, ordering the insects of the earth, the slugs & beetles, the preachers and gangsters, the lovers & lepers, & even the little, loving letter-writers like ourselves, on the maddest missions all over this altering earth. He may be a benevolent as the Alhambra, or gloomy as the Gate. Today he is bloody, and that is a bloody nuff for me.

Comment. Night

I read over what I wrote this morning. All is silly, but why should I cross it out or throw away. It's just a little more me for you to grapple with. Which sounds even more conceited than many of the other things I've put in my letters to you. I've often wondered—I thought of asking you, but am always so vastly happy with you that I don't like introducing morbid & egotistic subjects—whether you think me as conceited a little young man as I often think you must do. I'm not really; profoundly the other way. But I've noticed that when, for example, you—quite honestly and often misguidedly—run down your poetry, I never retaliate, as every true-blue poet should, by saying how very unsuccessful my own poetry is, too. I never say it, but not because I don't think it. I know it. And when you say, of a poem of mine, 'That's bad', & I try to argue & show you how good it really is—that, too, must sound conceit. Darling, it isn't. I'd hate you to think that I was all self-contented, self-centred, self-satisfied in regard to—well, only one little thing, the things I write. Because I'm not. And I'm not half as brave, dogmatic & collected in the company of Literary persons as I might have led you to believe.

Thank God it's dark. Now I can't see the people outside. I might be in a world of my own, owing nothing but the seeds of hate to all the dark passers, scuttling to the rub-a-dub-dub in the bebatted belfries of the stinking churches, scuttling homewards again or out on their half-frustrated amatory expeditions after the sin of love has been emphasised by St. Paul & his pimply apostles. I'm going to put on the light; the bad water-colours on the walls will be meaningless, Lake Como a lake of the brain, & even the naked Greek dart-throwers as human as the lumps of stone that clutter up the back garden. I don't want to see my books; a library is a sanatorium of sick minds. I don't want to see my papers all over the floor; why should I take my bed in the sanatorium? There's nothing better now but sitting in a circle of darkness, watching the shape of the body be shapeless, & hearing the intimate rustlings of the room louder & louder. Why aren't you here with me, in my little circle, holding my hand & braving the wicked world with me? Don't tell me—I know. The world is so wickedly wicked it won't let you brave it with me. I have just to go on hoping and waiting. I can make a shape of you to sit with me in this circle; I love the shape, but the shape isn't enough. I try to think of you marooned in your own dark island. Make room, darling. I'm as lean as Ugulino, I don't take much room. There, I'm comfortable now. Avaunt, you worm-faced fellows of the night. Pamela & me, on one circled island, sit & poke our fingers at you.

Comment. Tuesday Morning

Monday was a dead day, the hole in space you talk of, such a deep-damp hole as I must have fallen into when I last left you. I can hardly remember a thing about Monday, certainly not the rising and setting of the day. I don't think I read or wrote. I remember lifting up a cushion to see if you were underneath. You weren't. That was early in the morning, & it was after that, I believe, that I fell with a great clatter into space. After all, when you pick up a cushion to find nothing underneath—that's a terrible surprise. Of course it would have been rather a surprise if you had been there. But I haven't got over the idea yet that if I open a cupboard door very quickly, I might see you sitting and beaming inside. If you open a furnace door quickly, you'll see the devil, leering on a coal. But you have to shut the door even more quickly. And if, perhaps, you were in the pantry when I opened it one day, the shape of you I saw might—and would be, I think—no more than a very devilish trick. And when I touched you, as I undoubtedly would, I would not be surprised to see you change colour as rapidly as though I were a pinguid satyr, & disappear in an acrid flame through the holes of the cheese. Monday was dead. I know I wanted to write another section of this letter, & tell you in great detail how much I love you. But I died about ten o'clock, & I think you died with me. Now Tuesday, today, is quite a different sort of day. It's so abominably warm & bright that I shall have to satisfy my conscience which, like most other things, is bound up in you, by taking a bus to Gower & walking over the cliffs. I shall hate it because I shall be so lonely. But it shall be done; all your commandments shall be obeyed. I am writing this in a deck chair under the clothes-line. This should really be a very sexy note (it's not going to be), for above me and around me all the disembodied underclothes of this respectable Drive are doing a very naughty dance. Not so disembodied, though. Those spindle-shanked pants two lines away, have their own airy limbs; a spring demon has inhabited them: O inhabited pants! And that little vest, (mine, I think) is breathing up and down as though the Carnera wind were developing its chest beneath it.

Lunch. After lunch I go out to do my duty & your commands on the rocky fastnesses of Wales. And, late in the evening, I will finish this letter. Goodbye, —— I left the blank because I can't think of anything lovely enough to call you. Goodbye, darling. And I put such an inflection into the word that it sounds almost as lovely a word as I want to call you.

My latest song: 'Come into the garden, bawd.'

Wednesday morning

I couldn't write last night, was too tired after my medicinal walk which led me into the village of Llangenith, miles from anywhere, very near nowhere. Now, quite early on another bright blue day, I am sitting in the untidiest room you ever saw, writing the last few pages. I have just finished an incompetent drawing in pastels of a negro riding on a leopard down the clouds, & although it has made me feel in one of the most airy & unearthly moods, I'll try to answer your question.

I told you the answer over lunch one day, when you were misting the walls near our table with your long breaths of misery. I told you that however much I loved you I would still be able to say 'lousy' to anything lousy that you wrote, & tell you to take up raffia work if I thought that your poems had, and could have, no value at all. And I would. I've said 'lousy' to many of your poems, and will undoubtedly do so again, just as you have spat you of my angularities & my blonde bones. But, right, deep down in the pit of my belly, I know that you can be good, that you have been good, & that all the little lice in your Muse's ear will one day get up & depart. I can't enthuse over your poetry as yet, & you would know that I was wrong if I did. But I can say, honestly & honestly, that there is a thing in your poetry, in your Lotus Women, Symphonies, Lullabies, & Morning Suns, that is the thing of all true poetry. And if I can't name that thing, it is my fault & not yours. You couldn't give up writing. You know you couldn't. It would be criminal if you did. You have been given certain talents & facilities for the writing of poetry which you must, for the sake of all you believe in, love and live up to. What is wrong is your attitude, or, at least, much of your attitude, towards these talents. Because the talent, which is very easy to see in twenty out of the twenty four pages of your book, is not enough by itself; the work-woman in your poetess, the intellectual, the thinking craftswoman, has not had half enough to do. You must work at the talent as a sculptor works at stone, chiselling, plotting, rounding, edging & making perfect. You told me, too, over the same lunch, that you hadn't got the time & energy to do all this. My dear, I know; I know you haven't; and I know that it's wrong, as wrong as anything under the sun, that you have to work in a dull, methodical office, all the day, all the long, wild & wonderful day that waits for you and can never have you. But instead of going home in the evenings &, after dinner, sitting down to write a poem or two, why not sit down to write perhaps no more than three perfected lines? Instead of three or four mediocre poems, each with a line, a phrase, or a hint of beauty in it, you would, eventually, have one poem, or one stanza of a poem, that had all those collected lines, phrases & hints in it. You told me that the 'Lotus Women' was written very quickly, even though I thought it the best thing you had done. I still think so, but I liked it for no more than two lines & two phrases: the rest was ordinary. If, over that same poem you had spent as many hours as you spent minutes, each line would be one I'd like, & each separate phrase. This advice is easy to give & hard to carry out. But I want you to try to carry it out. You mustn't waste your little bit of genius. You mustn't read bad poetry, must forget your Tennyson & even your Housman. You must pack your poems tight, work at them every spare moment you have. Whatever you do, I believe in you. I believe in you at your worst & your best. Send periodicals and reviews to hell. Work at your poems. And send me every line you write. As long as I have you at the back of me I'm going to be good. And so are you, with me behind you. And I'm going to be behind you & with you always.

Wednesday afternoon. Soliloquy

You are my only friend. I say quite seriously that I have never really spoken to any other human being, & that you are the clear point of faith with which the psalmist lifted his eyes to the hills. When I went away from you, it seemed you had abandoned me to myself. And when I was with you, after all these years of pursuit, we were face to face, alone. And you were a tiny spirit floating around the room, flying faster and faster till you came invisible, & I could hear only your wings. It was a very quiet, monotonous sound, and came from a tail-less mangy dog which limped across the room. I raised my foot to kick it, but it was the toe of a giant who reached up to take the stars in clusters. Then you were behind me, whispering 'Juggle with these. Juggle I say. Go on'.

I wish I knew what that soliloquy meant. It means something very big, but I can't understand it. I know you weren't the mangy dog, dear. But who was? That's the worst of writing without thinking:

you write more than you think. I must have been the mangy dog, but I don't feel at all self-pitiful today. Damn the nonsense. Forget it. I seem very very near to you this afternoon. And being near you is worth all the nonsense in the world.

I'm going to drink some coffee now, & then finish this page. You'll have my letter tomorrow morning. Write over the week-end to me, so that I get your letter by Monday. Coffee. Even coffee has become a symbolical rite. The composition of my own letter and—best of all— the having of yours, has become the greatest event of my week, holier than the ritual of the bath, than the linking of sweet airs & phrases, than the night and its dreams. No more moujik, stomachic depression. No more worm for either of us, or if there must be a worm in our letters let it be the jolly, red-bellied one you told me about & not the grey-whiskered journeyman of the tomb.

> Fathom the wavy caverns of all stars,
> Know every side of every sand in earth,
> And hold in little all the lore of man
> As a dew's drop doth miniature the sun.
> But never hope to learn the alphabet,
> In which the hieroglyphic human soul
> Most changeably is painted, than the rainbow
> Upon the cloudy pages of a shower,
> Whose hinges a wild wind doth turn.
> Know all of each! when each doth shift his thought
> More often in a minute, than the air
> Dust on a summer path.

That's my great Beddoes. I wish to God we were lying by the side of the fire, reading his lovely gloom to one another ere the Spider make a thinne curtaine for our Epitaphes.

> Oh we are not at home in this December world,
> Cold sirs & madams.

Shall we live on an island, somewhere in the Mediterranean, writing & reading, loving & sleeping, singing our sweet rude rhymes to the seals? I love you darling. Goodbye.

Dylan

MSS.: Lockwood Memorial Library, Buffalo

On 22nd April 1934 he won the second major prize given by 'Poets' Corner', where it was announced that a volume of his poems would soon be published. Pamela Hansford Johnson's volume had just appeared.

TO PAMELA HANSFORD JOHNSON

25th April 1934

Introduction

When I received your mammoth envelope, I had no idea what it contained and began to wonder whether you had sent me your life-story in detail. I was quite expecting to see your letter open with, 'I was born on a cold and lousy May day in a garret in Park Lane', or something of the sort. Instead, of course, you gave me enough literary material to fill a book, and how on earth I'll be able to criticize it all by Thursday I've no idea. You see I'm writing this on Wednesday morning, although I received all those evidences of your teeming brain by the second post on Monday. I should have started writing before, but I've really been busy—what with my damnable walks (I'm awfully glad you've taken to them, too), rehearsals for a play (I don't know why I keep on doing this), drawing the drawings for the play (it's an arty piece of Coward), typing and revising stuff for Vicky, & attempting, quite uselessly, to finish a fairly long short story that I wanted to send you. So now I have only a very few hours in which to tell all the little that's been happening to me, to tell you once more that I love you and think of you all the time, and to do my best with your stories and poems.

My Dad read your book & liked it very much. He thought it was nearly all fresh and lovely. 'Graceful skimming' was his phrase, I think, &, on the whole, it's very apt. But you aren't going to skim any more. Today's poems—at least they are today's poems to me— are incomparably better. I wish they could have been printed too.

Thank God, now I can get a word in. You'll be interested to know that the B.B.C. have banned my poetry. After my poem in the Listener (Light Breaks Where No Sun Shines) the editor received a host of letters, all complaining of the disgusting obscenity in two of the verses. One of the bits they made a fuss about was:

> 'Nor fenced, nor staked, the <u>gushers</u> of the sky
> Spout to the <u>rod</u> divining in a <u>smile</u>
> The <u>oil of tears</u>.'

The little smut-hounds thought I was writing a copulatory anthem. In reality, of course, it was a metaphysical image of rain & grief. I shall never darken Sir John Reith's doors again, for all my denials of obscenity were disregarded. Jesus, what are we up against, Pam?

The poem you didn't like, along with 'When the Galactic sea was sucked', & a new poem which I'm sending you, is to be printed in the April New Verse. That particular poem isn't as bad as you think. There is no reason at all why I should not write of gunmen, cinemas & pylons if what I have to say necessitates it. Those words & images were essential. Just as some have a complex in regard to lambs & will never mention them even though lambs are necessary for their thought, you, my Christian, refuse to look a pylon in the face. I wasn't conceding anything. I wanted gunmen, and, shatter my hams (your oath, but such a wonderful one that you musn't be allowed to have it all for yourself) I bloody well had them. Ha! I'll be up as early as possible on Saturday, but don't hold anything up (I don't mean hold up a flag or an old man's adenoids in a bottle: you know what I mean), because I mayn't be able to leave Swansea until Friday night. More than probably I shall, of course, but I'm telling you this in case. . . . It's no good me saying I'm looking forward to seeing you again. You know how much I am. What are we going to do? Smile darkly over the fire? I want to see Congreve's 'Love for Love' at Sadler's Wells, if it's still on. Will you come? Or is there something else you'd prefer to see. There's the 'Country Wife'; that should bring out your best bawdy laugh. Find out if 'Juno & the Paycock' is still running. It isn't in the West End I know, but it may be in some obscure theatre.

What a chatty little letter this. Nothing but facts. It must be—it is—the effect of this pedantic day. The sky looks like the graph of a heavenly calculation.

No, I haven't been doing anything I shouldn't. I have smoked only two cigarettes since I last saw you. You can't—yes you can—realise how terrible it has been to give them up. I've chain-smoked for nearly five years; which must have done me a lot of good. I am allowed a pipe—mild tobacco, not too much. That keeps me alive, though I hate it like hell. I take walks in the morning and pretend there's a sun in these disappointed skies. I even go without a coat (sometimes) in this cold weather, & tread be-jumpered over the sheepy fields.

I've told you, I think, about the coughing sheep that plague my life. In front of my nice little villa is a field where bankrupt farmers pasture their animals before the time of the slaughter house. It's hard to believe how many of those doomed creatures are consumptive. Good old meat-eaters. In a week that particularly diseased sheep that keeps me awake half the night with its centenarian coughs will be done to death, cut up in various saleable lengths, and hung on hooks in butchers' windows. Some sweet little child will develop a sore throat one of these days, or suddenly his lung will break up like a plate (not a dental plate). So much for the carnivorous. One day I shall undoubtedly turn into a potato. You won't like me then. And, on that day of Transformation, I certainly shan't like you, salt rasher of bacon!

I like to be tidy-minded, but I so rarely am. Now the threads of half-remembered ideas, the fragments of half-remembered facts, blow about in my head. I can write to-day only awkwardly & uneasily, nib akimbo. And I want to write so differently: in glowing, unaffected prose: with all the heat of my heart, or, if that is cold, with all the clear intellectual heat of the head.

There were no shear-marks visible in my last letter for the reason that I had cut out nothing. I never shall in my letters, though the uncut material may, when I think back on it, hurt me very much. And how horribly easy it is to be hurt. I am being hurt all day long & by the finest & most subtle things. So on goes the everyday armour, and the self, even the wounded self, is hidden from so many. If I pull down the metals, don't shoot, dear. Not even with a smile or a pleasant smile or a rehearsed smile. (Like a speech from a Russian Drama. Look, little Ivanovitch, there are bodies in the Volga. One is your little Aunt Pamela. Go give her a snow-cold kiss. No, O little wretch, that is a dead postman. That is your auntie, the one with the poem in her teeth.)

What a biased child! 'Dolphined' is your word. Nothing shall take it away from you. All my words are your words (cue). The only reason I never finished the poem in which your word originally appeared was because I failed utterly to make it good enough. You are with me when I write (cue).

And now I shall rise from the lovely fire, jam my hat hard and painfully on my head, & go out into the grey day. I am strong, strong as a circus horse. I am going to walk, alone and stern, over the miles of grey hills at the top of this my hill. I shall call at a public house & drink beer with Welsh-speaking labourers. Then I shall walk back over the hills again, alone & stern, covering up a devastating melancholy & a tugging, tugging weakness with a look of fierce & even Outpost-of-the-Empire determination & a seven-league stride. Strength! (and I'm damned if I want to go out at all. I want to play discords on the piano, write silly letters or sillier verses, sit down under the piano & cry Jesus to the mice).

If I had money I would go round the world, looking for somewhere

where the sun was always shining, beautiful & near to the sea. And there I should build me a house as splendid as Keawe's, so that people should call it the house of light. All day there should be music, and olive-skinned virgins, bearing wine in lotus-coloured bowls, should wait on my littlest want. Women with the voices of harps should read to me all day long. And one day, leaping up from my scented couch, I should cry 'For Christ's sake give me a tram'.

MSS.: Lockwood Memorial Library, Buffalo

Geoffrey Grigson was at this time editor of *New Verse*. In 1934 and 1935 Dylan frequently appeared in that magazine. Later Geoffrey Grigson turned against Dylan's poetry and they quarrelled.

TO GEOFFREY GRIGSON

May 1934
5 Cwmdonkin Drive,
Uplands,
Swansea

Dear Grigson,

Thank you very much for writing. I'm sorry we could not meet for lunch, but your illness was a very real excuse. I shall be in London in about a month's time when I hope we can meet again. I'll let you know when I'm coming up.

I wonder whether it would be possible for you, when you are fit and about again, to see whether there is any chance for me to do some review work. I hope you won't mind me asking you this, but things are not going too well with me at present and I'd welcome any sort of journalistic work at all.

New Verse was awfully good this month, and I was pleased to see Carlos Williams given one in the eye.

The poem you said you'd read and tell me about is incomplete in the version you have. I enclose the complete poem.

Yours sincerely,
Dylan Thomas

MSS.: Texas

Pamela Hansford Johnson was now beginning to find her true vocation as a writer of prose, and was soon to start the novel *This Bed Thy Centre*, that was to make her name. Meanwhile she had sent Dylan a number of short stories, which he criticized, as usual, in mildly but acceptably sarcastic tones. I have omitted some fifteen hundred words of this criticism.

'Referee Poets No. 2' is, of course a reference to his forthcoming volume, she having been No. 1.

The 'Red Book' is the notebook in which he wrote down his short stories. It is now in the Lockwood Memorial Library, Buffalo.

The reference to a Mediterranean trip escapes me, as does the possibility of a visit to Russia.

'Percy' was a fictional character concerning whom he, Dan Jones and Pamela constructed fantasies.

TO PAMELA HANSFORD JOHNSON

2nd May 1934

Very Early

I have decided not to get up today, to lie serene in my bed and write of the things that go round me, the shapes of shadows on my mountainous knees, the curving of my immaculate breast and the life in my ever-scribbling fingers. I have put on nice new pyjamas, so this is going to be a pleasant day, and perhaps I shall not think of worms at all but only of the sun that I'm sure is shining in the curious world outside, and of other equally lazy people who, too, from the white islands of their beds are writing to ones they love on the commercial sea. In peril on the commercial sea. What is this death, this birth and apparent pain, this glib love—this rush to the head of so many extraneous creatures of the air that crowd my words and never let me stop a sentence at a nice, rhythmic stop? Don't tell me.

Which I think is about as nice an opening to a letter as any as I can think of. And having told you that I intend to spend the whole day in bed, I now contradict my own slothful intention and pull the sheets back. I shall go out immediately and commune with the sun—yes, I have established the fact: the sun is shining most strongly—or, on second thoughts, retire into a blowsy world of papers and pencils and write weak odes to a literary parhelion.

Now it's very obvious that I shouldn't begin to write so early. Half in, half out of sleep, I can't possibly write anything but a lot of high-falutin nonsense. Most words are Boogums at eight o'clock. And I can never say, 'Hark, hark the Snark' until at least after breakfast.

Well, why am I writing now? You have already risen and are staring, not very intelligently, at the stories of sudden death in the Express. Or perhaps it may be later than I think, and you are buying your cigarettes at the shop where the girl who thinks me jolly would be very much surprised if, tousled and red-eyed, livered and lachrymose, I was to walk in now. Or perhaps you are sitting in the bus, passing Chelsea or Kronsky, and wondering what the hell rhymes with piano. And here I lie, in a lukewarm bath of half-slumber, with the un-polished taps of words turned full on. Yes, why? I wanted to tell you the most remarkable dream I dreamed last night, in which I was climbing ladders all the time and waving to Pamela-faced horses on the top of asylum towers. But when I started to put the dream in order, it sounded Double Dutch, or, at least, Double Hatch, to me.

After Breakfast

It is still too early to be intelligent. Sometimes I think it always is, and that about fourteen o'clock I might really get up and say some-thing brilliant. But anyway you wouldn't like me if I did, and the hankering after cleverness is the hobby (wrong word introduced for the sake of the alliteration) that, theoretically, I most abhor. I should like to indulge in a rapid rifle rattle of Oscar wit—not necessarily concerning Oscardom (Pouff is the sweetest thing)—and say new clever things about sex and moths and hipbaths and all other luxuries in this bread-and-butter world.

The mention of Oscar reminds me of Oscar Browning, that divinely blue-blooded snob of the Oxford nineties. The last incident about him I read yesterday—I wish I could say I'd read it Gomorrah—in a book called 'Swan's Milk' by Louis Marlow. I'll repeat the very simple story, but first explain that Oscar was a little, very old, bald don, of the sort who always stops—in hopes—to read the writing on public lavatory walls. Oscar and another man were sitting on a mountain side, talking. 'What is the difference between a bob and a shingle?' the old don enquired. 'There's not much difference, only a shingled head looks like a boy's, behind.' 'A boy's behind' roared Oscar, 'A boy's behind. How can I sit here and listen to your obscene observa-tions. A boy's behind. I've never wanted to see a boy's behind. Any other simile. But a boy's . . . .' And in sheer joy he kicked a little dog who happened to be near them right over.

That's all. And that's enough for an hour. I want to read the crime page in the Telegraph. And I have, too, a violent desire to draw pin-men.

Noon

Or, at least, somewhere near noon. It's the word that attracted me. Have I ever told you of the theory of how all writers either work towards or away from words? Even if I have, I'll tell it to you again because it's true. Any poet or novelist you like to think of—he either works out of words or in the direction of them. The realistic novelist —Bennett, for instance—sees things, hears things, imagines things, (& all things of the material world or the materially cerebral world), & then goes toward words as the most suitable medium through which to express these experiences. A romanticist like Shelley, on the other hand, is his medium first, & expresses out of his medium what he sees, hears, thinks, & imagines.

A nice true chunk of dogmatism, superbly inept on such a May morning. I have noticed in my last few letters—you are guiltless as usual—a tendency to write a lot of immaterial matter, and then lump in all the actual replies at the end. So that half of your pages go uncommented, though never, my darling, unread. Let me be a model letter-writer for once, & reply to your letter page by page in strict order.

Our Future

I believe with all my heart that we'll live together one day as happily as two lobsters in a saucepan, two bugs on a muscle, one smile, though never to vanish, on the Cheshire face. But I will never exhaust my flow of pessimism, for, sadistically, it gives me a delight or a pain and a delight mixed in one, to imagine the most dreadful things happening to us, to imagine a long future of bewilderment and disillusionment ending in Tax Collectors (I never want to hear their bloody names again) match-selling and sterile periods of the production of cracker-rhymes that we, in our hopeless megalomania, will imagine as the disregarded fruits of genius. That one day you will vomit at the sight of my face, and I at the tones of your voice. That I go nuts and you go gaga. So let me occasionally chime in with a deep chord of misery, & throw myself over an abyss of hopeless and quite unnatural speculations as to the future of two small and harmless persons who, in accordance with everything God has said or has been said to say since the beginning of the world, love and want each other.

May 29

Is a date that has become very important on the calendar. I will, unless anything goes wrong and the winds of circumstances blow me helter skelter in my pyjamas over the Adriatic or the Caribbean, be seeing you then, and the twenty odd days to go will be more turtle-footed than any twenty days have ever been.

When I said that I must have something definite in mind when I came up, I did not mean that, otherwise, I should be starving all the miserable day in the bewidgeoned park. No, what I meant was the utter boredom I'd endure between the times of goodbye and hallo to you. So something definite there must be—Vicky's proud party, or a futile interview with an uncaring publisher, or even a few luncheon appointments with bad poets. I'll write and arrange something with somebody, and probably the result will be as vague as that. Trouble at home. What a mild, mad phrase. No, no, there's none, or, at least, none that matters. But my father and mother are going to leave here about the end of June & go to live in the country, God-knows-where. I won't go to the country. I'll come to town. And it will need a very philan-thropic deity, indeed, to tell me what I do or where I sleep or even—if it wasn't for you—why, why. I won't stay with my sister, either. I am going to find a high, conventional garret, there to invoke the sadistic Muses, get a little drunk on air, and wave my hand to you over the Dome.

.   .   .   .

Referee Poets. No. 2

Thank you for your abortive list of poems. I disagreed heartily with you. 'We see Rise The Secret Wind', 'In The Ten Paradoxes', 'The Eye of Sleep' & 'Thy Breath was Shed' are all very bad indeed. I have rewritten 'The Eye of Sleep' almost entirely, and it is now a little better, though still shaky on its rhythms and very woolly as to its intention (if any). But I know how hard it is to make any sort of comprehensive list for anyone else.

I am going to include some poems which have been printed, so 'Boys of Summer', though altered & double the length, is to open the book. Other poems are: 'Light Breaks Where No Sun Shines'. 'Before I knocked and Flesh Let Enter'. 'No Food Suffices' (revised). 'When Once The Twilight Locks' (revised). 'Our Eunuch Dreams'. 'A Process in the Weather'. 'The Force That Through the Green Fuse'. 'Where Once The Waters of Your Face'. 'That The Sum Sanity' (revised). 'Not Forever Shall The Lord of the Red Hail' (revised). And about six or seven others I am still in the process of pruning and cutting about. You say Vicky's obstinate. Well you know I am, too. And nothing that I don't want goes in.

Red Book

So that's where I left it. I was despairing of it. You are an angel not to read it. I confess that if you had left your book somewhere, & told me implicitly not to touch it, the first thing I would do when your back was turned would be to peep, with a nasty aren't-I-a-lad expression, into the pages. But I believe you, and I am glad you haven't read it because it contains more nonsense to the square inch than most wards in a home for people who imagine they are bath buns or postage stamps or maypoles etc.

I wish I could have disguised myself as an Old Girl—pince-nez, warts, & thin vowels are essential, I suppose—and come to hear your impassioned reading. Did you read your Symphony? If you intend to some other time, a good idea would be to cultivate—if that is the word, and I'm sure it isn't—a violent indigestion before beginning. Think how easy the tympani would be then. But I'm afraid you want artificial teeth to do full justice to the harp. What is it like, really, reading your own poems to a set of polite people who, in all probability, imagine trochee to be a new sort of lawn game? Were you nervous? I hope you were, you bitch, for you shouldn't read poems to Old Girls. I've a good mind to ferret an Old Boys Society, & read them the waxiest & wombiest efforts that I've got.

Answers. And Tit Bits

Play was 'Strange Orchestra', which we've done before. I played, as usual, a degenerate artist. But my drawings were good. One was a large abstract, done mainly in furniture varnish, titled from the Revelations: 'The Star Called Wormwood'. And the other two were early Victorian pastels of nude women rolling about in fields. A few of the audience were quite horrified, the con-Genital idiots! I can't think what plays we could do, but I think we'd be funniest as the Macbeths. But in our prospective society, I refuse to play incestuous fathers all the time. Let me have a change now and then, and play a homosexual butler. You, my dear, shall play whores & whores only. 'Sex', by Mae West, may be a good Starring Vehicle for us, though I refuse to appear without my trousers in more than two acts out of the three.

Would you like to play Mrs. Avling in 'Ghosts'? I'd love to play Oswald, even though he is your son. We'd give them neurosis with a capital F.

I'll look up some plays and show them to you when I come up. I'm enclosing a poem and a story. Darling, will you type the story for me so that I can send it to Lovat Dickson's. Perhaps you won't like it very much, but I refuse to anticipate that. Tell me what you think of it. Damn the details; just tell whether, as a whole, it's at all successful.

The poem is, I think, the best I've written—I've said that to you about a lot of mine, including all sorts of wormy beasts. It may be obscure, I don't know, but it honestly was not meant to be. It's too— I can't think of the word—for anything but New Verse to print. I'll get Grigson to do it. But it isn't Grigson's opinion I want. It's yours. And what are these 'new standards' you've arrived at. I hope they aren't too high. Only about an hour ago, a boy of fate, disguised as a telegraph messenger, came with a wire from 'New Stories' accepting my 'Enemies'. It was accepted by another paper a month or two ago, but refused at the last moment because of the word 'copulation' on the last page. Now 'New Stories' has it, copulation and all, & is to print it next month.

Try 'New Stories' 118 Banbury Road, Oxford. Address it to E. J. O'Brien—of the 'Best Short Stories of the Year'.

Money

Short stories of the sort I write hardly make anything. 'New Stories' for instance, perhaps the best story journal of the lot, doesn't pay at all. And poetry wouldn't keep a goldfish alive. Novels and popular, narrative stories are the things. I'm damned if I'm going to write for the Strand, even if I could, which I very much doubt, and novels are a long and arduous business. Besides, it's no use writing a novel merely for the sake of writing one. You have to have something to say that only the novel can express. My novel—I've done the first chapter —will be, when and if I finish it, no more than the hotch-potch of a strayed poet, or the linking together of several short story sequences. I shall scrap it in a few days. No, novels aren't for me—yet. So what's the alternative? Six months ago I'd have suggested the docks or the oven with the greatest equanimity. But now I've got to live. It's when I'm with other people more than when I'm by myself that I realise how much I want you and how very far away you are from me. I'm willing to work. I do work, but in an almost anti-mercenary direction. Which is no good at all for you or me. Something has to be done, but Christ knows what it is. And Vicky can't help. He can do little more than keep himself alive, & that not very comfortably. And the arty people I know are almost as broke as I am. There are all sorts of things I could do. I could get in with a bad repertory company in Coventry, or some place like that—I forget the exact place. But that's as far away from you as ever and quite futile. A man wants to take me for a long trip up the Mediterranean and I could go to Russia with a Welsh Communist organisation. All very nice, but what the hell's the good? I might have a good time, but I'd make no money at all, and if I thought about you when I was standing on the dockside at Odessa, I'd break my heart. So something has to be done. And with that nice, comfortable platitude, I sink back into a usual lethargy and continue to write of my uncommercial maggots.

Percy Droppeth Again

No more Percy again. I haven't got time. This has got to go by the last post. Percy, the ubiquitous, the inscrutable, & the entirely bafty will have to wait. But he'll come. What a profoundly unamusing book we might make out of him. I wonder how much madness the British reader takes to his ounce of nonsense. Can you imagine the Times Supplement reviewing 'The Quality of Percy'? 'This bafty book. . . .' 'Conglomerations of Youthful Horseplay, Senile Smut, & Lunatic Obscurity'. Mr. Gerald Gould . . . 'Hatcha!'. No, I can't imagine it either.

By the way, raw carrots are spendid. But raw potatoes are bloody. I've given them up, anyway, and had bread-and-milk for supper last night. It tasted pretty loathsome, but I got it down somehow & pretended it was good. No more yapping at my diet. My darling Pam, you don't eat half enough yourself. I won't be satisfied until we play a rousing game of hockey together. And, after the match, we'll retire into the woodshed—where all dirty things happen—& commit fel-o-de-se.

Again I haven't replied to half your letter, & again I've left too many things unsaid. I don't think that I've said that I love you. But I do. Oh I do. Goodbye, Pamela, & write soon, very soon.

Dylan XXXXXXX
a magic number, dear

Throughout most of May 1934 he was in Wales working on the poems which were to constitute his first volume, *18 Poems*.

'The Old Tin Kettle' was a music hall song.

Tom Warner was a close friend of Dylan's, a composer.

A. R. Orage was editor of the *New English Weekly*.

Dylan's 'weak, watery little' poem was 'Ears in the turrets hear', a poem generally regarded as one of his finest. At that time, however, it probably seemed to him too lucid, insufficiently dense.

I have omitted some four hundred words of criticism of her poems.

The end of this letter is missing.

TO PAMELA HANSFORD JOHNSON

9th May 1934

Yesterday, I received from Southampton a small, round tin of tooth powder, enclosed, in an explanatory note, at the request of a Mrs. Johnson of Battersea Rise. 'Eucryl destroys germs in every part of the mouth.' Was that the intention of your mother's much-to-be-thanked request? Or perhaps you sent it after my singular poem, in order that I may clean my mouth out with great thoroughness? Give my love to your mother, and thank her for the powder. Whether it will destroy the germs or not, I cannot possibly say. I hope not. I admire germs. And, if I remember, I shall bring a few more than usually bawdy paragraphs into this letter to satisfy their lecherous itches.

And, while I remember, too, let me raise one nasty growl about your unparalleled bitchiness in pinching my letter to the Neuburg. I wrote a stony, non-committal letter to him, received your pathetic appeal, and immediately tore the old effusion up and posted off a charming Micawberish affair. And don't you go about jeering at my Old School Tie. I hate Old School Ties. I haven't got one. I shall now attempt to light a Russian cigarette in a most rakish manner, and look all sexy at the mantel-piece. But it doesn't work. I am fated to be British under my Russian exterior. But don't always point at my tie. Just pretend it isn't there. Anyway it was a sweet letter, and, if nothing else, I meant what I said about Pamela Johnson, though if I had any idea that she would see the letter, I would have introduced a long and dirty paragraph all about her nasty little moist-nosed muse.

Again I am unwell. Melodramatic introduction, reminiscent of some wheezy Shylock, to a page of remorse and self pity. But no, it shall not be. Even more melodramatic. Sir Jasper Murgatroyd enters through the trapdoor with a snarl, and immediately opens his waistcoat and distributes, from his navel, Empire Marketing Board pamphlets on 'The Caul of the Colonies'. To put it plainly—it is an intellectual impossibility to put anything plainly—I feel about as much more use as (a sudden puritanism makes me delete this. Very indecent) (I am trying very hard to deny the Tooth Powder, and to devote all my bawdy and soul to the composition of Old Tin Kettle innuendoes. But it fails. This May morning is un-naturally church. The birds sing the Ave Maria. My germs tell me that Ave Maria sounds like a sexual disease. I whisper 'Poonah' to them, and display an invisible gout. They vanish). But I am ill, ill as hell. I have had a headache for a fortnight, and haven't slept for longer than that. I've lost all hope of ever going to sleep again. I lie in the dark and think. I think of God and Death and Triangles. I think of you a lot. But neither You nor the Triangles can make me sleep. I've drugged myself up to the eye-lids. I have a little box of tablets with an instruction on the cover not to take, on any account, more than three. I take nine, and still I remain awake. I have tried everything. I have tried getting drunk. I have tried keeping sober. I have counted sheep and bathchairs. I have read till I can't see any more. I have tried completely under the bedclothes & on top of the bedclothes, right way up, wrong way up, with pyjamas, without pyjamas. A good idea, of course, is to gas yourself just a little bit. But I can't think how that's going to be done.

No more, Darling, send me to sleep. No more. Perpetually pathetic, these daft little notes of mine can serve no purpose but to show you, again and again, how much I need you. And no Mediterranean for me. I'd love the sun, and I'd love the places the sun would take me to. But it's all useless, for, when I came back, I'd be just where I was before I went away—a little less pale perhaps, but as green as ever as to what I must do in this dull, grey country, & how one little colour must be made out of you and me. The chromosomes, the colour bodies that build towards the cells of these walking bodies, have a god in them that doesn't care a damn for the howls of our brains. He's a wise, organic god, moving in a seasonable cycle in the flesh, always setting and putting right what our howls at the astrologers' stars and the destiny of the sun leads us on to. If we listen to him, we're O.K. And he tells me, 'Don't go away now. You stick to your unamiable writings and your never-to-be-popular morbidities. You stick as near as you can to what you love'. So no trampsteamer up a blue sea for me. Give me Pamela and a Chatterton attic. Enough for the likes of me, and too much, too, for God knows why she loves this idiot writing & writing, precious as a herring, on this Old School paper.

It must be this ecclesiastical morning that drives me into such stagey melancholia. And so, by cunningly sitting in a room looking over the soot of Swansea chimney pots, I avoid the sun and all the priestcraft of May. I sit and devour the brick walls with my eyes, hoping to draw out a little of the mason's opium that, hot from their foul pipes, cemented these breeding huts together. But the room is stuffy, filled with the tobacco smoke it shouldn't be filled with & my naughty thoughts that leap, like Tom Warner's from clinical observatories in Vienna to syphilitic cabarets in Buenos Aires, from Builth Wells to Chimborazo, from the altitudes of poetical ideals to the rhyming of 'catalepsy' and 'autopsy'. I shall have nothing to send you. The old fertile days are gone and now a poem is the hardest and most thankless act of creation. I have written a poem since my last letter, but it is so entirely obscure that I dare not let it out even unto the eyes of such a kind and commiserating world as yours. I am getting more obscure day by day. It gives me now a physical pain to write poetry. I feel all my muscles contract as I try to drag out, from the whirlpooling words around my everlasting ideas of the importance of death on the living, some connected words that will explain how the starry system of the dead is seen, ordered as in the grave's sky, along the orbit of a foot or a flower. But when the words do come, I pick them so thoroughly of their live associations that only the death in the words remains. And I could scream, with real, physical pain, when a line of mine is seen naked on paper & seen to be as meaningless as a Sanskrit limerick. I shall never be understood. I think I shall send no more poetry away, but write stories alone. All day yesterday I was working, as hard as a navvy, on six lines of a poem. I finished them, but had, in the labour of them, picked and cleaned them so much that nothing but their barbaric sounds remained. Or if I did write a line 'My dead upon the orbit of a rose', I saw that 'dead' did not mean 'dead', 'orbit' not 'orbit' & 'rose' most certainly not 'rose'. Even 'upon' was a syllable too many, lengthened for the inhibited reason of rhythm. My lines, all my lines, are of the tenth intensity. They are not the words that express what I want to express; they are the only words I can find that come near to expressing a half. And that's no good. I'm a freak user of words, not a poet. That's really the truth. No self-pity there. A freak user of words, not a poet. That's terribly true.

> 'I'll not be a fool like the nightingale
> Who sits up till midnight without any ale
> Making a noise with his nose,'

is a quotation I write down for no reason at all. Neither do I feel it to be correct. For I'll be a fool like the hyena, sitting up till dawn without any pleasure, making a noise with his guts. This is out of mood with the day. I should be writing some sunny paragraphs, imagining in the words for you a green and blue expanse of Welsh country where the cattle, in accordance with all conventions, 'low', where the lambs 'frisk', and the glassy streams 'babble' or 'tumble' according to the rhyme. I'll walk this afternoon, and, perhaps, in the late night, when I write to you again the near summer loveliness will have gone into me so deeply that all the clowning and the pretentious stomachraking of the last two pages will be nothing but an echo that refuses to 'sing' in your ears or an odour that refuses to 'waft' to your nose. But, before I go out, very lonely and quite twice as pale and haggard as usual—I hardly weigh anything at all, eight one or under now—into my Gower bays, there are several matter of fact things in your last letter which I want to answer.

Now Orage, though a very pleasant and a very sincere man, is known to be almost entirely lacking in taste. He runs the literary sections of the New English Weekly by a system of filing. He has in his office literally hundreds of poems and short sketches and stories. Most of them are bad, but that doesn't matter. It's quantity with him, not quality, that counts. And week by week one or two of these stories and poems are taken down from their dusty shelves and printed. You just wait your turn, and then in you go. So there's really very little satisfaction in having anything printed in Orage's paper. He doesn't pay at all, and the standard he sets is so low it's hardly flattering to be accepted by him. He goes in for mediocrity. 'Headline', whatever its faults—and I begin to suspect that its main faults at the moment, may be my fault—is not mediocre, and not original enough —in subject, at least,—to startle him into an acceptance. I've no idea where you can plant 'Headline'. Its matter, I should imagine, would be too ordinary for 'New Stories', which deals with rather out-of-the-way affairs. 'The London Mercury' might like 'A Man And A Monkey', though I believe they keep you waiting rather a long time before they reply. The 'Everyman' prints stories. So does John O'London: but for the last, the more conventional the better. I'll have a look at some more of the magazines littered about the house. I can't remember the name of the story, but the one about the watch, the little girl, and the nasty old gentleman, is more of a commercial effort than any I can think of of yours. And, though you'll probably squeal to heaven at the suggestion, you might do worse than send it to a paper such as 'Nash's'. There are scores of papers like that, above the standards of the 'Strand' & 'Pearson's', that might stretch their standards of taste sufficiently to allow admittance to your cheery little story. And have you sent any poems to J. C. Squire? And have you sent to Harriet Monro? And what about a mild (very mild) poem to Frank Kendon, of John O'London's. He printed a terribly weak, watery little thing of mine—I've never shown it to you—last week (Saturday May 5th). These do seem dreadfully low brow suggestions. But they're not derogatory. Far from it. But you've struck such a curious <u>medium</u> in your poetry lately that publication becomes very difficult; there are so few medium papers left. By that I don't mean 'middlebrow' or anything like that. But you've brought 'conventional' poetry, descendent from Tennyson & the middle Victorians, to a point of near-perfection, and any modern, even any alive influence, is absent. So that editors of most periodicals are rather troubled at your poetry, for most of the editors (&, unfortunately, the editresses) look at the influences first and the individuality afterwards. If a poem, in the John Donne descendency, is fairly good, they print it; if very good in the Tennyson descendency, they refuse to. What they never realise—they cannot, of course, being, principally, caterers for the fashionable taste of the moment, and a taste which has spat Tennyson out & sucked up the good & the bad of John Donne in large mouthfuls —is that the convention, the heredity, of the poem doesn't matter a farthing. It's the individuality of the poet, an individuality that owes nothing to the Jacobeans or the Victorians, that really matters. If you, still (& inevitably) retaining the old Johnson individuality, were to tack on to your poems the conscious influence of Donne, Tourneur, Traherne or Manley Hopkins, you'd get published all over the place & be the moment's wow in every public salon. But you're not going to do that, because you realise that it's worthless, & that what Jack Common (entirely ignorant of everything outside intellectual socialism) refused for the Adelphi is far more valuable than most of the Donne-fathered babies he lets discharge inside his nice yellow covers.

. . . .

MSS.: Lockwood Memorial Library, Buffalo

Laugharne, the little seaside town which will for ever be associated with the name of Dylan Thomas, had been known to the poet almost all his life, but this is, I believe, his first description of it.

Glyn Jones, the well-known poet, short story writer and novelist, was a few years older than Dylan and one of his first 'literary' friends.

Richard Hughes's most famous book in 1934 was *A High Wind in Jamaica,* indeed a cosmopolitan novel.

The reference to Rimbaud is interesting in view of Dylan's subsequent self-identification with the boy-poet ('the Rimbaud of Cwmdonkin Drive'). Dylan knew no French, but had probably read him in translation by Edgell Rickword or Norman Cameron.

A. L. Basham was the third, and last, 'Poets' Corner' poet to receive the award of having his poems published in book form.

I have omitted a not very funny story about Mae West, the sex-symbol of those days.

TO PAMELA HANSFORD JOHNSON

11th May 1934

Laugharne

I am spending Whitsun in the strangest town in Wales. Laugharne, with a population of four hundred, has a townhall, a castle, and a portreeve. The people speak with a broad English accent, although on all sides they are surrounded by hundreds of miles of Welsh country. The neutral sea lies at the foot of the town, and Richard Hughes writes his cosmopolitan stories in the castle.

I am staying with Glyn Gower Jones. You remember I showed you one of his bad poems in the Adelphi. He is a nice, handsome young man with no vices. He neither smokes, drinks, nor whores. He looks very nastily at me down his aristocratic nose if I have more than one Guinness at lunch, and is very suspicious when I go out by myself. I believe he thinks that I sit on Mr. Hughes' castle walls with a bottle of rye whisky, or revel in the sweet confusion of a broad-flanked fisherwoman.

Incidentally, I showed him some of your poems, your latest poems. And he couldn't understand them at all. An ardent admirer of the Criterion, he fails to understand you. And it's quite true. You are getting pleasantly obscure, and much of what you write at the moment must seem quite mazy and difficult to almost anyone except myself. But then the reason is obvious. I, too, am mazy and difficult. We both are in our fleshy lives. And let me remind you that you will find my body damnably difficult to dispose of. 'That particular one' (your Bluebeard words) has found a widow. I will never find anyone except you. The only solution will be a little poison in my cup. Even then there would be the phantom Thomas, head under arm, three mackintoshed, weakchinned and blowsy, seeking you out and groaning his disembodied bawderies in your ear. Or, of course, you could garotte me as I nibble at my vermicelli. (Rose plot,

Fringed pool,

Ferned garotte.)

I always seems to be complaining that I cannot fit the mood of my letters into the mood of the weathered world that surrounds me. Today I complain again for a hell-mouthed mist is blowing over the Laugharne ferry, and the clouds lie over the chiming sky—what a conceit—like the dust-sheets over a piano. Let me, o oracle in the lead of the pencil, drop this customary clowning, and sprinkle some sweetheart words over the paper (paper torn slyly from an exercise book of the land-lady's small daughter). Wishes, always wishes. Never a fulfilment of action, flesh. The consummation of dreams is a poor substitute for the breathlessness at the end of the proper windy gallop, bedriding, musical brooding over the national dungtip.

My novel of the Jarvis valley is slower than ever. I have already scrapped two chapters of it. It is as ambitious as the Divine Comedy, with a chorus of deadly sins, anagrammatized as old gentlemen, with the incarnated figures of Love & Death, an Ulyssean page of thought from the minds of the two anagrammatical spinsters, Miss P. & Miss R. Sion-Rees, an Immaculate Conception, a baldheaded girl, a celestial tramp, a mock Christ, & the Holy Ghost.

I am a Symbol Simon. My book will be full of footlights & Stylites, & puns as bad as that, kiss me Hardy? Dewy love me? Tranter body ask? I'll Laugharne this bloody place for being wet. I'll pun so frequently and so ferociously that the rain will spring backward on an ambiguous impulse, & the sun leap out to light the cracks of this sow world. But I won't tell you my puns, for they run over reason, and I want you to think of me today not as a bewildered little boy writing an idiot letter on the muddy edge of a ferry watching the birds & wondering which among them is the 'sinister necked' wild duck & which the terrible cormorant, but as a strong shouldered fellow polluting the air with the smell of his eightpenny tobacco and his Harris tweeds, striding, golf-footed, over the hills and singing as loudly as Beachcomber in a world rid of Prodnose. There he goes, that imaginary figure, over the blowing mountains where the goats all look like Ramsay MacDonald, down the crags and the rat-hiding holes in the sides of the hill, on to the mud flats that go on for miles in the direction of the sea. There he stops for a loud & jocular pint, tickles the serving wench where serving wenches are always tickled, laughs with the land-lord at the boatman's wit, ('The wind he be a rare one he be. He blows up the petticoats of they visiting ladies for the likes of me. And a rare thirst he give you. Pray fill the flowing bowl, landlord, with another many magnums of your delectable liquor. Aye, aye, zor'. And so on), and hurries on, still singing, into the Hikers' Hostel, removes his pimples with a bread knife, and sprinkles a little iodine over the one and forty bats that ring the changes in the Hikers' belfries.

But the eye of truth, tired of romancing, turns back with a material squint on my self, and marks the torture in my too-bony hand and the electric livingness in the bodies of the goldfish I carry in the lining of my hat. Pamela, never trust the goldfish in the lining. They dribble lead over the nice, new felt. And their molten excreta drops, with the noise of the drums in Berlioz, on to the open skull.

I am tortured to-day by every doubt and misgiving that an hereditarily twisted imagination, an hereditary thirst and a commercial quenching, a craving for a body not my own, a chequered education and too much egocentric poetry, and a wild, wet day in a tided town, are capable of conjuring up out of their helly deeps. Helly deeps. There is torture in words, torture in their linking & spelling, in the snail of their course on stolen paper, in their sound that the four winds double, and in my knowledge of their inadequacy. With a priggish weight on the end, the sentence falls. All sentences fall when the weight of the mind is distributed unevenly along the holy consonants & vowels. In the beginning was a word I can't spell, not a reversed Dog, or a physical light, but a word as long as Glastonbury and as short as pith. Nor does it lisp like the last word, break wind like Balzac through a calligraphied window, but speaks out sharp & everlastingly with the intonations of death and doom on the magnificent syllables. I wonder whether I love your word, the word of your hair—by loving hair I reject all Oscardom, for homosexuality is as bald as a coot—the word of your voice. The word of your flesh, & the word of your presence. However good, I can never love you as earth. The good earth of your blood is always there, under the skin I love, but it is two worlds. There must be only half a world tangible, audible, & visible to the illiterate. And is that the better half? Or is it the wholly ghostly past? And does the one-eyed ferryman, who cannot read a printed word, row over a river of words, where the syllables of the fish dart out & are caught on his rhyming hook, or feel himself a total ghost in a world that's as matter-of-fact as a stone? If these were the only questions, I could be happy, for they are answered quickly with a twisting sense into the old metaphysics. But there are other and more dreadful questions I am frightened to answer. I am whimsy enough today to imagine that the oyster-catchers flying over the pearliest mudbanks are questioning all the time. I know the question and the answer, but I'm going to tell you neither, for it would make you sad to know how easily the answer drops off the tip of the brain. Fill up the pan of the skull with millet seed. Each seed shall be a grain of truth, & the mating grains pop forth an answer. (Bugger me black.)

I wish I could describe what I am looking on. But no words could tell you what a hopeless, fallen angel of a day it is. In the very far distance, near the line of the sky, three women & a man are gathering cockles. The oyster-catchers are protesting in hundreds around them. Quite near me, too, a crowd of silent women are scraping the damp, gray sand with the torn-off handles of jugs, & cleaning the cockles in the drab little pools of water that stare up out the weeds & long for the sun. But you see that I am making it a literary day again. I can never do justice to the miles and miles and miles of mud and gray sand, to the un-nerving silence of the fisherwomen, & the mean-souled cries of the gulls & the herons, to the shapes of the fisher-women's breasts that drop, big as barrels, over the stained tops of their overalls as they bend over the sand, to the cows in the fields that lie north of the sea, and to the near breaking of the heart as the sun comes out for a minute from its cloud & lights up the ragged sails of a fisherman's boat. These things look ordinary enough on paper. One sees them as shapeless literary things, & the sea is a sea of words, and the little fishing boat lies still on a tenth-rate canvas. I can't give actuality to these things. Yet they are as alive as I. Each muscle in the cocklers' legs is as big as a hill, and each crude footstep in the wretchedly tinted sand is deep as hell. These women are sweating the oil of life out of the pores of their stupid bodies, and sweating away what brains they had so that their children might eat, be married and ravished, conceive in their wombs that are stamped with the herring, &, themselves, bring up another race of thick-lipped fools to sweat their strengths away on these unutterably deadly sands.

But now a piece of sun comes out again. I am happy, or, at least, free from the morning's tortures. Glyn has gone fishing and in another half hour the 'Three Mariners' will have undone their waistcoats. I shall drink beer with the portreeve, & no crimping pussyfoot shall say me nay.

I forgot to bring your letter with me. It lies locked at home in the Pamela drawer. Its memory makes Laugharne a bit brighter—but still not bright enough—and it closed with the only words that should ever close a letter. But I can't remember many of its details. I'll reply to them again, or perhaps they can wait till I see you again. I shall look out for your tail-less story. I forgot to bring 'Anna' too. It is the best story you have written. You are becoming very competent, dear, and your stories are all your own. There are many things for me to say about 'Anna', but they, too, must wait.

Oh hell to the wind as it blows these pages about. I have no Rimbaud for a book or paper rest, but only a neat, brown rock upon which I have drawn three very ferocious travesties of your face—one eyeless, one toothless, & all entirely bloodless. And wee on the sun that he bloody well shines not. Soon I see you. Soon I kiss you hullo.

It's getting cold, too cold to write. I haven't got a vest on, and the wind is blowing around the Bristol Channel. I agree with Buddha that the essence of life is evil. Apart from not being born at all, it is best to die young. I agree with Schopenhauer (he, in his philosophic dust, would turn with pleasure at my agreement) that life has no pattern & no purpose, but that a twisted vein of evil, like the poison in a drinker's glass, coils up from the pit to the top of the hemlocked world. Or at least I might do. But some things there are that are better than others. The tiny, scarlet ants that crawl from the holes in the rock on to my busy hand. The shapes of the rocks, carved in the chaos by a tiddly sea. The three broken masts, like three nails in the breast of a wooden Messiah, that stick-up in the far distance from a stranded ship. The voice of a snotty-nostrilled child sitting in a pool and putting shellfish in her drawers. The hundreds and hundreds of rabbits I saw last night as I lay, incorrigibly romantic, in a field of buttercups & wrote of death. The jawbone of a sheep that I wish would fit into my pocket. The tiny lives that go slowly & languidly on in the cold pools near my hands. The brown worms in the beer. All these, like Rupert Brooke, I love because they remind me of you. Yes, even the red ants, the dead jawbone & the hapless chemical. Even the rabbits, buttercups, & nailing masts.

Soon I see you. Write by the end of this week.

Darling, I love you.

XX

Morning. Sunday 13.

But the night never comes. And two loose days have passed since I wrote these last ink words. They were loose days, and I accept the reprimand—before it comes—with a bowed head and a dim, canary mouth. I don't know why I do it. It's silly and childish, but somehow inevitable, especially on a sunny Saturday evening in a seaside village where, most of the afternoon, I had lain in the sun, trying to colour my face and look out-of-doors. I hate the little, minor disturbances of the world—the forgetting of letters, the losing of papers, the tiny falls, mishaps & disappointments which crop up, regular as the suicidal wish, each grassy day.

Last night, in the deserted smokeroom of a seaside pub, I found myself suddenly cornered by three repulsive looking young men with coloured shirts, who asked me, in a most polite & Turpin way, for my cigarettes. Since they all looked exactly like Wallace Beery in one of his less debonair moments, I gave them my cigarettes and enough money to buy three pints of beer. They then smiled—or rather showed me about ten (or less) broken teeth (between them)—

and persisted in drinking their illgotten beer in front of me & making rude remarks about the length of my hair. Now, I don't mind their communist ideas, or even the practice of them. But why my cigarettes, my beer, & my funny hair? It's little incidents like that that make one feel very weak & small in a country full of strong barbarians. Before they left me—probably to intimidate another lonely little person— they told me what was apparently a dirty story in Welsh. That was the last straw, & later the sun went out.

This morning, looking at Vicky's non-committal remarks about Dylan Thomas, the experimentalist, I found myself wondering who this sad named poet was, & whether he had any separate existence from the sadder person, of the night before, bullied out of his lawful cigarettes by three strong men & falling back, in the event of his comic cowardice, on to a stony pile of words. And why should the experimentalist be given so many lines in a national newspaper, & my Beery-mouthed desperadoes be consigned to the mortality of a letter page?

Anyway, I'm not an experimentalist & never will be. I write in the only way I can write, & my warped, crabbed & cabinned stuff is not the result of theorising but of pure incapability to express my needless tortuities in any other way. V.cky's article was nonsense. If you see him, tell him I am not modest, not experimental, do not write of the present, and have very little command of rhythm. My Pegasus, too, is much, much more spavined than that of A. L. Bashman, who is too selfconscious, or Pamela Johnson, whose latest published 'Poem' is sweet, girlish drivel. Tell him too that I don't know anything about life-rhythm. Tell him I write of worms and corruption, because I like worms and corruption. Tell him I believe in the fundamental wickedness and worthlessness of man, & in the rot of life. Tell him I am all for cancers. And tell him, too, that I loathe poetry. I'd prefer to be an anatomist or the keeper of a morgue any day. Tell him I live exclusively on toenails and tumours. I sleep in a coffin too, and a wormy shroud is my summer suit.

'I dreamed the genesis of mildew John
Who struggled from his spiders in the grave,'

is the opening of my new poem. So there. But I don't like words either. I like things like 'ungum' & 'casabookch' XXX, for you, my bleeder.

All of which, I think, must be owing to the condition of the liver. But never forget that the heart took the liver's place. •

My novel, tentatively, very tentatively, titled 'A Doom on the Sun' is progressing, three chapters of it already completed. So far, it is rather terrible, a kind of warped fable in which lust, greed, cruelty, spite etc., appear all the time as old gentlemen in the background of the story. I wrote a little bit of it early this morning—a charming incident in which Mr. Stripe, Mr. Edger, Mr. Stull, Mr. Thade and Mr. Strich watch a dog dying of poison. I'm a nice little soul, and my book is going to be as nice as me.

. . . .

Which leads me, quite naturally, to the end of this ridiculous letter. (Sorry. Had to cross this out. It was indecent). I love you Pamela, more every day, think of you more every day, and want to be with you more every day. Don't take much notice of my rantings and rumblings, and less of that horrid poem I sent you last week. I love you and love you. I only believe in you. Nice, round Pamela, I love you. All the time, always will, too. Write very soon and keep me alive. Sorry for all my letter. I'm not too well—perhaps it's that. You don't mind how daft the letter do you? If it's the mask I know, never lift it, my twice blessed. Love, & the crosses I can't write because there's not room enough. And now goodbye. I seem to be getting back into my old letter mood, and don't really want to stop writing. But I have to stop sometime, and I've already delayed this letter longer than I wanted to. Reply in a very few days, will you. And do be honest. Remember, I'm very fond of birds (Damn, that again!). Yes, do write back soon. Wave your hand to your mother for me, and kiss yourself good morning, and good night.

Dylan

PS. What do you want for your birthday? Books? Rings? Wurlitzer Organ?

MSS.: Lockwood Memorial Library, Buffalo

The dating of the very strange letter which follows is highly speculative. The deductions upon which the date is based are these. In her unpublished diary, Pamela Hansford Johnson noted, on Monday, 27th May: 'Appallingly distressing letter from Dylan. I cried . . . nearly all day and had to write telling him it must finish. So an end to that affair.' To no other letter that has been preserved from their correspondence could these words apply. He had recently been in Laugharne, and may well have stayed on there, or with his uncle across the estuary at Llanstephan, for another week.

His psychological motives in writing this letter to the girl with whom he was in love, but with whom his sexual relations were platonic, are clearly extremely complex. He was perhaps trying to prove his manhood, for he still fretted about his youthfulness.

TO PAMELA HANSFORD JOHNSON

? 26th May 1934
Sunday morning
Bed

Question One.　I can't come up.
　　　　Two.　I'm sleeping no better.

Question Three.　No I've done everything that's wrong.
　　　　Four.　I daren't see the doctor.

Question Five.　Yes I love you.

I'm in a dreadful mess now. I can hardly hold the pencil or hold the paper. This has been coming for weeks. And the last four days have completed it. I'm absolutely at the point of breaking now. You remember how I was when I said goodbye to you for the first time. In the Kardomah when I loved you so much and was too shy to tell you. Well imagine me one hundred times worse than that with my nerves oh darling absolutely at the point of breaking into little bits. I can't think and I don't know what I'm doing. When I speak I don't know if I'm shouting or whispering and that's a terrible sign. It's all nerves and more. But I've never imagined anything as bad.

And it's all my own fault too. As well as I can I'll tell you the honest honest truth. I never want to lie to you. You'll be terribly angry with me I know and you'll never write to me again perhaps. But darling you want me to tell you the truth don't you. I left Laugharne on Wednesday morning and went down to a bungalow in Gower. I drank a lot in Laugharne & was feeling a bit grim even then. I stayed in Gower with a friend of mine in the waster days of the reporter's office. On Wednesday evening his fiancée came down. She was tall and thin and dark and a loose red mouth and later we all went out and got drunk. She tried to make love to me all the way home. I told her to shut up because she was drunk. When we got back she still tried to make love to me, wildly like an idiot in front of Cliff. She went to bed and my friend and I drank some more and then very modernly he decided to go and sleep with her. But as soon as he got in bed with her she screamed and ran into mine. I slept with her that night & for the next three nights. We were terribly drunk day and night. Now I can see all sorts of things. I think I've got them.

Oh darling, it hurts me to tell you this but I've got to tell you because I always want to tell you the truth about me. And I never want to share. It's you & me or nobody, you and me and nobody. But I have been a bloody fool & I'm going to bed for a week. I'm just on the borders of D.T.s darling and I've wasted some of my tremendous love for you on a lank, redmouthed girl with a reputation like a hell. I don't love her a bit. I love you Pamela always & always. But she's a pain on the nerves. For Christ knows why she loves me. Yesterday morning she gave her ring back to Cliff. I've got to put a hundred miles between her and me. I must leave Wales for ever & never see her. I see bits of you in her all the time & tack on to those bits. I've got to be drunk to tack on to them. I love you Pamela and must have you. As soon as all this is over I'm coming straight up. If you'll let me. No, but better or worse I'll come up next week if you'll have me. Don't be too cross or too angry. What the hell am I to do? And what the hell are you going to say to me? Darling I love you & think of you all the time. Write by return and don't break my heart by telling me I mustn't come up to London to you becos I'm such a bloody fool.

XXXX Darling. Darling oh

MSS.: Lockwood Memorial Library, Buffalo

Dylan wrote Pamela Hansford Johnson a letter which she received on 30th May, 'pleading for another chance'. She gave it him, and she received another from him on 6th June, to which she replied, according to her diary: 'Wrote . . . forgiving him so hope for better luck next time.'

On 12th June he arrived in London again, and their love affair continued, happily. He was in London for two weeks. She was by now very much in love with him. And when he returned to Swansea he was determined to get away from the place as soon as ever he could. He apparently suffered from the delusion that Gertrude Stein could get him a job as a commercial traveller on a bicycle.

Pinker was a literary agent in New York, eventually convicted of defrauding his authors, whereas Curtis Brown was a literary agent in London of impeccable honesty.

I have cut the greater part of this letter, which consists of private jokes, criticism of her stories and gossip about 'The Vickybird' and his circle. It is, however, worth quoting his comment on his poem 'If I were tickled by the rub of love':

'I enclose my new poem. I hope you'll like it. It's going in *New Verse* this month. I took a long time over it and, at the moment, anyhow, I'm a little bit pleased with it. Not much—just a little bit.'

The end of the letter is very affectionate.

TO PAMELA HANSFORD JOHNSON

2nd July 1934

Excuses

This letter is short and late for two reasons: first, I have been waiting until today for a reply from Gertrude Stein, hoping, that as a result of her letter, I should be able to come to town very soon and with a good, if futile, excuse. Second, I turned out for a cricket team on Tuesday evening, finished with the remarkable analysis of 34 overs 60 odd runs & 3 wickets, 1 innings 0 runs, 2 dropped catches, & have been a physical wreck ever since, tortured with rheumatism & a stiff right arm. The Stein letter arrived this morning. To all intent it was quite bloody, but it furnishes an excuse of sorts, and I shall be in London on Wednesday or Thursday of next week. The Stein has, apparently, nothing to do with the bicycles which are owned by a Mr. Magnus Cohen. There's nothing in it for me of course, but I'll have a peep at him, & perhaps sing a few snatches of the Horst Wessel song outside his office door. I have given up my cricketing career, & can now cheat at Mah Jong with great dexterity.

Agents

What a beautiful word, too. Think of Rodin's Pinker, and the natural annoyance following their mistake in not attempting to make saleable what is only unsaleable to a mind counterfeited with slush magazine stories will fade into a proper prospective. As it is it's all right. Pinkers will sell 'Headlines' & the poem for you, and you, eventually, will sell the rest. That's the worst of being 'classy'. You have to look awfully high all the time. You won't be very popular, but dear! dear! you will be loved. Curtis Brown's don't like me very much either. I think they've got morbid minds, for the first two stories they are sending out are 'Martha' & 'The Vest'. Now, if they want smutty stories . . .

MSS.: Lockwood Memorial Library, Buffalo

Three days later he was writing to her again.

It is almost certain that Dylan Thomas never joined the Communist Party, and I am told by a friend who was with him that he did not actually attend the Mosley meeting.

The greater part of this letter is, once again, criticism of Pamela Hansford Johnson's writing, petty gossip about friends and pungent comments on poets now forgotten. I have therefore omitted a thousand words.

TO PAMELA HANSFORD JOHNSON

Week of July 5th 1934

Good Morning. I hope it is morning with you. If not, good morning still. The sun in my heart comes up like a Javanese orange: for similar images compare any poem in the Poets' Corner. I am at my open window again, looking out now on boys with red hair playing cricket. As always at this magically and dirtily casemented window, I am happy and aloof. Yes, I can think of you doing your usual things in your usual house, imagine your tattery up the Rise and your burning Minor in the bus. But I, to you, move in a fabulous, Celtic land, surrounded by castles, tall black hats, the ghosts of accents, and eternal Eisteddfoddau. Come down to see me, but come, my love, in the summer when we can move from this North London stuffiness near to the sea, and lie about on large cliffs by small villages, and fix my moustache not on a rolling, public bowl but on the edge of each private wave. To compensate for my disadvantage over you, here is an ambiguous, and totally inadequate, outline of my house and district. G.W.R. station. Shabby, badly built streets, unutterable melancholy blowing along the tramlines. Quarter of an hour's tram ride up a long, tired road. A square, a handful of shops, a pub. Up a treed hill, field on one side, houses on the other. Near the top of the hill a small, not very well painted, gateless house. Large room, smaller room, study, kitchen. Four bedrooms, w.c. lavatory. Space at back sufficiently large for wash-house, clothes' line, deck chair and three sparrows. Private school in field opposite. Nice field. Tennis court above. Very nice, very respectable. Not much traffic. Lot of sparrows. My own room is a tiny, renovated bedroom, all papers and books, cigarette ends, hardly any light. Very tiny. I really have to go out to turn around. Cut atmosphere with book-knife. No red cushion. No cushion at all. Hard chair. Smelly. Painful. Hot water pipes very near. Gurgle all the time. Nearly go mad. Nice view of wall through

135

window. Pretty park nearby. Sea half a mile off. Better sea four or five miles off. Lunatic asylum mile off. Workhouse half a mile off. All this sounds depressing, but you must come down. And come down soon, as soon as you can. If it's hot and summery we can have a wonderful time. And if it rains, we can fug all day and all night with the greatest pleasure in the world. You asked about Dad. He's no better, and has to see his London doctor even more often. My mother is weak but still garrulous. You won't like her. She talks too much, too often, and too unintelligently for it to be possible for you to like her. But she's very kind and would love to see you. So explore this Welsh darkness, my darling, I may even take you to Laugharne, which is the nearest approach under the sun to a Stygian borough.

Is this Political Work?

If you read the newspapers, you'll see that Swansea is the centre of the centre of all revolutionary activities this week. It is the week of the trial of Tom Mann and Harry Pollit. I have just left the Socialist Party, and offered my services to the Communists. I was in time for Mosley's meeting, and was thrown down the stairs. No harm done, however. I have just completed a seditious article attacking the shirted gentlemen. Cha!

. . . .

MSS.: Lockwood Memorial Library, Buffalo

Dylan spent most of June in and about London. This was perhaps the high point of his romance with Pamela Hansford Johnson. He was pressing her to marry him, and she very nearly agreed to do so. One evening they decided to get a licence next day, but in the morning she had second thoughts.

He returned to Wales at the end of the month, and throughout July and early August was writing to her regularly. Only one of those letters survives.

'Comrade Trick' was A. E. Trick, a grocer in those days and active in local Labour politics. With his customary exaggeration, Dylan used to refer to him as a Communist. Bert Trick, who also possessed considerable knowledge of poetry and wrote poems himself, was one of the first to encourage Dylan. Dylan and his friends used to meet regularly once a week in Bert Trick's flat above the shop to discuss art and politics. The political passage in this letter is a clear echo of those conversations.

The letter includes a not very funny story, omitted, and criticisms of her stories, also cut.

TO PAMELA HANSFORD JOHNSON

20th July 1934

Your letter made me very happy, too. I am listening to Monteverdi's Ballet of the Ungracious Ladies. And that is very happy music, in spite of Pluto and a coloratura Venus. I have only just finished reading 'The Stranger' of Algernon Blackwood—a very happy story, in spite of the ghost. I am smoking a good Turkish cigarette, and have pinched a glass of invalid port from my mother's bedside. Your letter is on the table in front of me, and, later in the night, Comrade Trick is coming to take me to a Fascist Demonstration. Nothing much could be better. Your presence would make everything all right. Through the body of words I tickle you a courteous salute under the chin. You now have a long white beard, and I find myself tickling General Booth of the Salvation Army. But these little snags of vision are to be expected. Yesterday I divined the position of a garden slug. There, under that particular tuft, that small square of soil (I said) lies a fat slug. I dug up the tuft, and there the slug lay, smiling like Mona Lisa. I now add to my list of recondite & entirely uncommercial attainments that of being able to unearth slugs at any given moment. If we ever possess a parrot or a canary, my gift will be distinctly useful. If not, it can still be used as a method of bridging over any awkward pause in the conversation. 'Find a slug for the gentleman.' 'Certainly, my dear.' And, so saying, I produce from the potato bed a black juicy specimen with a long mane.

. . . .

Back to the land now. No more talk of gangrene and sexual abberations. I'm enclosing a new story, 'The Vest' which will provide all that is needed of violence and general nastiness (General Nastiness of the Fifth Buffs).

. . . .

More (for no reason at all) of my long postponed Political Corners*

An economic system (he barked) must have an ethical sanction. If it can be forced home on the consciousness of people that the present

* I'm very fair anyway. I mark this section so that you can skip it.

137

economic system is ethically bad, the seed has been planted that may in time grow into a fine revolutionary flower. Convince people that a thing is bad, and they are ready to listen to a reasonable plan for its overthrow. There is and always must be a stream of revolutionary energy generated where society is composed, at the top and bottom, of financial careerists and a proletarian army of dispossessed. Out of the negation must be a classless society. But there is no great future for a political party based solely on the claims of the workers, as human labour in industry is almost obsolescent. The negation has emerged, & the future of politics must be in the synthesis of production & consumption. There is no use in the ownership of a national bank unless there is sufficient financial credit to make it function. The control of money—that is banking, credit, consumption—is the only key to the communal state. Industry is capable of giving the community a high standard of living, and it is only a faulty monetary system which prevents industry from delivering the goods. Aggregate prices are higher than the aggregate of communal incomes & wages. The monetary & credit system is only a system of book-keeping or accountancy. What is required is not a bloody revolution but an intellectual one. Alternatively, there is the confiscation of property by force. The revolutionary political parties are not in common agreement on that point. The communist party, with the faint endorsement of the I.L.P., advocates force to reach power. The Socialist League, the New Socialist Party, the Orthodox Labour Party believe in first attaining constitutional power and then putting their policies into practice. If constitutional government cannot, in the space of a year after the next General Election, fulfil their policies, then a united front must be made, the army and the police force must be subdued, and property be taken by force. No one can be neutral, neither worker, intellectual, nor reactionary, for the composition of the classes has changed. The class struggle is primarily the intellectual struggle, and, however remote it may seem from the economic process, it is nevertheless conditioned by it. All that matters is the right and the wherewithal to live, and all that remains is to discover, not by hypothecating, but by the trial experiment of constitutionalism, & then, if that fails, of force, the most scientific way to introduce the new society. The governing principle must be that of consumption. The worker is only a factor in production & nearly an obsolete factor at that. But a consumer is a perpetual factor in any society. All society ceases to be class-ridden when treated purely as a primary body of consumers. The most efficient and just organisation is under the direct control of the State. Those controlling the state shall earn in consumer credit no more than the worker who controls the drains of the state. Private profit must end. Reserves against depreciation must be the only charge on industry.

The release of humanity from toil is overdue. Long hours & low wages are anachronistic. The whip of poverty can only flog a dead horse. The shout of the ring-master is a dead language. Our heritage is machine-made leisure. We have the desire, the means, & the opportunity, but not the common and united front that is not frightened, if the ballot and the pressure of constitutional government fails, to advocate, & practice, the last reserve of communal force. The State of the future is not to be an economic despotism or a Christian Utopia. It is the State of Functional Anarchy.

And a fol fol dol and a reel of cotton. So much for that. I'm preparing a paper on Functional Anarchy from which, with the permission of my readers, I shall quote in the next open letter to the constituents of the Battersea ward.

This is a mess of a letter, too. It dribbles and mouths all over the place like Maurice Chevalier. I'll blame it on the weather which is an unhealthy mixture of blues and greys. As soon as I finish this letter I'm going to sit in the sun and watch a county cricket match. Even degenerates like myself have that old True-blue urge which naught can vanquish. I am looking for my School Tie which is, I believe, acting as a sort of strap around a pile of pornographic literature lent to me some months ago by a small man on the sands. I am also practising in a low voice to say 'well played son', & 'damned bad luck' when a ball hits the wicket-keeper in the pelvis. Happy, funny, bloody, wicked, dirty, beautiful world o'mine. Oh why aren't I with you, my darling.

And of course I'll see you before your holidays. I'll be up in August. And don't forget about Wales.

Write soon and write much. Tell me all there is to tell. Go on working hard. Don't draw moustaches on my photograph. Give my love to your mother. Do make another burn-mark in the Chelsea Bells. Have a drink for me. And kiss me good morning before I gird up my loins and go. All possible love whatever. Do call your cat Egypt.

Dylan

XXXX. Sometime in August. (I think I shall have someone to sit (again) on my face so that, meeting, you won't recognise me, and we can start being in love again. A dirty desire.) I love you. Bloody-face loves you.

Dylan returned to London early in August and lived in the house of Pamela Hansford Johnson's mother, where the next letter was written, until mid September. The strain of such propinquity in platonic circumstances began to tell on the two young people. He took to staying out late and coming home the worse for drink. A series of shattering rows followed those occasions, and she, although she remained in love with him, began to have grave doubts about the wisdom of her choice. Furthermore she was beginning to suffer from overwork. Not only was she working full time in a bank, but was also finishing her first novel, written at great speed.

Yet she was still more or less engaged to Dylan, and in mid September she and her mother accompanied him to Swansea, to meet his parents. The visit was not altogether a success. Mrs Hansford Johnson found Mrs Thomas a great bore. It rained for two weeks. Pamela discovered Dylan's true age, nineteen, and realized that marriage was out of the question. Finally she fell ill, a doctor was summoned and she returned to London with her mother.

Dylan was now quarrelling with Victor Neuburg about the selection of his poems, and there were difficulties with the commercial publisher. Eventually David Archer, of the Parton Street Bookshop, agreed to print the book.

Alfred Janes the painter was one of Dylan's closest friends. They were planning to share a studio in London, where they were joined by another Swansea painter of their own age, Mervyn Levy, and later, after they had moved, by yet a third, the Ulsterman William Scott. The Hansford Johnsons, too, were moving from Battersea to South Kensington.

The meeting of the John O' London literary society was used by Dylan as an opportunity to scandalize his townsfolk. The pattern of the *enfant terrible* was beginning to appear, as was that of the boy with the load o' beer.

TO GEOFFREY GRIGSON

Summer 1934

53 Battersea Rise,

(at the moment)

S.W.11.

Dear Grigson,

I know you'll excuse this note, but it is quite essential that I take advantage of the offer you made, I think seriously, last week. I can't go back to Wales yet, for even the foundations of the Old Home seem to be crumbling. If I had realised at tea yesterday that things were really as bad as they are, I wouldn't have had to trouble you with this undignified note. My world of good, dying fathers and bad, female poets is proving affectionately unstable. I don't mind the Garret and Crust at all, but I'd much prefer to borrow some money and to postpone such a conventionality. Again I apologise for the substance and the mood of this.

Five o'clock, Wednesday?

Very sincerely,
Dylan Thomas

MSS.: Texas

TO PAMELA HANSFORD JOHNSON

Early October 1934

PS. Jumper at end of week (mother).

Book It And See

First of all, to reply to the short letter marked bloody private and confidential. Runia seems to have given you a fairly correct summary of the correspondence between us. Another letter—written by Neuburg & Runia in collaboration, actually in different sorts of ink—came later, explaining very carefully a number of things that I can't understand at all, and asking—as you intimated—for a poem for this Sunday's Referee. Why, do you know? I suspect vaguely Caponeish measures. Vicky is, I believe, putting me on the spot. Though what spot, and why, God alone knows. My letters, as perhaps Runia told you, demanded the return of my book. But I'm no more likely to get it than I am to find Gibbon's History of Christianity in my navel. Only force remains. I can't seriously adopt the idea of a second selection of even more immature & unsatisfactory poems. I find, after reading them through again, that the poems in Vicky's confounded possession are a poor lot, on the whole, with many thin lines, many oafish sentiments, several pieces of twopenny Christ, several unintentional comicalities, & much highfalutin nonsense expressed in a soft, a truly soft language. I've got to get nearer to the bones of words, & to a Matthew Arnold's hell with the convention of meaning & sense. Not that it matters, anyway. Life is only waves, wireless waves, & electric vibrations. Does it matter, my little radio programme from Battersea, that the high or the low tension runs down? I have, of course, in the weakness of my spirit, sent some clumsy poem for the Referee. But, blast it, I will be firm, & the October date still stands. Much thanks for the Bloody private low-down.

House Lend a Little Chairful

In reference to my prospective studio. Janes and I will be coming up definitely about the second week of November, by car fortunately, bearing with us typewriters, easels, bedclothes, brassières for lady models, & plum cakes for Nelson's lions—a cherry or two for Eros, a copy of the London Mercury for Nurse Cavell. We want a room about fifteen shillings per week; it must be as large as possible, larger if possible, unfurnished, with good light. Preferably gas, electric is bad for our sensitive eyes & complexions. But don't worry about looking for one; we will procure one, even if it is a little out of Chelsea. But you might keep your eye open; one eye. Have you a mattress & a chair either to give or sell to two poor, unrecognised geniuses? I don't want to take a mattress up; it's too big, & I don't want to buy one because I'm frightened of getting rabies or ringworm. Don't throw any old furniture over the neighbours' walls. It would be vitally useful to us. If you have a fairly large & dirty table you don't intend taking with you, store it somewhere, & I'll buy it from you. Don't forget my prospectively philanthropic clothes, furnisher of the artistic poor! Table, mattress, chair! I don't want to buy them from a second-hand shop, owing to the possibility of disease; I would, if you had them, like to purchase them from No. 53 (going—gone) Battersea Rise.

.   .   .   .

Pursuit

Well, I wouldn't choose it. I'd let the damned thing go. Blood on the raspberry to it, for all I care. I think it's lousy, just lousy. There's no merit in it at all: it's coy, it's turgid, it's affected, it's nauseating. I cannot, I'm afraid, approve of the New Manner, which seems to me to be a bloodier way than ever of linking together old mannerisms. No, I mean you just *can't* go on like that. It's criminal. I know you're not well, but you can't blame the poor thing on a too-rapid heart. Sorry to be so rude. I can't give any constructive criticism.

.   .   .   .

John O' London's Circumcision

A definite success. There were thirty-five people in the audience, that's all, and thirty of them were women. But what women! All of a dim, uncertain age, most of them virgins, & all with some smattering of Freud & Lawrence. The Chairman, a big-bellied bore, introduced me as a Young Revolutionary (I was becomingly clad in red) who was tackling A Difficult & Courageous Task. I then gave them the works. At the beginning there was a frozen & horrified silence, but eventually I induced a few titters, &, at last, real, undeniable interest. A glassy look came into the eyes of the spinsters. I put in several wisecracks, & ended with 'Let copulation thrive'. Then the ladies, in one solid mass, bombarded me with questions. In the Communist Erewhon I had dealt with, would there be no perversions? What we consider as perversions, I replied (excuse the novelette form of this report) are, for the most part, healthy and natural bypaths of sexual life. How could a woman defend her honour in such a state? Tin drawers, I replied with Ready Humour. Do you believe in preventatives? The day, I replied, that legalised birthcontrol & clinical abortion came into practice, will go down as a French Letter day in the annals of history. And so on for two hours, until middle aged ladies, who before that night would have blushed or been horrified at the mention of pyjamas, were talking gaily about whirling-sprays, Lesbianism, sanitary towels, latrines, fornication & other everyday & normal things. Trick made a nice little speech about the inevitability of Revolution, a gentleman defended repression with a very bloodshot eye, Janes made a joke about gallstones, & the meeting closed. God knows what we've done to these ardent & earnest ladies, but I hope it hurts. The more I see of Wales the more I think it's a land completely peopled by perverts. I don't exclude myself, who obtain a high & soulful pleasure from telling women, old enough to be my mother, why they dream of two-headed warthogs in a field of semen. (I heard, later, that a committee meeting has been held, & that care must be taken in the future as to who is invited to lecture. Those bloody women woke up in the cold light of morning, & regretted those few hours of—if nothing else—verbal freedom.)

Last week-end I spent in Aberystwyth with Caradoc Evans. He's a great fellow. We made a tour of the pubs in the evening, drinking to the soon-to-be-hoped-for destruction of the Tin Bethels. The university students love Caradoc, & pelt him with stones whenever he goes out.

I have nothing to send you (except a pound of love), but have nearly finished a short story. I am working very hard on a poem; it is going to be a very long poem; I've completed fifty lines so far, it is by far the best thing I've done. I don't suppose I'll have finished it even when I see you, but you shall read what there is of it then.

How much more of your novel? Of course, I want to see it all before Pinkers have it.

—————————

Now love & goodbye, more love than goodbye, for I'll see you soon, but write soon and much, & do, my darling, get better for me. I don't like to think of you ill. (And you, very naturally, don't like being ill.) Don't forget any old furniture—specially mattress, table, chair. Give my love to your mother. Love again, and a terrible lot of it. XXXXXXX.

Dylan

MSS.: Lockwood Memorial Library, Buffalo

The questionnaire was one submitted to a number of poets, by *New Verse*, and published in that magazine in October 1934. Dylan Thomas's answers are reprinted in *The Life of Dylan Thomas*, pp. 161–3.

TO GEOFFREY GRIGSON

July 1934?

5 Cwmdonkin Drive,

Uplands,

Swansea

Dear Grigson,

Thanks for the note.

I have no poems at all at the present moment, or at least no poems which I should care for you to see. I hope in a few days to be able to send you two new poems, though.

I enclose my answers to the questionnaire. I'm afraid they sound rather priggish in places, but I couldn't avoid it. They make me sound, too, very contented with my work, which I am certainly not. If they are not what you want, or are too long, I'll be quite willing to do another set of answers.

You asked me to remind you, some time ago, about the books for review. I've been doing a certain amount of reviewing lately, & would be very pleased if you could, as you promised, send a few volumes along.

I'm sorry to have no poems ready. I'll send you some during the week, if I may.

Sincerely,

Dylan Thomas

I hope to be in London about the middle of August. I was up a little time ago, but heard that you were away on holiday. I was sorry to miss seeing you.

MSS.: Texas

TO GEOFFREY GRIGSON

July 1934

5 Cwmdonkin Drive,
Uplands,
Swansea

Dear Grigson,

Here are the two poems I said I'd send you. I hope it's not too late. More especially, I hope you like the poems. They are both very recently written. Do let me know if it is too late, as I may be able to do something else with the poems. But I hope, again, that you'll like them and be able to print them.

I'm coming up to town at the end of this week. Will you be away then?

Sincerely,
Dylan Thomas

MSS.: Texas

Dylan and his friend Alfred Janes, the painter, were moving to London early in November, where they were going to share a room.

Dylan had never then been out of England and Wales and certainly not to the Balearic islands.

T. S. Eliot was a director, and poetry editor, with the publishing house of Faber & Faber. Whether in fact he ever seriously considered publishing the volume which subsequently appeared with Dent's imprint entitled *18 Poems* I do not know, but it is probable.

Norman is Norman Cameron.

TO GEOFFREY GRIGSON

October 1934

5 Cwmdonkin Drive,
Uplands,
Swansea

Dear Geoffrey,

I've been meaning to write to you for the last month, and was awfully glad to get your letter. In answer to your questions: (a) I am in Wales, (b) I'm coming to London in about ten days, (c) I have been on the Balearic Islands occasionally, (d) I've died once or twice, too, (e) I am never lascivious. Penniless I retreated from London, and penniless I return. I've been staying all over the place, with Caradoc Evans in Aberystwyth, with an indulgent but ailing mother, as now, with a large lady and her hotel on the Gower Peninsula, and in a cottage in Carmarthenshire, glorying in the name of Blaen Cwm, where I lived on carrots, (no, that's not quite true, I had onions as well). But in ten days or less I'll be taking a room with another bloated aristocrat in town. I hope I'll see you and Norman very soon.

Have you seen Pope Eliot lately. He's doing funny things with my book. Three or four days ago his secretary sent me a letter by express post—I don't quite know what express post means, but you have to pay sixpence to the boy at the door—asking me to make no arrangements until I had heard from the Pope himself who was writing that evening. What earthly arrangements could I make? And I'm damned if he's written. I remember somebody telling me once that she had used a poem of mine as a sort of funnel to put in a bottle, as a sadistic doctor wanted a sample of her urine. Do try to find out if the entire staff of Faber and Faber are doing similar things with my twenty poems.

Of course you can use any poems of mine you want to. I've written a new one—bit better than the others, I think—which I enclose. Perhaps you'd like to use that too, or instead.

Thanks very much for the promise of the books. But it's hardly worth sending them if I'm coming up in ten days, is it? Do let me have some then, though, I'm relying on reviews to ensure the carrots and onions.

> Yours,
> Dylan

Do you think it would be better if the enclosed poem were *not* divided into stanzas? I've tried it that way, but it seemed more obscure.

Ross Williamson of the Bookman has given me some reviews. Do you think Janet Adam Smith would too if I wrote her a nice, cooing letter?

MSS.: Texas

Dylan and Fred Janes had moved to London on 10th November 1934. Neuburg had recently published in 'Poets' Corner' an appreciation by A. E. Trick of Dylan's poems.

'Vanoc' wrote the political article for the *Sunday Referee*.

As can be seen, Dylan had very rapidly moved out of the orbit of Victor Neuburg and the Creative Lifers.

Princess Marina married the Duke of Kent on 29th November 1934, which is why I have assigned this undated letter to early December.

TO BERT TRICK

December 1934
5 Redcliffe Street,
London, S.W.10

Dear Bert,

This seems a nice and suitable time to write the letter that I know I should have written at least a week ago. The *Sunday Referee* has done us both quite proud, although personally I do not think that Neuburg chose the most flattering passages of either your letter or Comrade Thompson's. Your criticism was good and naturally I agreed with every word of it. It contained, expressed in a beautifully condensed way, what you and I have discussed for so many hours and win the prize (what is the prize by the way?) it bloody well should. Comrade Thompson wrote at far greater length than you, explaining subtleties in my bad poem that I was, and still am not, aware of, and your Oxford Vanoc (who wrote the political article in the *Referee* letter) was just as good. I heard two anarchistic gentlemen arguing vigorously over it in a café last night. There is no news or there is all news. The city goes on, myself now a very insignificant part of it. I live with Janes just off the Fulham Road on the borders of Chelsea, Fulham, South Kensington and Brompton, in a large room with a bathroom and sort of inferior wash-up adjoining.

This is the quarter of the pseudo-artists, of the beards, of the naughty expressions of an entirely outmoded period of artistic importance and of the most boring Bohemian parties I have ever thought possible.

Slightly drunk, slightly dirty, slightly wicked, slightly crazed, we repeat our platitudes on Gauguin and Van Gogh as though they were the most original things in the world. There are, of course, scores of better people that I do meet, but these little maggots are my companions for most of the time. I think I shall change my digs quite soon.

Another Swansea boy—Hark, Hark the Parish Pump—lives in the room above us. He is Mervyn Levy, a small Jew who does small and cunning drawings, and, at present, does not work in the Royal College Kensington.

This bloody land is full of Welshmen, and, day by day, as I feast my eyes upon their mean and ungenerous countenances, I feel like Caradoc Evans whose books are, in a small circle at least, becoming a highbrow success owing to my uninterrupted praise of them.

I'm not at the moment working very hard. I find it difficult to concentrate in a room as muddled and messy as ours is nearly all the time. For yards around me I can see nothing but poems, poems, poems, butter, eggs, mashed potatoes, mashed among my stories and Janes' canvases. One day we shall have to wash up, and then perhaps I can really begin to work. As it is, most of the stuff that I brought up with me has been accepted by various periodicals. A new very high-brow magazine called very originally *Art* is to print my 'Burning Baby' in its first quarterly number in January 1935. The *Adelphi* is printing my 'Tree' this December. The next *Criterion* is printing my 'The Visitor'. That is in the middle of this month. *New Verse* is printing a long poem ('Ha' of the Fellow') that you have in your cuttings book, and also a review of Spender's new poem *Vienna*. And my book of poems will be out before Christmas. I have hopes too of a publisher, probably Spottiswoode, publishing my stories in the spring. To continue this egoistic survey: I met a number of new notabilities including Henry Moore the sculptor, Edwin and Willa Muir, Wyndham Lewis and certainly not least, Betty May. Now, how does your world go? Has the *Guardian* reformed and started to print your nasty little nigglings again? And what are you doing all these long winter nights, printing propaganda? Propagandish poems? Or writing more of those damnable indignant and abusive letters? Or reading more of those damnable facts that you manage to extract from all sorts of seditious quarters? I kept the *Daily Worker*'s Princess Marina supplement for you, but, as usual with all such things, I went and lost it. It was a special and particularly seditious pamphlet abusing the whole of the royal family and exhibiting almost bawdy cartoons of 'Enemy the King'. Very good. London was hell on the day of that royal ramp, the streets crowded enough to be almost impossible to walk in, the whole of the traffic disorganised and the pubs open till eleven all over the city. There were women and their babies, I saw them, who waited all night outside the Abbey keeping those perishing children in the cold and fog for at least twenty four hours. I told Norman Cameron about it and said that they all should be put in lunatic asylums. He said that there was no necessity, all that need be done was to keep them in England. Isn't this letter well typed? Write to me soon, telling me all that you know or would like to know, all about the *Guardian* and sedition in general.

As this is the first letter it must not, according to the rules of etiquette, be too long. There, you liar, it isn't etiquette I'm worrying about, it's just sheer laziness. Give my regards to Mrs. Trick and to Miss Trick, whose poems, so Vicky tells me, are by far the best and the most sincere that he receives. Write soon and don't forget all the news.

Dylan

I came across yesterday, in the possession of a fellow whom I don't know and can't borrow from, the first real literature of Fascism and Nazism. It is called 'Might is Right' and was printed in Australia in the 1890's. The author is called Raynor Redbeard. If you can by any method, get hold of it.

MSS.: Lockwood Memorial Library, Buffalo

At about the same time, and perhaps on the same day, he wrote to Glyn Jones.

Edith Sitwell's 'Aspects of Modern Poetry' had recently been published. Dylan's harsh judgment was shared by many others, and he had a personal motive for disliking the book in that it contained a parody of his own earliest poems. A few weeks later she was to praise a poem of his publicly, in the *London Mercury*. He met her and they became and remained good friends until his death.

TO GLYN JONES

London, early December 1934
5 Redcliffe Street, S.W.10

Many thanks for the letter, and many apologies that you should have had to write the first letter since I came up to town about a month ago. I seem to have been very busy and have written only two letters home during the whole time. I haven't written to any friends at all, and hope that they know me well enough by this time to realise that it's no more than a lazy carelessness on my part—though a lazy carelessness is bad enough, God knows.

Very, very glad to hear that you are coming to London about Christmas. I am looking forward to seeing you and to introduce you to Grigson. I am, as I think I told you when, during the famous Caradoc expedition, we last met, staying with a painter called Janes. We possess one large room in a quiet street in South Kensington—in

149

South Kensington, that is officially, but we are near Chelsea, Fulham and Brompton. Everything is in rather a mess, but if you don't mind that and I don't somehow think you do, then I do really wish you would sleep with us. Janes spends most of his time indoors and cooks his own meals, but I have most of my scanty meals in cafés—scanty not for the reason of utter penury, although I have had and do have and am having at the moment a particularly lean period, but for the sake of the demon alcohol who has become a little too close and too heavy a friend for some time now.

Pile in with us, will you? We shall also have the greatest pleasure in providing quite nice breakfasts free of charge. Does that induce you? Yes, of course it does. So when are you definitely coming up? I'm not, I don't think so at the moment at least, going home for Christmas. My book of poems is coming out then, and I hope to make just sufficient money to keep me happy for the few most important days of the holiday.

So you've been reviewing Edith Sitwell's latest piece of virgin dung, have you? Isn't she a poisonous thing of a woman, lying, concealing, flipping, plagiarising, misquoting, and being as clever a crooked literary publicist as ever. I do hope you pointed out in your review the real points against the book (you did, I know, but I like being dogmatic)? The majority of the book was cribbed from Herbert Read and Leavis, actually and criminally cribbed. She has misquoted Hopkins at least twenty times, reprinted many poems without the permission of publisher or poet. Yes, that was my poem, absurdly criticised. I duly sent my protest to Gerald Duckworth and he replied to the effect that so many protests of a similar sort had been received, that he could, as yet, do nothing about it. It is being hoped that he will have to withdraw the book. I would like to see your review of it.

What news there is can wait until I see you. Let it be soon and don't forget to let me know when that will be. You stay with us of course.

Dylan

Excuse me typing this, but I have only just found my pen and ink.

Dylan returned to Swansea for Christmas, but early in the new year he was back in London. By now *18 Poems* had been published (on or about 18th December) and had attracted attention in a very small circle.

Charles Fisher was one of Dylan's closest Swansea friends: they had

worked on the *Post* together, where Fisher was still employed as a journalist.
The characters referred to in the last paragraph are Swansea friends, mostly
connected with the paper.

TO CHARLES FISHER

London, February 1935

Dear Comrade Fisher,

Thank you very much for your letter to which I would have replied
sooner had it not been for about twenty reasons; the abominable cold
cramping the fingers, elongating the sweet hours of bed, and forcing,
eventually, the tired half sleeper to erect a small fire in an insufficient
grate; the sin of laziness, cancelling the positive virtue that regards
sin and virtue lazily, equally and equably; the lack of ink, my tame
harridan having, bless her breasts, spilt the contents of a full bottle on
the linoleum; the worries of a life that consists, for the most part, in
building the brain on paper and pulling down the body, the small and
too weak body to stand either the erection of a proper brain or the
rubbing of saloon counters: the pressure of words, the lack of stamps;
flu in embryo, a snotty chicken-faced foetus swimming, very red,
behind the nose; and another twelve reasons, all too complicated to
go into at the moment. The ink still staining the linoleum, and my
harridan asleep, I have got to type this letter. The keys are cold.

You asked me to tell you about my theory of poetry. Really I
haven't got one. I like things that are difficult to write and difficult to
understand; I like 'redeeming the contraries' with secretive images;
I like contradicting my images, saying two things at once in one word,
four in two and one in six. But what I like isn't a theory even if I do
stabilise by dogma my own personal affections. Poetry, heavy in tare
though nimble, should be as orgiastic and organic as copulation,
dividing and unifying, personal but not private, propagating the
individual in the mass and the mass in the individual. I think it should
work from words from the substance of words and the rhythm of
substantial words set together, not towards words. Poetry is a medium,
not a stigmata on paper. Men should be two tooled, and a poet's
middle leg is his pencil. If his phallic pencil turns into an electric drill,
breaking up the tar and the concrete of language worn thin by the
tricycle tyres of nature poets and the heavy six wheels of the academic
sirs, so much the better; and it's work that counts, madam, genius
so often being a capacity for aching pains.

About manuscripts. I'm very pleased and glad that you do want a
manuscript of some poems of mine, and I'll try to let you have what

you want. But my method is this: I write a poem on innumerable sheets of scrap paper, write it on both sides of the paper, often upside down and criss cross ways unpunctuated, surrounded by drawings of lamp posts and boiled eggs, in a very dirty mess, bit by bit I copy out the slowly developing poem into an exercise book; and, when it is completed, I type it out. The scrap sheets I burn, for there are such a lot of them that they clutter up my room and get mixed up in the beer and butter. Now what can I send you? A typed copy? Shall I write some out for you? Or preserve from the waiting fire the next batch of almost illegible sheets? Anything you like. I am at your service.

Write again soon. I write so few letters, and like writing them, even if my style is a little too heavy footed. Give my regards to Mr. Job; prevent Mr. Hatcher from taking too many Woolworth waitresses to the cinema: plant a rose in Reuben's hair; remember me to Bill Latham and to Tom Lucy; and tell Eric that Hennekey's devastating cider now costs two pence halfpenny a glass.

Dylan

PS. The manuscript, whatever it will be, I'll send on to you when you tell me what you want. I can't give you the exercise books for they contain the only copies I possess.

PSS. What are you doing with yourself? Do you write at all now? That is, apart from the daily hack work?

MSS.: Charles Fisher

Dylan's romance with Pamela Hansford Johnson faded out once he came to London, but there was never any definite rupture. This, the last of his letters to her, was probably written in the spring of 1935. 'This Bed' is a reference to her first novel: *This Bed thy Centre.*

TO PAMELA HANSFORD JOHNSON

Spring 1935

5 Cwmdonkin Drive,
Uplands,
Swansea

I've returned home, after a ragged life, for a few weeks' rest before I go to the country for the summer. I should have written what's much too long a time ago, because there's so much to explain and so much that, perhaps, will, and should, never be explained—it means such a lot of belly rubbing and really tearful apologies on my blasted part. But never mind that. Britons never will be slaves, and I'm a rat. I saw Janes before I left London, and he told me that he had had tea with you and that you were working hard on your new novel. He said, though, that you were having rather a lot of trouble with it. Would you like me to go through, in my usual naggy way, what you've written so far? You know—to say, 'No, no, no, this can't be, too lush, too lush', & 'this is impossible', & 'Cut, cut, cut' etc. I'd really like to; you write better when you've got someone to stand behind your shoulder sneering when you go purple & using a cruel pencil over your choicest peacock-greys. Would you like me to repeat my usual & my 'This Bed' sub-editing? If you would, and you still aren't too angry with me for all the silly and careless things I've done, send the MSS to me at home, & I'll send it back very soon & very carefully gone-through. Love to your mother and—always— to you.

Dylan

MSS.: Lockwood Memorial Library, Buffalo

Early in March he was back in Swansea. A pattern was being established, and one that was to last throughout his life. In London it was drink, talk and women. When exhausted by what he later called 'the capital punishment' he would return to Wales and work.

The meeting with Richard Hughes, who was away, did not take place until the following year.

In April he went to stay with A. J. P. Taylor, the historian, and his wife, Margaret, in Derbyshire, where they had a cottage.

TO GLYN JONES

Swansea, beginning of March 1935

Dear Glyn,

As you see, the trials of life have proved too much for me, the courts have found me guilty, and, rather hollow-eyed and with little real work to my credit, I've returned home for a few weeks' holiday. I'm leaving, I believe, in the first week of April, but for the country then and not for London—Surrey, Cheshire, Derbyshire, I don't know which. It's very lonely here in Swansea, and the few old friends I have spend their days in work and their evenings in indulging in habits which I've had quite enough of—at least temporarily. As it is I'm working on some short stories, but I don't know whether they're any good, and I would like you to have a look at them. Do you feel like coming down one Saturday before I go? There are crowds of things for us to talk about, and far more peace and comfort than we had in the pubs and that wretched room of mine in London.

How are you getting on? Have you sent any poems to Geoffrey G. yet? What about your story of the workman shitting over the cliff? The Adelphi hasn't printed the other story yet, has it? Has Papa Eliot replied? and all sorts of other questions.

And now I remember one of the main points of this letter. Some weeks ago in the gossip column of the South Wales Evening Post, there was a paragraph to the effect that Richard Hughes, in a long conversation with the gossip-writer about modern poetry, had said how much he admired my poems. That definitely gives us an introduction to him, doesn't it? What do you say if I write him a note asking whether we could call and see him in his castle one week-end? If your car is still alive, we could run down to Laugharne, visit him and his beard, and then either return to our homes—these things could be settled later—or stay with our relations around Llanstephan. I think we'd have an interesting time. I won't write to him, of course, until I hear from you.

Levy, by the way, who now has very fierce black whiskers almost down to his middle, sends his greetings to you and is going to try to get hold of you when he goes back to Cardiff at Easter. Will you be there then? His address is still 5 Redcliffe Street.

Drop me a line soon. I feel quite keen about visiting Richard Hughes.

Yours,
Dylan

PS. Roger Roughton also wishes to be remembered to you. He's just left for America.

Geoffrey Grigson had arranged that he review books for the *Morning Post*, of which Grigson was literary editor.

The statement that Dent's had brought out *18 Poems* 'unexpectedly' is a strangely ingenuous falsehood. Nor did Dylan ever learn any German.

TO GEOFFREY GRIGSON

March ? 1935

Dear G.

Thanks again for the books. I can't send any new poems now, as Dent has brought out my book—which had unpublished ones I wanted you to see—unexpectedly.

I liked the German poem. I'm trying to learn a little German myself. Here's something I made of it: I found it awfully hard, & had to paraphrase in bits. But all the meaning & the flatness and the metre & things are there.

Love,
Dylan

MSS.: Texas

The dating of the next letter is uncertain, but it was probably written in July or August of 1935.

The American artist was Rockwell Kent, and the cottage a cow byre converted into a studio.

Horatio Bottomley was a celebrated English demagogue of the First World War period, later sent to prison for fraud.

TO BERT TRICK

July ? 1935
Glen Lough,
County Donegal

Dear Bert,

Is it any good telling you that for the last three months or more I've been meaning and meaning to write a long letter to you, a sort of self-explanatory monologue and travelogue and a necessary lecture on the ways of a Welsh poet in the amazing world. I've been meaning to ask Twentieth Century about the economic ruptures, and whether the Guardian has managed to invent a truss for them yet, to learn

about the new Vanoc of socialism and the bollix of the old gang, to
inquire very politely and sincerely into the question of health, work,
and happiness. But I'm never very hot on meaning. It's the sound of
meaning that I like and so the long letter remained unwritten. The
months moved on and I shifted from the Derbyshire peaks to the
London saloons, from the upper reaches of the Thames to the edge
of the Atlantic, without saying hello or good-bye to you. How is
the family? How is the small world? (It's the big world really.) What
have you been reading and doing? Does John still dance with a
skeleton? Has the corpse of Mainwaring H. sprouted rhubarb yet?
How many times have you lectured on 'one syphilisation' of man
to the ingrown virginities of the prig-squared circle? Tell me all
about everything. I'm ten miles from the nearest human being, with
the exception of the deaf farmer who gives me food. And in spite of
the sea and the lakes and my papers and my books and my cigarettes
(though they're darned hard to get and I've few left of them) and my
increasing obsession with the things under the skin, I'm lonely as
Christ sometimes and can't even speak to my father on an etherial
wave-length.

I came here—'here' is a cottage studio, once owned by an American
artist, perched in a field on a hill facing a bit of the wild Atlantic—
with Geoffrey G. but he's gone back to town. And here is a wild and
unlettered and un-French-lettered country, too far from Andera, a
village you can't be too far from. Here are gannets and seals and
puffins flying and puffing and playing a quarter of a mile outside my
window where there are great rocks petrified like the old Fates and
destinies of Ireland, and smooth white pebbles under and around them
like the souls of the dead Irish. There's a hill with a huge echo. You
shout and the dead Irish answer from behind the hill. I've forced
them into confessing that they're sad, grey, lost, forgotten, dead and
damned forever. There are St. Brigid shapes crossed in the rafters of
my cottage, and these shapes are to keep away what and who should
be kept away. They're superstitious here, or mad, whimsy or barmy,
and the blood sports are blood sports, but I can break a trout's back
now as skilfully as Geoffrey (who gave me the killing rod) but with
more conscience.

My days these days are planned out carefully, or at least conveniently,
to the clock I haven't got (if time is the tick of a clock I'm living in a
funny dimension, in an hourless house): I rise at nine, I breakfast
and clean up till ten, I read or write from ten till one, I lunch at one,
then I walk over the cliffs to the sea, stay or walk about there till half
past three or four, then tea. After tea I write until the early dusk,
then I climb over the hills to the high lakes and fish there until dark.

Back, supper, bed. I have a little illegal poteen whiskey with my supper. I smoke black shag in a bad pipe. One day a week I shall walk the miles to Glendormatie where there is a shop and porter bar. It rains and it rains. All the damned sea-gulls are fallen angels. Frogs and storms and squids and clegs and mutton-birds and midges and killing beetles. Dead sheep in the bracken. But this is by no means a despondent letter. Words are coming nicely. And the rain can't get in through the roof. I have a blazing turf fire and the only sound is the sea on the million stones. I have a beard too, a curly ginger growth, nearly regular, sweetly disorderly. I'll keep it for good, I think, or long enough anyway for the Tricks and the Thomases and my Mumbles Mermaid (bless her hair and her tail) to admire and finger it. I have my home-sicknesses, but they vanish all right like all the thoughts of permanency and the Uplands and the Park go up in a wet smoke. In my sicker moments I think of my writing by my gas fire opposite the tall Greek nudes, or walking past your shop to the train stop, and rattling along to a beery and fleshly Oyster-mouth, of walking to your house in the Sunday rain and sitting by the fire until we've set the whole world straight, and the whole Welsh world is dark. But I wouldn't be at home if I were at home. Everywhere I find myself seems to be nothing but a resting place between places that become resting places between resting places themselves. This is an essential state of being, an abstraction as concrete as a horse-fly, that's always worrying the back of your neck, plaguing and worrying before it draws blood. I'm at home and the blood's spilt, but only until the pricked veins heal up again and my water and sugar turn red again, and the body and the brain, all the centres of movement, must shift or die. It may be a primary loneliness that makes me out-of-home. It may be this or that, and this and that is enough for today. Poor Dylan. Poor him. Poor me.

I wish I could provide you with notes on the financial, political, economic, industrial and agricultural conditions of this lazy and vocal land, but my powers of natural observation, never very clear, would give me less Marx every day. I find I can't see a landscape scenery is just scenery to me, botany is botany or Bottomley Horatio, oblique; little he wotted when he made the trees and the flowers how one of the Welsh chosen would pass them by, not even knowing that they were there. My own eyes, I know, squint inwards when, and if, I look at the exterior world, I see nothing or me; I should like very much to say that I see everything through the inner eye, but all I see is darkness, naked and not very nice. What can be done about it? The birds of the air peck my mustache. Idly I shoo them aside, engrossed in thoughts concerning the spiritual anatomy of the worms of Donegal.

This is a poor, dirty land, and the pigs rut and scrabble in the parlours. There are few political feelings in the west, though most people seem to favour a mild republicanism. My deaf farmer believes in fairies, and burns a red lamp under a religious magazine reproduction of somebody's hideous head of Christ; even his calendars are Christian. I always expect to find a cross in the soup, or find a chicken crucified by skewers to a fatty plate.

Have you heard from Fred Janes? He's living higgledy-piggledy in a ruin and a riot of a Kensington studio with Levy the bearded, and a couple of other irresponsible and wildly conventional painters. He might be returning to Swansea soon. London's lousy in hot weather. Fred loves Gower like a Rhossilli rabbit. He might, too, bring Scott, a little beard, with him. That'll be nice. Scott's well worth knowing, and Fred is more seriously and comically metaphysical than ever.

We stayed with Dan Jones in Harrow for a few days. He reads all the time, and is cleverer than ever, but his mind is a mess for he doesn't know any direction. He isn't sure either of music or writing, though he does both competently and often brilliantly. I shouldn't be surprised to see him turn into a first-rate literary critic, producing a standard study of a comparison of European literatures. He has all that Jamieson had with more wit, more sensibility, and, with his time limits, a far more comprehensive erudition. Trevor Hughes of the undiluted letters is no nearer the loony bin but the smell of the padded cells is floating about his nostrils. He has lately become a friend, counsellor, and admirer of Pamela J., who has spurned me as a small but gifted Welshman of unsocial tendencies and definitely immoral habits. Her last novel has sold well, and is now in a fifth edition. Her next honourable edition to the shelves of libraries and the welfare of widow wombs is to be called Blessed Among Women.

The rest of my acquaintances are very much as usual, thank you. Geoffrey G. has a small daughter, Caroline, and a new hedgehog. Norman Cameron has a book of poems appearing very soon. And my next poems will be published by Dent. Now the news fades. The rain is coming heavily and I am going to make myself some creamy tea. I'll write more, and more interestingly, I hope after the creamy tea. Good-bye, as is said, (and its a foul thing to say) for now.

For now was a long now, and it's morning again, with the wind sweeping up from the sea, and a straight mist above the hills. I've had breakfast, built a tiny stone bridge over the stream by my front door, fallen twice into the muddy gutters by the side of the stream, and banged my thumb with a hammer. In half an hour or less I'm going to work on my new story 'Daniel Dom'. Did I tell you about it when I saw you last? It's based on the 'Pilgrim's Progress', but tells of the adventures of Anti-Christian in his travels from the city of Zion to the City of Destruction. I've been commissioned to write it but I won't be given any money until the first half a dozen parts or chapters are completed. The agents are rather frightened of blasphemy and obscenity (and well they might be) and want to see how clean the half dozen chapters are before they advance me anything. The poor fish don't realise that I shall cut out the objectionable bits when I send them a synopsis and first chapters, and then put them immediately back. I've finished John's story, too, it's called 'Cora, the Vampire.' I'll send it to you to show John once I've had it typed.

Do you still take New Verse? A long poem of mine will be in the next one (Consternation!).

I don't know how long I shall be here; it all depends on how the silence and the loneliness attack me. I had thought of staying here until September, but the hot months are long months. And though I can't say I like my fellows very much and though my social conscience is becoming more flea-bitten every day, I can't indefinitely regard my own face in the mirror as the only face in the world, my beard as the only beard, my undiciplined thoughts as the only thoughts that matter under the sun, or the lack of light, and as the thoughts that revalue the egg-shaped earth. I will want more than an echo, sad, grey, lost, forgotten and damned forever to answer me in August, and more than the contaminated sheep to rodger on the high cliffs. But, if I can I'll stay here till September, come home for a few weeks, and then return to London when the season commences. I hope to have a certain amount of dramatic criticism or if that sounds too pompous, a little free entertainment on the stage and a little free love off-stage from any publicity-seeking actresses I can find. It's fairly honest to be a dishonest critic of a corrupted commercial theatre—as the best socialists suck all they can from the jaundiced ass-hole of an anti-socialist state.

Before I say good-bye, I must tell you about Vicky Neuburg. He's got a new residence in North London, a crazy room full of books, kippers and warming pans, a hot-as-hell conservatory with a fountain full of goldfish, and a jungled garden where the members of a strange Neuburgian clan, The Circle (I think) of Creative Art and Life, meet, talk, jibber, froth, growl and presumably do their practical best to fornicate among the rushes and wormy ferns. The creature himself —I must tell you one day, if I haven't told you before, the story of how Alisteir Crowley turned Vicky into a camel—is a nineteenth

159

century crank with mental gangrene, lousier than ever before, a product of the Jewish nuts factory, Oscar tamed, Runia Tharp is a believer in the voice of nature, and eases a fart in the bath in the fond belief that it resembles in pitch and tone the voice of some Wordsworthian spirit invoking a horsefly. Rest in purgatory.

Write soon and at great length, telling me all there is to tell in which you know I am interested, personal things, impersonal things, local politics, news, views, and all the etceteras you can think of. Give my love to everybody—even Mrs. W. I saw a seal like Mrs. W. yesterday.

Yours,

Dylan

MSS.: Lockwood Memorial Library, Buffalo

The poetry editor at Dent's—who had agreed to publish Dylan's second volume of poems, and who were to remain his English publishers for the rest of his life—was Richard Church, himself a poet of an older generation.

On 6th October 1935 Dylan, now back in Swansea, sent Richard Church 'most of the manuscripts', although the so-called sonnet sequence 'Altarwise by owl-light' was not yet finished.

It would seem that Richard Church did not grasp what it was that Dylan was attempting to do in his poems, and for this he can scarcely be blamed, for few people did. He preferred Dylan's simpler, that is to say his earliest, poems, and confused the density and occasional obscurity of his most recent poem with surrealism. To this criticism Dylan replied as follows.

TO RICHARD CHURCH

9th December 1935

5 Cwmdonkin Drive,

Uplands,

Swansea

Dear Richard Church,

Thank you for your letter, and for the candid criticism of my poems. I do appreciate the trouble you have taken to make your attitude towards these poems quite clear, and am glad that you value my work highly enough to condemn it when you find it—though wrongly I believe—to be influenced by such a pernicious experiment as surrealism. Far from resenting your criticism, I welcome it very much indeed, although, to be equally candid, I think you have misinterpreted the poems and have been misled as to their purpose. I am not, never have been, never will be, or could be for that matter, a surrealist, and for a number of reasons: I have very little idea what surrealism is; until quite recently I had never heard of it; I have never, to my knowledge, read even a paragraph of surrealist literature; my acquaintance with French is still limited to 'the pen of my aunt'; I have not read any French poetry, either in the original or in translation, since I attempted to translate Victor Hugo in a Provincial grammar school examination, and failed. All of which exposes my lamentable ignorance of contemporary poetry, but, surely, does disprove your accusations. As for being 'caught up in the delirium of intellectual fashion of the moment', I must confess that I read regrettably little modern poetry, and what 'fashionable' poetry I do come across appears to be more or less communist propaganda. I am not a communist.

I hope you won't object, but I took the liberty, soon after receiving your letter, of writing to a very sound friend of mine and asking him what surrealism was, explaining, at the same time, that a critic whose work we both knew and admired had said that my own poems were surrealist. In his reply he told me what he thought the principal ideas of surrealism were, and said that surrealist writing need not have any 'meaning at all'. (He quoted some dreadful definition about 'the satanic juxtaposition of irrelevant objects etc.'.) I think I do know what some of the main faults of my writing are: Immature violence, rhythmic monotony, frequent muddleheadedness, and a very much overweighted imagery that leads too often to incoherence. But every line is meant to be understood; the reader is meant to understand every poem by thinking and feeling about it, and not by sucking it in through his pores, or whatever he is meant to do with surrealist writing. Neither is the new group on which I am working influenced, in any way, by an experiment with which I am totally unfamiliar. You have, and no doubt rightly, found many things to object to in these new poems; all I wish to do is to assure you that those faults are due neither to a delirious following of an intellectual fashion nor to the imitation of what, to my ignorance, appears a purposely 'unreasonable' experiment inimical to poetry.

In conclusion, I have quite a number of poems, simple as the three you liked, to my mind not half as good as the ones you cannot stand for. Do you wish me to send those on to you, or would you rather we wait until we can discuss everything when I come to town in the early new year?

Again, I trust that you will not find this letter pretentious or impudent. I have thought a great deal about what you said in your letter, and my only excuse for the possible pretentiousness of my reply is that I really do want you to realise that you have—my obscurity is to blame—misinterpreted the purpose of my obviously immature poetry, and attributed to it experimental absurdities I hardly knew existed.

Yours sincerely,

Dylan Thomas

MSS.: Messrs Dent

Rayner Heppenstall, the Yorkshire poet and novelist, was three years older than Dylan. At the period of this letter he had not yet had a volume published, though poems and stories had appeared in periodicals. For the past twelve months they had been great drinking companions whenever Dylan was in London. Heppenstall has described their boozing and brawling in his book, *Four Absentees.*

Oswell Blakeston was another poet of this generation, considerably less rumbustious in his behaviour, and *Caravel* was a literary magazine.

Clerkenwell and Kilburn are working-class districts in London, extremely drab, whereas Limehouse is in the East End near the docks, and contains the Chinese quarter.

Thomas Burke was half of Burke and Hare, the Edinburgh body-snatchers of the early nineteenth century, and figures in the film, *The Doctor and the Devils,* that Dylan was to write with Donald Taylor ten years later.

TO RAYNER HEPPENSTALL

31st December 1935

5 Cwmdonkin Drive,

Uplands,

Swansea

I owe you a lot of apologies, five shillings, and a long letter. I haven't got enough news to make a long letter, I certainly haven't five shillings, but I do apologise for my delay in answering your letter, quite half of which I nearly understood. Green ink makes everything illegible, anyway, but your handwriting makes even a simple address look like a nice Sanskrit poem. From what I could gather, you'd come back either from the Rectory or the Fitzroy and were gassed hard. Purposely you were in a strong and came out only for impudent purposes. What a time you've been having. But thanks again, I'm frightfully glad to hear from you. I never think of cider without thinking of black eyes, and the mere mention of Clerkenwell brings back the years like the smell of old violents (what I meant to type was old violets, but I'm damned if I'm going to cross anything out). Now, on the last day of the year, I am sitting more or less seriously down to type you a long delayed but now most seasonable letter. I'm typing because my own handwriting is bloody and my hand shakes. As, with lynx eyes, you'll spot, I'm taking a at home far from the beards and bow ties, and will be here until the end of January. Let's meet when I come back to town and, over beer, roar our poems at each other like little Bellocs, and stamp up Bloomsbury waving our cocks.

I had a letter a little time ago from Oswell Blakeston, and he said he'd met you and a new black eye of yours in, I think, the Café Royal. He said that you had said you were now entirely tamed and pugnacious no longer. But do be pugnacious once more, just once more, and attack G.E.G. like a bloodhound. How is the book doing by the way? I don't read many periodicals now and have seen very few reviews. I see you're writing for Oswell's supplement to Caravel too. Do you know anything about Caravel? I've never, in my ignorance, heard of it before.

I spent most of the summer in Donegal and did a lot of good work there, but a wave of rather alcoholic laziness has set in since and I am only just beginning to put words together again. The poetry machine is so well oiled now it should work without a hitch until my next intellectually ruinous visit to the bowels of London. I want to go abroad this summer but I don't know where. Do you know anything about Spain? Can you get along without Spanish and without money? (The same applies to any country and I'll probably end up in a bed-sitting room off the Fulham Road.) But why Kilburn, Rayner, of all places? Why not a much cheaper place in the East End? If you don't object to vermin you can get a palace near London Bridge for about two shillings a week. Come and live in Limehouse with me and write books like Thomas Burke.

I told you there was no news. I live a comfortable, sheltered, and now only occasionally boozy life in Swansea, along with Fred Janes. I'm writing a very long poem—so are you, if I read your letter correctly—and a number of dream stories, very mixed, very violent. There is much to be said, if I may coin a phrase, for leading the conventional life. (But when I think of it I always have, for the shabby drunkenness of Chelsea was even more conventional than this.)

Write a letter sometime and tell me what you're doing.

> Good luck, and plug Grigson.
> Yours,
> Dylan

MSS.: Texas

Robert Herring was editor of *Life and Letters Today* and had published Dylan's 'Altarwise by owl-light' sequence of poems in December 1935.

As this letter shows, Dylan had no illusions about his own behaviour in London. Indeed he now wore his drunkenness as a mask, as he still, occasionally, wore his alleged tuberculosis.

'Miss S.' is Edith Sitwell, who was praising his poems and had expressed a desire to meet him.

Oddenino's was a large café-restaurant almost next door to the Café Royal, which was then the natural meeting place for writers and artists.

TO ROBERT HERRING

> 30th January 1936
> 5 Cwmdonkin Drive,
> Uplands,
> Swansea

Dear Robert Herring,

I'm sure the worst will happen; it always does; I shall get blind. So let's meet, shall we, on my first day in town? the 10th. Shall we meet somewhere in the evening; I mayn't be up for lunch. You can tell me all about Miss S. She isn't very frightening, is she? I saw a photograph of her once, in medieval costume. And thanks a lot: I'd like very much to dine on the 20th. Don't bother to write, unless of course, you aren't free on the 10th. I'll ring you in the afternoon to fix a time and pub. I shan't wear a gardenia but I am short with bulging eyes, a broken tooth, curly hair and a cigarette. Otherwise I am respectable enough even to go into Oddenino's (That's not a suggestion for a meeting place, but the Café Royal is, I believe, barred to me, and anyway I prefer places with things to spit in). Do you ever see Oswell Blakeston by the way? If you do, wave your hand at him for me. I hope to have a drink with him next month. And if you aren't free, then do suggest any other day after the 10th.

> Yours sincerely,
> Dylan Thomas

Eric Walter White was in those days best known as a critic of films and music. I quote this letter not because it is intrinsically interesting, but because it is typical of many that I intend to omit.

TO ERIC WALTER WHITE

8th March 1936

5 Cwmdonkin Drive,
Uplands,
Swansea

Dear Eric Walter White,

I am, by accident, not by nature, so abominably rude and unreliable that I have to spend the best part of the first week after my regular short visits to town in writing frantic letters of apology. Before these regular short visits, I work out my plans in the most pleasant detail; almost every day is arranged so that something nice happens in it. And then, when I do come to town, bang go my plans in a horrid alcoholic explosion that scatters all my good intentions like bits of limbs and clothes over the doorsteps and into the saloon bars of the tawdriest pubs in London. I was looking forward to meeting you and being taken to hear music; but minor nastiness followed rudeness (ringing you up for example,) (and then not appearing) and I heard no music at all and I failed to meet you. It would bore you to death to hear all the reasons, but I do really and deeply apologise for my behaviour.

I'm returning to town in about a fortnight, before I go into the country to work, and nothing so silly shall happen again. Will you have a meal with me then and let me apologise personally. Do say yes.

Yours very sincerely,
Dylan Thomas

MSS.: Eric Walter White, Esq.

Once again here is a letter that has little intrinsic interest, but that is typical in two ways. One is the protracted joke—that they were both mice. Dylan would pursue such jokes for weeks on end. The other is the manner in which he fits his tone to the mood of his correspondent—even in this case to the extent of apologizing for chasing girls!

The signature is a drawing of Dylan by himself, drinking, smoking, wild-curly haired.

The gramophone records are Jean Cocteau reciting 'La Toison d'Or' against jazz, Naylor making astrological predictions, and Burns and Allen singing 'Do you believe me?'

TO OSWELL BLAKESTON

7th March 1936
5 Cwmdonkin Drive,
Uplands,
Swansea

Dearest mouse my dear, You're awfully lucky, you and the little whisker friends, all smug and slimy, listening to Cocteau and Burns and Naylor & Allen behind the skirting board. Nobody ever heard of a mouse menace, and you are not a national danger, and people write poems about you and call you slinkie and nice and velvet. You'd be safe even in Chicago, where they'd give me a fifth leg. Every year sixteen thousand London brothers and sisters cornered caged and killed. They brought out an act to destroy me in nineteen nineteen, when I was only five years old. But they gave me a week! I haven't seen you for so long, not since we spent an evening in not going to the Queen's Hall, and not since I left you, outside the Café Royal very rudely for a silly Rat. I'm coming back, travelling under the seat all the way, nibbling brown paper, at the beginning of next month. Will you meet me? And this time I'll promise not to be bad: I'll powder my snout and not run after hen-rats. And will you send me some of my fan-mail sometimes? I'm so unpopular these days. Whenever I switch on the wireless it's an interval. I was abominable about the B.B.C. But I'll get what's coming to me: when I die I'll go to hell, and it'll be Rat Week always.

Much love to you, very much, Oswell.

From

(Dylan)

MSS.: Oswell Blakeston, Esq.

Rather earlier than the last two letters, he had been invited to Cornwall, to stay, in April. Wyn Henderson had been music and art critic in London for the Argentine paper *La Nacion*. Later she had been a typographer and publisher. She was to run Peggy Guggenheim's ultra-modern London art gallery. At the moment she was living between London and Cornwall, where she had a small cottage, and was to have, next year, a guest house. She knew everyone in the world of the arts.

Norman Cameron, who had become one of Dylan's closest friends, was worried, as so many of his friends were, by his drinking habits in London. He had suggested to Mrs Henderson that she ask Dylan to stay.

I do not know which of his stories 'The Phosphorescent Nephew' eventually became. There was a novel of the period called 'The Venetian Glass Nephew'.

TO WYN HENDERSON

9th March 1936
5 Cwmdonkin Drive,
Uplands,
Swansea

Darling (Dylan) Darling (Dylan again) Wyn, and Oswell (if he's about).

How nice of you to purr about me after dinner, two fed, sleek cat-rubbing against the table-legs and thinking about a scrubby Welshs man, with a three-weeks-accumulated hangover and a heart full of love and nerves full of alcohol, moping over his papers in a mortgaged villa in an upper-class professional row (next to the coroner's house) facing another row (less upper) and a disused tennis court. It was a lovely rolling letter, out of the depths of dinner, and a winy mantle of love hung over it, and thank you a lot, Wyn and Oswell.

Wyn privately: As your mascot and very welcome guest, I'd love to come to Cornwall more than anything else: it sounds just what I want it to be, and I can write poems, and stories about vampire sextons deflowering their daughters with very tiny scythes, and draw rude little pictures of three-balled clergymen, and go to pubs and walks with you. It's all too lovely to be good; and I'd enjoy it so much. I'm coming to town in about a fortnight: I've got to meet a few publishers and try to get money from them as I haven't any, and, I believe, to read some poems over the wireless. That won't take long: the publishers will (probably) pretend to be deaf, and the wireless will break down. If you are gone by then, chugging into Cornwall, shall I follow you and will you meet me, me lost with beer in my belly and straws in my hair? And if you haven't chugged away, but are still rampaging in Bloomsbury (or wherever you rampage mostly) we can go together, can't we? And that will be nicer still. (This letter, Wyn dear, is too excellently phrased. But I've just finished writing a story called 'The Phosphorescent Nephew'; and whatever I do now, bugger me it's literary.)

So thanks, Wyn, for the invitation. I do hope you won't be gone when I come back to London—even though you have to go away and leave me there temporarily—because there are lots of little things to talk about.

Much love to you, (and to old Slime, the State Parasite).

Dylan

TO RICHARD CHURCH

17th March 1936
5 Cwmdonkin Drive,
Uplands,
Swansea

Dear Richard Church,

I'm so sorry to have delayed sending my poems to you. I have been thinking about them a good deal, and about what we said when we last met. I promised to send two lots of poems, one lot containing the recent things, most of which you've already seen and one of more-or-less simple, unambiguous poems. But I don't think now that that's a very wise plan—or, to my present way of thinking, a very honest one. Just as you, as you said, would consider it almost dishonest to publish poems you could not explain to those people who might buy them, so I feel it would be dishonest of me to attempt to get published a complete book of 'simple poems'; I shall always go on trying to write simple, unambiguous things, but they can only be a very little part of my work ('my work' sounds awful but it can't be helped). What I want to do is to include a certain number of these 'simple poems' in each collection of new poems I, God willing, might publish in future years. The same with this present collection. As you'll see, most of the poems are the very recent ones you have, in the past, objected to—along with ones much less difficult. I should not like the simples or the not-so-simples to be published separately: after all they were written more or less at the same time and do, together, represent my work for the past year and more.

If, after this final reading—and believe me I'm not being snooty at all—you come to the conclusion you could not honestly print them in your series, am I at liberty to try and have them published else-where? I hope, of course, most sincerely, that you will be able to publish them: if not the day may come when none of my poems will be indecently obscure or fashionably difficult.

Yours sincerely,
Dylan Thomas

MSS.: Messrs Dent

He came to London in late March 1936, spent a few days there and then went down to Cornwall with Wyn Henderson.

· On 20th April he went back to London for a week or so. (This, the first of his letters to Vernon Watkins, is postmarked G.W.R. or Great Western Railway, which means that it was actually posted on the mail train.) He returned and stayed in Cornwall until late May.

Vernon Watkins, also a Swansea man some few years older than Dylan, had read *18 Poems* when first it came out and had called on the younger poet. They became close friends. Henceforth Dylan was to accept Vernon's detailed criticism of his poems as he accepted that of no one else, and was to seek his technical advice.

TO VERNON WATKINS

20th April 1936

Polgigga, Porthcurno, Penzance,
Cornwall. Monday

Dear Vernon,

Perhaps it's a bit late to say Sorry for not having let you know I couldn't come to see you that particular Sunday—whenever it was—and to tell you how much I missed you and the unwonted walk and the toasted things for tea and the poetry after it; but I want to say Sorry, and I hope you'll forgive me, and I hope, though that's the wrong way of putting it, that you missed your hearty, Britain-chested, cliff-striding companion as much as I did. I had crowds of silly, important things to do: pack, write formal letters, gather papers, and catch the Sunday night train; and I didn't get out of bed until all those things had to be scamped through. Now in a hundred ways I wish I hadn't come away; I'm full of nostalgia and a frightful cold; here the out-of-doors is very beautiful, but it's a strange country to me, all scenery and landscape, and I'd rather the bound slope of a suburban hill, the Elms, the Acacias, Rookery Nook, Curlew Avenue, to all these miles of green fields and flowery cliffs and dull sea going on and on, and cows lying down and down. I'm not a country man; I stand for, if anything, the aspidistra, the provincial drive, the morning café, the evening pub; I'd like to believe in the wide open spaces as the wrapping around walls, the windy boredom between house and house, hotel and cinema, bookshop and tube-station; man made his house to keep the world and the weather out, making his own weathery world inside; that's the trouble with the country: there's too much public world between private ones. And living in your own private, four-walled world as exclusively as possible isn't escapism, I'm sure; it isn't the Ivory Tower, and, even if it were, you secluded in your Tower know and learn more of the world outside than the outsideman who is mixed up so personally and inextricably with the mud and the unlovely people—(sorry, old Christian)—and the four bloody muddy winds.

I was in London for just over a week, and the same things happened there that always happen: I kept roughly a half of my appointments, met half the people I wanted to, met lots of other people, desirable and otherwise, and fully lived up to the conventions of Life No. 13: promiscuity, booze, coloured shirts, too much talk, too little work. I had Nights Out with those I always have Nights Out with: Porteous, Cameron, Blakeston, Grigson, and old Bill Empson and all—(Empson, by the way, has been very kind to me in print, in a review of the Faber anthology, saying, quite incorrectly, though than which etc. there could be nothing nicer for my momentary vanity, that little or nothing of importance, except for Owen and Eliot, comes between Eliot and ME. Ho! Ha!) Also I had lunch with Pope Eliot, as I said I would have; he was charming, a great man, I think, utterly un-affected; I had a spot of rheumatism that day, and nearly the whole time was spent in discussing various methods of curing it, ('I think it was in 1927 I had my worst bout, and I tried Easu Ointment' etc.) I left London with Life No. Thirteen's headache, liver, and general seediness, and have by this time thoroughly recovered.

Polgigga is a tiny place two miles or less from Land's End, and very near Penzance and Mousehole (really the loveliest village in England). We live here in a cottage in a field, with a garden full of ferrets and bees. Every time you go to the garden lavatory you are in danger of being stung or bitten. My hostess, or what you like, has unfortunately read too many books of psychology, and talks about my ego over breakfast; her conversation is littered with phrases like narcissist fixation and homosexual transference; she is a very simple person who tries to cure her simplicity by a science which, in its turn, tries to cure the disease it suffers from. I don't think that's my phrase, but here in this Freudian house it's truer than hell. But I shall tell you probably when I see you in the summer—a summer I'm looking forward to a lot. The one thing that's saving me—saving me, I mean, not from any melodramatic issues but just from sheer unhappiness—is lots and lots of work. I'm half way through another story, and have more or less finished a poem which I want to send you when I'm better pleased with it. But here again I'm not free; perhaps, as you said once, I should stop writing altogether for some time; now I'm almost afraid of all the once-necessary artifices and obscurities, and can't, for the life or the death of me, get any real liberation, any diffusion or dilution or anything, into the churning bulk of words; I seem, more than ever, to be tightly packing away everything I have and know into a mad-doctor's bag, and then locking it up: all you can see is the bag, all you can know is that it's full to the clasp, all you have to trust is that the invisible and intangible things packed away are— if they could only be seen and touched—worth quite a lot. I don't really know why I should be unloading any of this on you, and probably boring you—no, that's wrong, you couldn't be one of the bored ones of the world—at the same time. But you are—even if only momentarily—the one happy person I know, the one who, contrary to facts and, in a certain way, to circumstances, seems to be almost entirely uncomplicated: not, either, the uncomplication of a beginning person, but that of a person who has worked through all the beginnings and finds himself a new beginning in the middle—I hope, for your today's happiness—a beginning at the end. That's not clear, of course. You might, and would, I know, if you could, help me by talking to me. I don't fear—we talked about it, do you remember— any sudden cessation or drying-up, any coming to the end, any (sentimentally speaking) putting out of the fires; what I do fear is an ingrowing, the impulse growing like a toenail into the artifice. Talk to me about it, will you—it's probably a terrible task I'm trying to drag you into—in any way, any words. And tell me what you're doing and writing. I'll write you again soon, a clearer letter, less face-in-the-earth, less eye-in-a-sling.

Yours always,
Dylan

God, I almost forgot.

Are you rich temporarily? Would you like to lend me some money, a pound or, at the very most, two pounds? I have a beastly, vital debt—rather a lot—to pay in the next few days; I've got together most of it, but not quite all, and all has to be paid. I can—if you are penniful temporarily, and, if you're not, do forget it and go on writing the long letter you're going to write to me—let you have it back next week certainly. Of course you don't mind me asking you, but if you're broke or holiday-saving, I can get a few pounds elsewhere—though not, Mr. Watkins, with such lack of embarrassment as I can ask you for it.

Yours always again,
D.

[*Pencil PS.*]
Did the snaps—I bet they didn't—come out well, or at all?

MSS.: British Museum

It was during this visit to London in late April of 1936 that he almost certainly met his future wife, Caitlin Macnamara, for the first time.

Meanwhile Richard Church had agreed to publish his second volume of poems.

TO RICHARD CHURCH

1st May 1936
Polgigga,
Porthcurno,
Penzance,
Cornwall

Dear Richard Church,

I am so very, very glad that you are going to publish my poems. Knowing how you feel about their obscurity and (occasional) wilful eccentricity, and about your own obligations, both as a publisher and a poet, to the public you have already created by bringing out the work of so many of the more Intelligible Boys, I do appreciate your decision to let me and that public 'face each other'. I can only hope that the

poems will, in some little way, justify the faith you have in them—
a faith, perhaps, that goes against judgement.

In less than a month I shall probably be able to let you have the
other half dozen poems you need: two new ones, completing the
long poem of which you have the first eight sections, and four younger
ones selected and revised.

I'm very glad too that you liked my story in Comment. I've had
quite a lot of stories of more or less the same kind published lately,
and have got together enough to make a book. I know you don't
publish short stories at all; if you did, I should certainly have sent the
book to you to look sternly upon. (I'm afraid I can't make good
sentences on a typewriter.) At the moment I'm vainly squinting around
for some innocent publisher who doesn't mind losing money on
twenty difficult and violent tales.

One day I hope, as you suggest, to write a story about my earlier
world; but I don't feel sure enough of myself to attempt it yet in the
form of a novel. What I have been thinking of lately is a book about
Wales with a slender central theme of make-belief, a certain amount of
autobiography and also a factual Journey of the more popular kind
(the Bad Companion's English Journey, Muir's Scottish one, etc.).
It's difficult to write about this in a letter, but I should, when I come
to town in a month's time, like to talk it over with you. Could we
arrange to have a meal together? I'll let you know the exact date of
my return. I'm sure that if you would be kind enough to talk over
this Welsh idea with me, it would clear up nearly all the vaguenesses
and leave me something practical and (almost) commercial to work
upon.

Do excuse this very loosely written letter. And thank you again
for all your encouragement.

Yours sincerely,

Dylan Thomas

MSS.: Messrs Dent

He was in London for the Surrealist Exhibition in early June, went down to Swansea, and returned in late June to take part in a poetry reading, connected with the exhibition, in honour of Paul Eluard, on 26th June. Dylan read a postcard.

During this visit he saw John Johnson, then connected with Rupert Doone's Group Theatre, who suggested that he write a play.

Nigel Henderson is Wyn Henderson's son. The play was never written.

TO NIGEL HENDERSON

7th July 1936

5 Cwmdonkin Drive,
Uplands,
Swansea

Dear Nigel,

Thank you so much for the papers; I've been working on the poems and I've burned the indiscretions. I should have written and said thanks weeks ago, but I mislaid your address, and the letter you wrote has been chasing me all over the place; it arrived this morning. Sorry you didn't give me a nudge at the exhibition; it wasn't earnest conversation really; probably little jokes.

About the Group Theatre: I had some drinks with John Johnson about ten days ago, but hadn't anything much to offer him. I've been thinking of doing a Horrible play, mostly in prose with verse choruses and have got bits of the story mapped out; but I would like to meet Doone before I get down to it, as, without some sort of promise that it will be performed, I don't feel like devoting a lot of time to it at the moment—I can't as a matter of fact, because I've to review lots of crime stories in order to buy beer and shirts and cigarettes.

I'm coming up to town at the beginning of August. If you're about then, perhaps we could fix a Doone, you and me meeting? And if you've got a green hat of mine, do be an angel and send it along; it rains here all the time, and my brim's coming off.

I'll drop you a line as soon as I know definite London dates.

Thanks again,
Yours,
Dylan

MSS.: Nigel Henderson, Esq.

His first meeting with Richard Hughes took place on 15th July 1936. Augustus John and Caitlin arrived at Laugharne Castle on the same day. As John's subsequent account of the meeting shows, he was unaware, and remained unaware, that Dylan and Caitlin were already lovers.

TO RICHARD HUGHES

14th July 1936

5 Cwmdonkin Drive,
Uplands,
Swansea

Dear Richard Hughes,

I'm going to Fishguard by car tomorrow, and passing awfully near Laugharne. I do hope you'll be there because we—that's painter Alfred Janes and me—would like very much to call on you. We shall, shall we, some time in the afternoon? Hope I shan't miss you as I did last time.

Yours sincerely,
Dylan Thomas

MSS.: Richard Hughes, Esq.

Before leaving for Laugharne he wrote to John Johnson.

Betty Boop was a figure in a strip cartoon of the period, blonde, curly haired and with plump cheeks. John Johnson does not remember who she was, but recalls her sitting, silent, while he and Dylan talked. It seems probable that she was Caitlin.

The stories are his earlier, fantastic, macabre, even surrealist ones, some of which appeared in *The Map of Love* in 1939, while the others were published after his death.

TO JOHN JOHNSON

15th July 1936

5 Cwmdonkin Drive,
Uplands,
Swansea

Dear John Johnson,

Thanks for your letter. I was very sorry too, that we didn't have more time together, but it was—this is my weekly sorry day—all my fault really. I should have had a proper lunch with you, not a few bolted drinks with Betty Boop. I always find lunch in London a deliberate lie; next time we meet, let's make it Drinks.

I hope I'll be able to start a play quite soon; and I realise, of course, that there can't be a guarantee of production. So glad, though, that you're going to help make things easier.

I'll send you the stories, sixteen of them. Four or five of them sentimental and possibly worthless—I hope not, because I think they are readable at least—at the beginning of next week. I'm going away this morning to stay very richly with Richard Hughes in a castle, otherwise I could send them off earlier. Hope this isn't too long a delay. And thanks so much for wanting to take this trouble over them. But I doubt if an established, commercially established, publisher would be very keen; some people consider the stories dirty and, occasionally, blasphemous—which they probably are. But you shall see any way, and thanks again for wanting to.

I think I'll be in town sometime in August; let you know before-hand and we'll have some drinks.

Yours,

Dylan Thomas

MSS.: John Johnson, Esq.

Twenty-five Poems was published on 10th September 1936. A week before, he wrote to Edith Sitwell, who was presumably even then writing her enthusiastic review of his poetry for the *Sunday Times,* which helped, more than any other notice, to bring that book to the attention of the general public. This is the only letter of his to her that survives.

TO EDITH SITWELL

2nd September 1936

5 Cwmdonkin Drive,

Uplands,

Swansea

Dear Miss Sitwell,

I know I couldn't have expected you to answer my letter of so many months ago. I was dreadfully rude, not turning up and every-thing, and I do understand about your not answering my silly letter of apology. But I hope you aren't cross with me really, and I really do want you to believe that I regret—as much as anything in the world —not having continued the friendship I think we began. Will you meet me again, in spite of things? You're still a great encouragement to me—and always will be—and I do appreciate it.

Yours very sincerely,
Dylan Thomas

MSS.: Dame Edith Sitwell Estate

As this letter shows, Glyn Jones, who earns his bread and butter as a schoolmaster, had recently married. His review of *Twenty-five Poems* in the *Adelphi* had been most favourable, though with certain reservations.

Glyn Jones's first published volume of short stories was entitled *The Blue Bed*. Hamish Miles was an editor with the publishers, Jonathan Cape.

TO GLYN JONES

December 1936
5 Cwmdonkin Drive,
Uplands,
Swansea

Dear Glyn,

I was very glad to hear from you; it's been such a long time; and, though I knew more-or-less that a letter to your school address would still find you, I was, for some reason, really dubious about writing: you seemed to have vanished so successfully into Cardiff and marriage that I wondered whether you were cross with me in some vague way about a vaguer something or other that I may have said or done. I'm awfully pleased to know it's nothing like that, I think we both must have been just careless. How are you? I see you quite a lot in the Adelphi, but have you given up Grigson's paper and the rest? I hadn't heard about the book of stories; that's grand. What's it going to be called? I believe I've met Hamish Miles once. (bald?)

And about the review: of course I didn't think it was unfair; it's about the best I've seen of the book, and it helped me a lot; it really was constructive; I never knew, for instance, that I was such a numerical demon. And I agree with what you said about some of the poems being 'tidy enough' but so weak in contrast with some of the earlier bits of explosive bombast; that's true and perhaps I was silly in allowing those 'tidy' poems to appear more as a concession to obscurity-decriers than anything else. You're the only reviewer, I think, who has commented on my attempts to get away from those rhythmic and thematic dead ends, that physical blank wall, those wombs and full-stop worms, by all sorts of methods—so many unsuccessful. But I'm not sorry that, in that Work in Progress thing, I did carry 'certain features to their logical conclusion'. It had, I think, to be done; the result had to be, in many of the lines and verses anyway, mad parody; and I'm glad that I parodied those features so soon after making them, and that I didn't leave it to anyone else.

But, personally, I'm sorry you didn't mention the one particular poem in the book—'Then Was My Neophyte'—which I consider was the best. Nobody's mentioned it; perhaps it's bad; I only know that to me, it is clearer and more definite, and that it holds more possibilities of progress, than anything else I've done. But thanks a great, great deal for your review. I'm afraid I shan't be returning until the middle of next week. If you're still up, my address will be 27 St. Peter's Square, Hammersmith, W.6. I don't know the telephone number but you can get it from Directory Enquiry; it's Cameron's flat, but, as he's just moved in, I don't suppose his name will be in the book. And anyway, if you won't be up then, could you come down and see me for the day in the New Year? I'll be home most of January. Or could I come up and see you? I'm looking forward to either— very much.

Yours,
Dylan

Throughout the winter of 1936–7 Dylan was between Swansea and London. His literary affairs were now being looked after by David Higham, the author's agent, who contrived to handle Dylan's complicated and often non-existent finances until his death.

TO DAVID HIGHAM

9th February 1937

5 Cwmdonkin Drive,
Uplands,
Swansea

Dear Higham,

I do, really and deeply, apologise for my rudeness in not replying to your last letters. I've been ill, off and on, but not ill enough, I admit, to excuse my rudeness. I think the real reason why I haven't answered you before is that I felt—and still feel—ashamed, that is, about all this nonsensically careless business of my book of short stories. It's quite true what you heard: that Spenser Curtis-Brown had my stories, sent them to Church (who, incidentally, was forced to refuse them), and has now given them to Frank Morley. It came about in—my fault, of course—a vague and weak way: Curtis Brown wrote to me quite a time ago, enquiring about my stories and asking me to send them to him. I sent them more or less without thinking, though obviously I should have—and should greatly have preferred to—let you have them once they were ready. My capacity for even the simplest business undertaking is negligible: it sounds as though I am trying to please the notorious vagueness of the Dreamy Poet Type B classified by Punch, but really I'm a complete nit-wit when it comes to replying to people, organising anything, making any sort of deal, keeping my tiny affairs in order, and even, in this shame-making case, just sending to one agent the very little, and very un-commercial work I do. None of that vagueness is a respectable excuse, I know: but my New Year resolutions are for Punctuality and Order and I will keep them.

As for this project that I should do a book about Wales—I am very keen about it, and feel pretty sure that I could make a good job of it too. What I wanted to do was a Welsh Journey, from the top of the agricultural North to the Rhondda Valley, a journey suggested by Priestley's and Muir's though, of course, owing nothing to their method of approach, being far more personal and intimate: not a series of generalisations about Wales, or a survey of its position today, or a Nationalistic tirade, or a naturalist's rambling tour, or an historical text book about harps and castles, but an intimate chronicle of my personal Journey among people and places. I should want to do the journey alone, sometimes on foot, sometimes by bus or train, having a more-or-less definite route but being at liberty any time to interrupt it when any especially interesting incident, or people, or place, appeared. That is, I should map out for myself a set number of towns or villages on the journey from North to South, which I'd regard as my brief headquarters; what route I would take between those head-quarters would be decided by what incidents arose, what people told me stories, what pleasant or unpleasant or curious things etcetera I encountered in the little-known villages among the lesser-known people. This is all very vague, and is meant to be. I purposely do not want a too definite or binding plan to be put before a publisher; I want the Journey to be individual and informal; neither quite a picaresque travel book nor a personal journey, but a mixture of both; and certainly not a journey that blusters about the Open Road. It's difficult to explain, but somehow I feel certain it can have a commercial interest for publishers. (Augustus John will do a frontispiece for it—a portrait of me—and, if I can make him, some drawings. But the frontispiece is certain. I know lots of newspaper people in Wales, too, and can get as many photographs as are needed.) What I had in mind was that I should be paid expenses, preferably weekly, for the length of time the journey takes—expenses enough to pay my travel and accommodation bills (£5?)—which should be anything from two to three months. I realise that even a publisher favourably inclined might hedge a bit at undertaking to dole out expenses like this on a project which I am able to describe only so vaguely; and it occurred to me that perhaps he would pay my expenses for, say, one month, give me time to write up fully the chronicle of that one month's Journey, and then read it and see whether it's good enough to warrant him going on paying expenses for the rest of the time needed to complete the book. (I don't know whether I'm making myself clear; I know I'm writing very clumsily today.) Naturally I'd rather that some nice publisher would guarantee to pay expenses for the whole two or three months: but I know absolutely nothing about how far publishers allow themselves to go on a thing like this. I could, if necessary, draft out a rough map of the route I'd like to take. I intended calling on—and, in some cases, staying with a number of Welsh and Anglo-Welsh writers and painters who live in Wales—Richard Hughes and Caradoc Evans for instance—and of getting some Welsh sketches from Cedric Morris, the painter. I can't think of anything else at the moment.

I shall be in town next week for some days. Perhaps, if we met, I might be able to explain this Welsh project a little more clearly; at least I can try. Do let me know whether you'll be able to see me then, any time during the week, and whether this Journey business is, as I ignorantly believe it to be, of some practical value.

And, before I forget, Simon and Schuster of New York say they are interested in my work. Do you think it advisable to get in touch with them about 25 Poems?

Sincere apologies again for my rudeness and carelessness.

Yours sincerely,

Dylan Thomas

MSS.: David Higham Associates

On 6th July he wrote a letter, a desperate plea for money, 'even five pounds from Dent' to David Higham. Three days later he and Caitlin had moved to Wyn Henderson's guest-house.

TO DAVID HIGHAM

9th July 1937
The Lobster Pot,
Mousehole,
Cornwall

Tuesday

Dear Higham,

So glad Faber want the story for their Welsh book. And of course I accept.

I hope you've received my pathetic, and now even more disastrously important, letter. As you see from the address above, I've had to move from Lamorna, and I shan't be able to stay here long without some almost immediate money. It's hard to work at all under these conditions.

'The Orchards' is going to appear in the Faber Book of Modern Stories, too, isn't it?

Yours,
Dylan Thomas

MSS.: David Higham Associates

The first number of Keidrych Rhys's magazine *Wales*, with which Dylan had a desultory connection, had just appeared. It included a poem of Vernon Watkins's, which Dylan altered slightly, inverting one line and omitting another. Vernon Watkins had written Dylan an angry letter about this, and indeed had corrected such copies as he saw in the bookshops. He received this reply.

Nigel Heseltine is a writer and critic, the son of 'Peter Warlock', whose real name was Philip Heseltine, the composer.

TO VERNON WATKINS

Mousehole, Cornwall
15th July 1937

I'm sorry that this is such a
short and inadequate letter. I'll
do much better next time.

Dear Vernon,

If, in some weeks' time, you see a dog-like shape with a torn tail and a spaniel eye, its tail between its legs, come cringing and snuffling

up Heatherslade gravel, it will be me; look carefully at its smarmy
rump that asks to be kicked, its trembling, penholding paw that
scribbles, 'kick me', in the dust. It will deserve your anger. But,
really, the Grief of the Sea was this: I was fooling about with a copy
of the poem, playing the pleasant, time-wasting game of altering,
unasked-for, somebody else's work; and then, when I met Keidrych
with the manuscripts I had collected, blindly and carelessly I must
have included among them the for-my-own-benefit, not-to-be-shown
copy instead of the original. I hope you forgive me: that's the truth.
I was worried when I saw the first number of Wales, with that
Bowdlerized version in it, and should, anyway, in a few days have
sent off an explanation to you. Further than that I Cannot Go, but
you may still kick me when we meet in Pennard again—and I'm
hoping that will be soon.

Yes, I thought 'Wales' was good, too. I had actually very little
myself to do with the editing, though when Keidrych goes up to
Cambridge next year I shall probably—and with you as colleague,
or whatever it is, if you'd be—take it all over.

My own news is very big and simple. I was married three days ago;
to Caitlin Macnamara; in Penzance registry office; with no money,
no prospect of money, no attendant friends or relatives, and in
complete happiness. We've been meaning to from the first day we
met, and now we are free and glad. We're moving next week—for
how long depends on several things, but mostly on one—to a studio
some miles away, in Newlyn, a studio above a fish-market & where
gulls fly in to breakfast. But I shall be trying to come home soon for
at least a few days, along with Caitlin: I think you'll like [her] very
much, she ~~looks~~ like the princess on the top of a Christmas tree, or
like a stage Wendy; but, for God's sake, don't tell her that.

Write as soon as you can, and bless me.

Love to all the family.

Yours always,
Dylan

MSS.: British Museum

George Reavey, poet and translator, half Russian and half Irish, was
connected with a publishing firm in Paris, where he then usually lived. He
wished to publish Dylan's stories in England, and a long, fruitless correspondence ensued. This letter is characteristic of a lengthy correspondence,
culminating in frustration, which is not worth reprinting in this selection.

Anna Wickham was renowned for the violence of her poetry.

Dylan and Caitlin had gone, from Cornwall, to his parents' home near

Swansea. They had then moved to her mother's house in Hampshire. It is from that house, where they were to spend a great deal of time, that this letter is written.

TO GEORGE REAVEY

3rd January 1938

Blashford,

Ringwood,

Hants

Dear George,

I shan't be in London until the end of next week. We were, as you know, staying with Anna Wickham, but a difference of lack of opinion made us return to the country. I'm afraid I can't find a copy of 'The Orchards'. It was printed in the Criterion and reprinted in the Faber Anthology (also published by Faber).

I haven't a copy of any of these books, otherwise I'd tear the story out. I'm writing today to my home in Wales, asking if there is by any chance a copy there. That's the best I can do: I never manage to keep the manuscript of anything I write.

I'm enclosing a list of names to send to about the guinea edition. Something should definitely come from some of them.

Is it possible for you to write about the details of the book you mentioned in your note & on the telephone? Or would you prefer to leave it until I come back to town?

Anyway, let me know.

Yours,

Dylan

MSS.: Harvard

TO HENRY TREECE

January ? 1938

Blashford,

Ringwood,

Hants

Dear Henry Treece,

This is to thank you, deeply, for your presents; for I shan't regard them as anything else. I, too, will send you a present one day, and may you welcome it as gracefully as I did yours. The cigarettes tasted better than any I've ever had; I am, by preference, a chainsmoker, though usually all the links are missing. I am not hurt, I do not lift the nose, nor call you Boy Scout: Thank you very much for sending me two such very nice things; and I am grateful to you always. (It is more than a romantic fallacy to say that only a garret-poet can produce the immortal line; it's a realistic lie. One can write on bare nerves, but not on an empty stomach; the impulse of a poet is not affected by hunger and squalor, but the 'craft' needs time and concentration which a man nagged by hunger cannot afford to give it.)

I'll write very soon with, if possible, more suggestions and mss. Please don't bother to return anything I send you. Do you want the chapter back?

This is only a note of thanks, but the word is not 'only'.

Sincerely,
Dylan T.

MSS.: Texas

Dan is Dan Jones, now Dr Daniel Jones, the composer, and Dylan's closest childhood friend.

Augustus J. is Augustus John.

'Percy' was a fictional character invented by Dylan and Dan Jones long before, and already referred to in an earlier letter to Pamela Hansford Johnson.

Fred is Alfred Janes, the painter.

TO CHARLES FISHER

11th February 1938
Blashford,
Ringwood,
Hants

Dear Charles,

This is mostly to ask you if you could find out Dan's address for me. Tom, I suppose, knows it. I've been in London a lot since I saw you last, and meant to have a nostalgic re-union with Dan, but all I knew was that he lived at Sherwood Ho. Harrow. which didn't seem right. I'm going back to town at the end of next week, so could you let me have the address quickly? It would be very nice of you, and I'll leave you a sycamore tree in my will as soon as I've uprooted it from my wife's mother's garden. I miss our old meetings. Here, apart from Caitlin and a few very immediate people, there's no-one to talk to easily except Augustus J. who can't hear. Swansea is still the best place: tell Fred he's right. When somebody else's ship comes home I'll set up in Swansea in a neat villa full of drinks and pianos and lawnmowers and dumb-bells and canvases for all of us, and the villa shall be called Percyvilla. I have been writing quite a lot, being locked in a room every morning with beer and cigarettes and the implements of our trade. I've been lecturing too, to classes of London University. My stories are appearing next month, under the title of 'The Burning Baby: 16 Stories', published by the Europa Press of Paris & London, and in 2 editions—a general one, and a limited signed one, dear me. And my next book will be that reversed version of Pilgrim's Progress, & will appear with the Obelisk Press, Paris. Publicity over. Give my love to the boys—I can't write to them, because I don't know their numbers or roads—& when you write tell me how they are & what they're doing, & what you're doing and how you are?

Don't forget the address, will you?

Love,
Dylan

MSS.: Charles Fisher, Esq.

Mr Hermann Peschmann was at this time a lecturer, in English literature, with the Adult Education Department of Goldsmith College, University of London. He lectured to evening classes. He also ran a Poetry Club, to which Dylan read. He later ran the Reigate, Surrey, Poetry Club, and Dylan read there as well.

He had been asked by the *New English Weekly*, to review several volumes of poems, together with a number of magazines devoted to poetry. Among them there was a poem of Dylan's which moved him, though he was not sure if he had understood it correctly. He therefore wrote to Dylan with a request for elucidation.

The poem which Dylan here analyses is 'I make this in a warring absence', which had just appeared in *Twentieth Century Verse*, No. 8, Jan.–Feb. 1938, entitled 'Poem (for Caitlin)'.

TO HERMANN PESCHMANN   1st February 1938

Blashford,
Ringwood,
Hants

Dear Mr Peschmann,

Thank you for the letter. I'm glad my visit went so well, and hope I'll be able to come again.

You say you want to know what the poem (in Twentieth Century Verse) is 'about'. There I can help you. I can give you a very rough idea of the 'plot'. But of course it's bound to be a most superficial, and perhaps misleading, idea because the 'plot' is told in images, and the images are what they say, not what they stand for.

Still I hope this is of some assistance, even if not especially for your review. (Could you, by the way, send me a copy of that New English Weekly? I'd be very grateful, because I'm out of touch with everything here.)

Sincerely,
Dylan Thomas

The poem is, in the first place, supposed to be a document or narrative, of all the emotional events between the coming and going, the creation and dissipation, of jealousy, jealousy born from pride and killed by pride, between the absence and the return of the crucial character (or heroine) of the narrative, between the war of her absence and the armistice of her presence. The 'I', the hero, begins his narrative at the departure of the heroine, (Stanza One) at the time he feels that her pride in him and in their proud sexual world has been discarded.

(Stanza Two) All that keen pride seems, to him, to have vanished, drawn back, perhaps, to the blind wound from which it came. (Stanza Three) He sees her as a woman made of contraries, innocent in guilt and guilty in innocence, ravaged in virginity, (Stanza Four) virgin in ravishment, and a woman who, out of a weak coldness, reduces to nothing the great sexual strength, (Stanza Five) heats and prides of the world. Crying his visions aloud he makes war upon her absence, attacks and kills her absent heart, then falls, himself, into ruin at the moment of that murder of love. He falls into the grave: (Stanza Six) in his shroud he lies, empty of visions and legends; he feels undead love at his heart. The surrounding dead in the grave describe to him one manner of death and resurrection: (Stanza Seven) the womb, the origin of love, forks its child down to the dark grave, dips it in dust, then forks it back into light again. (Stanza Eight) And once in the light, the resurrected hero sees the world with penetrating, altered eyes; the world that was wild is now mild to him, revenge has changed into pardon. (Stanza Nine) He sees his love walk in the world, bearing none of the murderous wounds he gave her. Forgiven by her, he ends his narrative forgiveness—but he sees and knows that all that has happened will happen again, tomorrow and tomorrow.

MSS.: Texas

Tambimuttu came originally from Ceylon. As this letter shows, the first issue of his magazine, *Poetry*, had just appeared. The very mention of the late-Georgian poet who called himself John Gawsworth caused Dylan to burst with rage in those days.

TO TAMBIMUTTU

5th March 1938
Blashford,
Ringwood,
Hants

Dear Tambimuttu,

Thank for your cheque and for the first number of your beautifully produced magazine. The print's always a pleasure to read, even if some of the poems aren't. That's no sneer, believe me. I congratulate you a lot on the handsomest 'intelligent' poetry magazine I know of, and on the courage of your unfashionable introduction. I do understand that you have an extraordinarily large circulation, and that you can't, for that reason, weigh the paper down with too much difficult verse—and I'm not suggesting that the best is difficult, only that most of the best today is bound to be. I suppose there is, there must be, some reason why John Gawsworth, F.R.S.L., should appear with, say, MacNiece. I think that to include Gawsworth—I mean nothing personal—in a magazine most of whose contributors are, at least, and if little else unites them, nostalgic for nothing but a better present, is overdoing your ostensible wish to make 'Poetry' readable to a great number of people on first sight. (I agree, incidentally and only just, with a possible editorial policy which takes the view that if a number of people will only buy the magazine for the not-so-good verse that attracts them easily and immediately, the good verse may do its work on them in spite of themselves and the magazine may prosper.) I can see the point in beginning a new magazine with an easily conventional lyric or two, especially if the (problematical now, no fingerpointing offence) editor's real favourites of poems which appear later in the number contain such words as Marx, copulation, and pylon; words, very likely, and rightly likely, to put off bookstall tasters. But whether robins, rills, and Mercury woodcuts work the other way I wouldn't know. Please don't take this as a badtempered letter. I want, as much I think as you do, to see 'Poetry'—it's needed alright, verse magazines in England are very sad—grow into something extremely entertaining and popular. Poetry editors are mostly vicious climbers, with their fingers in many pies, their ears at many keyholes, and their tongues at many bottoms. You've shown, in your introduction, how much you believe in the good of poetry and in the mischief of cliques, rackets, scandalschools, menagerie menages, amateur classes of novitiate plagiarists etc. More subscribers and power to you. But one trouble I see is that, in an attempt to include many sorts of poetry, you're liable in the end to sacrifice poetry for variety. I know that you dislike as much as anybody whose dislikes have not been patterned for him, the sort of anthology that begins by saying, 'In this we aim to represent every school of contemporary poetry', and the sort of gushing, inaccurate, Professor Daisy textbook beginning 'It is now apparent that there were at the introduction of the twentieth century five poetical channels of thought'. To try, in paper or book, to represent the whole 'field' of contemporary poetry is to take a turd'seye view. Surely the only thing an editor can say about this particular point is, 'This paper's going to print the best poems that are sent to it, and let the contemporary field disappear up its own pansies'. (This may be irrelevant arguing, and I'm sure is badly put.) I lent 'Poetry' yesterday to the butcher's son here, so haven't got it by me to write you in detail about the poems—as you suggested I should try to do. I'll try in a later letter. Just received yours this morning. I heard one of your broadcasts, hope you'll be talking again soon. Lord, what a difficult business it must be, running a poetry paper: and afterward what heavy enthusiasm or condemnation from small and amateur pontifs like me. Don't take too much notice, only my sincere congratulations. I'm afraid I don't know when I'll be in London again, I can't afford to take a penny bus most days. But when I'm up, I'll let you know at once. Best wishes, Dylan Thomas.

I'll send my poem by Wednesday. Thanks for the extra time you're allowing me.

MSS.: Texas

Henry Treece is a poet, novelist and critic. He was soon to be one of the founders of the poetic movement called 'The Apocalypse' which recognized Dylan as one of their masters. Dylan, however, took a poor view of the talents of these Apocalyptic poets and refused steadily to have anything to do with them.

In his very voluminous correspondence, Dylan seldom discusses the work of contemporary poets. This letter to Treece is one of the few exceptions.

Unfortunately some of the names have had to be omitted for fear of causing offence.

TO HENRY TREECE

23rd March 1938

Blashford, Ringwood

Dear Henry Treece,

I wanted to write as soon as I had your long, explanatory letter and the first chapter of the book, but I suddenly became very busy trying to make enough money to let me be busy in peace. Now, having failed utterly to rake in or stave off, surrounded by the noises of disruption or ejection, at last and again on the doorstep, facing a butterless future, I can reply to you at ease.

Do you, I wonder and hope not, know what it is to live outlegally on the extreme fringes of society, to bear all the responsibilities of possessionlessness—which are more and heavier than is thought, for great demands are made of the parasite, and charity, though soon enough you can learn to slip it on with a pathetic feeling of comfort, is a mountain to take—and to live from your neighbour's hand to your mouth? I have achieved poverty with distinction, but never poverty with dignity; the best I can manage is dignity with poverty, and I would sooner smarm like a fart-licking spaniel than starve in a world of fat bones. A poem, obviously, cannot be begun with the strength and singlemindedness it demands and deserves unless there is enough money behind it to assure its completion; by the second verse the writer, old-fashioned fool, may need food and drink. I know I will be paid—and how well, how well—for a poem when it is finished; but I do not know how I am going to live until it is finished. If I am going to live on writing any longer, I shall have to give up living; or write in a vacuum. Now I go without cigarettes, the tubular white ants, in a smoking, swarming country. I feel in the position of the professor who was seen far out in the sea, spluttering, struggling and waving his arms and crying, 'I'm thinking, I'm thinking'. People on the beach who knew he was always thinking, did nothing; and he sank.

Yes, I have seen my poetry called 'considerable' and 'important', and so it is to me. I am not really modest at all, because, putting little trust in most of the poetry being written today, I put a great deal in mine.

You mention Cameron and Madge. Cameron's verse has no greater admirer than myself, and I respect Madge's verse, though with complete lack of affection. But when you say that I have not Cameron's or Madge's 'concentric movement round a central image' you are not accounting for the fact that it consciously is not my method to move concentrically round a central image. A poem by Cameron needs no more than one image; it moves around one idea, from one logical point to another, making a full circle. A poem by myself needs a host of images because its centre is a host of images. I make one image—though 'make' is not the word, I let, perhaps, an image be 'made' emotionally in me and then apply to it what intellectual and critical forces I possess—let it breed another, let that image contradict the first, make of the third image bred out of the other two together, a fourth contradictory image, and let them all, within my imposed formal limits, conflict. Each image holds within it, the seeds of its own destruction, and my dialectical method, as I understand it, is a constant building up and breaking down of the images that come out of the central seed, which is itself destructive and constructive at the same time.

Reading back over that, I agree it looks preciously like nonsense. To say that I 'let' my images breed and conflict is to deny my critical part in the business. But what I want to try to explain—and it's necessarily vague to me—is that the life in any poem of mine cannot move concentrically round a central image; the life must come out of the centre; an image must be born and die in another; and any sequence of my images must be a sequence of creations, recreations, destructions, contradictions. I cannot either, as Cameron does, and as others do—and this primarily explains his and their writing round the central image—make a poem out of a single motivating experience. I believe in the single thread of action through a poem, but that is an intellectual thing aimed at lucidity through narrative. My object is, as you say, conventionally to 'get things straight'. Out of the inevitable conflict of images—inevitable because of the creative, recreative, destructive and contradictory nature of the motivating centre, the womb of war— I try to make that momentary peace which is a poem. I do not want a poem of mine to be, nor can it be, a circular piece of experience placed neatly outside the living stream of time from which it came; a poem of mine is, or should be, a watertight section of the stream that is flowing all ways, all warring images within it should be reconciled for that small stop of time. I agree that each of my earlier poems might appear to constitute a section from one long poem; that is because I was not successful in making a momentary peace with my images at the correct moment; images were left dangling over the formal limits, and dragged the poem into another; the warring stream ran on over the insecure barriers the fullstop armistice was pulled and twisted raggedly on into a conflicting series of dots and dashes.

All this, of course, is not a comment on your chapter, but only a most unsuccessful attempt, again, at 'getting things straight', for myself. As for helpful comments, I'm afraid I have none. I shall be very interested to read your chapter on Hopkins's influence, because I have read him only in the most lackadaisical way; I certainly haven't studied him, or, I regret, any other poet. The comparison with the surrealists should give you a lot of scope, especially if, as I am sure you do, you think it little more than a highbrow parlour game. I haven't by the way, ever read a proper surrealist poem, one, that is, in French from the Breton boys. I've seen some translations by Gascoyne, but they were worthless.

Before I forget: New Directions, America, is going to publish both my books of verse and my book of stories, and also the long story I have been working on lately. It's the intention of New Directions to 'build' me in America; advanced writing apparently sells very well over there, they're such culture-snobs; and I should think that in some little time, the end of the year perhaps after my books are published, there would be no difficulty at all in finding a small snob publisher to do your book; it could be done in England. I really think it would be more successful, to begin with, brought out that way.

I want to send you the dozen or so new poems I've written and a bundle of reviews, but I will have to wait until they are forwarded to me from my last lodgings. Here, however, is one very new poem, which I consider—at the moment—to be more satisfactory as a whole than anything I've done. I hope you can understand the handwriting; I've no typewriter.

I'm sorry I can't suggest anything. If I do think of anything helpful, I'll write it down and send it to you immediately; and the other manuscripts won't, I hope, be long coming. My book of stories has been delayed, owing to the printers turning shy and calling certain paragraphs obscene. I understand new printers now have it in hand, and it is to appear on the 1st of April. I'll send you a copy, of course.

I have, suddenly, thought of a very little something, but it is a point, probably, that you have touched on, or are going to touch on, incidentally: the question of religion and the supernatural in my poetry. I know there is something I would like to write you about those questions: Shall I?

I am sorry not to be able to stamp this letter. My wife and I are here completely alone, and have no food and no money at all. Neither shall we have any until the end of next month. Until then, quite honestly, we starve. That is easy to write, but all the world's hells to know.

Yours very sincerely,
Dylan Thomas

James Laughlin IV was the son of a very rich American, and was of approximately the same age as Dylan. He had recently left Harvard, against his father's wishes, and had founded the publishing house, New Directions, which published what were then the most *avant-garde* writers.

At the time he had very little money, for his father had cut him off when he left Harvard, and he was living on $100.00 a month from an aunt.

He was the first American publisher to be interested in Dylan's work. In 1939 he published *The World I Breathe*, a collection of verse and prose. He remained, and remains, Dylan's American publisher.

TO JAMES LAUGHLIN

Blashford,
Ringwood,
Hants
March 28th 1938

Dear Mr Laughlin,

Thank you for writing, and for sending me the books; they interested me very much indeed, and I thought they were splendidly produced. I appreciate deeply the kind things you said about my work. I have, of course, no hesitation at all in accepting your offer of American publication, and in letting you have not only the books I have published in England but also the books that I am writing and shall write in the future. I should like you, that is, to be my American publisher for good and all.

About the books of mine that have been printed over here; my first, 'Eighteen Poems', which had a considerable success in its way, was brought out by the Parton Press; the copyright is mine, and you can have the book whenever you like. (Details about the sheets—and some, I think, may have been printed already, in preparation—can be gone into later, can't they?)

My second book, 'Twenty Five Poems', was published by J. M. Dent. I did not, by the way, know I had any American agents; in fact, I have not, and I have never heard of Ann Watkins Inc. The agent in England who handled my 'Twenty Five Poems' was David Higham, of Higham, Pollinger, and Pearn, 6 Norfolk St, Strand, London; Watkins Inc. may do their work in America: I just don't know. Neither have I heard from Watkins Inc. about your publication terms. Will you get in touch with Higham? I am writing to him by this post. I am quite sure there will be no possible difficulty in getting them to arrange for you the American rights, etc. of the Dent-published book. Dent has not, of course, any claim to the American copyright: my contract with them is for the British Empire alone.

My third book, 'The Burning Baby: 16 Stories', will appear on the first of May—it should have appeared sooner, but there was some unavoidable delay owing to the printers turning shy of some particularly harmless passages—from the Europa Press. I have already written to George Reavey, of that Press, telling him to correspond with you immediately, and suggesting to him, as you said in your letter, that he should, right away, print 500 sheets for you. That matter should be easily settled. Reavey's address is: Europa Press, 7 Great Ormond St, London, W.C.1.

Now comes the most difficult, and to me the most desperately important, part of this letter. I must say, straight away, that I must have some money, and have it immediately. I live entirely by my writing; it can be printed only in a small number of advanced periodicals and they pay next to nothing, usually nothing. I was married recently —against all sense, but with all happiness, which is obviously more sensible—and we are completely penniless. I do not mean that we just live poorly; I mean that we go without food, without proper clothes, have shelter on charity, and very very soon will not have even that shelter. I have now less than a shilling; there is no more to come; we have nothing to sell, nothing to fall back upon. If I can be tided over for a little time I think I will be able to work hard enough to produce poems and stories that will provide some kind of food and shelter. If not, there is no hope at all. I apologise for this recital, but every one of my hopes is based on the possibility that New Directions may be able to give me an advance on royalties: on royalties, perhaps, for books to come as well as for the books already published and which are, apart from certain arrangements, outside my province, with Reavey and my agent Higham, already yours. I will, of course, sign a contract with you stating that all my books, past, present, and future, are to be published by you—if you want them—in America. If New Directions cannot see its way clear—and its all extremely irregular, I know, and must be very annoying to you—to give me an advance on royalties now, before even the books have been published in America, I am more than willing to dispense with my future royalties and take whatever sum you can give me for the complete American copyright of all books I shall write. For what I need now, and more urgently than I can tell you, is money to continue living. And, unfortunately, money at once: that is the important thing. I hope to finish a long prose work soon, perhaps next month—that is, if I can procure lodgings and buy necessities, for we must leave this address the moment we can buy a railway ticket to anywhere—and have it published in London in the autumn. That book, too, I can deliver, and will deliver, to you quickly as some further exchange for the advance I hope to the lord you will be able to forward me when you receive this letter, this unavoidably miserable letter for which I again apologise. I had hoped to write all this in a businesslike manner, but I failed. I failed because, although I know nothing about the business of publishing or the agreements that can be made between publisher and author, I know enough to realise that my most sincere appeal for an immediate advance on the work you wish to publish is unorthodox and, possibly, insolent. I am sorry I had to write this, but I am forced to do away with dignity and formality, and ask you this question: Can you, at once, give me money for which, in return, I promise you all the work I have done and will do? I wish very much to be published by you. I hope, beyond all things, that you will answer me. I'll try to make my next letter to you a less wretched affair than this.

Yours very sincerely,
Dylan Thomas

MSS.: James Laughlin IV

In the spring of 1938 Dylan and Caitlin went to live in Laugharne (pronounced Larne) in Carmarthenshire, South Wales. This was to be their home for the next two years. Richard Hughes, the novelist, had found them a cottage near to his own home. In late July they moved into a larger house, 'Sea View', at the other end of the town.

TO HENRY TREECE

16th May 1938   Gosport Street, Laugharne

Dear Henry Treece,

I've been moving house. That is, I've left, with trunks and disappointment, one charitable institution after another and have found and am now occupying, to the peril of my inside and out, my rheumatic joints, my fallen chest, my modern nerves, my fluttering knutted pocket, a small, damp fisherman's furnished cottage—green rot sprouts through the florid scarlet forests of the wallpaper, sneeze and the chairs crack, the double-bed is a swing-band with coffin, oompah, slush-pump, gob-stick and almost wakes the deaf, syphilitic neighbours —by the side of an estuary in a remote village. (The village also contains bearded Richard High-Wind Hughes, but we move, in five hundred yards, in two or more different worlds: he owns the local castle, no roof and all, and lives in a grand mansion by its side and has a palace in Morocco. These legendary possessions were acquired half by whimsy, half by influence. I could beat out an Elfin cadence with the best, be naughty, delightful, naive, adult, shrewd, bewitching and pawky about children—'He has the fairy alchemy': H. Wolfe— but all the influence I could raise wouldn't buy me a paper bag of tripper's shit from Merlin's Cave.) And that is my excuse for not writing, for not thanking you for the Hopkins chapter or enclosing the MSS I promised. It's taken such a time to settle down and up. I hope you'll forgive me.

I was much impressed by the Hopkins chapter, which means I enjoyed it and thought much of it was true. What a lot of work you've put in. I never realised the influence he must have had on me. As I told you before, I have read him only slightly. I have read far more Francis Thompson. I've never been conscious of Hopkins' influence. As a boy of fifteen or sixteen, writing in all sorts of ways false to myself, composing all sorts of academic imitations, borrowing sometimes shamelessly and sometimes with the well-supressed knowledge of a pretense to originality, I find—from looking over many hundreds of those very early poems—that there was, and still is, to me, not a sign of Hopkins anywhere. (And I had read him then, as I had read a great deal of poetry, good and bad; or, rather, I had read through his book). The people most to be found in those early poems were, I think, the Elizabethans and George Peele, Webster and, later, Beddoes, some Clare (his hard, country sonnets), Lawrence (animal poems and the verse extracts from the Plumed Serpent,) a bit of Tennyson, some very bad Flecker and, of course, a lot of bits from whatever fashionable poetry—Imagists, Sitwells—I'd been reading lately. But out of all that muddle, some poem-sections of which I enclose unaltered, I see no Hopkins. You might see it; you've already proved several things to me in that extraordinary chapter. Sometimes, I think, the influence of Swinburne is more obvious than that of Hopkins in a couple of the quotations from my poetry that you use: 'All all and all the dry worlds couple', for instance. This is rhythmically true, at least.

Very much of my poetry is, I know, an enquiry and a terror of fearful expectation, a discovery and facing of fear. I hold a beast, an angel and a madman in me, and my enquiry is as to their working, and my problem is their subjugation and victory, downthrow and upheaval, and my effort is their self-expression. The new poem I enclose, 'How Shall My Animal', is a detailed enquiry; and the poem too is the result of the enquiry, and is the furthest I can, at present, reach or hope for. The poem is, as all poems are, its own question and answer, its own contradiction, its own agreement. I ask only that my poetry should be taken literally. The aim of a poem is the mark that the poem itself makes: it's the bullet and the bull's-eye; the knife, the growth, and the patient. A poem moves only towards its own end, which is the last line. Anything further than that is the problematical stuff of poetry, not of the poem. That's my one critical argument, if it can be called that; the rest is a poetical argument, and can only be worked out in poems.

I've been looking through some old reviews, hoping to find some vague material for you. Desmond Hawkins' review of 25 Poems in the Spectator was one of the best, I remember, but I haven't a copy of it. He said several very good, clear things. Here are a few reviews which might give you some opportunities for remarks etc. There's no point in sending you ordinary, straightforward damning or congratulatory reviews, is there—This is great, This is punk? Stephen Spender, by the way, said in a review of the year's poetry some time ago—in the Daily Worker—'The truth is that Thomas's poetry is turned on like a tap; it is just poetic stuff with no beginning nor end, shape or intelligent and intelligible control'. Do you think that's worth mentioning and refuting? It's a belief held by many fancy poets like Spender. (I should like to know, too, how much that complete bit of nonsense was caused by a review I once wrote for New Verse of Spender's 'Vienna' operetta. Have you a copy of that review?) I know that you wouldn't want to introduce into your book any particular bickering, but Spender's remark is really the opposite of what is true. My poems are formed; they are not turned on like a tap at all; they are 'watertight compartments'. Much of the obscurity is due to rigorous compression; the last thing they do is to flow; they are much rather hewn. Now Spender himself has no idea of form; His poetry is so much like poetry, and so remote from poems, that I think most of his work will become almost as unreadable as the worst of the Georgians—and very soon.

Another remark I came across in a review—by Julian Symons of Hart Crane in 20th Century Verse—is: 'No modern poet except Thomas is, for me, more affecting, more able to twist words to the shape of the reader's tears.' Are you going to mention Hart Crane? Three or four years ago, when I first knew Norman Cameron, he told me that the most obvious influence in my poetry was Crane, a friend of his. And he was astonished, and at first unbelieving, when I told him that I had never heard of Crane before. He showed me some of his poems then, and I could certainly see what he meant: there were, indeed, two or three almost identical bits of phrasing, and much of the actual sound seemed similar. Since then I've read all Crane's poems, and though now I see the resemblance between his poetry and mine to be very slight, I can understand that some people might still think I had come under his influence.

You ask me about the Middle Ages. I know nothing about them. You must remember I've had no education—I left a provincial secondary school when I was fifteen or so—and I've never read anything except Modern English. Also, I can't read French, although I've often been called an imitator of the surrealists etc. I'm looking forward to the chapter on surrealism, and the 'straight' poems.

I want to let you have this very inadequate letter straight away. There's been too much delay between our writings, but it was all my fault and now I'm settled, however precariously, once again. I'm not enclosing in this letter a selection of very early poems; I'll try to get them typed tomorrow and will then send them off straight away. I haven't forgotten about religion and the supernatural, but it seems to me now like an essay that has to be written, so it will be better if I say what I think about it, at random, informally, from time to time. One of the times will be when I send off the typed poems, tomorrow or the day after. Again, forgive me. I've got a lot of material about—reviews, about ten exercise books full of poems, a few articles on poetry etc.—and they only need a little weeding and cutting before I can let you have them. If you've got any questions that might have arisen from the chapters you've done or from the plan for the rest of the book, do let me know.

All best wishes,
Dylan T.

MSS.: Lockwood Memorial Library, Buffalo

Edith Sitwell was among the first to proclaim Dylan a genius. In September 1936 she had praised *Twenty-five Poems* in the *Sunday Times* and a furious correspondence had ensued.

Michael Roberts was a poet and critic, influential in the literary world at that time.

Clifford Dyment was a young poet who contributed to Geoffrey Grigson's *New Verse*, among other publications.

David Gascoyne was a surrealist poet, slightly younger than Dylan.

TO HENRY TREECE

1st June 1938

Gosport Street, Laugharne

Dear Henry Treece,

I think Edith Sitwell would be very pleased to read the book. I don't know if she likes me, personally, now, or not. I have the idea she's offended, but this may be incorrect. I wrote her some two months ago at her Paris address, but have had no answer; perhaps she's away, perhaps the letter hasn't been forwarded, perhaps the address is dead, perhaps she has been insulted by my very long delay in replying to her letters, perhaps she too has gone lazy or bad-mannered (this I doubt extremely). Anyway, she still likes my work and she'll undoubtedly like yours; and her London address which won't be dead unless this Girton and county and deaf middle-aged ladies' institution has been raided, is c/o The Sesame Club, 49 Grosvenor Street, W.1. The Paris address is 129 rue Saint-Dominique, VII.

About her review, and the subsequent letters, in the Sunday Times some of which you said you might mention or include—She makes a few interesting mis-readings or, rather, half-readings. She says the 'country-handed grave' in my poem 'A Grief Ago' is 'that simple nurse of grief, that countryman growing flowers and corn'. My image, principally, did not make the grave a gentle cultivator, but a tough possessor, a warring and complicated raper rather than a simple nurse or an innocent gardener. I meant that the grave had a country for each hand, that it raised those hands up and 'boxed' the hero of my poem into love. 'Boxed' has the coffin and the pug-glove in it. Edith Sitwell's analysis, in a letter to the Times, of the lines 'The atlas-eater with a jaw for news/Bit out the mandrake with tomorrow's scream, 'seems to me very vague and Sunday-journalish. She says the lines refer to 'the violent speed and the sensation-loving, horror-loving craze of modern life'. She doesn't take the literal meaning: that a world-devouring ghost creature bit out the horror of tomorrow from a gentleman's loins. A 'jaw for news' is an obvious variation of a 'nose for news', and means that the mouth of the creature can taste already the horror that has not yet come or can sense it coming, can thrust its tongue into news that has not yet been made, can savour the enormity of the progeny before the seed stirs, can realise the crumbling of dead flesh before the opening of the womb that delivers that flesh to tomorrow. What is this creature? It's the dog among the fairies, the rip and cur among the myths, the snapper at demons, the scarer of ghosts, the wizard's heel-chaser. This poem is a particular incident in a particular adventure, not a general, elliptical deprecation of this 'horrible, crazy, speedy life'.

You say you intend showing the book to Michael Roberts who will be 'sympathetic towards us'. You are not treading on my corns when you call Roberts a good Thinker, but I personally can do without his condescension. He commented in the London Mercury that 'it is a pity D.T. should sometimes give the impression of us ng a large and personal vocabulary merely to make a schoolboy exhibition'. The phrase I object to is not 'a schoolboy exhibition', for I'm not afraid of showing off or throwing my cap in the air, but 'It's a pity'. What function has this patronising 'pity' in criticism? Do I need a critic to weep over my errors of taste? Let him point them out, tell me, if he likes, how to rectify them: but, for Christ's sake, not sympathise.

Yes, I should certainly write to James Laughlin of New Directions (Norfolk, Connecticut). I've had a lot of letters from him lately about plans for publicity for my stories and poems in America, and I know he'll be very interested in your book. He seems genial and very earnest and has been giving me small sums of money regularly, though now they've ceased. He talks about 'his' poets, and takes an avuncular interest in obscurity.

I wonder whether you've considered writing anything—perhaps only a few paragraphs—about the Welshness of my poetry: this is often being mentioned in reviews and criticisms, and I've never understood it. I mean I've never understood this racial talk, 'his Irish talent', 'undoubtedly Scotch inspiration', apart from whiskey. Keidrych Rhys—editor of the very good little magazine Wales— always has a lot to say about it. He's an ardent nationalist, and a believer in all the stuff about racial inspiration etc. If you felt like it, you might drop him a line (C/o J. F. Hendry, 20 Vernon Road, Leeds) and tell him about your book and ask him what he thinks about the Welsh in my work. Anyway you'll get back a long and interes ing letter: he's the best sort of crank.

Yes, the oompah is a swing-band term. I enclose a glossary from a story in a swing magazine: Black Trumpet.

I think the method you adopted in the surrealist chapter—the clearing away of superficial misconceptions by attack and contrast of quotations—is the only effective one, and I thought the whole chapter extremely well argued and formed. You know Gascoyne's poem, in a very early number of New Verse, that begins something like 'White curtains of tortured destiny'? There are some lines in that I feel sure you could make use of, lines far more engaging and precociously lunatic than any in his Magritte poem. I've nothing to argue about in this chapter and, apart from the Gascoyne poem for quotation, no suggestions. It's a fine piece of work, and has convinced me once again that my own sane bee in the bonnet can never be a pal of that French wasp forever stinging itself to a loud and undignified death with a tail of boiled string.

Did you tel' me, in a early letter, that you might spend some of your summer noliday in Wales? Why not come and see us here? There's room for you, and food.

Yours,

Dylan T.

I'm looking forward to the other chapters, and will try to let you have the poems I promised you—early ones—very soon. They're not being as easy to arrange as I imagined.

MSS.: Lockwood Memorial Library, Buffalo

The story referred to is 'The Peaches', which was republished in the following year as part of the *Portrait of the Artist as a Young Dog*.

Robert Herring was the editor of *Life & Letters Today*.

TO HENRY TREECE

16th June 1938   Gosport Street, Laugharne

Dear Henry Treece,

I'm very glad indeed that you both will come and spend some time with us in the summer; any time, for any time. I warn you that our cottage is pokey and ugly, four rooms like stained boxes in a workman's and fisherman's row, with a garden leading down to mud and sea, that our living and cooking is rough, that you bathe or go dirty. You will find my wife extremely nice; me small, argumentative, good-tempered, lazy, fumbling, boozy as possible, 'lower middle class' in attitude and reaction, a dirty tongue, a silly young man. I hope you like drinking, because I do very much and when I have money I don't stop. There are three good pubs here, the best bottled mild in England, and no prohibitive drinking hours. There are walks, and boats, and nets to pull, and colossal liars to listen to. There is a double bed in one room, two single beds in the other; you can sleep in the double bed, or in the two beds, or sandwiched in a single one. There is an earth lavatory and it smells like a shit-house. Welcome; and let me know when. (By the way, what do I call you? Throw your Treece away.)

This is a bad time for me again, and I can't buy a stamp for you. I haven't a single penny, or half-penny, or filed French slot-coin. Smokeless and breadless, we face a bad weekend. We wait for shillings which we have no right to expect. Bitter, cruel Laugharne; my pipe is full of butt-ends from the grate, my table crowded with the dead ends of poems, my head full of nonsense. The sun is shining on the mud; my wife is out cockling. I am writing to a critic in Northumberland. A little girl has called with buns; I say, 'no buns', though all my everlasting soul shouts for them and my belly is turned by the sight in the kitchen of two poor dabs we caught, two out of all the breeding monsters in the sea, with a broken net yesterday. Last week I finished a long story about my true childhood, and here's a letter from Life & Letters saying they will print it and pay for it in September.

> O Chatterton and others in the attic
> Linked in one gas bracket
> Taking Jeyes' fluid as narcotic;
> Drink from the earth's teats,
> Life neat's a better poison than in bottle
> A better venom seethes in spittle
> Than one could probe out of a serpent's guts;
> Each new sensation emits
> A new vinegar;
> Be a regular
> Fellow with saw at the jugular.
> On giddy nights when slap on the moon's mask
> A madman with a brush has slapped a face
> I pick a stick of celery from the valley
> I find a tripper's knicker in the gully

And take another nibble at my flask.
What meaning, voices, in the straight-ruled grass,
Meaning in hot sock soil? A little cuss
Can't read sense in the rain that willynilly
Soaks to the vest old dominies and drunks.
Dissect that statement, voices, on the slabs.
Love's a decision of 3 nerves
And Up or Down love's questions ask;
On giddy nights I slap a few drunk curves
Slap on the drunk moon's mask.
Rape gulp and be marry, he also serves
Who only drinks his profits
And would a-wooing go around the graves.
Celibate I sit and see
Women figures round my cell,
Women figures on the wall
Point their little breasts at me;
I must wait for a woman's smile
Not in the sun but in the dark;
The two words stallion and sterile
Stand in a question mark.
The smiling woman is a mad story,
Wipe it away, wipe a crumb
From the preacher's table.
I offer you women, not woman,
A home and a dowry:
3 little lusts shall your dowry be,
And your home in a centaur's stable.

That's better; but the trouble is I can quite easily feel like that these days, and when I said my head was full of nonsense I meant it. I'm an expert at aping my own moods: now I could wear Dowson's invisible hat, and my throat can encompass Chesterton's dead rattle.

When I mentioned Life & Letters, I thought that that paper might easily be interested in any chapters of yours you might like printed separately. Herring's a friend of mine, more or less, and why not write to him? And do tell me what poem, or piece of poem, you'd like me, for a footnote, to analyse in detail? I'll send you some things very soon, and try to answer your questions. You might send me the 'straight' chapter sometime. Apologies for muddled letter, for the lack of a stamp.

Dylan Th.

MSS.: Lockwood Memorial Library, Buffalo

6th or 7th July 1938

Gosport Street, Laugharne

Dear Henry,

I should have written ten days ago and acknowledged your kind and welcome bungift, six days ago and acknowledged the chapters, and should have answered immediately your short note about August 2. But rudely I've put all off, wanting time to read the chapters carefully, to write about them, to analyse a poem, to answer your questions, so that I could send one long, full letter. Even now, when I do write at last, these ambitions are only partly realised and still full of holes, and the analysis, Freud help it, must wait until next time. I'm working, hard for me, though there's very little to show for it: some incomplete prose about a dwindling woman, a tame poem, a taste of nice words in the head.

I'm especially glad you can come to stay for August week, as this is the week of great celebration here: a carnival with queen, a regatta with prizes, a dance with soaks. Laugharne—pronounced Larn—will be almost gay and certainly crowded. The High Wind blows its trumpet, few that can walk from their houses will walk back, there will be speechmaking, drunkmaking, sickmaking and we must all dress up. Perhaps it won't be like that at all, but it is a good week for a visit anyway. I'd been hoping that, by the time you arrived, we would have been in our new house, but that's unlikely now. And I don't know how you get from here to Harlech, but I know you can quite easily; North Wales is just a bit further on, one way or the other. And I don't know how you get to Laugharne from Northumberland; somehow, I do know, you must get to Carmarthen or to Tenby: we lie about midway. From London it's easy (but unhelpful): Paddington to Carmarthen direct, half an hour's busride from there. There is no railway station here, but we have a nice townhall. From where will you travel? (And no, before I forget, I wasn't in Baker St. Post Office Christmas 1936). (Were you in the Knitted Buoy department of Llantrisant Naval Museum on Mother's Day? Why Baker Street?)

I thought the Straight-Poems chapter was convincing and concise. Do I understand, from your Eliot quotation at the head of the chapter, that the poetry in these straight poems is a calculated escape from the personality-parade of my loud and complex poems? I don't know if they are at all, and I really don't see how they could be. I wrote them, most of them anyway, quite a long time before the other poems in the 25 volume. The straight poems in 25 were, indeed, with a very few exceptions—I'll be able to show you all dates when we meet, but I can't now remember the exceptions because I haven't got copies of the two books—written before most of the poems in the 18 volume. But I don't want to muddle things now; we can go over all my manuscripts (if you care to, of course) and see properly how these poems do genealogically work. It might have very curious results. Both books contain poems written over about eight years; there is no definite sequence. I have a great deal of material still, in MSS books, to shape into proper poems: and these I will include, quite vaguely (that is, without considering an easily marked, planned, critical 'progress') in future published books. But we can talk about this. (Those above are teastains.)

I was interested in what you said about my lack, except in that little finger-poem, of any social awareness. I suppose I am, broadly (as opposed to regimented thinkers and poets in uniform) antisocial, but I am extremely sociable. But surely it is evasive to say that my poetry has no social awareness—no evidence of contact with society— while quite a good number of my images come from the cinema and the gramophone and the newspaper, while I use contemporary slang, cliché, and pun. You meant, I know, that my poetry isn't concerned with politics (supposedly the science of achieving and 'administrating' human happiness) but with poetry (which is unsentimental revelation and to which happiness is no more important—or any other word— than misery). (I'll elaborate that, if you'd like me to. Not that it's obscure, but it may, in some way, be helpful to add to it.) But the idea you gave me was that you actually consider me unaware of my surroundings, out of contact with the society from which I am necessarily outlaw. You are right when you suggest that I think a squirrel stumbling at least of equal importance as Hitler's invasions, murder in Spain, the Garbo-Stokowski romance, royalty, Horlicks, lynchlaw, pit disaster, Joe Louis, wicked capitalists, saintly communists, democracy, the Ashes, the Church of England, birth control, Yeats' voice, the machines of the world I tick and revolve in, pub-baby-weather-government-football-youthandage-speed-lipstick, all small tyrannies, means tests, the fascist anger, the daily, momentary lightnings, eruptions, farts, dampsquibs, barrelorgans, tinwhistles, howitzers, tiny death-rattles, volcanic whimpers of the world I eat, drink, love, work, hate and delight in—but I am aware of these things as well.

Another very small criticism: in your Introduction you say that I 'do not, like other poets of (my) age, lean over gates, seeking kinship with daffodils and sheep'. Do you mean other poets of my age-in-years, of my generation, or of my century? I ask you, what other poets of my age do lean over gates? It's a crack at young Georgians, not at New-Versers, intellectual muckpots leaning on a theory, post-surrealists and orgasmists, tit-in-the-night whistlers and Barkers, Empson leaning over his teeth to stare down an ice-cold throat at the mathematical mystery of his doom-treading boots, Cameron riding on the back of neat graves. And, actually, 'seeking kinship', with everything, daffodils, sheep, shoehorns, saints, bees, and uncles is exactly what I do do. I think, with all due lack of respect, that it's a futile crack anyway.

It's nearly post-time and I've done almost nothing except get noisy about very little matters. I think I'm putting most of my comments and criticisms off until August. But I'll write soon, properly soon, with more about these chapters. I took several notes which need only a little filling-out to make a long, vulgar, enthusiastic, argumentative letter proving nothing at all. Write when you can. I'm returning the Introduction.

Yours,
Dylan T.

I haven't, of course, read the chapters you've sent me in any order, but, from what I have read, it seems to me that you've quoted that make-it-clean-boys part of my 'Answers to an Enquiry' about half a dozen times. This is probably due to the irregular way I've read. How does the plan of the book stand now? I'll certainly let you have a poem-analysis for a footnote, and more material you'd care to use may come out of our future joint examination of piles of MSS.

Dylan

MSS.: Lockwood Memorial Library, Buffalo

Tom is Tom Warner, the musician, another close Swansea friend.

TO CHARLES FISHER

Late July 1938
Seaview,
Laugharne,
Carmarthenshire

Thursday

Dear Charles,

We've moved house & tilted our noses. Our previous house, once a palace, is now that cottage. How we ever existed there is beyond us. Here we could have two bedrooms each, which is quite useless.

Will you give Tom this note.

When are you coming to see us. Henry Treece is down next week to stay. Come along & meet him? Bring some poems.

Love,

Dylan

MSS.: Charles Fisher, Esq.

Money worries continued to plague Dylan throughout the summer of 1938, as indeed they were to do for the rest of his life. John Davenport, the poet and critic who was and remained a close friend, had recently returned from Hollywood, with his wife Clement. He helped Dylan directly, and also attempted to get others to do so. He then suggested an appeal on Dylan's behalf to the Royal Literary Fund, and sent Dylan a list of possible signatories to such an appeal.

As to the persons referred to in this letter, they are, with their names correctly spelled:

Ralph Straus, author and critic; Brian Guinness, now Lord Moyne, poet and patron of the arts; Cyril Connolly, author and critic, soon to edit *Horizon*; Aldous Huxley; John Hayward, editor, biographer and anthologist, a close friend of T. S. Eliot; E. J. O'Brien, editor of the annual *Best Short Stories of 193–*; Arthur Calder-Marshall, short story writer, novelist and critic; John Collier, short story writer and novelist; Stephen Spender, poet, and at that time propagandist; William Empson, poet, critic and philosopher; Laz Aaronson, critic; Peter Quennell, poet, biographer and critic; Edgell Rickword, poet.

TO JOHN DAVENPORT

Laugharne,

Carmarthenshire,

31st August 1938   S. Wales

Dear John,

Thank you very much. What a list of the boys, the nibs of the P.E.N. Club, pipe-sucking, carpetslippered, New Statesman in pocket, 'Mr Y has timbre', symposium contributors ('I write in white ink in a kneeling position'). How can I chose from such richness, rule out a Strauss for a Guinness? No, but I leave it to you if you don't mind choosing, because perhaps you know what sort of writer the Royal Literary Fund will have most faith in. I myself have written to Eliot (who has replied, and has already written 'strongly' to the Secretary) and to Connolly, who hasn't yet replied (is he in England, do you know?). I should think the more, and the generally better known, names the better. Huxley? He is famous and respectable, isn't he? but I doubt very much that he knows my name. Does that matter? I heard from the Secretary this morning; he said that his committee doesn't meet again until October, a cold and cheerless way off, so he intends to approach the Government on my behalf for an immediate spot. To do this, he needs, at once, a few letters 'authenticating the merits' of my case. So the point is: which of the names you suggest— (it really is terribly kind of you to take this trouble)—would be most likely to write, of their own initiative, an immediate brief letter okaying me? Would it be better to try to choose a few names that have been known to like my poems? Or would some of the eminent say, if you asked them, a couple of nice words in a short letter, just for friendlinesses sake and the brotherhood of Art? Of the names you wrote down, I'm known to John Hayward—I mean by 'known' that I know I'm known to them—E. J. O'Brien, Calder Marshall, Collier, Spender, Empson (though I think he's in China, isn't he? and I must have, in my favour, some at-once responses), Aaronson, Quennell, Rickword. But I should think more or less middle-aged people would be safer. It would be grand if you'd write to 3 or 4 of these, telling them about things and asking them to write as soon as possible a short letter to:

H. I. C. Marshall
Secretary Royal Literary Fund
Y. Gell
Trelyllyn
Nr. Towyn, Wales.

How quickly I get money—and God how much I need it depends on how quickly any of these people will write an 'authenticating' letter.

.   .   .   .

I've just had, from Reavey, at last, a lawyer's list of the objectionable words, phrases, passages & whole chunks in my short stories. The word 'copulation' (used by me in reference to a tree, most innocently), 'pissed', I said that a man spitefully pissed against the wind in order to wet somebody behind him), 'All Pauls Altar', the actual description of a murder committed by a naked woman (especially the phrase 'her head broke like an egg on the wall'), 'the holy life was a constant erection to these gentlemen', and about 20 long passages, none in the least way tittivating, none using obscene words, none evasively or circumlocutionarily to do with fucking,—all have to go in the English edition. And anyway I'd rather tickle the cock of the English public than lick its arse, which is what even this small and comparatively unimportant piece of censorship would have me do.

Thank Clement very much for her offer of infant clothes, which Caitlin would love to accept. There won't be any need until about the end of the year, before which perhaps we'll see you. It's very kind of her. Our thing, we hope, won't be too small or monstrously big for the clothes. Write soon and tell me what members of the troupe will perform for me. Thanks again v. much.

Love to both,

Dylan

MSS.: Texas

The notes to the following letters are by Vernon Watkins, as published in his *Dylan Thomas: Letters to Vernon Watkins*.

'The poems "The Tombstone Told When She Died" and "A Saint About to Fall" accompanied the next letter, and its two paragraphs are concerned with them in that order. The second poem, on which he had been working continuously, was written in anticipation of the birth of his first child in January.

'The postscript about "ogre" refers to the poem "On No Work Of Words Now" which I had typed and sent back to him.'

TO VERNON WATKINS

14th October 1938

Sea View, Laugharne

Monday:

Dear Vernon,

I'm sorry not to have written before, I've been awfully busy with my own work, with reviewing, & muddled up with trying to get money from a sinister philanthropic society. Here's my new big poem and—with no anger at all—the Hardy-like one. I considered all your suggestions most carefully. A 'strange & red' harsh head was, of course, very weak & clumsy, but I couldn't see that the alliteration of 'raving red' was effective. I tried everything, & stuck to the commonplace 'blazing' which makes the line violent enough then, if not exactly good enough, for the last. In the last line you'll see I've been daring, & have tried to make the point of the poem softer &

subtler by the use of the dangerous 'dear'. The word 'dear' fits in, I think, with 'though her eyes smiled', which comes earlier. I wanted the girl's terrible reaction of orgastic death to be suddenly altered to a kind of despairing love. As I see it now, it strikes me as very moving, but it may be too much of a shock, a bathetic shock perhaps, & I'd like very much to know what you think. No, I still think the womb 'bellowing' is all right, exactly what I wanted; perhaps it looks too much like a stunt rhyme with heroine, but that was unavoidable. 'Hurried' film I just couldn't see; I wanted it slow & complicated, the winding cinematic works of the womb. I agree with your objection to 'small'; 'innocent' is splendid, but 'fugitive' & 'turbulent' are for me, in that context, too vague, too 'literary' (I'm sorry to use that word again) too ambiguous. I've used 'devilish', which is almost colloquial.

As to the big poem—only provisionally called 'In September', & called that at all only because it was a terrible war month—I'm at the moment very pleased with it, more than with anything I've done this year. Does 'Glory cracked like a flea' shock you? I think you'll see it must come there, or some equally grotesque contrast. The last line of the 2nd verse might appear just a long jumble of my old anatomical clichés, but if, in the past, I've used 'burning brains & hair' etc too loosely, this time I used them—as the only words—in dead earnest. Remember this is a poem written to a child about to be born—you know I'm going to be a father in January—& telling it what a world it will see, what horrors & hells. The last four lines of the poem, especially the last but two, may seem ragged, but I've altered the rhythm purposely; 'you so gentle' must be very soft and gentle, & the last line must roar. It's an optimistic, taking-everything, poem. The two most important words are 'Cry Joy'. Tell me about this, please, very soon. I'm surer of the words of this poem than of the words in any recent one. I want mostly to know what the general effect of the poem is upon you (though of course you can criticise, as you like, any detail).

Sorry you couldn't come this weekend. Do try to come next. I'm afraid we are much too poor to be able to come up to see you for a long time. So do your best.

All Love,
Dylan

The following typed quatrain was sent on a separate sheet of paper with this letter: it was printed that winter in the magazine 'Seven':

I, the first named, am the ghost of this sir and Christian friend Who

writes these words I write in a still room in a spellsoaked house:
I am the ghost in this house that is filled with the tongue and eyes
Of a lack-a-head ghost I fear to the anonymous end.

On reverse of envelope :

Can you send me a typed copy of the long poem?
   The word is OGRE, not orge or orgy &, as Pritchard would say,
I'll listen to no criticisms of it.

MSS.: British Museum

Lawrence Durrell was two years older than Dylan. They had met a
year or so earlier, but did not know each other at all well. Dylan at this time
admired Durrell's writing, particularly the *Black Book* which had been
published in Paris earlier that year. Later, as will be seen, he was to have
second thoughts.
   Durrell had come to London with Henry Miller, another writer whom
Dylan greatly admired. They were at that time editing an English language
magazine in Paris together, originally called *The Booster* and later *Delta*.

TO LAWRENCE DURRELL

December 1938?

Blashford,
Ringwood,
Hants

Dear Lawrence Durrell,
   I would have liked to see you too, after that first short meeting in
Anna's house, in a clean pub with an evening before us and pockets
jingling and lots of fire and spit and loud, grand affectations and
conceits of Atlases and London coiling and humming: but Caitlin
and I went away in a pantomime snow, thrown out at midnight, and
we spent the night very coldly and trained back without tickets to
charity in the morning. Now this warmth is ending, and we'll train
back without tickets to London and live there in a bad convention.
   I think England is the very place for a fluent and fiery writer. The
highest hymns of the sun are written in the dark. I like the grey
country. A bucket of Greek sun would drown in one colour the
crowds of colours I like trying to mix for myself out a grey flat insular

mud. If I went to the sun I'd just sit in the sun; that would be very pleasant but I'm not doing it, and the only necessary things I do are the things I am doing. Unless by accidents, and my life is planned by them, I shall be nearer Bournemouth than Corfu this summer. It will need a nice accident for us to live anywhere: we are stages beyond poverty; completely possessionless; and we are willing but angry; we can take it but we don't want it. I liked your Stygian prose very very much, it's the best I've read for years. Don't let the Greek sun blur your pages as you said it did. You use words like stones, throwing, rockerying, mossing, churning, sharpening, bloodsucking, melting, and a hard firewater flows and rolls through them all the time. . . . And it's so brave too; you used the sudden image of Christ with incredible courage. I mean to borrow the typescript of the Black Book as soon as I get to London.

But I wonder what Anna will make of Miller's books. I know her well. Morals are her cup of tea, and books are just beer: she swallows them down without discrimination of taste or body or brew, and judges them by the effect they have on her bowels. For her a good book produces a bad poem from her, containing an independent moral judgement, but the poem could really have been written without the book. And I think it insulting to books to take them as a purgative in order to void material which, with a little constriction of the muscles, could have been voided anyway. My own book isn't nearly ready. I am keeping it aside, unfinished, and writing off, now, the things which would be detrimental to it if I were to continue. You said on the back of the envelope that you wanted a poem for a special number; I have one I can send but Miller, in his letter, said he did not know when two prose pieces of mine would appear, owing to some unexplained difficulties, and it's rather silly, isn't it, sending you stuff to keep and not to print. But do tell me; I'd love to send you the poem of course.

Sincerely,

Dylan Thomas

MSS.: Lawrence Durrell, Esq.

A few days later he was writing to Henry Treece, who had meanwhile been to stay. To judge by Dylan's letters to others, the visit had not been an unqualified success. The arrival of Augustus John, 'The Old Master', made the sort of conversations Treece wished to have with Dylan wellnigh impossible.

The 'Jewish drawer' is Mervyn Levy, the painter and a childhood friend.

TO HENRY TREECE

1 September 1938   Sea View, Laugharne

Dear Henry,

Every apology, true and false, for not having written before. The Old Master stayed on several more days after you left for Harlech; his varnish was cracking visibly; he left us bloated, and dumb from his deafness. Then a friend of mine, a Jewish funny drawer with lots to do and say, hitchhiked here from London, on his way to Ireland. He stayed on, occupying all my time in ways you know by now and Caitlin's for over a week until my mother-in-law and a neuter friend came for a holiday in the pub. Now they're all disappeared and I'm forced to work. Thank God the sun has gone in and I needn't go out; we've nothing left but our wits and paper. Please forgive me. I really have had no time even for politeness—and anyway I know you too well now to need to be polite—and certainly not for a long letter.

The only things I've written have been letters to the Royal Literary Fund, asking them for a grant, and to some respectable persons—Mr. Eliot and minor deacons—asking them to support my application. What I need now urgently is some small regular income. The garret's repugnant; I can't keep a steady hand and wag a wild tongue if worry like a bumbailiff sits silently nagging by my side. Poverty makes me lazy and crafty. I'm not a fineweather poet, or a lyrical tramp, or a bright little bowl waiting for the first fine flush, or a man who cuts his face with a grand phrase while shaving; I like regular meals and drink and a table and a ruler—and three pens. Eliot has supported me strongly—he's staying in Wales now, thirty miles from here, and is coming For Tea—and the Fund secretary is, apparently, going to apply for me to the Fascist Government. Mr. Chamberlain is crazy about modern verse, and I shall send a photograph of myself, in bowler and gasmask, rhyming womb with tomb.

This is only a note to let you know I'm alive, and to apologise, and to say how much we enjoyed your staying here and how much we hope you'll come and stay again and that we'll meet again soon. Little awkwardnesses may have arisen—you took the up path, I took the Brown—but they weren't I hope, anything serious; and one day I'll walk ten miles with you, and you shall sit ten hours in a saloon chair with me.

Perhaps none of us got really going; in your short stay I had toothache, hangover, rheumatism, and seasickness, and was all the time perfectly healthy. Nelly had a bad Welsh cold; I hope she's better now. Over this weekend I'll write the good letter, with analysis etc. That's a promise.

I asked John about a drawing; he'll do it when he comes back from France in the autumn. If he does it quickly, in one go, it should be good, and might help the commercial success of your book.

More very soon. Terribly sorry about this rude delay.

Love, Dylan

Caitlin wishes all the right things for you and Nelly.

MSS.: Lockwood Memorial Library, Buffalo

The Royal Literary Fund refused his application for a grant on the grounds that he was not an 'established writer'.

'Beachcomber' was the pen-name of D. B. Wyndham Lewis, who wrote a sarcastic and humorous column in the *Daily Express*.

Charles Williams, who is usually described as the author of 'theological thrillers', was also an editor with the Oxford University Press.

Boots the Cash Chemists used also to run a lending library which catered to the tastes of the unintellectual middle-class.

TO JOHN DAVENPORT

Laugharne,
Carmarthenshire

23.ix.38

Dear John,

It's disappointing of course, but I expected it. I know that tolerant sadness, that liberal shrug in the rustling gloom; I've heard 'rather a forlorn enterprise' (resigned but still whimsical), 'there it is what can we do' (palms lifted, ash dropped on the untidy waistcoat drooping on a wrong button), 'we're only the intelligentsia you know' (arch, self-deprecatory and twisted smile), 'yes, Spain is terrifying' (serious suddenly, the eyes studiously dilated) echo, like the pad of old slippers

213

in a room carpeted with the competition-pages of the New Statesman, on late summer evenings when nostalgic Hampstead lies half asleep in a briar cloud and the air is full of the soft cries of reviewers and the gentle choosing of books. I react like Beachcomber, and could raise up my club Lewis. The little pessimisms of these Boots-minded thrush-watchers—calculated to make appear difficult the too-easy occupation of writing—could drive me to not drinking. When does anyone 'establish his claim to be a professional writer'? When he makes enough money not to want assistance? Are my needs less because I'm young? Must I live celibate on bread and poems until my Novel is Accepted? Anyway, something may come, I suppose, of this lion-prodding; I'd like to print the growls. Eliot and Charles Williams—he's very respectable and enthusiastic—have written letters for me. Will one of the people you've approached do anything? I hope so. The 'exceptional circumstances' must be stressed.

And about what, if anything does happen, will the Fund slip over? Any idea? Do write if there's any news, or if there isn't.

                                                      Dylan

Haven't managed to get 25 Poems yet. My new book of poems is almost ready. I've no idea who to give it to.

MSS.: Texas

Seven was a small poetry magazine edited by Denys Val Baker. The poem referred to in this letter is 'A saint about to fall'.

TO HENRY TREECE

(16 October 1938)   Sea View, Laugharne

Dear Henry:

If it wasn't that I know bitterly how wild it makes a man or a Caitlin, how it puts into the head a sense of injury that was perhaps not there before, I'd say Now don't be huffy. Of course—as you should know; am I a quivering bundle of temperament, all wind and wet conceit, that I can imagine I could, even if I wanted to, be rude to my equally unconceited, un-nonsensical friends?—I haven't any wish not to fulfil my promises, not to write you lots of times and lots of pages. It's only that I'm lazy about writing, and deeply depressed. You mustn't be offended because I'm a lazy pig. (I know, I bitterly know: 'Who's offended? damn your presumption, jerry-headed conceit that makes you think your lack of writing can offend me'; and that's true, but I always mean one way less than I say and the other way more; it is my ever present conscience, concealed under a Punch humour, that forces me to make each fact dubious, to attempt to add suspicion to straight details.) I've wanted to write so often, have thought about you, what you're doing and why, and several times have written Dear Henry down, stared at the paper, sunk into coma, picked my nose and made a small salt meal, though there were many things to tell you and, even then, many apologies to make. I'm depressed about facts, which no-money makes dubious; debts are climbing, tradesmen barking, the Government is too busy, the Royal Literary Fund regards my literary claims as insufficient (you have, I think, to be a Georgian, a writer of faded belles-lettres), we will have to abscond from here one day next week, leaving a furnished (now much better, and more fully furnished than when you were here) house behind, a lovely town, some friends. At least, if not abscondence, a holiday from debts; and that will not pay them. We will go to Swansea for a week or two, then Hampshire.

(On this Tuesday, the 18th, I'm going to Manchester, to broadcast with Auden, MacNiece, Spender etc., in a programme, called the 'Modern Muse', compered by M. Roberts. I suppose it would be quite impossible for you to meet me in Manchester that evening? I know only that you're North; I've no idea where. If you could, come to the B.B.C. offices.)

Now about your last, full letter: It was odd to hear that Donald Duck of the New English Weekly has decided that I'm too young for your book. He wrote me last week, saying that he had met you, that he would encourage the book all he could, and also that I was a swell reviewer. He was enthusiastic, quacked for pages. What did he tell you? He must change his mind very quickly; and what a mind too! I'm glad Seven is doing the surrealist chapter. They want one or two new poems of mine to go in the same number with it; I sent some short ones yesterday, but it may be too late. Your offer—which I should have thanked you for a long time ago—of a percentage of anything that comes from your book is terribly generous. It was nice of you to think of it, and I accept it very gratefully. I hope we'll both make out of it, and be able to meet to spend. I'll try to be in London at Christmas; you must meet some of my disreputable friends; I have one of the best collections. Caitlin won't be with me; she looks increasingly robust and our little half-formed monster is kicking and smiting.

There haven't been any visitors here for some time now, and we live very quietly. We have a supper a week with the Hugheses, and they have one here. I am writing poems, and will send them to you

215

as soon as they are typed. One, I think, is as good as anything I've done: a longish poem to my unborn child. You shall see it next week. I want to post this off now because it's late, and I'm going to Swansea tomorrow morning and then on to Manchester. This is the first of a regular series of dull letters. And I've nearly finished for you an analysis of two poems.

Yours ever,

Dylan

I'll send, too, the address—when I can find it—of a new American quarterly edited by Ransom. The first number appears in December. They want new critical work.

MSS.: Lockwood Memorial Library, Buffalo

Fordingbridge was where Augustus John had his country house. In fact they were going to stay with Caitlin's mother, Mrs Yvonne Macnamara, at Blashford, which is a few miles from Fordingbridge.

John Davenport's house was at Marshfield, near Chippenham.

The book called *In The Direction of The Beginning* (the title of one of the short stories) was never published. Seven of the stories, which Richard Church did not regard as obscene, were published by Dent's. What was to have been the title story was not among them. The book was therefore renamed *The Map of Love*, the title of another story, and published in August 1939.

TO JOHN DAVENPORT

Sea View,

Laugharne,

Carmarthenshire

4 November 1938

Dear John,

How very nice and kind of you. That five pounds helped an awful lot, and now our debts are almost all paid off. We want to leave, the middle of this month, to stay in Hampshire, and perhaps now we'll be able to leave owing nothing, which will be grand. Thank you so much.

Last night we went to Hughes to dinner—you know he lives here, don't you; in the ruined castle—and he gave me a great lot of his prize bitter and this morning I don't know what I am.

I've heard nothing yet from the Royal Literary Fund. Are they definitely reconsidering their decision? How did you work it? When you said they gave away forty five thousand a year, didn't you mean four to five? I'm waiting anxiously, twitching every time the postman walks over the cockles to our door.

A couple of weeks ago I read some poems on the wireless in a programme called The Modern Muse. All the boys were in it, and what a mincing lot we were. Did you hear it? All the poets were born in the same house, & had the same mother too.

I'm sending a copy of 25 Poems, but I couldn't get a first edition. Will this do?

The monster clothes came this morning. Can any child be as small as that? Thank you, Clement. Caitlin's writing a note.

Is Chippenham full of bedroom suites? And is it far from Fordingbridge because we'll be there—or very nearly there—in a fortnight & we must meet. Let me know.

Did you like the poem I sent you? I think the Hogarth Press, under John Lehmann, is going to do my new book: it's called 'In The Direction of The Beginning'.

Thanks a lot. This letter's very weak because of bitter but my gratitude isn't.

Love to you both

Yours

Dylan T.

MSS.: Texas

The dating of the next letter is uncertain. It may have been written in 1939.

TO JOHN DAVENPORT

16th November 1938

Sea View,

Laugharne,

Carmarthenshire

Dear John,

We're going to be able to get away from here, which is killing us a bit this winter, for a week in December, might go to Ringwood, and would be delighted to be invited to stay with you for a day or two. My previous letters weren't answered, and this is a last request

for a little word. It would be nice to have somewhere to go; & we'd
like to see you. Do you know Frederic Prokosch's poem, The Dolls.
I've seen it in lots of anthologies lately. Do try & get hold of it for
Spender-voice reading. I've done an almost exact imitation of it
which you might like: but you must see the original by its side:

The Molls

I found them lying on the floor,
Male shapes, girl-lipped, but clad like boys:
Night after night their hands implore
Emetic Percies for their joys.

They retch into my secret night
With stale & terrifying camp
And offer as the last delight
A crude, unhappy, anal cramp.

Gently they sigh to my behind
Wilde words, all buttered, badly bred,
And when I dream of them I find
Peacockstain's poems on my bed.

The real last line of the poem is: 'Small tears of glass upon my bed'.
I couldn't beat that & I didn't try.

Love to all,
Dylan

MSS.: Texas

'Crane' in this letter is Hart Crane. Goodland, Cooke and Moore were
concerned with the magazine *Seven*. John is Augustus John.

TO HENRY TREECE

31 December 1938   Blashford, Ringwood

Dear Henry,

Your indignation shames me. In the note of December 19th, it's
'Ever, Henry'. Between that time and the 30th a poison has worked,
a bird has told you, and 'Yours sincerely, Henry Treece' stares and
floors me. I had your nice last letter in Laugharne, and was proud and
glad to have it. You liked me as a man but did not admire me (the past

tense is open to correction), which is just as it should be; I have the same feelings about myself. My selfish carelessness and unpunctuality I do not try to excuse as poet's properties. They are a bugbear and a humbug. The selfish trouble is that I myself have had to put up with these seriously annoying faults for so long that I've almost come to think other people can bear them. I am the one who wakes up nearest to myself, and the continual horror that comes from the realisation of this individuality has made me almost believe that the reactions of others to my horrible self—that would not be itself did it not possess the faults etc. that make me now write this simplified confession of complicated egoism so untidily—are small enough, in comparison, to be counted as the others' loss or to be beaten down by one unsulky thought. But of course I apologise, and sincerely. My silence is never the result of promises for noise. My every intention to be in London over Christmas was kicked in the wish by the thought of becoming a father. We were taken away from Laugharne with a rush, and never seem to have recovered. I don't know why your letter returned 'unknown', unless it was a post-official hint at the subsidence of my already rickety reputation. Perhaps this letter to you will be returned, marked 'No Such Person'. Nothing is above red ribbon except a heart.

Answering your first letter: I won't sign, with or without argument, the Apocalyptic Manifesto. I wouldn't sign any manifesto unless I had written every word of it, and then I might be too ashamed. I agree with and like much of it, and some of it, I think, is manifestly absurd. That's not giving my own variety of bird to a thing over which you and others have spent considerable time and thought; it's only to say that the language of such documents is strange to me, that organic reality is all my cock. I cannot see how Auden is unaware of Donald Duck, unless Donald Duck is supposed to be a symbol and not a funny bird. Donald Duck is just what Auden is aware of. To him (Auden), what this problematical squirrel of ours stumbles over is more important than the squirrel act of stumbling. Auden often writes like Disney. Like Disney, he knows the shape of beasts (and incidentally he, too, might have a company of artists producing his lines); unlike Lawrence, he does not know what shapes or motivates those beasts. He's a naturalist who looks for beasts that resemble himself, and, failing that, he tries to shape them in his own curious image. The true naturalist, like Gilpin, offers his toe to the vampire bat; Auden would suck the bat off. I liked very much your reasonable contradiction of the quotation from Marx. But it's all rather like flogging a dead force. Another thing that's admirable is the insistence, without irrational prejudice, on man's dissolution. I like the title 'Apocalypse:

The Dissolute Man' more than yours. But this isn't the time to argue with a statement of belief in which I mostly believe but with which I cannot sympathise wholly (or even dissolutely), owing to my own dogma of Arrogant Acceptance. If I'm given time—you know I write slowly, and not too often to be interfering—I'd be very glad to write for Apocalypse, whole or corner. I'll try to write something about Crane, but it will come slowly. That's not, I know you know, an affectation. Would you like that chunk of prose I was working on—copying out, once, in affectedly microscopic writing—in Laugharne. The first half is finished. And I'll have a poem, not a very long one, completed by the middle of January.

I shan't quarrel now—this is meant, however misguidedly, for a patching-up letter—with your promise of Apocalyptic 'publicity'. Don't you believe me when I say that I don't want to be publicised? Or don't you? I have all the publicity that my small output deserves, and because some other people's small output has more and undeserved publicity, should I worry? Publicity will not get me more money; the little work I produce is paid for as highly as the rags I contribute to can afford. Publicity would not increase my output—indeed, the opposite—nor would it make it saleable to better-paying magazines, nor would it make pay at better rates those magazines that still would print me.

About the manifesto quotation from that letter of mine: Don't you think, looking at it coldly, that its effectiveness (if any) would be increased by cutting out '... but I am aware of these things as well'. Surely, my conscious catalogue implies that? I think those last few words—whoever wrote them—sound smug. Imagine me suggesting that I was not aware of Oxo, Damaroids, and Bunny Austin. Can't you end the quotation at '... tick and revolve in'? Please; and that is, too, if you have to use the bit of silliness at all.

I'd written half this letter when I heard from Henry Miller, who'd come to London for a few days; and luckily I managed to get driven to see him. Also I met that sap Goodland, the blue-and-water-eyed contactman, yes-man, no man. I just missed the other boys, Cooke, Moore, etc. They're better than Goodland?

I have reminded John of the picture. He now has two portraits finished of me. One I'm going to use in my next lot of poems; the other John is entirely willing to be let used in your book. An expert photograph will have to be taken of it; your publishers will, of course, have to see to that. I'm working on an analysis of a few of my poems now, but there have been so many interruptions lately. Now they are over.

I'm glad to hear you're getting married so soon. Remember us to Nellie. Are we seeing you this summer? Thank you for your open house. You know about ours too. Write soon. This has been an awkward letter to write. I'm sure all our next letters will be easy. Regards from Caitlin.

Yours sincerely,

Dylan Thomas

Ever,

Dylan

MSS.: Lockwood Memorial Library, Buffalo

Dylan's and Caitlin's first child, Llewelyn, was born on 30th January 1939. Sketty is a part of Swansea.

Bob Rees is at present chief librarian of Swansea Public Library. He was a school friend of Dylan's.

Fred is Alfred Janes.

Dan is Dr Daniel Jones, whose childhood home, where Dylan had spent so much time as a boy, was a villa called Warmley.

TO CHARLES FISHER

January 1939

We hope to be back in Laugharne   Blashford,
at the end of February. Don't forget   Ringwood,
us then: Liberty and Calamity hall,   Hants
where a naked man may bury his
towels in peace.

Dear Charles,

I was glad to hear from you; living is even more miserable for all your absences; I should have written a long time ago to find out how all that curious collection is carrying on in the last days of the fall of the British Empire, but I am fat and slothful, sentimental and un-scrupulous, a bag of a boy in the flush of his pulled youth. This flat English country levels the intelligence, planes down the imagination, narrows the a's, my ears belch up old wax and misremembered passages of misunderstood music, I sit and hate my mother-in-law, glowering at her from corners and grumbling about her in the sad, sticky quiet of the lavatory, I take little walks over the Bad Earth. Our baby should be born at the end of next week, we wait and it kicks. Lack of money still pours in.

And I'm glad you're all working, on levitation, rainbow's promises, the drama, & Sketty organs. I heard last week from Bob Rees, who said that he wrote to Fred to find out my address and that, to his great surprise, he got a real letter back from the old umbrella himself. Bob says that he's going to write a book one day, to be called 'The Life and Letter of F. Janes'.

Will you give me, some time, Dan's new address. I still feel Warmley.

Love to you all,
Dylan

MSS.: Charles Fisher, Esq.

Keidrych in this letter is Keidrych Rhys, the editor of *Wales*.
It would seem fair to assume that Mrs Macarthy is a fictional character.

TO HENRY TREECE

26 January 1939   Blashford, Ringwood

Dear Henry,

Thanks for the good letters. And straightaway I must say that I haven't got anything for Seven. Half a poem's on my table, and that's all. I'm sorry my name has to remain on the cover, but, after all, I had not promised to contribute to this number. Apocalypse is a different affair, isn't it? I mean, surely Seven hasn't taken that as a new name? Actually, I still have that large chunk of prose I told you about, and from which I read you bits; but that's got to be bought. I've spent so much time on that that I don't part with it except for real money; and I'll stick to that even if it prevents the thing ever being printed. It applies to my promised contributions to Apocalypse, too. From now on, I'm going to be paid, and paid fairly, for every line of mine that's printed. Cash-minded Dylan, that's me—if you know the reference. I'll sell Seven seven pages of glamorous prose. Any offers?

Glad you're feeling better now. I'm not feeling better. I'm worried and lazy and morose. I've got a hundred headaches and a barbed mouth. I hate every living person with the exception of a Mrs. Macarthy who lives in Chelsea. I can't write this letter.

Keidrych is hysterical. Why should I be interested in the blurb for

Glyn Jones's book in America? And why, anyway, should he send it via Lincolnshire? He's always doing things like that; once he sent me a lot of used stamps and the bibliography of Arthur Machen.

Thanks for the warning about our literary friends' correspondence circle. I don't want to hurt anybody—much. But your friend is a sap, 19 or 20. His blue eyes are pools of piss—aristocratic piss. He's got fallen arches in his mouth. You say that he might have been frightened of me? Of me? I'm like a baby in the dark.

More when I feel good. Caitlin is still waiting; the baby's overdue by three days. No worry, though. She sends her regards to you and Nelly. This letter's really to tell you about Seven and me. More, about me, when I don't feel so sick and angry.

Love,

Dylan

and more soon, too.

MSS.: Lockwood Memorial Library, Buffalo

This undated letter was written either in January or February of 1939.

Lawrence Durrell had noticed, in the British Museum, the extraordinary resemblance between Dylan's small, neat, backward-sloping hand and that of Emily Brontë, and had sent Dylan a photograph of a manuscript poem she had written.

TO LAWRENCE DURRELL

February 1939?

Blashford,

Ringwood,

Hants

Dear Lawrence,

I forgot to thank you for the pound, crisper than celery and sweeter than sugar oh the lovely sound, not through ingratitude, it's as welcome as a woman is cleft, but through work (half a poem about energy), sloth (in a chair looking at my feet or the mirror or unread novels or counting the patterns on the floor to see if I can work out a system for my football pools or watching my wife knit or dance), depression (because, mostly, there weren't more pounds from more people), small habits (from bar-billiards to broadcast talks, slick-bonneted Hampshire roadhouses and socialist teas), love, unqualified, the nearness of Bournemouth, colds and pains in the head and your Black Book about which more in another and longer letter. I liked too very much your eggy poems in Seven. Thank you for the Emily Brontë poem; I thought at first sight it was a rejected manuscript of mine: a great likeness, and yes I can read nearly every word of it. Why are you still in London, has somebody moved Corfu? And do you want another poem from me, got seven shillings and sixpence? Regards to your wife and muse, to Heppenstall if you see him, not at all to Goodland.

Dylan

MSS.: Lawrence Durrell, Esq.

David Higham, the author's agent, had been looking after Dylan's literary affairs for some eighteen months by this time.

'A Prospect of the Sea' was not in fact included in *The Map of Love,* which contained three further stories, 'The Tree', 'The Mouse and the Woman' and 'The Dress'.

TO DAVID HIGHAM

20 February 1939

Blashford,
Ringwood,
Hants

Dear Higham,

I'm sorry to be so long returning these stories and suggesting, for Dent's, the ones which I should like to be included in my book of verse and prose. But I've been trying hard to raise enough money to keep my wife and son going for the next month or two, and unsuccessfully. Now I'm relying entirely on Dent's. They've got the mss of the poems, and here are the stories. Of the stories I suggest The Orchards, The Enemies, The Map of Love, A Prospect of the Sea, and The Visitor. Those are all stories to which no objection, other than literary, could be taken, and anyway they're the best—especially in a book also to contain poems. Church has, among the mss of the poems, part of a prose-piece called 'In the Direction of the Beginning' —a title I originally intended as the title of the whole of the book. I have, however, been considering this piece, and have now decided to make it part of a much longer work which I want to spread over many months to come. But that decision doesn't alter the book: there are still sixteen poems and five stories; and two poems, now finished but not polished up enough yet, to be added. So that Dent's have the whole mss of the whole book, only not yet finally arranged in order—surely a small consideration considering that the book will not be published until after the spring. (Church can, of course, choose other stories from the enclosed collection if he wants to, but I'm sure my choice is right for the purpose of this book). And, having the mss in their hands, can't they be persuaded to give me the £30 promised on 'Completion of Mss'? If they can't be persuaded, then I'm sunk. And this is no begging or joke. I can't return with my family to Wales until some important debts there, principally for rent, have been settled; and there's no money, other than Dent's promised money, coming to me in the world. Do please do your very best for me. After all, here is the book they wanted. The John portrait they can photograph any time they want to—I have all his permission. (By the way, have you heard if they'll do it in colour or not?) And the only thing left to do is to arrange the order of contents. I have, I know, altered the original idea of the book by wishing to cut out the prose-piece already in Church's possession, but I must do that, and five stories and eighteen poems—the two extra ones will be ready and typed by the end of the week—is quite as big a book as Church said he wanted. Please, Higham, do try and get that advance immediately. We've got to move, and we can't until our Welsh village has been pacified financially. I can rely on you, I know, to do your best for me as quickly as you can.

Yours,
Dylan Thomas

MSS.: David Higham Associates

Barker is George Barker, the poet.

Tambimuttu was a young Sinhalese who was financing a new magazine called *Poetry*.

Jan and Bill Brewer are characters from the Devonshire folk song called 'Widdicombe Fair'.

TO HENRY TREECE

March 1939
Blashford, Ringwood

Dear Henry,

Sorry not to reply sooner. I'd decided, until your postcard this morning, not to write a word for some weeks, not a word of anything.

It wasn't a moral decision. I wanted to go and play billiards at the Conservative Club, etc.; all day long. But I'll have to do that little analysis now before you shame me to incoherence, and certainly before your marriage, upon which I congratulate you with all the sincerity of a smug, happy, penniless husband and father. I'll finish over this weekend the strongly promised stuff.

I don't know why you have to work yourself up into such an indignant rage when you say that you won't pay me for the analysis. Nobody asked you, sir. It never occurred to me.

Of course I don't associate you with Goodland. You're my friend.

I hadn't heard anything about the anthology. Naturally I'd like to contribute to most things you're likely to do or intend doing, but I won't have anything much to contribute for some time. All my new poems belong to the book which Dent are bringing out in the summer definitely. Your anthology couldn't appear before then, and obviously the same poems couldn't appear in both things. I'll have a few poems, I suppose, but I'll have to get them published in magazines—if the anthology isn't under way by that time—as soon as they are completed because I need every halfpenny. I have nothing with which to bring Llewellyn up—he's six or seven weeks old. Nothing is O, not an inadequate income. Is the anthology Apocalyptic?—whatever that means.

I saw your Seven article, and I'm looking forward to seeing another one in Poetry. Glad the first one was disliked by Grigson and Symons. What a fancy magazine Poetry is with its wig-and-scroll cover, treesnaps, and woodcuts, Barkers, whistlers, pukers, masturbative monologues, Tambimuttu—although I admire the courage of the queer introduction—wetting his Ceylonese, Spender with life still Nestling on his lips. The postwar man, as Tambimuttu might have said in his first Indian letter, struggling for watered spirits. The English poets now are such a pinlegged, nibcocked, paperhearted crowd you could blow them down with one bellow out of a done lung. I'm not taking, conscientiously, the inverted attitude, even if it isn't inverted, that insists on the worthlessness of the intelligentsia and the great qualities of those outside it, especially as I am living now—but not for long, Laugharne in April—in the country where the English romantic outlaw is at his loudest in praise of characters and soil—'I wouldn't share a piston with Stephen or Wystan but I'd roll in a sewer with Jan and Bill Brewer'—and I suppose that in finding my sympathetic friends where I mostly do I'm at last on my own level. Don't get me wrong, I'd always prefer to see a street full of lords to a street full of other unemployed. Not that this matters.

Don't worry that anyone else will get hold of your letters: I have no clique, no correspondence club. You know how I live—I'm not, I hope, sentimentalising over this point; over other points I am happy at any time—and that life doesn't contain letter or culture snooping. What you say to me is safe from any but my own mis-interpretation.

I'll write more when I send what you want. Sorry about the flimsy delays.

Dylan

MSS.: Lockwood Memorial Library, Buffalo

Pamela and Kerith are the names of Bert Trick's children.

TO BERT TRICK

March 1939
Blashford,
Ringwood,
Hampshire

Dear Bert,

This is to tell you with variations what I'm sure you must know by now—that I'm the father of a son named Llewelyn, aged six weeks, a fat, round, bald, loud child, with a spread nose and blue saucer eyes. His full name is Llewelyn Edouard, the last being a concession to Caitlin's French grandfather. But in spite of this he sounds militantly Welsh, and, though this is probably national pride seen through paternal imagination or vice-versa, he looks it too. Before anything else, before apologies, recriminations, and news, how are your wife, Pamela and Kerith? Please do remember me to all of them, though Kerith I suppose remembers me as nothing but a shifting blur with a mop on top.

For well over a year now we've failed to keep in touch with each other. Was it my fault or yours? Mine, perhaps. I'm careless, I know, and appear rude but never feel or mean it—though you've not written either. I hear nothing from the boys. Is Fred still pine-appleing and knifing? Consummation in the cinema? Expressing down Walters Road with his head full of fruit and stars? Has Tom erased himself completely yet? So, nothing about you. Oh, I'm set in life now—two stone heavier, but not a feather steadier. Though never again will

I fit into Swansea quite so happily and comfortably as I did, for I'll be a hundred jokes and personal progressions behind all my friends. I'll be almost a dead face. Or, worse still, a new face, in which nothing will interest them but the old shades and expressions. I'm strong and sentimental for the town and people, for long filled-in Sundays with you and scrapbooks and strawberry jelly at the end. For readings and roarings with all the grand boys. I'm not meaning to talk like an ancient village outcast—no more than two years separate me. I'll have all the summer, and every summer, I hope, in Carmarthenshire. But one small close society is closed to me. And a social grief is natural. We're all moving away. And every single decisive action happens in a blaze of disappointment.

What's been happening to you? How are the town-hall and councillor schemes? Here in this flat, narrow-chested, and bowed county full of fading squires, traditional English romantic outlaws, sour gentlewomen and professional ostriches, I long for my old but never properly mounted soapbox of bright colours, and my grand destructive arguments learned so industriously and vehemently from you on winter evenings, after Cwmdonkin sonnets and Lux to sweet ladies. You gave my rebelliousness a direction. And on the black back-to-the-wall umbrella-man's day, I'll have you to blame, which will be a small recompense.

We'll come back to Wales in the first week in April, to Laugharne where we'll rent—though the landlord would disagree—a crumbling house. On to Swansea for a day or two to let my mother see Llewelyn in all his shit, sweetness, and glory. I must see you then. You'll recognise me by my belly, black hat, and a nostalgic flavour of the Uplands. I want you to see my new poems which will make a book in the summer—not quite a book, because the whole thing is called THE MAP OF LOVE and is 15 poems and 7 stories. Old stories mostly, but cut and pruned to buggery or sense. I've got so many questions to ask you that I'll keep them all until we meet. Do write a little soon and let me know how things are and what you are doing.

Love,
Dylan

MSS.: Lockwood Memorial Library, Buffalo

Dylan and Caitlin returned to 'Sea View', Laugharne, with the baby, early in April 1939.

The Fitzroy was a public-house in London, much frequented at this time by writers and painters: the reference is thus to the pubs of Salisbury, about half way between Mrs Macnamara's house at Blashford and John Davenport's at Marshfield.

Roger is Roger Roughton; Lord Tredegar (Evan Morgan) was a millionaire and, in some measure, a patron of the arts; Norman is Norman Cameron; Lynette Roberts was Keidrych Rhys's wife.

TO JOHN DAVENPORT

Laugharne,
Carmarthenshire,
S. Wales

May 11 1939

Dear John,

It's good to hear from you, I'm very sorry too we never met again in the Fitzroys of Salisbury—(I looked about, after you'd told me of Salisbury's literary reputation, & saw crowds of New Forest writers, some tweed and briar, some lankly titled, many going sandalled after Russian tea)—or that we couldn't afford to move across to each other. Yes, of course, Caitlin and I will be looking forward a lot to your all coming here, & make it soon. How is Roger, I haven't seen him for two years or less, he was magnificently prosperous when I did see him, and dressed, I was glad to see, like a capitalist. I say come soon because I'm going to be summoned for a few small debts and unless something happens I shall spend Whitsun picking opium. I haven't dared answer the door all this week; who knows what wired fortunes I've missed that way, invitations to sherry and princesses with Tredegar, fan-mail from Dowlais. When we stayed with you in Marshfield I was richer than I've ever been, I may have spoken scoffingly of small sums, my vistas were misproportioned, even in my mind rustled and clinked. I'm so penniless—the stamp on this letter's stolen—that I'm thinking of trying to work out a small income for myself on these lines: to get as many people as possible, people that is, of assured incomes and some little interest in whether I do or not avoid the debtors' jug, to promise to send me five shillings (5/-) a week each; if I could get ten people, we'd flourish. I've thought of a possible few, including yourself and Norman, and what do you think of the idea? I've done nothing, except this letter, about it yet. It's not as crazy as it may sound; I do very much want to go on working here, but I find it very hard when I can't go out in the street for fear of a woman with a shilling owing to her chasing me into the mother sea. As I can't make money by what I write, I think I should concentrate—Miller, incidentally, believes in this too, as you may have found out—on getting my living-money from people and not from poems. Do tell me what you think. But it's all a plan for the future, it would take some time to get started; now, now I'm trembling for Saturday which is the final day. Yes, I believe, too, that Durrell, a very pleasant chap, is over-rated, but I can sympathise with the people who did boost up the Black Book so vehemently when it appeared because the first reading of it does, I think, shock you into emotional praise; it is, on the surface, so much <u>cleverer</u> than Miller, and anyway many reviewers of the Black Book hadn't, remember, read a line of Miller before. Durrell's verse is a bad show-up or down; but I think Miller's city night life is new and tremendous. We can agree when we meet. My book 'The Map of Love' is due in August; definitely, a notice appears in the Dent's summer catalogue. There wasn't any need after all for us to have gone through the stories, for fish-like Richard Church did the simplest thing by cutting all the best stories out. The ones left are, mostly, very tame, & there will only be the poems—the book is 17 poems & 8 stories—to save it. One story had 'its moments of sensuality', so out it went. Caitlin and Llewelyn are strong and well. I hope you all are too. Write soon, & come here soon. My love,

Dylan

A few of the people I've thought of approaching about my five bob fund are: Edith S., Norman, John Davenport, Richard Hughes, here, Lynette Roberts, Peggy Guggenheim, Augustus, Robert Herring. But of course they won't all agree. I want more possibilities for this Trifling Subscription.

I do not know who Hendry was, nor what anthology this is.

TO HENRY TREECE

May 1939
Laugharne

Dear Henry,

Congratulations on your marriage. Late, of course, but true. Our son is screaming outside the window; because this is scrappy and dim blame him. Thank you both for the cake; Caitlin ate it immediately.

I'd heard about Hendry's anthology before you wrote, from Keidrych, who was here some weeks ago being consciously queer and talking little magazines until the air was reeking full of names and nonsense and the rooms packed to the corners with invisible snobs. But I didn't know that you were handling it with Hendry: I'm glad you are. (What, by the way, is Hendry's criticism like? His poetry seems to lack it.) I can't keep up with the quarrels that surround Seven, Delta, and the rest, and only hope that you can work them out to our advantage: to provide one magazine that publishes without venom but with some point. About my own contributions to the anthology: I haven't got anything new—all I've been working on are straightforward stories, sold now for large (to me) sums to Life and Letters and Story—but you can, naturally, reprint what you like. When is the anthology appearing? My own book, under the title of The Map of Love, comes out on the 1st of August. By that time I should have a new poem, and may have, though it's unlikely, finished an article on Miller that I've been preparing since he first hit me in the belly. Sorry to be so unhelpful. I've done nothing yet on Crane; there's not, in an isolated article, much to say (I think) and it's better to read him. Print, of course, your article in Poetry. How could the publicity offend me? Only one thing: do, for friendship's sake, cut out that remark of mine about 'I have a beast and an angel in me' or whatever it was; it makes me sick, drives me away from drink, recalls too much the worst of the fat and curly boy I know too well, he whose promises are water and whose water's Felinfoel, that nut-brown prince.

At the moment your letter, with blank postcard, dropped through the door. I found sinister the absence of any comment on my cowardly delays, but thank you very much for being so good with me, so consistently good in spite of what must seem my arrogance and selfish irresponsibility. If your and Hendry's anthology is appearing in July— that is, before my own book appears—then it's no good your printing much of mine that will be in my book. The contents of my book should come as new to people who buy it—most of the stuff's been in little magazines, but not many people read them—and for them to be printed (I mean, for many of them to be printed) in an anthology brought out almost simultaneously with my own book is obviously absurd. (That's very loose writing, the baby's louder, I hope the meaning is clear.) I suggest therefore that you reprint no more than one of my newer poems—either 'A Saint About To Fall', which came out in the first number of Poetry, or 'How Shall My Animal', a copy of which I'll enclose, and one story, 'A Prospect Of The Sea', which is not appearing in my book but which Life and Letters printed some time ago. I think it's about my best story to date; Church refused to let me include it in The Map of Love—sixteen poems and seven stories—because it has 'moments of undeniable sensuality'. You'll have to ask Herring, I suppose, for permission, which of course he'll give; sorry I've no copy at all of the story; could you get one direct from Herring, do you think, and charge it, if necessary, to Apocalypse —is that the finally decided title?—accounts? I wish I had something fresh to send you; if I do, shortly, you shall have it.

Tell me the new gossip soon. Caitlin and I are well and strong now, happy here as always among friendly people, and in debt to many of them. Is Nelly well? Our regards. I doubt very much that we'll be able to move out of Laugharne this year, in spite of your nice invitation to us. I'd love to move North, though, for a week or two. Are you coming here? There's room and welcome always you know that. We work, play darts, don't read enough, spend a couple of evenings a week with the hospitable but whimsy Hugheses. I get stouter, burlier, squarer every day: twelve and a half stone now. We have a few visitors, Keidrych, Vernon Watkins; Roughton is coming down soon, probably for Whitsun; there's a possibility of Miller in the summer, though what a city-hound like that will do here God knows. No, no truculence now, hardly ever disgruntled. Tell me the names of the new rackets and the number of balls. It'll be nice to hear from you. I've kept to the last the shocking admission that I can't—at the moment anyway—write those analyses you want me to, and which I want to do too. By can't I mean just that: the words won't come. I've tried a hundred times, and have never got further than the lines of a new poem or a series of completely side-tracking ideas. But I'll go on trying. Tell me about your book.

Dylan

MSS.: Lockwood Memorial Library, Buffalo

Apart from the unending money worries, the spring and summer of 1939 were perhaps the happiest period of Dylan's adult life. But already, in July, the coming war was casting long shadows even in distant Laugharne.

The 'straight autobiographical stories' are the *Portrait of the Artist as a Young Dog*.

TO HENRY TREECE

July 1939
Seaview, Laugharne

Dear Henry,

I was glad you wrote to me; I like hearing, and I'd feel, I know, very angry if you wrote to me as badly and as irregularly as I do to you. I mean always to send you regular letters full of news and opinions, but what happen are occasional flat bits of grumbling and promises, fully felt and meant, of small worth for your book. And, though I want to be bright and full of opinionated news, this letter won't be any better either, for I'm deep in money troubles, small for some, big as banks for me; my debts are rising, it's raining, my new troubles and poems won't move, and what have I got to sparkle about I'd like to know?

We've been staying for a fortnight with my father and mother, who are nice, warm-hearted people forced, by silliness and an almost hysterical greed for safety, to be so penny-cautious, so impatient for my success (which means for me to have money, a position, and property), that I could run right out and exchange all my happiness for something entirely useless like an old bird-bath or a book of MacNeice's poems. Money and property I should like, but my life's set now towards not getting them. My father's house is stuck on a crowded piece of beautiful landscape—This Way to the Cliff scenery —and surrounded by 4000 Territorial soldiers. Girls hot and stupid for soldiers flock knickerless on the cliff. We're returning to Laugharne tomorrow. There are only 50 soldiers there.

What are you doing for your country? I'm letting mine rot. A girl I knew, sweet and reckless, is Captain Mabel now. Liberals are talking of Hitler's unscrupulous sincerity. MacNeice on the radio asked F. R. Higgins on the radio, and both, if you ask me, were pissed, 'Would it be honest of me, in the present state of the world, to go and live in a little cottage in Ireland and let war and its rumours roar?' (I distrust people who question their own honesty; such people walk critically behind their actions, observe the action of writing a poem before the poem itself; wherever you go and whatever you do your honesty, or lack of it, goes, and acts, with you). A schoolmaster in Wales wrote asking me if I would join a Society of Welsh writers and help to attack and crush provincial dilettantism and the feeling of unimportance and loneliness, which young provincial writers are, he says with knowledge, possessed by. (If they feel so unimportant as writers, it is, perhaps, because they are: and loneliness from anything except friendship hasn't hurt anybody.) A speaker on the wireless said that English dogs don't like foreigners. My liver's rebelled against me, and I have sudden attacks of overwhelming temper; blood rises to my head, and I stamp my little feet. Are you happy in your new state and house? We'd like to visit you—Caitlin and the baby are well— but won't be able to until we can find travelling and during-Lincoln-shire money, which may never be. The little I get goes, after a few

233

pleasures, to tradesmen and two landlords. We must, I suppose, live. And I do get little; I am hoping to sell some new straight autobiographical stories in America for a whole pile of England-trotting money; I'm hoping for retaining money from Dent. My book comes out on the 24th of August, but I've had all that matters from that and now there are only reviews to come. Have you found a paper to review it for? What about, if nothing with a larger circulation is willing to let its poetry go to anybody who likes poetry (the dramatic critic of The Times for the theatre), the New English Weekly? I should like very much to see your article in MacDiarmid's paper. Could you send me a copy? If you have only one, I'll return it quickly. I'm sure, by the way, that the Oxford University Press, however kind, will not do your book; Charles Williams, who works for it, is a friend, but he could not, only two years ago, persuade, by any means, the Press to publish my poems; they mightn't be inclined to bring out a book of criticism about work they did not 'see fit to' print themselves. Why won't Symons publish it? He's produced some books, hasn't he: Confusions about Symons by X, etc.? Will you send me your long poem? Handshakes to Nellie.

Love,
Dylan

I've got quite a lot to tell you. Next letter soon. The baby Llewelyn is singing and eating paper, I can't think now of anything but that. Let me have your news.

MSS.: Lockwood Memorial Library, Buffalo

Dylan's father was a sick man now. Dylan and Keidrych Rhys were to have broadcast an anthology of poems by Welshmen on 6th September. This, however, was cancelled because of the outbreak of war.

TO D. J. THOMAS (AT MARSTON)

Seaview

August 29 1939

Dear Dad,

Grand, magnificent dictionary. A lovely surprise. Thank you very much for it. I will take good care of it and use it often. It is a most valuable thing for me to have; & it appears to be an extremely good dictionary too. Immediately, I looked up all sorts of obscure words;

234

& the results couldn't have been better. Exciting to open the important looking parcel this morning & find just what I have been wanting. Thank you for the dedication too; I'm glad you enjoyed the Map of Love. Do please tell me what you like best in it, & what seemed most difficult & unattractive. I haven't yet seen the Spectator review, though Vernon wrote to tell me it had appeared and was good and sensible. I saw Fisher's article which was really about how well he knew me. I haven't seen any other reviews. Was there one in the Observer? I couldn't get hold of it last Sunday.

Yesterday I had the first work done on my teeth: 4 fillings. There is one extraction to come—an unnoticeable stump at the back—and about 6 more fillings. Then, with care, my teeth should last me for good. I wasn't hurt, although, because the teeth needing repair were scattered all about my mouth & not in a cluster, no injection could be made.

These are awful days & we are very worried. It is terrible to have built, out of nothing, a complete happiness—from no possessions, no material hopes—& a way of living, & then to see the immediate possibility of its being exploded & ruined through no fault of one's own. I expect you both are very anxious too. If I could pray, I'd pray for peace. I'm not a man of action; & the brutal activities of war appal me—as they do every decent-thinking person. Even here the war atmosphere is thick and smelling: the kids dance in the streets, the mobilised soldiers sing Tipperary in the pubs & wives & mothers weep around the stunted memorial in the Grist. Our own position is, so far, quite comfortable.

I hope you enjoyed your queer, lackadaisical day here—in spite of bookshelves and Polly's snailing—as much as we did. If there's no disturbance before September 6, I hope to see you in Swansea on that day. We must make arrangements later.

Thank you for everything you brought us on your visit. We were really grateful, although perhaps, we found it difficult to say much.

And thank you greatly for the very fine dictionary. I am proud to possess it.

I hope mother's well, or better than she has been.

Love to both of you
from us both,
Dylan

This shd have been posted yesterday, but just before the post went I found I hadn't any envelopes—& wasn't in time. Sorry.

MSS.: Dylan Thomas Estate

When the war broke out, on 3rd September 1939, Dylan Thomas had achieved a measure of happiness and even a sort of equilibrium. He was happily married with a home and a baby. His third book had just been published, and he enjoyed a considerable fame, if only in a very restricted circle. His first book was about to appear in the United States, and he could sell any poem or story he wrote, though the payment might be trifling.

Now, as he realized immediately, all was threatened. Not only were the little magazines faced with immediate extinction, and with them his small income, but he himself was liable to be called up. The prospect was excessively gloomy. Meanwhile he continued at Laugharne, and completed the volume of short stories that was to appear, next year, as the *Portrait of the Artist as a Young Dog.*

TO GLYN JONES

11th September 1939

Seaview,
Laugharne,
Carmarthenshire

Dear Glyn,

Thank you for the Miller book back. I'm glad you enjoyed most of it, and I mostly agree that it is not the super book I sometimes blurb it to be to fellows who haven't read it. As writing it is unoriginal, but it has, sentimentally speaking, more guts and blood in it than new English prose books have. The only recent prose I've had as much pleasure out of, loud, meaty pleasure, has been another American book —Nightwood (far different, with original writing too). I remember you said, in Laugharne, that you hadn't read it: would you like to? I like the idea of Miller's anti-literature, but it is a pity he writes, so often, in the old literary way to achieve it. He's always got the same cracks to grind, but, after all, good fucking books are few & far, & if you look at Tropic of Cancer as the best modern fucking book, & not—perhaps my sincere enthusiasm—as a universal life-&-death book, then I know you must enjoy & admire it enormously. (The adverb is also, I notice, on the back of the book.) Yes, it is, to date, his best book, but passages from Tropic of Capricorn which I've read in magazines are really much better, wider, less repetitive, & contain the best descriptions of America I've ever read. But I'm too annoyed and unsettled to write clearly, even about Miller's books which I do know well and feel about clearly. I want to get something out of the war, and put very little in (certainly not my one and only body). I'm trying to get some profitable civilian work; that will probably be impossible. Does your school go on? Do tell me what you intend doing when, after registration, you are called up? Prison & the Medical Corps are both disagreeable to me. Regards to your wife from us both.

Dylan

I want to see your review in Welsh Review. Will it appear now?

The reference to the 'Boys' Fire League' in the next letter is explained by the fact that many poets and artists who wished neither to join the armed forces nor be conscientious objectors were at the time volunteering for the Fire Service.

TO JOHN DAVENPORT

14 September 1939
Seaview,
Laugharne,
Carmarthenshire

Dear John,

Although you haven't answered any of my letters since you came down here in June—and one of the letters was important, about the 5 bob. flotation scheme which has now come to nothing; I don't know if it would have come to anything even if you had helped me —I'm still trying to get a word out of you, and this time again writing for advice or assistance. If you don't answer I shall know something is wrong, though I shan't know what the something is, unless, as I said before in one of my letters-to-the-void, you were so unspeakably bored with your visit that you've decided not to speak. It's this War. I am trying to get a job before conscription, because my one-&-only body I will not give. I know that all the shysters in London are grovelling about the Ministry of Information, all the half-poets, the boiled newspapermen, submen from the islands of crabs, dismissed advertisers, old mercuries, mass-snoopers, and all I have managed to do is to have my name on the crook list and a vague word of hope from Humbert Wolfe. So I must explore every avenue now, I can't afford to leave an Edward Marsh unturned. Because along will come conscription, and the military tribunal and stretcher-bearing or jail or potato-peeling or the Boys' Fire League. And all I want is time to write poems, I'm only just getting going now, and enough money to keep two and a bit alive. The only thing I can do, apart from registering myself on the official list of writers to be kept available for possible abuse by the government, is to write to people, friends

237

and acquaintances or just people who might be able to help, and to ask them on knees not yet broken, whether they can give me a job or suggest to whom or what I should apply. For my little money-sources —(apart from anything else)—are diminishing or dying. Soon there will not be a single paper paying inadequately for serious stories and poems. Do you know of anything for me? I can speak and act too. Does the film-world want an intelligent young man of literary ability, self-conscious, punch-drunk, who must (for his own sake) keep out of the bloody war, who's willing to do any work—provided of course that it pays enough for living? I'm not expecting plums from the war —after all, they must go to the kind of chaps who refused to give me anything out of the Royal Literary Fund—but I do want something. Will you tell me if you know of any chances, if, in your clubman rambles, you meet persons who might be just even likely to consider me for some job, if there is, to your knowledge, any vacancy in films of any sort, and, most important, if you are willing, after such a long silence, to try to help me? Otherwise, I don't see how I am to continue here, or anywhere else, even for a very short time. As soon as war was, bills were popped in; the attitude of the tradesmen is changing rapidly; there's a great difference between a rich pacifist and a poor coward. Is it worth, (do you think, & also, of course, if you are willing to think), my coming to London to pull, lick, and see? Please write to me.

Love from us both to you both,
John & Clement,
Caitlin & Dylan.

MSS.: Texas

Sir Edward Marsh had been private secretary to many prominent politicians, including Winston Churchill. He had been a close friend of Rupert Brooke's, about whom he had written a book. He was a well-known patron of the arts, besides being a most influential person.

I have not seen the original of this letter. This extract is taken from *Edward Marsh*, by the late Christopher Hassall (Longman's 1959).

I understand that Marsh sent Dylan a small sum, perhaps £10 or £20.

TO EDWARD MARSH

14th September 1939

I am writing to you, a patron of letters, to ask for any help that you may be able to give me. You may have read some of my work, or

heard it spoken of. If not, I can refer you to Miss Edith Sitwell and
Mr. T. S. Eliot, who will tell you that I am a poet of some worth and
deserving help. I have a wife and a child and am without private means.
For the last few years I have been earning just enough money to keep
my family and myself alive by selling poems and short stories to
magazines. These sources of income are now almost entirely dried up.
It has occurred to me that you, with your connections with the Government, might be able to obtain some employment for me, either in the
Ministry of Information—though that, I am told, is overrun with
applicants, stampeded by almost every young man in London who
has ever held a pencil or slapped a back—or elsewhere, any other
place at all. I have been a journalist and an actor in a repertory theatre;
I have broadcast, and lectured. I am 25 years old.

I suspect that this letter is one of many similar that you are receiving,
and must apologise for giving you this additional trouble.

I have never, even in my most desperate moments, begged or
attempted to seek any employment outside my own limited and under-
paid profession. But now I must have work—I want to be able to go
on writing, and conscription will stop that, perhaps for ever—and I
beg you to help me.

I would very much like to give you, if you wanted it, any information about me and my work. Or I could, again if it was needed,
attempt to come to London.

Bishopston was a village outside Swansea where his parents now had a
small house or cottage.

TO BERT TRICK

29 September 1929 [*in error for 1939*]

Seaview,

Laugharne

Dear Bert,

And I never managed to see you in Swansea after all. I was there
for a few days about two months ago, but I was stuck all the time in
Bishopston, pennilessly. I didn't write asking you if you would come
down to see me, because I didn't know when my pennilessness would
end, and allow me suddenly to come to Swansea and Brynmill for the
day. This state did not end and hasn't ended yet. Now it is harder

than ever, poor or not, to move from this cockled city, even to Carmarthen, overrun with soldiers and war urgers and rememberers.

I wish it were possible for you to visit us. Laugharne is so sweet and quiet, and our house big enough to conceal all the Tricks in the world. How are your wife and children? Tell Kerith I agree with him when he said, 'Damn that' about my being a poet. Damn it forever, it makes uncomfortable life even harder and bonier and gives a poor man a wild beast of a conscience. Now I'm trying to complete by December a book of short stories, mostly potboilers, called temporarily *Portrait of the Artist as a Young Dog*, stories towards a provincial autobiography. They may be amusing eventually, but the writing of them means the writing of a number of poems less. They are all about Swansea life: the pubs, clubs, billiard rooms, promenades, adolescence and the suburban nights, friendships, tempers, and the humiliations. The book is on contract. I get too little regularly for the job. I am commissioned to write another prose book by the middle of next year, but there is apparently no clause in the contract forbidding obscenity and I'll give Dent the whole fucking works. Hope you get hold of my autobiographical book. You know all the stories, but the poems are new. I'd love to know what you think of them.

Llewelyn is bursting with energy; soon he probably will burst. He's eight months old now and has the familiar Thomas puffed innocence about him, lollypop eyes and nose that looks to heaven. His eyes are blue. If I can find one later I'll send you a photograph of him discussing philosophically with himself the alternatives of crowing or blowing. As one Daddy to another, what are you doing in the War? I'm very puzzled. When it's necessary I'm going to register as an objector, but also because I want to get something out of the mess if possible. My little body (though it's little no longer, I'm like a walrus) I don't intend to waste for the mysterious ends of others. If there's any profiteering to be done, I in my fashion wish to be in on it. But my natural and, to me, sensible greed and opportunism will come unfortunately to nothing; I'm sure of that. I know a few wires but they only tinkle when I pull them. So I'm afraid that I shall have to take the tribunal. Is there any possibility of getting a job in Swansea? I don't know how you feel about all this, but I can't raise up any feeling about this war at all. And the demon Hitlerism can go up its own bottom. I refuse to help it with a bayonet. To talk about keeping Hitlerism out of this sink of democracy by censorship and conscription, mystery-mongering and umbrella-worship, atrocity circulation and the (thank God mostly unsuccessful so far) fostering of hate against bewildered and buggered people. How long? Only to encourage the rebellious pacifism of anti-social softies like myself.

Write soon and tell me all about the war. I have only my feelings to guide me; and they are my own, and nothing will turn them savage against people with whom I have no quarrel. There's a need now for some life to go on strenuously and patiently outside the dictated hates and pettiness of war and that life I, for my own part, shall continue to support by my writing and thinking and by living as coolly, hotly, and as well as I know how.

Our love to you all,

Dylan

PS. And do tell me all the news too. I miss the boys and the smoky nights. Here everything is so slow and prettily sad. I'd like to live in a town or a city again for a bit. Let there be one town left, and we'll fill it with ourselves.

MSS.: Lockwood Memorial Library, Buffalo

By October of 1939 Dylan had decided that he would be a conscientious objector, and was writing to other writers in an attempt to persuade them that they endorse his point of view. He wrote letters similar to this next one to Henry Treece, Glyn Jones, Rayner Heppenstall and many other friends.

TO D. S. SAVAGE

27 October 1939

Sea View,

Laugharne,

Carmarthenshire

Dear D. S. Savage,

I'm trying to get together a number of statements of objection to war from young writers. These I want to get printed in Life & Letters Today: or, if they become too squeamish, in some smaller, independent paper. I don't know how you feel about this, so, in a first letter, will only say that the objections must not be just general ones— 'war is bloody, criminal, & absurd, everybody knows that, & I object to it heartily but I suppose I shall have to do something when the time comes'. Now, more than at any other time we have known, definite objections are needed. If you intend not to support the war

241

and to take no part in it, will you write, fairly briefly, your reasons?—
in whatever way you like, of course. I have written to several people
and have statements of objection, so far, from Desmond Hawkins,
Glyn Jones, Keidrych Rhys. I've been promised statements, too,
from Barker, Heppenstall, N. Moore, McDiarmid, and others. Any
names—whether or not you yourself are a thorough objector—you
can suggest? I needn't tell you that, if you are an objector, the fact
that you contributed to a thing of this sort, in face of public opinion,
and against most even of the intelligentsia, will not be in your disfavour
if, & when, you appear before a tribunal. Glyn Jones told me that he
believed you stood with us. I do hope so. Write to me, if you will,
anyway.

Yours,
Dylan Thomas

MSS.: Texas

Rayner Heppenstall refused to contribute to this symposium. His novel,
The Blaze of Noon, had just been published.

TO RAYNER HEPPENSTALL

Laugharne,
Carmarthenshire,
S. Wales

November 2 1939

Dear Rayner,

I am not 'making a stand against war'—which I doubt was the
expression I used; if I did use it, it was for convenience quickly and
not for argument, not to be offered as an expression of my own
thinking or feeling for you to put into inverted commas and throw
back to me; certainly not as a militant priggishness. I am banging no
drum for a Right, right, left or wrong; I am not forming fours to
oppose sixes and sevens—to 'justify my existence' (back the phrase
comes, dolled up in self-conscious punctuation. I too can recognise a
cliché and must let you know, as you let me know, that I recognise it
as one) but to prolong it. In asking you to 'contribute to my symposium' I was merely asking you, as a man I know who writes, to let
me have your individual objections to war; these objections, if they
existed, could take any form; I was not attempting to form a common
or rarefied front or backside; because I thought people might like to
read them, I set out to collect individual objections from some of my

friends and acquaintances. Also, of course, because I wanted to read them; I wanted to know what my friends and acquaintances are going to do when they are told by the State to fight not their enemies. My own 'stand' is a sit, and it will be on my own sit me down.

I'll certainly use your 'bit of nonsense'—which is what I do believe it to be—and thank you for bothering. Your question, 'Who's to stop me letting my rifle off up the colonel's arse?' has only one answer: 'plenty of people'.

And it's no use telling me, with heavy underlining, that you won't have an attitude to the war, much less to WAR. I don't care a bugger whether you won't or will: I wanted to know if you objected to war and why and whether you were going to 'serve' or not. My curiosity, I imagined, might have a journalistic interest. Others might like to be told that the only pacifists you come across are sexual perverts (crossed out and tut tut) or elderly ladies worried about dividends. You must have been living in a curious world—and there's no reason why you shouldn't have—to come across no other kinds of pacifists. Those are the kind that Beachcomber hopefully imagines make up the whole 'forces for peace' in this country. Perhaps the only socialists you come across are teetotal fruitarians.

When you come to talk about one's duty as a writer, then one can only say that his duty is to write. If to undergo contemporary reality to its most extreme is to join in a war—the evil of which is the war itself and not the things it is supposed, wrongly, to be attempting to exterminate—against people you do not know, and probably be killed or maimed, then one can only say flippantly that the best poems about death were always written when the poets were alive, that Lorca didn't have to be gored before writing a bullsong, that for a writer to undergo the utmost reality of poverty is for him to starve to death and therefore to be, as a writer, useless.

Three more reasons of yours why you will probably join up are, to me, even more doubtful; and by that I mean that the honesty that made up those reasons is in doubt. You say you may join up because you could not cash in on the Ministry of Information. Does that mean you can not? Is it any worse to receive a good salary for muddling information, censoring news, licking of official stamps, etc., than it is to kill or be killed for a shilling, or less, a day? You say you could not work on the land as one of a chaingang. Again, I do not see how that is any worse. One large lot of people is nearly always as 'congenial' as any other lot, and the matey folk-warmth of the trenches can only make for hysterical friendships, do or die companionships, the joking desperate homosexual propinquity of those about to die: the joy of

243

living and dying with a Saturday football crowd on an exploding ground. You say you could not languish like a martyr in jail, why a martyr anyway? The only reason one will go to jail is if a tribunal refuses to register one as an unconditioned objector and then if one will not do the services, substitute for military services, which the tribunal enforces. The individual can do what he likes: whatever he does, he is punished. I wanted to know which punishment you preferred.

How is the nest of fairies? Dan Jones told me something or other. Nice to hear you're having a baby. You or Margaret? Take no offence, Mr. H., but you said in your letter that you were pregnant. I'll get the Blaze of Noon, if I can, for review in The New English Weekly.

I'm living extremely quietly here, with Caitlin and Llewelyn. No money, of course, and we can't, even if we wanted to, move. I've nearly finished a book of straight, autobiographical stories: Portrait of the Artist as a Young Dog. Dent's give me a little miserable allowance which pays for cigarettes, light and coal. We're always warm, but badly in debt.

Will you be in London in December? I hope to come up for a week. And is Durrell there too? I'd like to see you very much.

Love to you and Margaret.

Dylan

I'll let you know the hour of my birth after I see my mother. The date is 27 October, 1914. The place, Swansea.

MSS.: Texas

The symposium was never published. Dylan was becoming bored in Laugharne, and nostalgic for Swansea. The Kardomah was a café in which he and his friends used to spend a great deal of time when he and Charles Fisher were reporters on the *Swansea Daily Post*.

TO CHARLES FISHER

December 1939?

Seaview,

Laugharne,

Carmarthenshire

Dear Charles,

I did enjoy hearing from you about yourself and the local lads with whom, in the intervals between Fitzrophobia, attempted 19th century dissipation, artgraft, amateur poncing, I condescended to muck provincially about. But the lads themselves are splitting up, perhaps even cracking up. Vernon should write the Glamorgan Lad and tell how, one by one, we reach the gallows, the marriage-bed, the grave, Harrow, Windrush or the Air Force. I'm coming to Swansea to swell your numbers, in Christmas week, or, if I happen to see an old blind lady crossing Laugharne High Street and I rush to her aid and later she turns out to be Lady St. Clears and leaves her fortune to the last person who did her a service, earlier. I am, at last, fed up with this retreat, the day has come, the castle and the pretty water make me sick. I want to see our beautiful drab town, I want to have smuts in my eye in Wind Street, I want to hear the sweet town accent float into my ears like the noise of old brakes. Keep some days for us when we arrive; show us round the town; reserve two seats (and one seat specially sawed down) in the Kardomah my Home sweet Homah. Perhaps Mabeley will be about too unless he's almost a Warden. I'm glad the Spy Service didn't take you: you would always have given up your papers to Dolores (the password is cocksnap, knock a hundred times on the onionseller's door, his name is Tabash, call him Dickinson) even if they were the wrong papers. I like your standard war joke; you should give the healthier-looking waitresses white feathers. I'm not doing anything about the war; resigned to personal neutrality, I wait until I am called up, and then I will probably scream and wheedle and faint.

There's a story of mine about me and Dan in the December Life & Letters, by the way.

See you all, or both, soon. Love, to you and Fred.

Dylan

We never see the Keidrych Rhyses now. I'm number one on the list, Mrs. R's list, of people who have a bad effect on hubby. That's what she thinks. I tell him bad things about poetry.

MSS.: Charles Fisher, Esq.

They spent Christmas with Caitlin's mother, and remained at Ringwood until late in March.

The prospect of being called up was now looming ominously. At the suggestion of Augustus John, Dylan wrote to Sir Kenneth Clark, then head of the Ministry of Information, in the hope of a reserved job. But Sir Kenneth could do nothing for him, beyond sending him a small cheque.

TO SIR KENNETH CLARK

25 March, 1940

Laugharne,
Carmarthenshire,
S. Wales

Dear Sir Kenneth,

I wonder if you got my letter of just over a week ago? I sent it to a Portland Place address, which Augustus John had given me, and which was in the telephone book. Augustus wasn't sure, though, whether you still lived there. If you have had my letter, I apologise for bothering you again; but I daren't take the chance that you have had it. I do hope this reaches you through the Ministry of Information; I wanted to write to your private address, because you must be bombarded with letters at the other place.

Augustus said he'd written to you and talked to you about me, about my chances of getting a job, any kind of job I'm capable of doing, to avoid conscription. And he told me that you'd said you'd look out for a job, but that, anyway, you didn't think I would be conscripted. In my letter, which perhaps has gone astray, I asked you if you'd be kind enough to tell me how probable my exemption was, and, if it wasn't very probable, could you help me to get some work, which would exempt me? I'm to register on April 7, which leaves me hardly any time, and if I do have to register it will have to be as an objector. I don't want to do that, because, though I will not fight, I am perfectly willing to do some kind of work; and I think it would be wasteful and silly for me to be made to work at something I know absolutely nothing about and at which I would probably always be inefficient. Augustus told me, too, that you knew some of my writing. I've got a year's work planned out, I'm halfway through a long book, and I do very much want to go on with my work. Conscription, or objection, must, I know, stop that work altogether—objection too, because I hardly think a tribunal, especially in Wales, would pay much attention to my nonreligious, nonpolitical reasons. I know it's presumptuous of me, as a complete stranger to you, to worry you with my worries, but I've no-one at all to turn to, no-one to advise me, and very little time left. Also, Augustus said that you were very willing to help me; and I shall be grateful for ever if you can.

I wrote my first letter to you from Hampshire, where I was staying, and asked you if you could arrange to meet me in London; if there would be a reason in my coming to London; if you would care to see me. I waited in Hampshire until the end of last week, hoping to hear from you, but now have had to come home to Wales. Will you let me know if I shall come to London to see you? Or, anyway, tell me about the possibilities of exemption or any kind of exempting work? I wish I could have made this letter shorter. I do hope you will answer me.

Yours sincerely,
Dylan Thomas

MSS.: Sir Kenneth Clark

Lady Clark had suggested to him that he volunteer for Victor Cazalet's anti-aircraft battery, as many other writers and painters had done. He did so, in late April, but was graded C3, probably because of asthma.

Meanwhile Stephen Spender, Herbert Read and Henry Moore had launched an appeal, through the magazine *Horizon,* to raise money on his behalf.

TO STEPHEN SPENDER

c/o Marston,
Bishopston,
Nr. Swansea,
Glam.

13 May, 1940

Dear Stephen,

Thanks for your letter. I do know it isn't an easy job for you to work out and carry out this appeal. But I misled myself and you when I told you that, as the medical board had graded me 3, I wouldn't be called up for a long time. I've been told now, authoritatively, that grade 3 people will be called up at exactly the same time as the other, 1 & 2, people in my age-group—though, of course, for different work: mostly, I gather, noncombatant. It was the first kind of excitement following the result of the medical examination that led me to wish-imagine I wasn't, therefore, wanted for the army. But in your letters, surely none of these details need be gone into: the fact is that I shall be called up when the rest of my age-group is. That can be truthfully and simply said: whether I'm called up to fire bullets or peel spuds doesn't make much difference, does it? I didn't realise, anyway, that the whole grounds of your appeal would be that I was being called up. I thought that the filthily desperate state of my money life at the moment was the important reason for help.

You asked for a few particulars—I've had to sneak my family away from our home in Carmarthenshire, because we could no longer obtain any credit and it was too awful to try to live there, among dunning and suspicion, from hand to mouth when I knew the hand would nearly always be empty. I've had to leave all our books and clothes, most of my papers etc., and unless I pay our most important debts, quickly, everything will be sold up: the beds & china & chairs & things that we've managed, with difficulty, to collect over three years. Now, until some money comes, we're staying here in my father's house: he's a very poor man and finds it, himself, hard to live: we're almost an intolerable burden on him, or, rather, we will be very soon. I'm writing only poems now, those extremely slowly, and can expect very little money for them. I do not want to write another straight prosebook yet; it would eventually get me some money, I suppose, but it would mean ten or more poems less, which, I think, would be sad and silly for me. And when I am called up, if only to be a latrine-minder, I shall obviously have less and less time in order to gain me even a few occasional pounds. My wife & myself have not a private penny. I do, a lot, want to return to Laugharne, Carmarthenshire, pay our debts, find ourselves in our own home again, live there working quietly until I am needed; & then to leave my family there, knowing they are, at least, clothed and housed. My debts amount almost exactly to £70. If I could get £100, I could settle everything & make a new start there: ensure food for the two others for a long time to come. If I cannot pay these debts & have a little to live on, there's no hope at all: everything we have collected and built up will go & I do not see where & how my wife & child can merely live. I cannot go away leaving them nothing but debts & their lodgings in another's poverty. I'd sooner die with them, & this little money worry is making a nervous fool of me when I want to be, and can be, solid and busy.

Thank you & Herbert Read & Henry Moore. I do hope something will happen from your kindness. And I hope this letter explains.

Yours,

Dylan

MSS.: Harvard

The result of this appeal was that Dylan and Caitlin were able to go on living in Laugharne until July 1940. By then the war was truly serious: France had fallen and a German invasion of England was believed imminent. It was not only Dylan's world that had collapsed.

Furthermore, the money raised by the *Horizon* appeal had been spent, and the small monthly cheques that Dylan had been receiving from Dent's also now ceased. It was impossible to go on living in Laugharne. John Davenport had invited them to come and stay with him in Gloucestershire, and thither they went. It was to be nine years before Dylan returned to live in Laugharne or had a real home of his own.

From July to September of 1940 Dylan and Caitlin were staying with John Davenport. I have no letters of any literary interest from this period, apart from those to Vernon Watkins, already published in *Dylan Thomas: Letters to Vernon Watkins*. Most of his letters that have survived from the first half of the war are to his publishers or his agent, and are concerned almost exclusively with business and with pleas for money.

In the autumn of 1940 he went to London and obtained work with a documentary film company, Strand Films, run by Donald Taylor, who was to become a close friend. Dylan was also writing programmes for the B.B.C. at this time. For the next two years he travelled between Wales, where Caitlin and Llewelyn were, and London, where the money was. In January of 1941 he was staying with his parents at Bishopston, just outside Swansea.

In this letter that follows, Pulham is Peter Rose Pulham, the painter and photographer; Archer is David Archer, who had once run the Parton Street Bookshop and had been Dylan's first publisher; Lord Howard de Walden, at John Davenport's suggestion, had given Dylan the £50 which had enabled Dylan to go to London and find work; Peter Watson financed *Horizon*, and gave Dylan money on several occasions—the poem referred to is *The Ballad of the Long-legged Bait;* Archibald Harding was a B.B.C. producer; Clement was John Davenport's wife; Arnold Cooke and Lennox Berkeley composers; Antonia White a poet and novelist; the Canary is *The Death of the King's Canary,* a fantastic novel on which Dylan and Davenport had been collaborating.

TO JOHN DAVENPORT

Jan 8. 1941
c/o Marston,
Bishopston,
Glamorgan

Dear John,

I had a telephone by my side last night so I had to ring you up. It was lovely to hear Clement. It was good to see you in London too, and I liked the Queens lunch with rednose and his belonging girl, and shabby humped elegant Pulham, and barmy Archer apologising for eating, and us, and port and mussels. It was grand just like the old times we never really had together in London. But the second meeting was an absolute daze to me, and I slept in the dark bombed room like a pig and I was obstreperous and over-confident, closing one eye, and weepy and repetitive, during the moments awake. I hope I wasn't too much for you, for a rather sinister countryman in his town club, menaces of churches, of devious and improbable connections, living up to de Walden's income, the largest host in London. 'So this is what they call a host. I'd forgotten.' Remember that architectural beard at the beginning of the 4 hours lunch? I rang you up the next morning, but you'd gone with Dawes to the country, so we went after lunch, travelling for about nine hours, and some officers in the restaurant car thought I was a spy—me—and asked to see my identity card which I didn't have all because I wore a black hat and because a young Welsh boy in a naval uniform was sitting opposite me, copying out his poems on small bits of paper and handing them to me slyly across the table.

After buying a few useless things—did Clement get her salonscene? —the Watson money disappeared, quick as a sardine, and we've been cooped up here, in little, boiling rooms, for nearly three weeks, quite broke, waiting for the second instalment: or, anyway, waiting for little sums to carry us over while we wait. Today the pipes burst, and Caitlin, in a man's hat, has been running all day with a mop from w.c. to flooded parlour, while I've been sitting down trying to write a poem about a man who fished with a woman for bait and caught a horrible collection.

I finished the Czech script, three weeks late, and sent it on to Morley with a rude note, as thought it were his fault. The script uses five announcers. 'War. The shadow of the eagles is cast on the grazing lands, the meadows of Belgium are green no longer and the pastures are barbed with bayonets. War. War.' Five announcers, and a chorus of patriots crying 'Siberia', 'Freedom of Man', 'Strengthen us for the approaching hour' like a bunch of trained bulls.

I told Clement on the telephone that we were thinking of going back to Laugharne to live, for a time; sharing a house there with the owner of the buses, the garage, the pub, the electric plant, the cockles, and, no doubt, eventually us. As soon as I can I'm going down to inspect. Perhaps you & Clement will come to see us, once, and if, we're settled?

I know I did apologise, in town, for my not writing after that morning rush away from Marshfield, but I haven't apologised to Clement. All I can say is: I was very muddled and unhappy, and didn't feel a bit like having any contact at all—until the muddles were straightened in my head—with anyone in the place where for so many months I had been so happy. You gave me a wonderful time; the summer talked itself away; and our book was the best of its kind or unkind, and Arnold and Lennox and Eric Dawes were fine new friends, and I loved our Club of Bad Books, and Antonia, buttoned, unbuttoned, dame, flapper, was always a charmer and a caution. I had the nicest, fullest time for years. Thank you both.

If I can—and Clement said I may—I'll try to come to Marshfield next weekend. We must do the last pages of the Canary then, and have it published quickly and make some money and enemies.

MSS.: Texas

The following letter to Bertram Rota, the bookseller, while of no literary merit is biographically of the greatest importance. The notebooks referred to are those into which he had been writing his poems between the ages of sixteen and nineteen, and from which he had quarried a very high proportion of the poems, then rewritten, which formed his first three volumes. This sale of his notebooks is thus a definite break with his past. By the time this volume of letters appears those notebooks, which are now with the Lockwood Memorial Library, New York State University, Buffalo, will have been edited by Professor Ralph Maud and published.

The long ballad is the *Ballad of the Long-legged Bait*.

TO BERTRAM ROTA

8th April, 1941

Marston,
Bishopston,
Glamorgan

Dear Mr. Rota,

Thank you for your letter. I am very interested in selling my manuscripts. The trouble is that most of my poems I write into exercise books, and that each exercise book contains a lot of poems, including utter failures that I shall never print. The same goes for my stories. If you would care for me to send a few of these books along, I'd be delighted. I think it would be a pity to disfigure the books by tearing a few poems out. I do not know, of course, if there would be a market for such work in bulk, as it were. Will you let me know soon? I should like to sell them, if possible, as I am in need of money.

In the meantime I enclose, for your offer, a small group of manuscripts: five poems and a story.

Yours very truly,
Dylan Thomas

PS. I have almost completed what I think is my best work so far: a long Ballad, which *Horizon* is printing next month. The manuscript of that, comprising a great deal of drafts, corrections, and alterations, is certainly the most interesting I have. Perhaps you would tell me if you'd like to see this, too?

D. T.

MSS.: Bertram Rota, Esq.

Roger Roughton, who had edited *Contemporary Poetry and Prose* before the war, had committed suicide in Dublin.

John Davenport had taken a job as a schoolmaster at Repton.

TO JOHN DAVENPORT

25? April 1941
Marston,
Bishopston,
Glam.

Dear John,

Deeply, really distressed to hear about poor, dear, old Roger. Although I hadn't seen him for more than two years, and wasn't likely to see him for years to come, if ever, I've always known that he was about somewhere with his little eyes and his cigarette, calm and treble in the middle of the crumbling system; I knew that he was always somewhere, perhaps driving a Bugatti with the radio full on, or riding a ladies' broken bicycle. It was nice to know that one always could see him. Now I find that, straightaway after your letter, I miss him an awful lot. I can understand how upset you are. You won't forget, will you, to let me know how he died, and as much of the why as we'll ever be able to know.

There won't, I suppose, be a single obituary line anywhere. I think we should do something, John. It may be silly, but I think it would be right. A letter—New Statesman?—saying that there are so many deaths now that the death of Roger Roughton will perhaps pass unnoticed, and that we, the undersigned, don't want it to. We could say just a few things about him, his work for the Communist Party, his publishing, his parties, his poems, himself. And get a few chaps— Bert Lloyd, maybe Enoch Soames, & Henry Moore, you'll know who to get—to put their names. What d'you think? You'll know better than I would. Roger shouldn't be allowed to pass out, in the middle of a bad war, in dirty Dublin, without his friends publicly recording it and their gratitude to him. We should do it quickly, too. Do let me hear from you very very soon.

I've nearly finished the Canary typing now. I'd have been quicker, but have had to borrow Vernon's typewriter for short, irregular periods. Can you send me the last few pages of the last part? Do you remember, we did a little that per-Repton weekend? In small exercise books. I wrote about half a dozen pages, nearly up to the Blackpool dinner from which Chronos escapes. The exercise book is probably in the pubroom somewhere. When I've finished all the typing, & the quick end of the book, I'll write or wire you, & then perhaps you'll be able to ask me up to Repton & we can correct it all.

I told Vernon that a stamped envelope to him had probably been on your desk for weeks. He quite understood. Faber's are bringing out his poems this year. I'm very glad. Provisionally titled 'Gratitude of a Leper', though I'm not quite sure myself.

I've just finished my ballad. Too late, unfortunately, for the May Horizon. It's about 220 lines long, a tremendous effort for me, & is really a ballad. I think you'll like it. At the moment, I think it's the best I've done.

I'll write to Antonia today about the script. Thanks.

MSS.: Texas

In late April or early May of 1941 they went to stay for several weeks with Frances Hughes at Laugharne Castle. Richard Hughes was away, in the Navy, and Dylan himself was often in London.

Tambimuttu was a Ceylonese who financed and edited *Poetry*; Henry Reed is a poet; Henry Treece's book about Dylan, *Dog Among The Fairies*, had not yet been published, though chapters had appeared in various periodicals; Geoffrey Grigson had edited *New Verse* before the war; Runia Tharpe had assisted Victor Neuburg, who had recently died, with his 'Poets' Corner' in the *Sunday Referee*.

TO MR TAMBIMUTTU

9th June 1941

Laugharne Castle,

Laugharne,

Carmarthenshire

Dear Tambimuttu,

Thank you for the post-dated guinea; and sorry to have been a bother about it, but even in a castle one must eat and smoke I suppose.

I hope number six goes well, though I'm not looking forward to Treece's article after his ridiculous overpraise of Reed:—
'All Elizabethan tradgedy, all the colour and violence of the ballads,' or whatever the words were in some such ice-cream line as 'O O Antonio'. I think the article did Reed a disservice, for the natural reaction to it was ridicule and that, unfortunately might embrace Reed's own dull, honest poetry too. If someone says a line is better than Shakespeare and it's really just an ordinary pleasant line, one's inclined, I think, to pass over the ordinary pleasantness of it by attacking the humbug, or gutter eye, that sees it as superb. I hope Treece doesn't say that there's all metaphysics in some ordinary line of mine.

A thing I don't like about 'Poetry', now that I'm feeling like this, is its plague of dedications: 'For Nigel', 'To Nicholas', 'From Basil' and the letters with all the Christian names and the back-pats and kicks. It's too much like 'Hi Gang' on the wireless. The intimate magazine should be circulated only among the family, and I'm damned if I belong to your family or Nigel's or Basil's. The public's got a right to demand that it's entertainment should be public; and if the public likes all this matey to-you, for-you, we're all pals together hugging and buggering party exhibition, then the public, as nearly always, is wrong.

What I do like about 'Poetry' is some of its poems; which is as it should be. Let's have less about them and more of them.

I'll write again when I get number six. Best wishes for it.

Yours,

Dylan Thomas

Sorry, I haven't got a copy myself of my 18 Poems. And I'm sorry some cad removed yours, but if your copy was inscribed by me to Runia—an old friend—then some cad must have removed it from her.

Yes, I'd love to send you some drawings, or illustrations. I'll have a shot right away.

MSS.: Texas

In the next letter Fred is Alfred Janes, known for the slowness with which he painted his meticulous pictures; Tom is Tom Warner; Dan is Dan Jones.

TO CHARLES FISHER

July 15, 1941.
Laugharne Castle,

Carmarthenshire

My dear Charles,

While looking through a drawer to find something it was not my drawer so I did not know what the something would be though I hoped for tinned food—I came across an old letter of yours to me, and with your home address which I'd lost. It really took the wind out of my sails (I was a yacht at the time), finding your handwriting in somebody else's drawer where peas at the very least should have been. It was like, not very much like, I admit, burgling a safe and finding an old friend inside it not a day older than one foot two. I thought I'd better write at once, before I found a drawing of Fred's (Still Life: One Egg. June 1936—June 1940) behind the hatrack in the music room or a manuscript of Tom's (Mabinogion, a Tone Poem for Horn and Kardomah) behind the butler in the cook's room. Especially as there is no music room and no butler and the only hatrack is a bust of Dante on which some child has written 'Odd Job'.

I saw too little of you in Swansea last time; hat and moustache for half a quick evening among the good-shows of the young lieutenants and Peggy and Betty and Babs the dancing dailies. I remember reading some of my unfinished Ballad—the whole is coming out in this month's Horizon—in a thick, confidential voice, being bought two pints at a time, giving my belly what-for; but the date we made for later I forgot at once, and spent the next evening trying to be in three Gower pubs at the same time, waiting, wondering which of them I had arranged to meet you in, then remembering too late that the meeting was to have been in Swansea, a large town. After months and months, and if you remembered the date yourself, forgive me, and do write.

I think that quite soon I'll be made to do work in a factory, so that this is my last bit of as much freedom as one can expect to enjoy without any money. I haven't seen a coin for weeks. Do they still sing as you spend them? Jesus, I loathe my poverty. Caitlin will, I hope, be able to stay on here while I am being thrown to the high explosives. My upper lip is a board, but still I am very miserable.

I am writing now, a long story about London, called 'Adventures in the Skin Trade'. Miller and Wodehouse. Do you know Tom's address? I want, through him, to find where Daniel is, that Lost Tribe in himself.

Tell me how you are, what you're doing, and be good to the Generals.

Love,
Dylan

And just a poem, finished today.

MSS.: Charles Fisher, Esq.

In late 1941 Dylan and Caitlin moved to London, where Mrs (now Lady) A. P. Herbert lent them her husband's studio. The name of the recipient of the letter which follows is omitted for obvious reasons.

TO MISS ██ ██   May 1942?

The Strand Film Company Limited,
Managing Director's Office,   as from
1 Golden Square,   13 Hammersmith Tce., W.6.
W.1.

> No Not any longer after Saturday.
> So will you—if you will
> write, please—please write
> to the film address.

Your letter—thank you very, very much for it; I was terribly glad to hear—came just after I had been seeing you on the films, you with your wand, showing a ladderless leg in the wings. You looked, if I may or mayn't say so, pretty good to me, and I wish you were in London, where even the sun's grey and God how I hate it, and not in Preston with a lot of sillies. I do hate the life here, the grey gets in your eyes so that a bit of green nearly blinds you and the thought of the sea makes you giddy as you cross the road like a bloody beetle. You wrote to me on a moor, and I write to you in a ringing, clinging office with repressed women all around punishing typewriters, and queers in striped suits talking about 'Cinema' and, just at this very moment, a man with a bloodhound's voice and his cheeks, I'm sure, full of Mars Bars, rehearsing out loud a radio talk on 'India and the Documentary Movement'. I wish I were on the Halifax moor talking to you, not to dishonest men with hangovers. Perhaps I shall be able to give a long-postponed talk to the Cambridge English Society during the week of June 8, which would be wonderful because perhaps you don't work all day and perhaps you would come out with me, walk somewhere, watch me drink a pint, and talk and talk and talk. Would you like that? If you would, then I could try very hard to come up for a day. Let me know will you?

You said you wrote a bad letter, and you wrote a lovely one, though too short. I said, horribly, that I wrote a good letter, and I'm almost inarticulate. What's a good letter anyway? To put down a bit of oneself to send to someone who misses it? To be funny and self-conscious or selfconsciously formal, or so very natural that even the words blush and stammer? I only know I'd prefer to talk to you, but as I've got to write because you're a million miles away, in the mild and bitter north, then I must write anything, anything or everything, just as it comes: into the thing that keeps my collar from vanishing into my hat. First, how very very odd it was, coming across you out of the blue, out of the black, out of the blue-and-black bruise of a smutty town at the end of a witless week, when everything had gone wrong, had gone wrong, as I didn't know then, only to come extravagantly right. I saw, suddenly, a human being, rare as a Martian, an actual unaffected human being, after months and months, and years indeed of meeting only straw men, sponge and vanity boys, walking sacks full of solid vinegar and pride, all the menagerie of a world very rightly at war with itself. (And now even the ink is spitting.) I felt, at once, so at ease with you that I can still hardly believe it.

Thank you for saying about Llewelyn. He's going away tomorrow, for a few weeks, to his grandmother, quite near Salisbury. Just outside Fordingbridge. I have to move from Hammersmith Terrace, and am trying to get a house in St. Peter's Square to share with some people who have furniture. You don't know, I suppose, anyone who has any furniture stored in London and who would want to give it a good home? The only things I have are a deckchair with a hole in it, half a dozen books, a few toys, and an old iron. These would not even fill a mouse's home. It is very good sometimes to have nothing; I want society, not me, to have places to sit in and beds to lie in; and who wants a hatstand of his very own? But sometimes, on raining, nostalgic Sunday afternoons, after eating the week's meat, it would, however cowardly, whatever a blanketing of responsibility and conscience, be good to sprawl back in one's own bourgeois chair, bought slippers on one's trotters. But to hell with it, I want to talk about you, I know too much about myself: I've woken up with myself for 28 years now, or very nearly. But I can't write about you—and now the spitting pen is broken and the ink over documents ostentatiously and falsely called Important—because though I feel much, I know so little. So goodbye for a time, and the smaller the time the better—at least for me. You will write? And I will see you?

love,

Dylan

T. W. Earp was a poet and, for many years, art critic on the *Daily Telegraph*. Although considerably older than Dylan, they became very close friends.

Caitlin had returned to Wales and was living at Talsarn, where Dylan spent as much time as he could.

A joke current at the time maintained that the Russian Marshal Timoshenko was really a Welshman named Timothy Jenkins, or maybe an Irishman called Timmy O'Shea.

The Ladder and the Jubilee were afternoon drinking clubs in London.

Banting is John Banting, the painter. Who Ann or Anna was, I am not sure—she might be any one of several.

TO T. W. EARP

Gelli,   as from,
Talsarn,   Strand Films,
Cardiganshire.   1, Golden Square,
                                                                            W.C.1.

30th August 1942

Dear Tommy:

On-and-on General Bock is driving a wedge among pincers,
Timothy Jenkins feints on the flank and the rouged Duke is wan,

The war is sweet with the summer breath of the panzers
And the dehydrated choirs of day welcome the dawn.
As I tossed off this morning over Talsarn Bridge to the fishes,
At war myself with the Celtic gnats under a spitfire sun,
Reading that twenty poems make fifteen cartridge cases,
Commandos are trained to be cannibals and bombs weigh a hundred
ton,
Poison is dropped from the sky in the shape of hipflasks and cheque-
books,
Pigs can be taught to firewatch and hens to lay handgrenades:
O the summer grew suddenly lovely as the woodland rose in a phalanx
And the painted privates I thought were bushes
moved in their Nash parades.

I have been here for over a week with Caitlin, with milk and mild
and cheese and eggs, and I feel fit as a fiddle only bigger; I watch the
sun from a cool room and know that there are trees being trees outside
and that I do not have to admire them; the country's the one place
you haven't got to go out in, thank Pan. I missed you last Friday, and
was not in time, (as I thought, up until the last moment, that I would
be able to catch the Thursday-night train), to let you know. I hope
you did not wait nor were cross, and that the Monico made up for the
lack of green tooth and pot belly, for the absence of one ventripotent
scortatory Krut. I'm returning tomorrow, Tuesday, and will be in
London until Friday night. Can you come up during the week, or
on Friday? A visit will make up for London after Wales. I want to
bring my bit of a novel with me, and let's try the Ladder & the Jubilee
and have a gala climb, without banting and unanned. I do hope you
can manage it. Will you write or wire?

Ever,
Dylan

MSS.: Ohio

By the summer of 1943 Dylan and Caitlin were installed in Chelsea, at
8 Wentworth Studios, together with the new baby, Aeronwy, who had
been born that spring. Llewelyn was with his grandmother at Blashford.

Tommy Earp and his wife May were living in the country, but he came
frequently to London. The telephone number is that of Donald Taylor's
Strand Films, where Dylan was now working almost full time. But 'full
time' did not mean that Dylan could not manage an all-day pub crawl with
a friend.

The reference to Lewis Carroll in the first line escapes me.

Frisco had a night club; the Ladder was an afternoon drinking club; Johnny Banting, the surrealist painter, was a close friend.

In the fourth line 'the Swiss' was a pub in Soho—this may be a reference to Dr Spooner, to whom spoonerisms are, erroneously, attributed.

Marcelle Quennell, Peter Quennell's ex-wife, was usually to be found in the Ladder Club at this time. Who Ruth was, I do not know. John Davenport was one of several friends with that Christian name who were frequently in the Antelope, a pub off Sloane Square, as was Augustus John. It was, if my memory is correct, slightly more expensive than most pubs; on the other hand, Penny may have been a girl.

The back bar of the Café Royal was one of Dylan's favourites: 'Dr Mabuse', the famous German horror film directed by Fritz Lang, was also one of his favourites.

Jim Phelan, the author of *Lifer*, who had served a life sentence because of his activities in the Irish Republican Army, was a good friend and drinking companion.

Welsh Peggy was a barmaid in a drinking club called The Horseshoe, in Soho. I believe there was another drinking club, also in Soho, in Wardour Street, run by a woman whose last name was Smith.

TO T. W. EARP

July 1. 43   Ger. 6304

Dear Tommy:

When next shall we stumble to the stutter of our lewis-gun carols
From Bombazine-bosomed bar to a bliss of barrels,
Two period percies friscoed with ladders and banting,
Two spooned swiss pillars, tumble falsetting and ranting?

O when, marcel-bound, shall we ruth our swine's way to the many-
johned
Penny-fond antelope's cavern from the royal back-bar of beyond,
Or, sinister self-mabuses ripe for the phelon of the withy,
Peggy-legged limping in bottle-dress hooved from the Wardour-
street smithy?

MSS.: Ohio

Peter Baker was at this time a publisher. This unfinished novel is *Adventures in the Skin Trade*. To the best of my knowledge, no more of it was ever written. Peter Baker did not buy it.

TO PETER BAKER

26 January 1944   Film Centre, W.1.

Dear Peter Baker,

Here is the manuscript of the first thirty thousand words of the novel we were talking about. This represents roughly half of what the whole novel will be. It may look a little formless now, but actually the whole conception of the book is made to a most formal pattern.

It might be worth while my saying in a few lines what happens in the rest, the unwritten, as yet, part of the story. The hero, as you will notice, is in the gradual process of losing his clothes; and as the story progresses so he loses more and more clothes, bit by bit. He loses these clothes through a series of incidents and in a number of places that are not connected by content or atmosphere with any of the incidents that came beforehand. That is, he does not progress through any ordinary drunken romantic picaresque movement, but through all kinds of sober, grisly, embarrassing, mortifying, but always readable, I hope, adventures in the wilderness of London, from Kilburn to Cockfosters.

Eventually, of course, he winds up without any clothes at all, and finds himself outside Paddington Station a moment before dawn. Standing there naked, having had every garment fall simultaneously with the acquisition of every new experience, he wonders, 'Now I am here, outside Paddington Station, just from where I began my pilgrimage, as naked as the day I was born. What'll happen to me? Will a very rich woman in a Rolls-Royce and a fur coat pass me by in the almost dawn, stop her chauffeur, and befriend me and lard me with charity and nymphomania? Or will a policeman pick me up for indecent exposure, my having shed all the skins of my semi-proletarian, bourgeois, provincial upbringing? Or will a romantic tart clutch me to her used bosom, in the Catholic tradition of Francis Thompson? Or, when dawn breaks, shall I see everyone walking about the streets, going to work, conducting traffic, going about their daily dulness, as naked, as utterly naked as I?'

That's how the book will run. Sorry if it sounds pretentious, but it's difficult to summarise the plot of something that's supposed to be nasty <u>and</u> funny. Will you write me at the above address when you've read this; and I do hope you can do something about it. Details, if any, until then.

Sincerely,

Dylan Thomas

TO T. W. EARP

February ? 1944

Far End,

Bosham,

Sussex

Dear Tommy:

Everything went wrong last lost London meeting. Jobs came up and Tennant fell down and I couldn't reach the Ladder and Tennant couldn't remember if it was the Ladder we were to reach and I looked-in at the Antelope and it drawled with moustaches. An awful day. Now we're moved to a house in Bosham—very nice, too, looking over water and perhaps Russell Flint—but I'm keeping the Manresa Studio on. I'll be up in London twice or more a week, but always on payday Fridays. Let me know, at Film Centre 34 Soho Square, when you're coming up. We must meet.

Almost as important—but perhaps a thing to be talked about when we meet in London—is that Petersfield is on the main London line from Bosham. Isn't Petersfield your market-town? And I would, I would like to meet there one morning.

Please don't forget to write. We have a dog now.

Dylan

TO T. W. EARP

postmarked 13th April 1944

Far End.

Saturday.

Bosham,

Sussex

Dear Tommy,

Very very disappointed I couldn't manage our Petersfield meeting. Donald wired urgently for my help on the rebuilding of Coventry

Cathedral, so I had to hurry up and help him rebuild it in Henekey's. I do hope the wire, my wire, reached you before you started out.

When can the next date be, in Petersfield? Tuesday would suit me, this coming Tuesday, admirably, at the same time, 12.20, in church or pub opposite. Would it suit you? There'll be no cathedral-call this time; a country-town few hours would be very pleasant.

I'm looking forward, so is Caitlin, to your coming down here. I have found some nice places, and there are no Pauls or Ninas, however goodhearted, at all: only the worst people I've ever met and not to talk to. Grand if I could bring you back here with me after Tuesday's Petersfield. Write or wire about Tuesday.

And will you ask May, please, about Bosham, and send her my love?

I have poems to bring on Tuesday, and hope Pera has been busy too.

Yours,
Dylan

MSS.: Ohio

TO T. W. EARP

Far End,
Bosham,
Sussex

Sunday 15 or 16 April '44

Dear Tommy:

It was distressing not to meet you so many times. I can't remember in detail how we missed each other so successfully; once, I think I wired confirmation of a wrong Petersfield date too late, and, by going to town, missed your wire confirming the right one. Then I was sent to Coventry, a visit of a few days which confused things for many more, and went to a wedding, and had such a fall into melancholy I couldn't even get round to Lysol or the utility blade but could only whimper in bed and fail to understand detective stories. In one communication you too hinted at the coming on of coma from which I hope you've now recovered enough to meet either this Tuesday or this Friday. On Tuesday I shall be, anyway, but with hope, in Mooney's Cambridge College from half past twelve. On Friday I can be anywhere you like at any after-twelve time if you'll write, or wire, before then to Bosham. But Tuesday will be best, of course, because it is nearest.

Here is a poem in three parts. One part, the second, I've already shown you in London when I probably forgot to mention that it was incomplete. Also another short poem. I would love to hear what you think about them when, at last, our bi-paths join in some coal-hole, some cheese-hole, or in any other reputable and, almost essential, acquaintanceless sewer.

Yours,

Dylan

MSS.: Ohio

For reasons given in the introduction I have included in this selection very few of Dylan's letters to Vernon Watkins. The note that follows is by Vernon Watkins, and is reprinted, with his permission, from *Dylan Thomas: Letters to Vernon Watkins*. Dot is one of Vernon Watkins's sisters.

'After a long deferred service I had left for the Air Force in December 1941. Although we continued to keep in touch, and to see each other fairly frequently, I lost all the letters that came during the next two and a half years.

Dan, mentioned in paragraph 7 of the next letter, is Dylan's lifelong friend, Dr Daniel Jones, the composer, whose Fourth Symphony is dedicated to his memory. His parents lived in a house in Swansea called "Warmley", the house described in the *Portrait Of The Artist* story, "The Fight".

The poem referred to in paragraph 8 is "Ceremony After A Fire Raid", a printed cutting of which accompanied this letter.'

TO VERNON WATKINS

27 July 1944

Dear Vernon,

I didn't think it was so long since we saw each other, or since I wrote to you. We were three months in Sussex, and two months near Beaconsfield. So it's nearly half a year and what a year and what a pity and what the hell. We must (always my fault that we haven't) write regularly to each other now, if only to report that a little tepid blood is still trickling, that there is still a faint stir somewhere in the chest, that we can still put pen to paper, paper to bottom, thumb to nose, the world to rights, two and two together, put and take.

The Sussex months were beastly. When it wasn't soaking wet, I was. Aeroplanes grazed the roof, bombs came by night, police by day, there were furies at the bottom of my garden, with bayonets, and a floating dock like a kidney outside the window, and Canadians in the bushes, and Americans in the hair; it was a damned banned area altogether. They worshipped dogs there, too, and when a pom was born in one house the woman put out the Union Jack.

Near Beaconsfield, where Chesterton sat on his R.C., it was better. We stayed with a man who runs the film company I fool for, and the country was green and okay, but the well-off people were dry and thin and grieved over their petrolless motorcars and played bridge like ferrets, and the poor snarled and were all named Body.

Now we're with my mother and father in Llangain, near Llanstephan, where everyone goes into the pubs sideways, & the dogs piss only on backdoors, and there are more unwanted babies shoved up the chimneys than there are used french letters in the offertory boxes. It's a mean place but near Laugharne where we will go next week.

Is Dot in Carmarthen? Let me know. We'd love to see her.

I've found that I can do most of my filmwork outside London, (which soon will be shelled terribly by things that scream up into the stratosphere, passing the queen bees, and then roar down on to Manresa Road), and so we are looking, again, for somewhere to live in the country. In Laugharne, if possible. In Wales, preferably. And we'll stay here, getting on my father—for he's one bald nerve—until we find a house, a flat, a room, a sty, a release.

By the way, I have a new complaint. Itching feet. There is nothing to see, the feet just itch. I have to take my shoes off many times a day and rub the soles with my socks. Ask Dan if he knows what it is—he's learned in little woes. How is Dan? I'd write to him but have lost his address. Ask him to write to me; I feel very Warmley to him all the time, and would very much love to hear.

Here is a poem (printed in 'Our Time') which perhaps you haven't seen. I didn't print the Lorca lines above the poem. Will you tell me about it? It really is a Ceremony, and the third part of the poem is the music at the end. Would it be called a voluntary, or is that only music at the beginning?

Keidrych & Lynette are in Llanybri. Lynette, who cannot read Welsh, is revising the standard nineteenth-century book on Welsh Prosody, and also annotating a work on the Hedgerows of Carmarthenshire. I hope she becomes famous, and that they will name an insect after her.

I am writing poems, and have three new ones I'll send you when they are typewritten and after I have heard from you about the Ceremony.

Write very soon, please, & tell me everything.

Love,
Dylan

MSS.: *British Museum*

Dylan and Caitlin had returned to Wales in the late summer of 1944, and had rented a bungalow at New Quay, Cardiganshire. They remained there for the better part of a year, though Dylan was frequently in London, in connection with his film work and, later, the B.B.C. broadcasts.

Pera is an anagram of Earp.

Philmayicity House is a typically elaborate pun. One of the buildings in which Dylan worked was called Magicity House. Phil Lindsay, the historical novelist, was a close friend who also worked there. May was Mrs Earp, but Phil May was also the famous cartoonist.

Donald is Donald Taylor, then running Gryphon Films, the successor company to Strand Films; Heard is Gerald Heard, the mystic who had emigrated to Hollywood; Peter de Polnay is a well-known novelist, who was at this time frequenting many of the same bars as Dylan.

Ockham was where T. W. Earp was living at this time.

TO T. W. EARP

Majoda,
New Quay,
Cardiganshire

September 1st 1944

So much meux has flowed under the bridges
You could drown London town, which would be just,
Since we met in the spring and drank religious.
If we don't meet again I shall throw away my trust.
And bitter's gone up and bombs have come down
Since Pera and pal like a pair of mouse
Squeaked in the liquorish wainscots of the town
And thumbed their whiskers at Philmayicity House.
It's a long way from London, as the fly bombs,
And nothing of Donald's guile can lug me
Away from this Wales where I sit in my combs
As safe and snug as a bugger in Rugby.
We've got a new house and it's called Majoda.
Majoda, Cards, on the Welsh-speaking sea.
And we'll stay in this wood-and-asbestos pagoda
Till the blackout's raised on London and on me.
But meet we must before the dove of peace
Drops in my eye his vain and priggish turd
And England's full of cultural police,
(For you, at once, a sentence of three months Heard,
For me a year on bread and de Polnay, Peter),
And verse inspectors kick up a mingy din

Demanding, at pistol point, to read your metre,
And oh the significant form troops mincing in!
How shall we meet, then, since countries lie between
The Rimbaud of Ockham and Swansea's Villon?
O fly the miles in Stephenson's machine
And spend a month with

Yours ever
Dylan

MSS.: Ohio

TO T. W. EARP

postmarked 21st September 1944,
Cardiganshire

Dear Tommy, please, from far, sciatic Kingsley
Borrow my eyes. The darkening sea flings Lea
And Perrins on the cockled tablecloth
Of mud and sand. And, like a sable moth,
A cloud against the glassy sun flutters his
Wings. It would be better if the shutters is
Shut. Sinister dark over Cardigan
Bay. No-good is abroad. I unhardy can
Hardly bear the din of No-good wracked dry on
The pebbles. It is time for the Black Lion
But there is only Buckley's unfrisky
Mild. Turned again, Worthington. Never whisky.
I sit at the open window, observing
The salty scene and my Playered gob curving
Down to the wild, umbrella'd, and french lettered
Beach, hearing rise slimy from the Welsh lechered
Caves the cries of the parchs and their flocks. I
Hear their laughter sly as gonococci. . . .
There stinks a snoop in black. I'm thinking it
Is Mr. Jones the Cake, that winking-bit,
That hymning Gooseberry, that Bethel-worm
At whose ball-prying even death'll squirm
And button up. He minces among knickers,
That prince of pimps, that doyen of dung-lickers.
Over a rump on the clerical-grey seashore,
See how he stumbles. Hallelujah hee-haw!
His head's in a nest where no bird lays her egg.
He cuts himself on an elder's razor leg.

Sniff, here is sin! Now must he grapple, rise:
He snuggles deep among the chapel thighs,
And when the moist collection plate is passed
Puts in his penny, generous at last.

On Saturday Augustus comes, bearded
Like Cardy's bard, and howling as Lear did.
A short stay only but oh, how nice. No
One more welcome than the oaktrunked maestro—
No-one but you who'll never come unless
I send the million-miscarriaged Welsh Express,
A train of thought run on wheels within wheels.
But on October 1 I show my heels
To New Quay, Cards, and then shall brave V.2.
And come to London. Remember me to
May. Is there a chance of one I never see
Coming up, also? Write me: Ever,

D.

Dylan was at this time adapting *Twenty Years A-Growing* by Maurice O'Sullivan as a feature film for Donald Taylor to produce. He never finished it.

Another film company had offered him terms to write a script about Dickens. Donald Taylor eventually took this over, too, but the script was never written.

TO DONALD TAYLOR

Gryphon Films,
2–6 West Street,
W.C.2.

28 October 1944

Dear Donald,

Now who could be writing to you from Gryphon? Why, bless my soul, it's the little Welsher. This is only to thank you for your wire, and to tell you that though work on 20 Years has been going so slowly and badly that at one time I thought we'd have to alter the title to 40 Years, now I believe I can get ahead with it properly. Reason for the badness and slowness is that this little bungalow is no place to work in when there's a bawling child there too: the rooms are tiny, the walls bumpaper-thin, and a friend arrived with another baby with a voice like Caruso's. Now, however, I have just taken a room in a nearby house: a very quiet room where I know I can work till I bleed. So little's been done on 20 Years—I've spent my time running out to look at the sea, away from the greater sea of noise within—it's not really worth discussing or sending. But now I shall get down to it with axe, concentration, and blow-lamp.

I hope the censors have finally come to heel. Let me know what happens from time to time about all our films, made, halfmade, unmade, readymade, secondhand, if you can.

A very nice fellow here, who runs a Nautical School, asked me how to get 16 mm films to show. All kinds: they're tough boys. I asked him to get in touch with you, who would—I hoped—tell him, in turn, who to get in touch with. Hope you can help.

How are things? Have a drink for me, only make it beer, as a new resolution, now a fortnight, nearly, old, has banned all other drinks—for a long time, I trust and believe.

Ever,

Dylan

Will write again soon, with *much more encouraging Twenty Years* news.

MSS.: Lockwood Memorial Library, Buffalo

Oscar Williams was an American poet, perhaps better known as an anthologist. He had a great admiration for Dylan's poems and for some years had acted as a sort of unpaid agent for him in the United States. His own first volume of poems, published in 1940, was entitled *The Man Coming Towards You.*

TO OSCAR WILLIAMS

As from
Gryphon Films,
Guild House,
2–6 West St.,
London, W.

31 December 44

Dear Oscar,

The signed anthology for 1942 has arrived, and the Man has come Towards me. Thank you very much for both. I haven't yet read more than a scattered few of the poems in your own book, stopping with delight and surprise at many knock-me-down lines, and shan't try to write anything to you until I have read the whole book carefully, and more than once, through from torpedo to cloudburst. Of the 1944 anthology I like a great deal. I like all that I have read of Alfred Hayes: has he had a book out there? And Shapiro's poem, and most of W. R. Rodgers', and, as always, the lovely poems of my friend Vernon Watkins (who certainly should be published in book-form in America). And much more, of course. I don't agree with you at all about Timothy Corsellis, and think that you have anthologised, in Henry Treece's poem, two of the worst lines since man began to write:

> 'And the green shark-cradles
>   with their swift
> Cruel fingers settling the
>   ocean's curls.'

Treece has written his own criticism in one almost comparably bathetic line: 'In the beginning was the bird'.

Oh yes, and while I'm feeling like that, let me curse you to the company, eternally, of novelists and actors for tacking on to the end of my poem, 'When I Awoke' the last verse of my poem, 'On A Wedding Anniversary'. I do not like either poem, but they are better apart. I expect a printed apology and an orange.

I am looking forward to a few cheques from magazines to which you sent my new poems. Thank you so much. I'm very glad to be able to send things to you, knowing that you'll get them printed. I am extremely poor at the moment; there is no chance of getting any money out of poetry in this country, no Guggenheims, no literary dibbers, only a few magazines, which pay nothing or a pound, and a handful of greyfaced young men with private incomes, weasely habits, and no inclination to give one anything but melancholia or dysentry.

I'll try to write something on war and poetry during the next week, but can't promise anything. I shan't know until I start writing whether I have clear ideas on this, or on any other, subject. I prefer what I think about verse to be in the verse.

I meet Dunstan Thompson sometimes in London, and find him quite charming. I asked him what you yourself were like & he made an elegant movement of his long sea-green hands, signifying, to me, nothing but the efforts of a man to play the flute without using his mouth.

Thank you, again, for the books & the good wishes, & for sending my poems around.

It is the last evening of the bad year and I am going out to celebrate myself sick and dirty.

Make what you can of 1945.

I shall try to write soon, sending the letter by airmail (or in a sealed man).

Yours,

Dylan

MSS.: Harvard

'B. & H.' are Burke and Hare, the body-snatchers in *The Doctor and the Devils*. James Bridie had written a play on this same subject, *The Anatomist*, and Dylan and Donald Taylor were anxious to avoid any appearance of plagiarism.

TO DONALD TAYLOR

8 February 1945 Majoda, New Quay

Dear Donald,

I feel very badly about it that our conversation some evenings ago should have disturbed you, and I do apologise now and immediately, knowing that the disturbing influence was, however it sounded, quite unintentional. I can only say that I'd just come out of a gastric chamber, had had a few hurried drinks to see if I were still alive, and then spoke to you, not in a quiet box as I usually do when I ring up, but against a background of maudlin sea-captains and shrewd, if stunned, travellers in petrol. One ear was hearing you and the other ear busy shutting out the buzzing of those Cardy drones, and I spoke, I know, hurriedly and stupidly. Please take no notice of what I said about Labour: I'm proud to be asked to try to do the script; my only fear is that I shall not do a very good job of it. I am not, as you know, politically very acute, and will have to rely, as always, upon emotionalism. But I will send off the opening sequences in a few days, and you will be able to tell from them whether I should go on alone with the scripting or whether I should work at it closely with you and, alone, do only the dialogue (whose indications we could map out together) and the descriptive-visual writing. Another reason for my unfortunate—and, again, really unmeant—disturbing conversation was that I was enormously pleased by the good news of the Suffer Little Children film, and very keen on getting on with it at once. I

271

know the short films have to be done, and I am sorry that I gave the impression of wanting to get away from them; it is, of course, the big-scale film of ideas that we both wish to work at, work hard and work soon, but Labour, too, is a job of work and I have, in my proper self, no intention of trying to escape it. I do want to say again that I think Suffer Little Children a superlative idea, and I am longing to talk about it in detail and around it, to discuss it at great length with you, and to work upon it as soon as possible and to produce the completed script more quickly than any other we have done. I'll come up as soon as you want me, but you will have the opening Labour sequences in your hands first. Sorry again. What news of B. & H.? I think I forgot to tell you the new name I had thought of for Dr. Robert Knox: Thomas Rock. This is very near, in vowels and general feeling, to the original, and does, I think satisfy Bridie's complaint: it does sound the name of a man who could be very distinguished and great in science. What do you think?

Let me know if you wish me to ring you again soon; and this time I shall choose the privacy of a public booth not the propinquity of a public bar.

Ever,

Dylan

I have just finished reading—and will send on under separate cover —the autobiography, called The Islandman, of Thomás Ó Crohan (The Blaskets, 1856–1937). It is the very first book about the Blaskets, written in 1926, published 1929. Ó Crohan was, apparently, a great and famous man, a Celtic scholar and authority, and lived all his eighty-one years on the Blaskets. It is most extraordinary that O'Sullivan makes no mention of him: he was, of course, very much alive on the Island all the time O'Sullivan was living there. It is also very odd that George Thompson should study Irish under a boy like O'Sullivan when there was already on the Island an acknowledged (by Yeats and everyone else interested in the folklore and the language) Irish scholar and taleteller. There is no mention, either, of O'Sullivan in Ó Crohan's book.

The Islandman, Twenty Years, and Robin Flower's own book— The West Island, is it?—represent all the available written literature of and upon the Blaskets: literature, that is, of general appeal, for there must be many, and probably untranslated, essays and papers on folk-lore, dialect, etc., etc., written by visiting scholars. But we should be able, from those three books, to tell the story of life on the Island in its entirety. I do not suggest that we use the actual material of Ó

Crohan's and Flower's books, but that we study them as background. I should very much like to see a copy of Flower's when I come up to town.

D.

MSS.: Lockwood Memorial Library, Buffalo

·

Betty and Sophie were the two principal characters in a script, *Suffer Little Children*, which Dylan was at this time writing for Donald Taylor. The film was never made, though part of the dialogue was later used in the Diana Dors film, *Good Time Girl*.

The Lion is the Black Lion, a pub in New Quay which Dylan frequented.

The introduction to Selected Writings was eventually written by J. L. Sweeney.

TO DONALD TAYLOR

Tuesday, 27 March 1945   Majoda,
                                                              New Quay

Dear Donald,

Today, limp in the hut, watching the exhausting sea, lost in our Betty—Betty dark?—drowned in our Sophie—Sophie fair?—but writing little until tomorrow, first, cold thing in the morning, with the dew on the grass, and the Captains in bed, and the trees talking double rook. I was so sorry you went back. Did you get a sleeper? And even the Captain is gone, with all his wheezy rumbling as though he were trying to bring up from his cavernous inside a very old, rusty, seaweedy anchor. Frank sparkles still, but the Lion lies down. This is only to say (1) I hope you'll be back soon, (2) I do hope you can, somehow, manage a little money this week, by some not-so-verity ruse, (3) I'll work as hard as I know on the synopsis or whatever we call it, as long as we call it good, and (4) Please don't forget to have a shot at doing those 'personal' thousand words for the introduction to my American Selected Writing. Let me see what you bang out. If you're too busy, I can ask Tommy E. to do something, but I hope you aren't. You've got Laughlin's letter, haven't you? He wants the thing very, very, very soon. Let me know.

Tomorrow morning I shall be fit as a tuba again, and will work, work, work,

Ever,
Dylan

MSS.: Lockwood Memorial Library, Buffalo

Even before the war was over Dylan was trying to get to America.

Majoda,
New Quay,
Cardiganshire,
Wales

March 28 '45

Dear Oscar,

Many thanks for the letter and for Poetry's cheque. I'm very glad you don't mind sending my stuff to the magazines. Here are another five poems: one longish one, four short ones. The longish one, I'm glad to say, has taken a great deal of time and trouble, and has prevented me from writing filmscripts on Rehabilitation, Better Housing, Post War Full Employment, etc. for the socialist film department of the Ministry of Information. If it surprises you that the Ministry, or any Ministry, have a socialist department, I can say that none of the scripts approved by that department get further than the next where they are shelved among a million dead ideas and periodically reshuffled by dead young men with briar pipes that are never lit in the office but which they always have protruding from their mouths like the cocks of swallowed bodies. By such so-quickly-to-be-buried work I earn enough to live on if I do without what I most like. So I'd love a little ladleful from the gravy pots over there—a lick of the ladle, the immersion of a single hair in the rich shitbrown cauldron—though naturally I expect nothing. It is very very good of you to try to fish something up for me. In this country, it would be the skull of a boiled fawner who, smelling the gravy steam, fell in and died, to the especial pleasure of his mother who had borne him piping. The war, they say, is all over bar the dying; and, when it is, I want to come over to America. How could I earn a living? I can read aloud, through sonorous asthma, with pomp; I can lecture on the Trend of Y, or X at the Crossroads, or Z: Whither? with an assurance whose shiftiness can be seen only from the front row; I can write script and radio films, of a sort; I can—and so on with the list that could be, and is, supplied by every person fit for nothing but his shameful ability to fit into the hack ends of commercial, intellectual, or personal, advertisement. I hope you'll get the five poems printed. Perhaps 2 or 3 of the short ones together in one magazine? You know. I hope you like them, or some of them. I've forgotten if the address you have of mine is the one at the top of this letter or the one of the Gryphon Film Company. If it is Gryphon, please do use that when—and I do hope you do, soon—you write. That is more-or-less permanent. The Welsh address I leave, for nowhere, some time in June. My poems are coming out this spring and, though by that time you will have seen all the poems in it—several, however, in very altered versions—I'll send it on at once. I'm looking forward to yours, and to the War Poets. Laughlin is bringing out a 'Selected Writing' of mine—when, I don't know—with a critical introduction by J. L. Sweeney. Though I know his name, I don't know his writing. It is very lovely here; I have a shack at the edge of the cliff where my children hop like fleas in a box—in London, the only remaining flea-circus I have seen is pushed about the streets in one half of a child's pram—and my wife grumbles at me and them and the sea for the mess we all make, and I work among cries and clatters like a venomous beaver in a parrot house. A letter full of nothing.

Yours,

Dylan

MSS.: Harvard

The script referred to in this letter is *Suffer Little Children.* The trial was that of a man who had threatened, and indeed attempted, to murder Dylan. The story of this sad little incident, so far as it can at present be told, will be found in my biography of the poet.

TO DONALD TAYLOR

10th April 1945

Majoda,

New Quay

Tuesday.

Dear Donald,

I'm sorry that my telephone calls are always about the same dear little thing, but I can't help it. I just can't get straight, ever since five pounds was, quite justly, deducted from my weekly pay, the week you were down. I really am in a mess, and am likely to get in more of one. And I must say that I can't live on eight pounds a week. Can't. Ten is hard enough to get on with, with a pound worth about eight shillings, but eight pounds is impossible, and I don't know what to do. If only somehow one could manage until this film is sold—as it really should be, it seems to me to have everything. But on eight a week, one can't. It means I cannot do anything that requires more than about a pound;

I can't get Llewelyn down for this incredible April, I can't buy a pair of trousers though my bum is bare to the sun, I can't join a library, and I shouldn't even smoke. All the eight, or even, really, the ten, does, is to pay rent, food, oil, and coal. Enough? No. Christ no. There are a hell of a lot of other essential things, and I can't get them. And, once in debt for anything over a pound or so—as I am, as I am—that debt can never be paid, and grows and grows into proportions beyond any hope. All this is, I know, familiar to you; but things have reached a climax for me, and I can't go on with this amount of money. I don't know what the hell to do, and wish to the Lord we could fix something together. I've got such great faith in the films we'll make together, it seems so silly to be grumbling about money now when, soon, we should be crinkling all over. But there it is.

I hope the script will be finished in a week. The trial, necessitating my getting my mother here from another county to look after the children, hindered it a lot; as all this petty hell about money is still doing. But I do think: a week. I'll send it off with notes; there are, I think, four or five sticky constructional points, but I have only in one case altered a constructional detail from our original. I have, too, cut out the jewels in the empty house that B. and S. and the boy break into. It seems to be too forced, too much of a coincidence, that Betty's downfall should come, both times, through jewels left so absurdly open for anyone to take. So I think that just 'breaking and entering' is enough to send B. and S. to School for three years. Other suggestions etc. I'll write about at length when I send the complete MS.

Sorry for most of this letter, but I had to say it. And I still don't know what to do.

Ever.

Dylan

MSS.: Lockwood Memorial Library, Buffalo

Blaen-Cwm where this next letter was written was a pair of semi-detached cottages near Llanstephan. Dylan's parents now lived in one, his uncle, Bob Williams, in the other.

Theodore Spencer, poet, was teaching at Harvard.

TO OSCAR WILLIAMS

as from
Gryphon,
Guild House,
2–6 West St.,
London W.C.2.

July 30. 1945

My dear Oscar,

Many thanks for many things.

For the cheques from periodicals, they couldn't have been more welcome, they seethed in their envelopes, which sounds like Lawrence, and burst in a shower of drinks and cabrides and small hospitalities to the dour and filmy mackintoshed bar-flies who work, or don't, with me.

For the anthologies, all of them so heavy and in such large lovely type, so dear, and with such lovely ladies and gentlemen to be seen out at the back: all portentously smoking (the pipes of bedpan), prinking, profiling, horizon-eying, open-collared and wild-haired in the photographers' wind, facing America and posterity and the music, shy as professional novelists caught accidentally in an arc-lamp, framed against rock and ruin, musing in cactused, glass-haired, first-editioned, (ooh, Cyril, a Kafka's missing), Paul-kleed brown studies, some smelling visibly of just-a-little-rice-and-bamboo-shoot-dish-my-wife-found-in-Mexico, or of peanut butter and homebrewed cider, some painted, some by painters, some by themselves, some just painted, one self-drenched and solemn under a coat of Celtic jam, one bow-tied to his explosive cross, the pin-up poets, oh how I love you all.

For your own book of poems. You've let down your hair, hard and loud on the one real ground, and sometimes you fall over it into a boiling black Belsen of your own. The poems never relax or play fair or explain or whine about their condition or are ashamed, but conduct their prolific unpretty lives in front of the nose of your nerves. They are pieces that fly, hot and violent and exuberantly unhappy, off a poem in the making. The wheels go round, crying, protesting, denying, on rails that are laid out only as the wheels express towards them. The rules, the form, spring up urgently as the temper of making needs them.

For your letters, too long unanswered but cherished next to my heart, hair, identity disk, razorscar from a Poetry Tea, the tattooed hoofprints of Dali's mother—It is hysterical weather where I am writing, Blaen Cwm, Llangain, Carmarthenshire, Wales, in a breeding-box in a cabbage valley, in a parlour with a preserved sheepdog, where mothballs fly at night, not moths, where the Bible opens itself at Revelations; and is there money still for tea? My son, in the nonstop probably frog-filled rain, is performing what seems, from this distance, to be an unnatural act with a beaver. Looking closer, I see he is only destroying his sister's doll—the little pixie. I can hear, from far off, my Uncle Bob drinking tea and methylated spirits through eighty years of nicotine-brown fern. My father, opposite, is reading about Hannibal through a magnifying glass so small he can see only one word at a time. I could lie down and live with Hannibals. And my wife is washing an old opera.

For the crust you offer in America. It is already nibbled, and I am the mice. Hands, and teeth, across the ocean.

For reading this.

Next morning. Still raining, and not daffodils. A farmyard outside the window, sows and cows and the farmer's daughters, what a day of dugs. I've been reading all Lawrence's poems, some aloud to no-one in this bombazine room, and liking them more & more. Do you remember:

O the green glimmer of apples in the orchard,
Lamps in a wash of rain!
O the wet walk of my brown hen through the stackyard!
O tears on the window pane!

Nothing now will ripen the bright green apples
Full of disappointment and of rain;
Brackish they will taste, of tears, when the yellow dapples
Of autumn tell the withered tale again.

All around the yard it is cluck! my brown hen.
Cluck! and the rain-wet wings;
Cluck! my marigold bird, and then
Cluck! for your yellow darlings.

Yes, there's his brown hen cluck in the gambo-swished mud, scratching for Christ, cackling in droppings, Gladys's pet lamb-now-sheep follows her maa-ing for poor, unloved Gladys's unmade milk, an Italian prisoner is scraping hay off a hedge, one Fontamara-brown-sly-innocent eye in the back of his head fixed on her black bloomered bottom as she bends to scatter grain for the yellow darlings. The rainy robins tic tac at the pane. Over the hill, the hoarse noise of a train carrying holes to Hugh's Castle. Near, a grey gulled estuary, and sheepshanks, corpses of cats, cowteeth, bottles of ether, jellyfish, frenchletters, indecipherable messages in jars (the secret of the Marie Celeste, the Number of the Beast, the name of Cain's wife, pyramid riddles, Tibetan acrostics, next year's newspapers) on the foreshore. I'm trying to establish my geography. Up the hill lane behind this house too full of Thomases, a cottage row of the undeniably mad unpossessed peasantry of the inbred crooked county, my cousins, uncles, aunts, the woman with the gooseberry birthmark who lies with dogs, the farm labourer who told me that the stream that runs by his cottage side is Jordan water and who can deny him, the lay preacher who believes that the war was begun only to sell newspapers which are the devil's sermon-sheets, the man who when his pony could work no longer because of old age, hanged it on an apple-tree to save a bullet, the woman who cries out 'Cancer!' as you pass her open door.

I should have written long before this, but couldn't bring myself to write only Thank You so very much for distributing my poems and for the sweet money, or to send you grunts of salutation from my trough. I have been trying to find out what legal etc. complications I will have to go through before leaving this country for America. First of all, because I have no financial independence, I have to be assured—or, rather, the American Embassy over here will have to be assured—that, on arriving in America, there is a job, or there are jobs, waiting for me; that I will not become a liability to the United States. There must be a sponsor, or sponsors, who will sign a declaration saying that I & my independents will not be allowed to become liabilities. So what is my first step? The American Embassy has given me several printed forms to be sent to whoever I imagine will employ me in the States & guarantee me a living. If I send those official forms to you, could you do anything about them? That is, could you approach TIME—whom you suggested as possible employers, if only for part of my time—and get some definite promise, however small, from them? If that could be arranged, then, after the returning to the American Embassy here of the signed 'We-won't-let-the-bugger-starve' declaration, and after the final examinations, interviews, and okayings, physical & political, I could sail within three months. So that, supposing with your help some job, appointment etc. could be fixed, I should be able to arrive a Migrained Father, in the early spring of next year. I have not yet written to Theodore Spencer, because I have lost your letter with his address in it, and with the particulars of the work he might be able to give me in Harvard. Also, I did not quite know how to approach him. I have found that he is an old friend of a very old friend of mine here, Augustus John, who sends him every greeting and asks him to do what he can. Perhaps Augustus has already written, I wouldn't know, when I saw him last he was chasing a woman in uniform through the Zoo, horned & goat-bearded. If Spencer could assure me—that is, again, if he could assure, on a form I could send you to send him, the Embassy here that Harvard will engage me in any lecturing or librarying—of some work, it would work wonders. Otherwise, a patron would do just as well, to say that he will look after me & mine in luxury, New York, or even in a kennel, Texas. I should most like to read, library, or lecture at Harvard. Time & Harvard. A promise of work from T & H from next spring on would settle, I think, everything—apart from money to travel with, & this I must try to rake up from the gutters in which I pretend to work. I'm asking you a lot, causing you bother, heaping responsibilities on your shoulders, prematurely crust-gulping. Will you do what you can? If you say yes, I will send the Embassy forms to you straightaway. I shall not write to Spencer until I hear from you.

I should bring my wife, my son aged now $6\frac{1}{2}$, my daughter aged now $2\frac{1}{2}$. Their names are Llewelyn and Aeronwy. They are quite nice hell. My wife's name is Caitlin, she is Irish. We would all come together because I do not want to return to this country for a long time.

The rain has stopped, thank Jesus. Have the Socialists-in-power-now stopped it? An incometax form flops through the window, the letterbox is choked with dockleaves. Let's get out, let's get out.

Later. I have been out. I went to the Edwinsford Arms, a sabbath-dark bar with a stag's head over the Gents and a stuffed salmon caught by Shem and a mildewed advertisement for pre-1914 tobacco and a stain on the wall, just above my head, that I hoped was beer. I had some beer with a man who said he was shot in the groin in the last war, and who, unable to have a woman ever since, blames it on the dirty Jews. He said, 'Look, what they did, the moochin', and showed me a scar on his calf. I said that I thought he said he had been shot through the groin. 'And the calf, and the calf', he said in a terrible temper. 'And the calf, the bloody yids.' He is an official in some Department—a Department set-built for the early German films—that investigates the authenticity of discharged soldiers' pension-claims. 'Every time I see "Psycho-neurosis" on a discharge paper, I say, Lead-Swinger.' He told me the best way to boil lobsters, which was detailed and painful. I told him Norman Douglas's recipe for raping a dog: catch the dog, open the drawer of a desk, put the dog's head in the open drawer, and then close the drawer. He told me how he had once made a child of six drunk. It began to rain again, great wrathful drops. We parted enemies. I rode back on a bicycle through the justice-must-be-done-let's-rain-on-sinners rain, and the bicycle wheels through the pools & slush on the roads asked the same monotonous & inane questions as the boiler-pipes once asked Gorki: Have you got any rubber? Do you want some fish? Cows under crying roadside trees, looking over the estuary, weed and webfoot mud, waited for Royal Academicians. Snails were coming out; A P.E.N. Club of slugs crossed the road; Manchester, Manchester, fetch a pocket handkerchief, said the engine over the hill; you could hear little boys in desolate back-gardens facing the depressed water slapping each other on the stomach.

And back to a cardtable holding up a jamjar full of cigarette-ends, the rough draft of a ten minute film on the Kitchen Front, your War Poetry anthology, a spool of film showing a pair of hands over a sink, Why Birds Sing, Llewellyn's Stampalbum, the large sheet of paper with the first line of a poem at the top: 'O'. I must, this week, at this table, finish the Kitchen Front, write a broadcast talk to be called 'Memories of Christmas' for the Children's Hour, write a begging letter to a Sir, write another line to come after 'O', fill up my £1000 People's Crossword, observe ill-nature, stop doodling, be natural, not sniff, not put ash in my coatpocket, remember that we all are brothers—'but not a trace of foul equality, nor sound of still more foul human perfection'. You need not clear the world like a cabbage patch for me. Leave me my nettles, let me fight the wicked, obstreperous weeds myself, & put them in their place. I don't at all want to annihilate them, I like a row with them, but I won't be put on a cabbage-idealistic level with them. I don't agree. Judy O'Grady and the Colonel's Lady and Lamarr Hedy and the Workers' Mayday, we're all bothers and blisters under unoriginal sins. For Whom Omar's Bowl Tells. The Censury of the Common Man. All Men My Enemies. O God, O Aren't we all.

I liked the War Poetry immensely. Everything I liked, much I didn't know. I could have done with some Lawrence though.

> Surely you've trod straight
> To the very door!
> You have surely achieved your fate;
> And the perfect dead are elate
> To have won once more.

281

Now to the dead you are giving
Your last allegiance.
But what of us who are living,
And fearful yet of believing
In your pitiless legions?

But probably no, he is too unequal. Thank you for the two copies one for each age. And I don't like the verses I have quoted above, either. Some of the contributors' views on War & Poetry I was glad to read; by others, especially by Treece's, appalled. War can't produce poetry, only poets can, and war can't produce poets either because they bring themselves up in such a war that this outward bang, bang of men against men is something they have passed a long time ago on their poems' way towards peace. A poet writing a poem is at peace with everything except words, which are eternal actions; only in the lulls between the warring work on words can he be at war with men. Poets can stop bullets, but bullets can't stop poets. What is a poet anyway? He is a man who has written or is writing what he, in his utmost human fallible integrity, necessarily communal, believes to be good poetry. As he writes good poetry very rarely, he is most often at peace with the eternal actions of words and is therefore very likely to be caught up in any bang bang that is going. When he is fighting, he is not a poet. Nor is a craftsman a craftsman. I think capital-lettered War can only in subject matter affect poetry. Violence and suffering are all the time, & it does not matter how you are brought up against them. And so on. But this is all vague and loose, like myself this rainy moment, and all I want to say before we bid a reluctant farewell to colourful Carmarthenshire is : Thank you again for books, periodicals, letters, cheques, friendship, and the help I know, I hope, you will give me in trying to get to America—which can succeed only if the authorities are informed that a position or positions—cut-glass for job or jobs—is or are waiting me in America, in your more-than-European idealism, like a be-aureoled bleached skeleton hovering its cage-ribs in the social heaven, beneficient. Lawrence again; oh leave me, you talking prick; oh to be where the Lady Loverlies shatter and the blackguards ride no more. Write soon.

Dylan

MSS.: Harvard

By now they had given up their bungalow at New Quay. The matter of finding a home was becoming desperately important, particularly since Gryphon Films was about to be wound up, and Dylan would have to rely entirely on free-lance work, either with other film companies or with the B.B.C., which necessitated his being within reach of London.

David Tennant owned the Gargoyle in those days, a night club popular with writers and painters.

TO DAVID TENNANT

28 August 1945

as from
Gryphon,
Guild House,
2–6 West Street,
W.C.2.
TEM. 5420

My dear David,

Across the counties, from mean, green, horse-thieving Wales, I raise one Playercoloured aspen hand to salute and supplicate. The last time I saw you, you had just gone from the Prince of Wales, and who am I to blame. The rest of the day was dark, shot with fire, a humming-top of taxis and glasses, a spinning sight of scowls and leers seen through the wrong end of a telescope made of indiarubber, a rush of close-ups, strange mouths and noses flattening themselves on one's own in places that seemed to be now a turkish bath, now a lavatory, now a gymnasium for midgets, bar, hothouse, hospital, knockshop, abbatoir, crematorium, revolving cathedral and, at last, a bed only an inch from the ceiling. I'm coming to town again on Thursday, and would love to see you. This time I shall be collected, calm but gabbling, a patient on a monument: beer only, for me, for weeks, for health, forgive me, for Christ's sake, for sanity, four freedoms. Can you ring me? A City, or at least a Fleet St. morning would be lovely. Do you know of any flat, small house, in London or fairly near that I could rent? I am getting desperate now. We have to move. There has never been, for me, anything more urgent than this. I have to find somewhere to live in, if only for a few months. Do you know of anybody? Would you ask some of the people you see? God, I'd be grateful. I'm going out of my mind here, and can do no work. There must be somewhere. Do do, do do do ask and see for me, David. I can't go on like this, travelling eight hours to spend a weekend with Caitlin. We must be somewhere fairly near London, if not in it. This is the supplication I referred to at the beginning. Can you, will you, help in any way by asking any who might know, who could know, who would be kind? It is spoiling everything, having nowhere permanent to live. I want so much to work, and cannot without some certainty of surroundings. A house, a flat, two rooms. I have managed to write one new poem and will bring it up to show you when we meet, I think you will like it, it's a poem for evenings and tears. I shall look forward to you ringing. Don't forget, please. Let's hug the counters of nasty reporters' pubs, and drink to the Only Atom. I think I could lie down and live with men, they are so unplacid and so unselfcontained, they sweat and whine about their condition; I like that. I'll be, I hope, seeing you soon. Do your best for me, about finding some hole in the wind to lay down my two heads.

Everything to you.

Dylan

MSS.: The Hon. David Tennant

They came to London in the autumn, though they had nowhere to live. Llewelyn was sent to his grandmother's, at Blashford; Dylan and Caitlin and the baby, Aeronwy, stayed with friends for varying periods of time, until at last they moved into the basement flat of the house in which lived Caitlin's sister, Nicolette, and her husband, the fashionable portrait painter, Anthony Devas. They spent Christmas 1945 in Oxford as the guests of A. J. P. Taylor, the historian, and his wife Margaret.

This letter contains over three thousand words of detailed criticism of her poems, which I omit.

TO MARGARET TAYLOR

Oxford, late 1945

Holywell Ford,
Guests' Bedroom

My dear Margaret,

I was so glad to be allowed to see the poems and to keep them for such a long time: too long a time, perhaps, though we did talk about them for a little and (on my part) a mostly inarticulate minute. I kept them so long, not because I had nothing to say about them but because I had so much. I find it awfully hard to say, about another's poems, just 'I enjoyed them', or 'I didn't like them', or, humming and ha-ing, to mumble something about 'the influence of X' or how much 'you could learn from Y'. The only way I know to talk about poems—another's poems—(unless they are all perfect, which means unless they are written in Heaven with a Gabriel-winged-Waterman dipped in nectar and God's blood)—is to try to go through them in detail for sound and shape and colour. The meaning of a poem you cannot, as a poet, talk about in any way constructively: that must be left to theoreticians, logicians, philosophers, sentimentalists, etc. It is only the texture of a poem that can be discussed at all. Nobody, I think, wants to talk, either, about how a poem feels to him; he finds it emotionally moving or he doesn't; and, if he does, there's nothing to discuss except the means, the words themselves, by which this emotional feeling was aroused. It is, of course, far easier to point out what one disagrees with than it is to comment sensibly upon what one finds good. One disagrees with a line of poetry because one discovers, immediately or after re-reading, that it is not inevitable, it could be changed, the wrong words have been used, or the right words in the wrong order, indeed one changes them about in the mind as one reads; but when the inevitable line appears, what is there to say? The music is made, the magic is done, the sound and the spell remain. This is only a (I'm afraid) repetitive, pedantic, platitudinary preliminary (God help us) apology for the few comments I want to make on each of the poems. I'm very conscious of how little, if at all, I can help to make these poems, or your future poems, nearer, in texture and intensity, to what you yourself would wish them to be. I can only burble like an old bird with its beak full of bias and soap; and you can but curse yourself for ever having given your poems to such a turgid rook.

MSS.: Texas

. . . .

This letter to Vernon Watkins is also, in my opinion, suitable for inclusion in this selection. Again I quote his explanatory note:

'My paper on Wilfred Owen, written ten years earlier, which Dylan had read at Pennard, and which I later read at Oxford, had been stored in a friend's house with other things during the war, and a long search failed to produce it. It turned up again, when I was not looking for it, two or three years later.

'Alfred Janes had been, before the war, a fantastically slow painter, working seven or eight hours a day for perhaps six months at a single picture,

usually at that time a still life, a geometrical study of fish or fruit. His close
friend Tom Warner, whose musical composition had given Dylan the title
of his story "A Prospect Of The Sea", had left Swansea and was teaching
in England.'

TO VERNON WATKINS

April 27th 1946

Holywell Ford,
Oxford

My dear Vernon,

There's never been such a long time between our letters, and I hope,
atom willing, there won't be again. (Somewhere in the wet Magdalen
trees a bird makes a noise exactly like Doctor Ludwig Koch.) It's
been my fault of course, that goes without whining, but I'm heavy
with reasons like Doctor Magnus Hirschfeld.

Right below where we live—it is, I think, a converted telephone
kiosk, with a bed where the ledge for directories used to be—there is
a vole-run. (Do not tell this to Fred who said that I could not speak
for half a minute without mentioning vermin or Dracula, and that
was five years ago.) The run is so narrow that two voles cannot pass
each other. Suddenly, an elderly, broad vole with a limp came quite
fast down the run from the left just as an elderly, broader vole with a
limp came from the right. From where I am sitting, expectantly nervous
and ill like patients on an imminent, I could see what the voles were
thinking. They never stopped running as they thought, as they neared
one another. Who was to turn back? should they both turn back?
should they fight, kiss, call it a day, lie down? They never stopped
their limping running as I saw and heard the decision made. With a
wheezing like that of a little otter, with a husky squeaky updrawing
of shining arthritic legs, the elderly broader limping vole jumped over
the back of the other. Not a word was said.

We've been here about six weeks, just behind Magdalen, by river
and vole-run, very quiet, Aeronwy in a day-nursery near and sleeping
in the next-door house or house-proper, Caitlin and I going our
single way into the vegetable kingdom. I haven't worked for a long
time, apart from reading, every week, over the air to the Indians: an
audience of perhaps three, and all of them bat-or-Tambi-voiced. I'm
reading Hardy on the ordinary service on May 19th. Probably about
eleven at night. Try to remember to listen. I've written a long comic
poem, not to be published, to keep the uttermost cellarmen of depression away and to prevent my doing crosswords. I've written a few
pieces, nearly all quotations, for the Eastern radio, on Edward Thomas,

Hardy, and some others. And I'm going to do a programme on Wilfred Owen: though all my job is the selection of the poems for the professional readers to (badly, usually) read, and the interpolation of four-line comments between each. I'd love to see your essay on Owen. Could I? I'd be very careful with it and return it spotlessly un-Aeronwied. And I want to write a poem of my own again, but it's hard here with peace and no room, spring outside the window and the gas cooker behind the back, sleep, food, loud wireless, broom and brush all in one kiosk, stunted bathing-hut or square milkbottle.

About Owen: Siegfried Sassoon has a lovely chapter about him, completely new, in his latest book, Siegfried's Journey. You would like it very much.

It's strange to think of you, and Fred, and Tom sometimes, in Swansea, again. How is that blizzardly painter, that lightning artist, that prodigal canvas-stacker? Has he reached the next finbone of the fish he was dashing off before the war? Please give him my love.

And Cwmdonkin Park. I wish we were there now. Next month some-time I'm going down to see my mother, who has been very very ill, outside Carmarthen, and will stop at Swansea on the way back? Have you a little sheetless, must be sheetless, dogbox with nails for me to sleep in? Any shelter for a night? Unless you've been mending the roof. Then we could, maybe, all spend one evening together, wipey-eyed, remembering, locked in these damned days, the as-then-still-forgiven past.

You and Fred and Tom and, shame, no Dan whose future's stranger than ever, his multiplying harrassed women trailing children like seaweed, his symphonies shouldering out in his head to unplayable proportions, his officer's trousers kept up now by three safety-pins. And me too: I had a little time in hospital but I'm out again now and fit as an old potato.

Love to you all, Gwen, Rhiannon, yourself, from Caitlin, Llewelyn — in Cornwall for a month—Aeronwy and myself. Please do send a photograph of Rhiannon. And the Owen?

Dylan

MSS.: British Museum

In March 1946 they had moved to Oxford, to a one-room studio-cottage in the garden of Mr and Mrs Taylor's house. They remained there, living in acute discomfort, for a year. Dylan's principal source of income was now the B.B.C., which entailed many, usually drunken, visits to London.

I know nothing about the recipient of this letter. I include it, not only for its intrinsic interest but also because it reveals Dylan's extreme kindness to others, particularly to other poets.

TO MR KLOPPER

Holywell Ford,
Oxford
May 30th 1946

Dear Mr. Klopper,

Thank you for your letter, and for letting me see the nine short poems from your long poem to be called 'The Vision'. I meant to reply long before this, but have been away; Do forgive me: the delay wasn't caused because I could think of nothing to say about your poems, but because I had too much to say and too little time to sit down and say it. Even now, I'm very much rushed for bread-and-butter work, and can put down only a few short and, I'm afraid inadequate comments on the poems. Perhaps, if you'd be kind enough to let me see the second part of the long poem, when it is finished, I could write my own, frankly, personal, impressions of it at greater length.

Let me say, first of all, that I do appreciate the difficulties you must feel in writing poetry in a, comparatively, recently acquired language, especially when you are, as you mentioned in your letter, cut off from all literary activities. This last, in the case of a poet writing in his native language, might indeed be more of an advantage than a hindrance; but, in your case, I can see that it must be grievously hard not to be able to share, with anyone sympathetic to the writing of poetry, in some discussion of the problems that arise out of it. I can imagine that one of the gravest disadvantages you encounter is that of feeling yourself—even though temporarily, and at inevitable moments of depression and self-mistrust—incapable of appreciating how an ordinary reader of English poetry would react to the texture and movement of your words, not to their meaning (for the meaning that any poetry can convey is common to all readers and writers in every language) but to the stuff itself out of which the poetry is made. Though you may be certain of the logical development of the argument of each poem, you are, I believe, uncertain of the feel of it. Too often, unmarried words limp together towards the consummation of the last line, only to find it entirely unsatisfying, unrewarding of the intellectual passion that had forced them towards that end.

All I can say that might be interpreted as even remotely constructive is that you must endeavour to feel and weigh the shape, sound, content of each word in relation to the shape, sound, content etcetera of the words surrounding it. It isn't only the meaning of the words that must develop harmonically, each syllable adding to the single existence of the next, but it is that which also informs the words with their own particular life: the noise, that is, that they make in the air and the ear, the contours in which they lie on the page and the mind, their colours and density.

So that in these poems—no, not individual poems but pieces of poetry moving towards a poem—I see that the abstract words rarely harmonise, or live together, with the concrete. In piece I, for instance, the 'avarice of shuffling feet' is, to me, quite discordant, I always feel that one should be very reluctant of putting down any abstract words at all, or at least of abstract words that one has not previously, or is not going to later, define.

I believe, referring to the line in piece I, that it is better to put down an avaricious word, an avaricious image, than a vague abstraction, the undefined word that means so many different things to so many different people. That is, to put down something like 'where all the shuffling feet are misers' (that's only the first tentative suggestion that came into my head) rather than 'the avarice of shuffling feet'. I admit this is an absurd suggestion: I'm not attempting to rewrite your poem, God forbid, but merely to instance, concretely, something of what I mean by saying that the juxtaposition of a vague word and a particular word is, to me, nearly always satisfactory.

Later, in the second piece, I confess that I can never make anything much of such a phrase as 'the measureless depth of fears'. I like, in poems, to be told why or how this 'depth' is full of fears, and even exactly what the 'depth' is. Such a line as 'The untellable deep squid-crowded sea' would, in spite of its impromptu silliness, mean more to me.

Certain lines of the second piece I like; and the repeated lines, though they do contradict what I said about the juxtaposition of vague and particular are moving.

The opening of piece III seems, to me, to be intellectually confused, the images mixed in some sort of evocative pudding.

It is, of course, far easier to point out what one disagrees with than it is to comment sensibly upon what one finds good. One disagrees with a line of poetry because one finds that it is not inevitable, it could be changed, the wrong words, quite simply, have been used; but when the inevitable line appears, what is there to say? The music is made, the magic is done, the sound and the spell remain. And so it is easy for me to say that I find most of piece IV unreal: the words speak to a dictionary-in-the-head, even to a dictionary of synonyms for I do not believe the words to be exact, to be 'just'.

But pieces VI and VII, because the words are objects, make an immediate impact, 'Yes', one says, 'this is what it is about; he is looking through windows at the rocks; I can understand, I think his grief and transitory omnipotence'. And I think the rhythms of all the pieces could be tautened; but that tautening will emerge itself as each word is valued according to its individual life.

But how little I can help you! How profoundly difficult it is! I can only burble like an old bird with its beak full of bias and soap; and you can but curse yourself for ever having given your poetry to such a turgid rook.

Send me some more any time you like, and believe me that, in spite of what I have said or only half said, I was grateful to you for having read them.

And do let me know if you want the poems back.

Yours sincerely,
Dylan Thomas

MSS.: Charles Feinberg, Esq.

Most of his correspondence during the summer and autumn of 1946 consists of business letters: to his agent, his publishers, to various B.B.C. producers concerning future contracts and to Donald Taylor about films. There is, however, one cheerful and characteristic letter to his old friend, Dan Jones.

TO DANIEL JONES

Holywell Ford,
Oxford
Monday, June 24, 46

My dear Dan,

I've only just got, dear God, your letter. I've been in London & Birmingham and jeopardy & hazard.

I'm eely and oily.

I'm hot trottered toast.

I'm my cup of toe.

I hate the earth: oh to hell with that
                        incommensurable cowpad.

Cleopatra smells of Marmite.

Come again, King Cain, and have a cosh, I'm Abel.

It was terrible to miss you. I wanted so much to help with mothers, aunts, children, luggage, eartrumpet.

In my reeking way, I'd forgotten you were going so soon.

I'm weevil.

I haven't forgotten the other help and shall send it as quickly as possible. Or, best, give it to you here. I had a job every day to do, last week, shouting 'Hi' in the North & 'Varlet' in Portland Square.

How long will you be in Swansea? Will you write by return?

And this is important. When can you come, alone or with your piece of Exeter oatcake, to Oxford? It must be in the next fortnight. Margaret Taylor, my hostess, has an empty (but for 5 children) house for a fortnight and sends an invitation: there's a big bedroom waiting, & three lavatories.

I have a cricket bat & a hard ball and a choice of lawns.

I wish beyond anything you would come.

I have a room in Magdalen to read, write, dance & destroy poems in.

I am negotiating the purchase of a barrel of Flower's Best Bitter.

There is a grand piano, a harpsichord, & a large library of records (with gramophone).

We are on the river, & there is a punt.

I shall have some money.

Will you write at once?

Caitlin is looking forward very much to seeing you & Irene; or you alone; or Dan first & then Jones after.

If you cannot possibly come, I will try to come to Swansea.

But for the next few weeks I think it will be difficult for me to move all that way from London, as I am waiting for a job.

Oh, it will be good here if you come.

My love for always, & my truly deep apologies for not being able to come down with them, to your mother & Aunt Alice. I am so glad they are home again, at last.

And I will see them soon. But we must be here first.

I shall sharpen the cricket-bat in anticipation.

We have a tame robin, & the swan calls on Mondays.

Love from your old friend,

Dylan

> By return, write.
> And all regards to Vernon & Fred.

MSS.: Dr Daniel Jones

In the period immediately after the end of the Second World War Graham Greene was much involved in the film world. (Among other films he wrote the script of *The Third Man* at this time.) He was also a director of the publishing house of Eyre & Spottiswoode. Finally, he has often taken great pains to help a fellow writer in distress. It was therefore quite natural that Dylan should turn to him for help in getting *The Doctor And The Devils* screened, or published, or both.

Though this first fragment is not dated, from internal evidence I take it that it precedes the letter which follows.

Tod Slaughter was a barn-storming actor who specialized in Grand Guignol-type plays, such as *Sweeny Todd, The Demon Barber of Fleet Street* or *Maria Martin and the Red Barn.*

TO GRAHAM GREENE

January 1947?

The brief and, I'm afraid, ignorant history of a script, tentatively called 'The Doctor & The Devils', about Dr. Knox, the Edinburgh anatomist and Burke & Hare, the murderers.

This script was written by me when I was employed as a scriptwriter by a small company called Gryphon Films which was formed as a result of the dissolution of the documentary-making Strand Film Company.

The director of the Gryphon unit was Donald Taylor. (His private address is Hill Cottage, Hedgerley Village, near Slough, Bucks.) He resigned from Gryphon Films at the same time as myself: September, 1945, just as the Film Producers' Guild Ltd was being formed.

Gryphon Films had its offices in Guild House, (which now houses the Film Producers' Guild), St. Martin's Lane, W.C.2., and was somehow financially connected with Verity Films Ltd., which is still there. I do not know any details at all of the financial connection between Gryphon & Verity. But Donald Taylor, under whom I directly worked and on whose orders I wrote 'The Doctor and The Devils' must know. I have always been under the impression that the copyright is his.

Some of the research necessary for the scripting of this film was done by a member of Gryphon Films. And I also worked upon the preliminary roughing-out of the script with Taylor who took, throughout, a lively producer's interest.

The script was shown to a couple of wellknown producers, or companies, who—so I gather, but only at secondhand as Taylor told me little or nothing once the script was finished—were most enthusiastic about it and wished to do it but refused when Taylor demanded that he should direct it himself. I have, as I said, no firsthand proof of this.

I do know that Michael Redgrave, who read it, was extremely keen to play in it.

I also know that the script was sent to James Bridie whose play, 'The Anatomist', is on the same subject. Taylor wished to have it clear in writing that the script owed nothing to the play and that should the script be filmed Bridie could in no way object. Bridie replied satisfactorily.

When the script is seen, and if it is thought to have cinematic possibilities, Taylor is, of course, the one man to approach on the question of copyright.

Dylan Thomas

MSS.: Graham Greene, Esq.

TO GRAHAM GREENE

Holywell Ford,
Oxford
January 11 1947

Dear Graham,

Thank you such a lot for your letter. And, please, forgive me for not having answered it straightaway. I've been working in London, and very muddled too about where to live—here is feverish—and how and why. And about many other things, one or two of which I want to worry you with if you don't terribly mind. I know you're so busy, as publisher, writer, man and all, but if you could, though I've no right in the world to ask you, help, I'd be grateful always. I'm so sorry Margaret Taylor nagged you about the filmscript over Christmas: I only heard afterwards how she had written and phoned and plagued and plugged, all through kindness towards me I know; I didn't realise she was making such a business of it. I felt and feel, vague and nervous about it myself, and about sending it to you and trying to make some of my problems, if only for a moment, yours.

But, first, thank you very very much indeed for reading the script. I am so glad you liked it—if anyone could like such a nasty thing. And for writing to say what you thought about it. And for getting in touch with Michael Redgrave: it's good to think he hasn't forgotten the script & still wants to do it, in spite of the old B picture and Tod Slaughter's Plans.

About publishing the script. I'm pretty sure Dent's wouldn't touch it with a pole, and I'd very much like you to do it. But the question of copyright remains, of course, the same as when I wrote you about Donald Taylor and the other complications.

What I want, frightfully urgently—and this is the chief of the worries I want to worry you with—is some money for or from it or the chance of getting some, and ever so quickly, I can't tell you how quickly I need it, some money from Rank. I've got a pile of doctors' bills for Caitlin and for my son Llewelyn who is never, I'm sorry, well; and a looming writ; and another one on the doorstep. I'm in a hell of a mess. And now. So what I want to ask is, is there any chance of Rank & his boys giving me some money at once, either on account of this script or on account of another script I could—and very much want to—write for them. I know that 'The Doctor & The Devils' might never, because of horror & copyright, ever be produced. But I should like it to be regarded as a sample of what I can write for the films. I want, naturally, to write a hundred-times-better script, and I'm sure I can. I can write other than horrible stories, and I want to. Would there be anything in the suggestion that I cd write a film specially for Redgrave? Would the reading of this D. & D. script make it clear to Rank and boys that I am capable of writing for the screen? and, if so, would they think of giving me some money, or putting me under contract?

On top of bills & writs, all howlingly pressing, I must get out of here & find somewhere else to live at once. And that will take money, which I haven't got. All I earn I spend & give to past debts. I'm in a mess all right. But I know I could write a good new script. And I wish Redgrave & Rank would pay me to do it.

Sorry about this breathless letter. Shall I ring you next week? and can you help, with the film boys, in any immediate way? Thank you again for your letter.

Yours,

Dylan Thomas

MSS.: Graham Greene, Esq.

I print the letter which follows more for its tone than for its content. Dylan was always most respectful towards his parents, particularly his father, and anxious to show his own life in the best possible light.

Ernest Stahl is now Professor of German in the University of Oxford.

Sir William Walton writes me that he never met Dylan, nor ever planned to write an opera with him. However, the visit to Gravesend certainly took place and ended with Dylan's arrest on a charge of being drunk and disorderly. Doubtless Michael Ayrton, the painter, intended to approach Walton.

Neither the Magdalen College Cottage nor the sharing of a house at Richmond with Bill and Helen McAlpine ever materialized.

TO MR AND MRS D. J. THOMAS

Holywell Ford,
Oxford
January 12 1947

Dear Mother and Dad,

I haven't written since before Christmas: it seems years ago. So much, and nearly all petty, has happened, so many plans made and broken. I wish I had written much sooner, to wish you a peaceful and well New Year but I've been busy as a hive and mostly in London where, without a headquarters, I find it hard, even impossible, to settle down at borrowed desk or friend's table to write. Every proper wish now, though so late, and I do hope to see you soon. I'm glad you're back home; it's wicked weather to move about in. But I'm sure Hetty & Ken were awfully good and kind. How is Arthur? I haven't seen him since—was it in London, when he & you came up about poor Will? How long ago? Will you send him Caitlin's love, and mine, when you write.

We had rather a gay and noisy Christmas here. Oxford's a very sociable place on occasions like that, and we went to several parties. We had Christmas Day lunch very quietly, just Caitlin & Aeronwy & myself in our snug summerhouse: we ate the biggest of the two delicious and tender chickens Mother sent, and a rich dark pudding made us by the Taylor cook, Florence, whose baby is due any day now, and a bottle of caustic red ink called Algerian wine. Aeron had some crackers. She loved her teaset and gives an assortment of dolls & bears daily parties. She had quite a lot of presents altogether, including a tricycle from us, books, a little mangle, a Noah's Ark, a golliwog, and a stocking full of nonsense and tangerines. Then Christmas Day Dinner with the Taylors, with turkey. Boxing Day dinner with some friends of ours here called Veal—he's a young composer, and son of the University Registrar—and Saturday dinner with a Corpus Christi don called Stahl, & his wife. Our second fat and luscious chicken we added to the Veal's table. One of our troubles here is that we can't invite anyone back; so instead, we take along a few things to their flats, rooms, or houses. The day after Boxing Day I had to go to London to give my after-the-news talk. A lot of people found the talk eccentric; perhaps it was; it wasn't, certainly, what most people expected to hear after the news. I've had quite a big post from it: half of it enthusiastic, the other half calling me anything from obscurantist to poseur, surrealist comedian to Bedlamite. The Manchester Guardian reviewed it very cheeringly; the News Chronicle with boos.

On New Year's Eve we went, with lots of other people, mostly BBC, to the Chelsea Arts Ball at the Albert Hall. Never been to it before. 5000 people there, all in fancy dress. A tremendously bright affair. I went as a Chinaman, Caitlin as a grand Spanish lady. It really was very exciting: wonderful to look at: all the boxes round the great hall packed with parrots, ballerinas, costermongers, Elizabethans, pirates, courtesans, tigers, Dutch Dolls, empresses, clowns, & the huge floor rainbowed with dancers. Valentine Dyall and Michael Ayrton— do you ever hear him on the Brains Trust?—were two of the company.

The day after that Dyall & I took part in 'Richard the Third' on the overseas Service of the BBC. Eastern & Overseas Services I now do quite a lot of work for: scripting, acting, & reading. They do a potted Shakespeare play a week. Last week it was Titus Andronicus, which I'd never read and probably never will again,—but it was great fun to do. There was a very fine actor, George Hayes once of the Old Vic, playing Aaron, the damned Moor.

Last week I read my story 'A Visit to Grandpa's', too. Did you hear it? 10-30 pm on Wednesday, in the Home Service.

I haven't many reading engagements for the near future. I'm talking about Sir Philip Sidney on the 24th, from the West. Can you get that? It will be repeated later in the Third Programme. And, for the Shakespeare series I mentioned, I'm arranging the programme on 'Merchant of Venice'. But that's impossible to hear in England, without a short-wave set. I've finished, & recorded, the first of two programmes about Oxford—the first was an exchange programme with Princeton USA—and very soon will be able to do my 'Return Journey' Swansea's programme. A day in Swansea, & the rest in Blaen-Cwm.

Did I tell you about the opera-libretto I have been asked to write? A full-length grand opera for William Walton. I have to turn out a very rough synopsis before I am definitely commissioned. This I hope to do next week. Michael Ayrton, who will do the decor, & I are going, on Wednesday, for a few days to Gravesend, Tilbury, & all around there, as I want to set the opera in a near-docks area. A very modern tragic opera, in the bombed slums of Wharfland. If this ever comes to anything, it will be the biggest English operatic event of the century. Really it will. A whole Covent Garden season in 1949 is contemplated. If, & when, I am commissioned to write the libretto, I should be able to stop doing any other work & devote about six solid months to it.

I've got a new book out in America: 'Selected Works'. I've had some good American notices—I enclose one from the New York Times. Can you return it afterwards, as I'm trying to file all American stuff for future use, when, one day, we go across there—but so far only one copy of the book which I can't, at the moment, find. As soon as other copies come, I'll send you one at once. It's a nice-looking book.

Do you ever listen to the series 'Poet & Critic' on the Third Programme? I'm the next Poet, the Critic being T. W. Earp. There'll be either three or four programmes, half an hour a week, starting the end of this month. I'll let you know exact dates later.

As to domestic news: we're well on our way to getting a cottage here, in Magdalen grounds. But I shan't know finally for about six weeks. It will be fine, if it works. The cottage is an old mill-house, on the Cherwell, surrounded by gardens. It is Magdalen property, and, if I get it, will be on a very long lease and at a very small rental. It will be a proper home for us. In the meantime: at the beginning of February, Caitlin & I think of moving to Richmond, to share a house—a big house—with Helen and Bill, the people we went over to Ireland with last summer. It's a house just by Richmond Bridge, right on the river. I do hope you'll be able to come & stay with us in it in the early spring. There's tons of room, & it's extremely comfortable. I'll tell you more about this—an almost certain plan—later on. Our idea is to share both the Richmond house & the Oxford cottage with Helen & Bill, one part of the mixed family being, probably, 'in residence' in Oxford while the other part is in our 'town house'. The Richmond house belongs to Helen, so our rent will be most reasonable. It's all pretty ambitious, but may come off.

Caitlin & I are going to lunch with Edith Sitwell in London tomorrow. She's on her way to Switzerland.

Last weekend, we went down to Ringwood & brought Llewelyn back with us for a week or so. He likes it here, with the two small Taylor boys. It's Giles's birthday-party today, Sunday, & there's a hell of a row going on all over the house. They're playing Murder, by the sound of it. Llewelyn's very pale and frail, but full of life. Caitlin's taking him, this week, to see a Dr. Walker here, a famous children's specialist. He's been suffering all the winter from asthma, and he's frightfully nervous too and has a peculiar way of walking. If the Doctor says he needs a change of climate—which the Bournemouth Doctor recommended—Margaret Taylor has, voluntarily, promised that she will pay to send him over to, & keep him in, a kind of holiday-school in the Isle of Wight for about 3 months. But we'll know the Doctor's opinion on this on Wednesday. Whatever happens, we're not going to allow Llewelyn to go back to Ringwood for any length of time. He must have the company of children of his own age, & also he must get away from the flat, damp New Forest district.

Llewelyn's a great reader. He reads everything, except poetry which he 'hates'.

And now I can't think of anything else. Oh yes: interest has been revived in my filmscript. Did I ever thank Dad for sending it on? Anyway, thank you very, very much.

Caitlin will write this evening. Thank you for all the Christmas presents. I can't tell you how welcome they were. And for the pound, which filled Aeron's stocking full. Llewelyn was awfully pleased, too, by his Christmas gifts from you. I wish you could see him, & hope that you soon will.

I'll write later, with news of Llewelyn's Doctor & whether he'll be sent to the I. of Wight or not. And etcetera & etcetera.

Please write and tell me something, as soon as possible.

All love from
Caitlin & myself,
Aeronwy & Llewelyn,
Dylan

MSS.: Dylan Thomas Estate

Dylan's friends were worried by his obvious and rapid physical deterioration and also by the fact that he was now writing no poems. The Authors' Society disposed of a Travelling Scholarship Fund, and Edith Sitwell, among others, arranged that he be free of money worries, for a period of three or four months, in Italy.

T. W. Earp was doing a series of broadcasts about Dylan produced by Commander King-Bull.

TO T. W. EARP

Holywell Ford,
Oxford
March 1st 1947

My dear Tommy,

Thank you so much for your letter.

The people who told you about my health, when you were last in London were all correct, & at the same time. I was roaringly well, then, some minutes after, a little mewling ruin. I would very nearly run down one street, to cringe, very nearly on my belly, up the next. In Finch's I was a lion; in the Duke of York's a piece of cold lamb with vomit sauce. Now I am back in ordinary middle health again, headachy, queasy, feverish, of a nice kind of normal crimson & bilious. I think that I am nearly well enough not to have to go out this morning in order to feel well enough to work this afternoon: a preposterous process, as it means I go to sleep with my face in the pudding & wake up sticky & fretful & bite my nails to the shoulder-bone. I hope, very much, that you are well too. I liked the first & second do's on me, & am looking forward to the third tonight which will be your fourth. I mean, the third section, supposed to be my reply, will now end the series.

The Commander writes to tell me that, owing to rushed Third Programme planning, your 4th (now 3rd) section is cut to 15 minutes, which means the loss of 'Fern Hill' & 'Vision & Prayer'.

I found the greatest difficulty in writing my piece, & have become rather hysterical in my generalisations. My references to your critical remarks are warm-hearted and dull. So am I.

Write me when you'll be in London, and, unless some film-work I am rushing at the moment in order to get some money for Italy prevents me, I'll be there, fit as a fuddle.

It was a great pleasure to me to hear you on the wireless; and thank you, very deeply, for all the extremely kind & penetrating things you said.

I hope to see you very soon.

Yours ever,
Dylan

MSS.: Ohio

Dylan and Caitlin set off for Italy in early April with their two children, Caitlin's sister Brigit and her small son Tobias. They went first to Rapallo.

TO MR AND MRS D. J. THOMAS
Villa Cuba,
San Michele di Pagana,
Rapallo,
Italy
11th April 1947

Dear Mother and Dad,

I don't know which will arrive first: this letter or a postcard of Rapallo. But the object of both is the same, and a pretty obvious one too: to tell you that we have all—Caitlin, Brigit, Llewelyn, Aeronwy, Tobias, & myself—arrived safely in Italy after three days' travel. Three very exhausting days. We had booked through from London to Rome—you have to book sleeping-reservations a long time ahead— before we knew where we were going. And so when we decided on Rapallo, we still had to travel on the Calais–Milan–Rome express, which meant that we had to go through Switzerland. If we had booked through to Genoa, we would have missed the whole Swiss loop. We'd have shortened the journey by a day. But it couldn't be helped. One of the nuisances was that our baggage got left behind at the Swiss-Italian frontier, and Caitlin & I had the hell of a job next morning, while Brigit looked after the three children, of chasing the baggage through the bowels of Milan station, endlessly interviewing bureaucratic officials in a jumble of languages, queueing up before wrong ticket-offices, bribing the Customs with English cigarettes, changing pound-notes into Black Market lire, dragging the children out of the hotel into rude & reckless taxis, & just managing to catch the train. Milan is a giant, nightmare city. The snow & the rain had just ceased before we arrived—a day or two before. The immensely long, wide streets, which run the entire length of the city, or seem to, were bakingly hot & dusty, clanking with great, packed, racing trams, buzzing with little toy motor bikes; there were stop-me-&-buy-one bicycle boys selling, not ice-cream, but bottles of Chianti, & set-faced sinister armed policemen. Brigit stayed in the hotel, and Caitlin and I went round the city & the cafés in the boiling sun, speaking our lame Italian. I have a dozen phrases, half probably wrong; Caitlin makes long & impressive-sounding speeches, which few can understand. But I hope we will pick up a working vocabulary fairly soon. Nouns I can remember; grammar, no. I shall have to learn it the dull way, I'm afraid, through a text-book.

The worst part of the journey was the shortest: from Genoa to Rapallo: an asthmatic train creeping & bumping over the bridges, over the bridges just erected or actually in the process of being erected. Nearly all the bridges along the Italian Riviera were blown up, but whether by the Germans or by the British I have not yet been brave enough to ask, or linguistically capable of asking.

San Michele is about a mile outside Rapallo: half way between Rapallo & Santa Margerita: not far from Porto Fino. It's a lovely village. Our little hotel—expensive; we can't stay here long—is right on the sea; our bedroom balconies are over the water. High hills above the village, covered with villas, fir-trees, olive-trees, wonderful villas, pink, red, white, turreted, pinnacled, baroque Christmas-cake;

the sea's bright blue, the very bright blue sky cloudless. It's so lovely, lying by the sea in the sun; incredible after this winter. I wish you could both be here. Do please write soon, very soon, and tell me how you are. Especially Dad. The last time Mother wrote, he was ill again, and in pain. I do hope, above everything, that he is better now. Do let us know at once, now that you have our (temporary) address. It seems all wrong, us here in the great sun, on the Riviera, & Dad ill, who would, I'm sure, feel so much better for a complete change of climate.

We walked to Rapallo this morning, but didn't have much time there. The front is all enormous, expensive hotels & cafés, packed with the rich: like Nice, or Mentone. But the little of the town itself that we saw is heavenly. Max Beerbohm lives here, though I don't know where; in some wonderful villa up in the olive groves, perhaps. Here Ezra Pound used to live; here it was he went mad too.

I had a letter from Edith Sitwell this morning, who is mostly responsible for us being able to come here. She is the chairman of the Authors' Society Travelling Committee, which occasionally gives writers money to move about. Talking about money: the Bank give you nine hundred lire for a pound; the Free Market, as it is known, gives you eighteen hundred. This part—indeed, much of the North, I think—seems well off for food. We have had excellent food, superlatively cooked, for the last two days; dinner being some form of very good spaghetti in a rich sauce, followed by bread & cheese (all kinds of cheese; my favourite gorgonzola), followed by apples or oranges or figs, & then coffee. Red wine always with the meal.

It's lovely to see the oranges growing around us.

Write soon, & so will I. Next week I am going, alone with Caitlin, to Rome, to see about British Council lectures. I hope also an introduction to one of the heads of Italian films, an American Russian Jew. I'll let you know what happens.

Now write soon, & tell us everything. I hope to God Dad's better. All with me send their love. And I send all mine.

Dylan

MSS.: Dylan Thomas Estate

Villa Cuba,
San Michele di Pagana,
Rapallo,
Italy

12th April 1947

My dear Margaret,

I was profoundly sorry not to see you; up to the last grey, ruinous moment I thought that, somehow, I could return to say au revoir, thank you for too many thousand things to count, above all your loyalty to me when I was wretched, ill, mean, drawn taut, lost, utterly unworthy of faith or affection, of anything but a kind of kicking pity. I wanted to thank you for your more than kindness to Llewelyn and Aeron, whom you helped to make well; to Cat and me, whom you housed when we were in a sick muddle; to me, to whom you were almost gentle. I do hope that you can help us to find a house in or near Oxford, so that we can see each other again. I want, so much to come back to Oxford. Oh, anywhere a house. I am lost without one. I am domestic as a slipper, I want somewhere of my own, I'm old enough now, I want a house to shout, sleep, and work in. Please help; though I deserve nothing.

The journey was first good, then baddish, then disastrous, then good again, then bad. The disaster happened at the Swiss frontier, when we lost our luggage. We should not have gone through Switzerland anyway. We found the baggage at last, after eternities deep, deep down under Milan station, through Ufa corridors, in Kafka cells and temples of injustice. Our lack of Italian helped. In steel-barred rooms, where Mussolini personally had whipped and interrogated, we faced row after row of tiny, blue customs-officers in wide hats, who smoked our cigarettes, spilt sugar on the clothes, joked at a great speed, ogled Caitlin, and cut our luggage labels off with scissors.

San Michele is a very pretty village; the sea's blue under our balcony; there's a wind, but the sun's hot; our pension is small, sweet, dear; there is lots of food & wine. The front at Rapallo, a mile away, is far too much of a rich playground, with enormous hotels, women from Phillips Oppenheim, international millionaires, &, this morning, us. But the town behind the swagger front is full of most lovely houses cafés, chianti, gorgonzola, markets, orangetrees. We are going to Portofino tomorrow. I do not know if I can start working here. There is no escape in a small hotel from the too many children. And besides, we must live in the country. This is sophisticated as Nice.

Caitlin & I will go to Rome next week to see film-&-British Council-men.

Write & tell me Nish-news. How are you? Don't, don't be unhappy, please. Write soon. And you will help about a house, won't you? I am as homely as a tea-caddy, but have no pretty pot.

Thank you, dear Margaret, for everything.

Yours ever,
Dylan

Caitlin sends her love. Could you, do you think, send a couple of thrillers or a magazine? I am forced to read poetry only.

Write soon,
D.

MSS.: Texas

Dylan managed to do some sightseeing in Italy, or so he told his parents.

TO MR AND MRS D. J. THOMAS

May 5th 1947

Villa Cuba,
San Michele di Pagana,
Rapallo,
Italy

Dear Mother and Dad,

Since writing last, Caitlin and I have been to Rome & to Florence—not on the same visit. In betweenwhiles, we came back to Brigit, Llewelyn, Aeronwy, and little Tobias: all of them fat and contented by the sea and in the sun.

Rome is a frightful journey from Rapallo. All travelling, over any distance, is bad. There are few trains or buses, and all the bridges have been blown up, or nearly all, either by Allied bombers or by retreating Germans. We went by bus to Rome: four in the afternoon till eight the next morning. And a damned uncomfortable bus too. The children could never have done it in one go. Rome was, I am glad to say in my little travelogue letter, Rome. We stayed in the oldest hotel in the city, directly behind the Pantheon. We had about five days there altogether, but, most of the time, just wandered round rather than going on vast exhausting tours of inexhaustible galleries & churches.

We did spend one morning in the Vatican City, dizzily moving down marble miles, craning and panting in the Sistine Chapel which is more wonderful than I could have believed, staring down from a great height into St. Peter's itself, from huge cool galleries that seemed the size of public squares and corridors like the terraces of Gods. We met a great number of people, writers, painters, musicians, mostly through the good offices of the British Council who, housed in the Palazzo di Drago or Palace of Dragons in the Street of the Four Fountains, give sumptuous parties, in tapestried rooms, to visiting intellectuals. The Council, whose director in Rome is a poet, Ronald Bottrall, whom I knew in London, gave a very good party for us; and after it we had the addresses of many people whom we met on subsequent days. They all talked English, which is shaming to foreigners who can only just catch buses, order wine, & count their change in Italian. There was one American writer, Frederik Prokosch: has Dad read any of his novels? The one or two I've come across are very good. One most learned scholar, Mario Praz, author of 'The Romantic Agony' & an authority, abroad, on English metaphysical poets. I made a couple of film contacts—nasty word—but they have, so far, come to nothing. It was very lovely strolling about Rome in the bright bright sun. We couldn't face the bus back, and flew from Rome to Genoa in an old army-plane: nearly everybody got very sick. The dock-front of Genoa is marvellous. Such heat and colours and dirt & noise and loud wicked alleys with all the washing of the world hanging from the high windows. We were there only a few hours, but the next day I took Brigit and Llewelyn there—it's an hour and a half from Rapallo— while Caitlin looked after the small children. Llewelyn was very excited, and ate much glorious ice-cream in garish cafés & felt like hell returning in the bus.

Then four days later, Caitlin and I went to Florence: not such a bad journey: 8 hours by bus through wonderful country. We stopped at Pisa, saw, of course, the Leaning Tower, & then, in Florence in the evening, met a lot of young Italian poets to whom, from Rome, we had introductions. Again, we were terribly lucky in our hotel right in the centre of the city, in the Cathedral square, by the great Dome, and the Baptistery, and Giotto's Belltower. Next morning, we met, by accident, in a sidestreet, Stephen Spender, who was there, just like us, only for a few days. We had lunch and dinner together. We saw the Pitti Palace & the Uffizi. I'd just been reading Romola, and could follow the city, almost, from my memories of that. The lovely, more than lovely, Ponte Vecchio was left untouched by the Germans, but the other lovely bridges were blown to hell, and also the little hanging houses round the Ponte Vecchio, old as Dante.

And the next day we rented, until the end of July, a little house some five miles from Florence, up in the hills, looking over the city, among pines and olives, beautifully green and peaceful, a cool, long house with a great garden & a swimming pool. The rent, in English money was £25 for 2½ months. If my money holds out until the end of July, we will, I know, be peaceful and happy there. The garden is full of nightingales and orangetrees. There are vineyards all around us. We move there next Monday, May the 12th.

The address is:

Villa del Beccaro,
Mosciano,
Scandicci,
Florence.

From there I will write again, at length, & tell you how we fare.

We do, with all our hearts, all of us, hope Dad is better & that Mother is able to carry on. Mother, in her letter, says the sun was shining. I hope it will be a lovely summer.

We are all well. Llewelyn is a fat boy now, but he misses the company of English boys of his own age to play with. He reads a lot. Now he is reading the Three Musketeers, in tiny print, in the same edition I read it in. Nelson's Classics, I think.

This afternoon, they are all out in a rowing boat in the still blue bay. I can see the boat from our window.

I'll let you know all about food etc. in my next letter.

The English tobacco situation is dreadful, isn't it. Here there are nothing but Black Market cigarettes. We bought a pile of coarse black tobacco from a sailor in Genoa, and are rolling that.

Love from all to both. Caitlin is writing. And you, please, write soon.

Best love,
Dylan

PS. When I can buy a big envelope, I will send on some American reviews of my Selected Writings, which Laughlin of New Directions has just forwarded.

MSS.: Dylan Thomas Estate

To begin with he loved the villa outside Florence.

TO BILL AND HELEN MCALPINE

Villa del Beccaro,
Mosciano,
Scandicci,
Florence
May 20th 1947

My dear Helen and Bill,

I'd have written much, much sooner—did you get a postcard?—
but waited until we had a house of our own to write from. Up to now,
we've been staying in hotels and pensions: expensive and unsatisfactory. And the Riviera sea was too tidy. Now, on the hills above
Florence, some five miles from the centre, we have found a lovely villa
in the pinewoods: beautiful, nightingaled gardens, cypresses, pillared
terraces, olive trees, deep wild woods, our own vineyard and swimming
pool, very tasty. There is a big room waiting for you. The cellar is full
of wine. We live on asparagus, artichokes, oranges, gorgonzola, olive
oil, strawberries, and more red wine. We have the villa until the last
day of July. Can you come? We'd love it, so much. Write at once, and
forgive this delay. Best love from Cat and me.

Yours ever,
Dylan

I will let you know all, if any, details when you write.
I am writing poems.
Are you married?
Brigit's son Tobias has just fallen in the swimming pool.
Have you got your passports? Do hurry.

D.

MSS.: William McAlpine, Esq.

Peter Quennell is the poet, essayist and historian. Stephen is Stephen Spender and Natasha Litvin is his wife.

TO MARGARET TAYLOR

Villa del Beccaro,
Mosciano,
Scandicci,
Florence
May 20th 1947

My dear Margaret,

At last we've found, in pinewoods on the hills above Florence, a house until the end of July. The pooled ponded rosed goldfished arboured lizarded swinghung towelled winetabled Aeronshrill garden leads into our own (dear God) olives and vines climbing to a mutes' conventicle, a Niobe's eisteddfod, of cypresses. What seem to be armoured belligerent emerald wasps bang and bully the bushes; one-noted birds blow their brains out in the pines; other very near birds, which I can see, birdily fox me with very distant cries from the wrong trees. I can smell the sun. There is a swimming pool into which I have been only once—by mistake. Caitlin, Brigit, and the children are seals and newts there. Masciano, the nearest village, is thin and tall, shouldered like Peter Quennel against the church. (The Marquis of Q I met in Rome. He was spending a week with the British Ambassador, drinking, by the gallon, grappa, which, to me, tastes like an axe.) Florence sparkles at night below us. In the day we see the Dome. It is perhaps five miles away. To get to the city we suffer by trap and tram. But there's so little need to move. The pinehills are endless, the cypresses at the hilltop tell one all about the length of death, the woods are deep as love and full of goats, the house is cool & large, the children beastly, the wine ample, why should I move at all until July the 31st. And then to the lovely unfound house in Oxfordshire, the house built round the desk you bought me? Oh I do hope so. And thank you thank you for the desk.

Did you receive the postcard, overcheerily scribbled with messages, after a big red dinner, by Caitlin, Natasha, Stephen and myself? Stephen was very gay, Natasha British as a hockeystick: I hadn't seen her like that. In flatheeled shoes she thumped the hot Florence pavements, gawky as an Arthur Marshall schoolgirl, shouting English, elbowing the droll Florentines from her gym-knickered way. I have met many of the young intellectuals of Florence, who are rarified and damp: they do not write much but oh how they edit! They live with their mothers, ride motor-scooters, and translate Apollinaire.

And thank you, so very much indeed, for the books and papers which came to Rapallo and which were terribly welcome, all of them, Sunday papers, thrillers, Listeners. And for your lovely letter and for all it said. Do, do write again, and soon. Tell me all your news.

I wish I had heard you read my poems, and Vernon's, and Alun Lewis's, and Roy's 'Skull In the Desert'. I wish I had heard you reading, on the Macedonian lake, from my orange stamp-book. And the changing fish and the living fossils of that deepest legendary water! God's pulling your leg.

It is all so widely quiet here, and the valley vining away to the church towers. In the next room, in her rest hour, Aeronwy is singing an obscene song. Brigit's Tobias, a spotty frog-boy, is screaming in the lavatory. Llewelyn, in the garden, is trying to cut a boat out of a pinecone with a breadknife and has several fingers left. Brigit is superintending the screaming of the boy-frog. Caitlin has shut herself away and is learning Italian—undoubtedly by looking through the window at the trees. I am sitting in a half-shuttered room over the vineyard, writing to you who are in Oxford, and thanking you for everything always, and sending my love.

Write soon.

I read anything in English.

Yours ever,

Dylan

MSS.: Texas

Soon though he began to feel lonely.

Rodney is Rodney Philips, who was financing a magazine, *Arena*, with which John Davenport was connected in an editorial capacity.

TO JOHN DAVENPORT

Villa di Beccaro,
Mosciano,
Scandicci,
Florence,
ITALY
29th May 1947

My dear John,

This pig in Italy bitterly knows—O the tears on his snub snout and the squelch in the trough as he buries his flat, Welsh head in shame, and guzzels and blows—that he should have written, three wine vats gone, a porky letter to Moby D. or two-ton John; but with a grunt in the pines, time trottered on! the spirit was willing: the ham was weak. The spirit was brandy: the ham was swilling. And oh the rasher-frying sun! What a sunpissed pig I am not to dip a bristle in Chianti, and write. I have so many excuses, and none at all. A few days ago I climbed a tree, forgetting my shape and weight, and hung this shabby barrel from a branch by my white padded mitts: they were torn neatly up the middles. Also, very slowly, I am trying to write a poem, moping over it, every afternoon in a room in the peasant's cottage: our little spankers make so much noise I cannot work anywhere near them. God grenade them. It was so good to hear from you, and to know you will be in Florence in July. Of course you must stay with us, but I had better explain that we are some miles from Florence itself, up in the hills. To get to the city, we go by horse-and-trap to Scandicci and then suffer in the tram for twenty-five minutes. One can order a car from Florence, but it costs about 3000 lire—thirty shillings. But we will, of course, manage somehow. We are all looking forward to you enormously. Will Rodney be with you? If he has his car, everything will be so easy. If he hasn't, it won't be such a problem anyway. We are in very beautiful country, and there is lots of room and wine in the house. No, I don't know Edward, but we were going to see him when we first came here: he wanted to let half his villa to an English or American family. We have got to know lots of the young intellectuals of Florence, and a damp lot they are. They visit us on Sunday. To overcome the language, I have to stand on my head, fall in the pool, crack nuts with my teeth, and Tarzan in the cypresses. I am very witty in Italian, though a little violent; and I need space. Do you know anybody in Florence nice to have a drink with? I met Stephen Spender there a few weeks ago. It was very sad. He is on a lecture-tour. He is bringing the European intellectuals together. It is impossible. He said in a lecture I saw reported: 'All poets speak the same language.' It is a bloody lie: who talks Spender?

I am going to write to Higham about Philips and Greene this week. Thank you for sending Greene's letter.

Write soon. It will be lovely to see you here. Love to all from us all here. And to Tommy, if you see him, to whom I must write.

I don't know what my plans are yet; they depend on money, and not mine. We have been offered a house in Parma when we leave here on July 31st, and I should like to go. Also the Oxford Taylors have wired about taking us a house in Witney, to which, I suppose, we'd have to return. It's very difficult. I am going to write a radio

play when this slow poem is finished. How are you? Give Kingsmill
a punch for me.

Yours ever, and see you soon.

Dylan

MSS.: Texas

The house at South Leigh, which Margaret Taylor had bought for them,
was to be their home for two years, after their return from Italy.

TO MR AND MRS D. J. THOMAS

Villa del Beccaro,

Mosciano,

Scandicci,

Florence

June 5 1947

Dear Mother and Dad,

How are you both? It's a long, long time since a letter came from
you; or is it that time moves so slowly here and one looks forward
as much to the postman? or postwoman, rather, a little woman too,
who walks about twenty miles a day, up & down these steep Florentine
hills, in the baking sun. Whatever it is, we do want to hear from you
soon. Letters from England seem to take, on the average, five days to
get here.

I hope it is sunny in Carmarthenshire. I read in the Sunday papers
Margaret Taylor sends me that it's going to be a wonderful year for
fruit in England. Here we have had strawberries and cherries galore,
lemons, and oranges from Sicily—too early for the more Northern
oranges. Peas, beans, asparagus, artichokes, I don't know if we'll be
here for the peaches. We do very well indeed for food, though it
isn't cheap, by any means. You can get anything, if you have the money.
Not as in England. Recently there was an English Exhibition in Rome,
organised by the British Council, to show what goods etc. England
was producing, what films it was making, pictures painting, books
writing, etc; and how much food it was eating. One person's total
rations for a week were exhibited. And the reaction, even among the
intelligent visitors, was: 'Yes, I see. That's the amount of sugar, or
butter, or tea, one person's allowed in England. And very small too.
How much does he have to pay for Free Market sugar, butter, tea,
etc?' And everybody downrightly refused to believe that that was

the amount you got, that and no more, and that you could not buy any more. They just did not believe that the Black Market in England is a tiny affair. In Italy, it is the White Market that is the tiny affair. The ration for cigarettes is 15 a week, I think. At every street corner, in every town, men, boys, & women, sit with great trays of cigarettes, English & American the dearest & the most popular. (We smoke the cheapest, rough Italian cigarettes: Nazionali, all stamped as the property of the Italian state. These we buy openly illegally at any shop, at any corner, for about 1/2 for twenty—twice the logical price.) Vegetables we get from gardeners here, but they aren't cheap either. The pound is worth, officially, 900 to 1000 lire; but by some wangling I cannot follow, the Bank will give you about 2000 lire for it. If you walk down the street, however, you will be stopped by any amount of touts and offered—at the present moment—2,450 for it. Into whose hands the English Pounds & the 'hard' currency Swiss francs and Swedish money go, I don't know. Some speculators are hoarding them against preposterous inflation. It is almost impossible to achieve any money perspective here. A big glass of good wine costs 20 lire, about 2½d. A small bottle, less than half a pint, of extremely thin beer costs about 60 lire. The horse & trap we go in down the hill to Scandicci costs 350 lire, each way. Sugar costs about 10/- a pound. I don't know offhand the price of rice & spaghetti, but I do know that the poor can afford to buy only the rationed amount per week, which is minute; & spaghetti is their staple dish. Nor can they buy more than the rationed amount of bread & flour: also tiny. And not only the real poor. It applies to the professional classes too. Only the profiteering rich, the already rich with well protected money, & foreigners can buy the goods with which the shops are stacked. And English foreigners, at any rate, not for long. The Americans, of course, can bring as much money as they like into the country. I hope to be able to last out, financially, until the end of our tenancy here: that is, the last day of July. But it won't be easy: neither Caitlin nor Brigit is a good manager. And, after the 31st of July, unless a miracle happens, we return. The best news is: We have a house. Margaret Taylor, a great friend to us, has found it. It is in South Leigh, which is 25 minutes by train from Oxford, 10 minutes from Witney. Aynsham is 2 miles away. Bablock Hythe about 3½. South Leigh is on the branch line which runs from Oxford to Yarnton, Aynsham, Witney, Bampton, & on up the Thames past Kelmscot to Lechdale. The house is called South Leigh Manor, but Margaret says that its name must not give me a dream picture of a moated, mullioned grange with coats of arms etc., but that obviously the Manor itself has vanished long ago and the house must be the old farmhouse that belonged to it. Its rent is £1 a week plus a couple of shillings a week rates. It has three bedrooms, two rooms downstairs, a tiny kitchen, & a washhouse where Margaret proposes installing a bath. It has a good garden in front & a bigger piece at the back. It is down a small farm drive. Attached to the house at the back is a cottage inhabited by an old couple who work for the neighbouring farmer—but looking the other way, and quite apart. The village is very small; one shop, one church (Margaret says it is lovely), one pub, and this is a Free House. But Witney, quite big, is only 10 minutes away. The House is 5 minutes from the station. I think we are very fortunate. Margaret has been going around by car for nearly 2 months, looking all over Oxfordshire, and this was the only place. She says she is going to move our Wentworth Studio pieces into it very soon; they are stored with her at Holywell Ford. All except the big bed, the beautiful studio bed, which, as I think I told you, was stolen by our tenant. Also Margaret has several bits & pieces for us. Now as to the furniture in Waunfort. Shall I let you know as soon as Margaret lets me know that she has settled about the house? and can Hobbs then move the furniture to Oxford, picking up Margaret on the way? You must let me know what Hobbs will charge, and I will send a cheque. We need, of course, every stick of furniture, every cup or frying pan, we can lay our hands on. We will be starting, once again, with no utensils or anything: I'll write to you about all this immediately I have definite information from Margaret.

I think I told you, before, that an Italian composer, Gino Managni Rocca, whom we met in Oxford—he is a friend of my friend Elizabeth Lutyens—has offered me part of his country house near Parma, after July, & is coming to Florence this month to see me & to talk about it. But obviously I cannot go there without money. Anyway, there is almost a stronger reason for our returning to England after our stay in this villa. Llewelyn must go to school; he must be with English boys of his own age. I'm afraid here he is getting very fed-up. There is so little for him to do, with only grown-ups and two small, bawling children. And, God, how they do bawl. They are, I'm afraid, bad for each other. Aeronwy is once more rather fractious and hysterical. There would be so much for Llewelyn to do with a boy of his own age here. The woods are beautiful; the garden one of the loveliest I've seen. There are wild groves and streams: paradise for cowboys & Indians. But he can't play all day alone. He reads a great deal: Dickens, Marryat, Arthur Ransome, Encyclopedias, Captain Cook's Travels, Stevenson, & anything he can find here, thrillers included. But he can't read all day, either. He makes elaborate paper games of his own. We have just hired a wireless, & he footles with this, getting the BBC Overseas Service mostly—but it doesn't come through very well. It's not much of a life for him though he is very well now, and brown, and fattening out. On Sundays, a family from Florence come out for the day with their two little boys: the man is editor of a literary quarterly here, and has translated lots of my poems. But the language barrier prevents Llewelyn & his boys really getting together.

It is terrifically hot to-day: ever since June began. It is useless to try to do anything between midday and 4 in the afternoon. And it will get hotter day by day. Florence lies below us, through the vines & olives, in a rippling haze.

Today there is a fiesta in Mosciano, & Brigit & Caitlin & the children are going. I am going to work. I cannot work usually in this house, even though it is large. Aeronwy & Tobias make a terrible din together, though Aeronwy is good enough by herself. So I work in a room in the peasant's cottage which is part of this estate: a good room, small & plain, looking into a wild wood. I am working on a long poem, but so slowly. And after it is finished, I want to write a radio play. Has my Swansea broadcast been on yet? I know it's due some time in June. Do tell me about it when you hear it.

My 'Portrait of the Artist' book of stories is also due this month on every bookstall in the shilling Guild edition. 50,000 copies to begin with.

I enclose a few American cuttings.

Can you give me Nancy's address when you write? She wrote to me very nicely, but I lost the letter & want to reply.

How is Idris? Remember me fondly to him.

Is Mabli a home dog again? Write soon.

And, so far as I know, & I hope, we will be seeing you, as usual in August.

Caitlin is writing. She sends her love.

And all my love,
Dylan

PS. I'm sorry: I can find only one American cutting, after all, from the best of the American University-sponsored quarterlies, the Southern Sewanee Review. Others when I can find them.
PPS. I have just had sent to me—Margaret again—'One Hole In The Wall' by Arthur Morrisson, & W. W. Jacob's 'Dialstone Lane' —both in the new Century Library. Both excellent. Also a very good thriller 'Deadlier than the Male' by Ambrose Grant, worth reading.

MSS.: Dylan Thomas Estate

Dylan was beginning to feel lonely, and found the heat oppressive. But he was writing poems again, or rather a poem, 'In Country Sleep'.

John Arlott, a famous commentator on cricket, was also a B.B.C. producer, of verse programmes among others.

TO JOHN ARLOTT

Villa del Beccaro,
Mosciano,
Scandicci,
Florence
June 11th 1947

My dear John,

Thank you for writing. It was very good to hear from you. Though I hear your voice every day: from Trent Bridge, at the moment. You're not only the best cricket commentator—far and away that; but the best sports commentator I've heard, ever; exact, enthusiastic, prejudiced, amazingly visual, authoritative, and friendly. A great pleasure to listen to you: I do look forward to it. Here, in the hills above Florence, I lead the quietest life I ever remember leading: it is sizzling hot, the hill to the nearest village is a spinebreaker, I am far too limp and lazy to go often to Florence, and I can work only in the early mornings and evenings: never my best time: I'm used to working from after lunch until pub-time, which in the country used to be about seven. Here I drink in the garden, alone or with Caitlin: we have no social life: I am a sun vegetable: I live on red wine, cheese, asparagus, artichokes, strawberries, etc. The etc. is usually more red wine. We have our own vineyard. The villa is enormous. So, probably, am I, after two months. I'm coming back in August: if the lire last till then. I was given some travelling money by the Authors' Society; otherwise I'd have been back long ago. And I'll be broke when I return, so any bits of booming—I heard Rape of Lucrece today; is Shakespeare over? and what is the next series?—narrating, etc., will be very welcome. Also, I'd love to write any programme you think I could do: and, scrupulously, on time.

Yes, of course I'd love some dollars, but I have so far, no poem. It would be useless giving you a chunk of the long one I'm twisting and gnarling: it's got to be read as a whole. If I do manage to write any short ones in between, I'll send them to you straightaway.

I can't afford to go to Venice. I've spent some time in Rome, in

Genoa, in Siena, and on the Riviera. But now I can just afford to
stay here on my sunburnt behind. I would like to go to Venice though.
Perhaps I can seduce your girl: or am I the wrong shape?

I'll be ringing you in August. Love to you & your family. Remember me to Val, when you see him. My daughter has fallen in a
cactus bush.

Yours,

Dylan

MSS.: John Arlott, Esq.

By mid July the heat and the solitude were getting him down.

TO T. W. EARP

Villa del Beccaro,

Mosciano,

Scandicci,

Florence

July 11th 1947

My dear Tommy,

> In a shuttered room I roast
> Like a pumpkin in a serra
> And the sun like buttered toast
> Drips upon the classic terra,
> Upon swimming pool and pillar,
> Loggia, lemon, pineclad pico,
> And this quite enchanting villa
> That isn't worth a fico,
> Upon terrace and frutteto
> Of this almost a palazzo
> Where the people talk potato
> And the weather drives me pazzo—

I am awfully sick of it here, on the beautiful hills above Florence,
drinking chianti in our marble shanty, sick of vini and contadini and
bambini, and sicker still when I go, bumby with mosquito bites, to
Florence itself, which is a gruelling museum. I loved it in Rome, felt
like Oppenheim on the Riviera, but we have been here, in this villa,
two months and I can write only early in the morning, when I don't

315

get up, and in the evening, when I go out. I've wanted to write to you, and have longed for a letter from you. We're coming back, some brown as shit, some bleached albino, one limp and carmine, all broke, early in August. Will you be in London, or visiting? I do hope we see each other often this autumn. I am told the bitter's better, and I will be writing a filmscript to buy same. We really do have an enormous swimming pool, (into which I have been only once, by mistake), and our own vineyard, olives, mosquitoes, and small Italian mice with blue chins. I have written a longish poem which I'd like to send you when it is typed by an Italian professor of English in Florence. I asked the professor about Elba, where we thought of going, and he said—it was the first remark I heard him make—'Plenty di fish-dog'. He translates Henry James and Virginia Woolf. Give my love to May and yourself. Write when you can, before August if possible, and tell me where, if you're in London, as you said, last time we met, you might be, I can write. Now I am going out to the cicadas to shake my legs a bit.

In the very opposite of haste,
Dylan

MSS.: Ohio

He had hoped that friends from England would visit him, but none came.

TO BILL AND HELEN MCALPINE

Villa del Beccaro,
Mosciano,
Scandicci,
Florence
July 14 1947

My dear Helen and Bill,

What a really big pity, and everybody waiting, from the torpedo lizards in the hairy pool—remind the gardener to change the water!—to the pick-axed and pneumatic-drilled mosquitoes in the guest's bedroom—remind the parlourmaid to take the bottles and the gorgonzola off the bed! We had planned such a lot of things to do, and all with wine: picnics, prickstrips, titlicks, nipsicks, gripwicks, slipthicks, tipsticks, liptricks, etcetera etcetera etcetera, parties, expeditions. Perhaps we can all come to Italy next year, and do things on a pig scale.

We are trying to arrange to spend our last weeks here in Elba, but have nearly exhausted our money and are twisting for more. We return on August 11th, and will be in London on the 13th. Will you be at home? And can you put us and our bags up for one night? Llewelyn, the next day, will go to his grandmother in Hampshire, & Cat, Aeron & I will go to Wales to see my mother for a fortnight. Then we return to a house Margaret has found us, in South Leigh, half an hour from Oxford: near Witney: small and a bit battered, but right in a village and in good country. I hope you'll be coming down, so much, and having beer and words: no, not having words.

The first two parts of my poem are finished. I'm working on the third. It's not as long as it sounds. I'll show it to you, please, when I come back.

The best to John.

What a pity you couldn't come.

Llewelyn is teaching English to some little girls nearby. As I write, in the garden, I can hear them doing their lessons, very loud: Funny bloody fart, funny bloody fart.

I do hope you'll be able to put us up that one night: we'll be rather lost.

Are you writing stories, Bill? I do hope there's a lot for me to read.

Love from both to both.

Dylan

MSS.: William McAlpine, Esq.

On 20th July 1947 they moved from Florence to Elba, which they loved. This is a postcard.

TO BILL AND HELEN MCALPINE

postmark 26th July 1947

A message from Albergo Elba, Rio Marina, Isola d'Elba, Italy. Lucky Napoleon! This is a most beautiful island; and Rio Marina the strangest town on it: only fishermen and miners live here: few tourists: no foreigners. Extremely tough. Something like a Latin Caherciveen. Notices 'Fighting Prohibited' in all bars. Elba cognac 3d. Of course, no licensing hours. Bathing wonderful. Regret your absence. Looking forward letter. Returning August 11th.

Love to both from all.

Dylan

Albergo Elba,
Rio Marina,
Isola d'Elba,
August 3rd 1947

My dear Margaret:

The heat! Old Elbanites on their flayed and blistered backs whimper about the heat. Sunblack webfooted waterboys, diving from cranes, bleed from the heat. Old scorched mineral-miners, fifty years in the fire, snarl at the heat as they drag the rusty trolleys naked over the skeleton piers. And as for us; The children all sun-and-sea-rashed, Brigit peeling like the papered wall of a blitzed room in the rain. And I can hardly hold this pen for the blisters all over my hands, can hardly see for the waterfall of sweat, and am peeling too like a drenched billboard. Oh, oh, oh, the heat! It comes round corners at you like an animal with windmill arms. As I enter my bedroom, it stuns, thuds, throttles, spins me round by my soaking hair, lays me flat as a mat and bat-blind on my boiled and steaming bed. We keep oozing from the ice-cream counters to the chemist's. Cold beer is bottled God. If ever, for a second, a wind, (but wind's no word for this snailslow sizzle-puff), protoplasmically crawls from the suffering still sea, it makes a noise like H.D.'s poems crackling in a furnace. I must stop writing to souse my head in a bedroom basin full of curded lava, return fresh as Freddie Hurdis-Jones in Sodom, frizzle and mew as I sit again on this Sing-Sing-hot-seat. What was I saying? Nothing is clear. My brains are hanging out like the intestines of a rabbit, or hanging down my back like hair. My tongue, for all the ice-cold God I drink, is hot as a camel-saddle sandily mounted by baked Bedouins. My eyes like over-ripe tomatoes strain at the sweating glass of a Saharan hothouse. I am hot. I am too hot. I wear nothing, in this tiny hotel-room, but the limp two rivers of my Robins'-made pyjama trousers. Oh for the cyclonic Siberian frigidity of a Turkish bath! In the pulverescence of the year came Christ the Niger. Christ, I'm hot!

But the Island I love, and I wish I were not seeing it in one of the seasons of hell.

Today is Sunday. On Thursday we go back to Florence, which is said to be hotter. On Monday, we catch our incinerator home.

Thank you, so much, for the £5. I hope you got my euphemistic wire. It was so welcome. And more, perhaps in the post now, will be welcome, welcome again. You are good to, & for, me. And the house! You find it, furnish it, scythe the garden, soften the bureaucrats; we are known, before we go, to the coaled & carred publican. Salute Bob Russell!

I will ring you as soon as we get to London, on the evening of the 12th or the morning of the 13th, and we will meet.

My brains are hanging out like a dog's tongue. I must go, looking for God, ice, impossible air, blister-biting blimp-blue bakehouse sea.

Till the 13th, about, goodbye.

I have altered several words in my poem.

Dylan

MSS.: Texas

Back in Oxfordshire in September he resumed the essentially unsatisfactory life that he had been leading before the Italian visit: commuting to London for the B.B.C. or for filmscript conferences, drinking too much when he got there, and doing very little serious work.

John Davenport was a member of the National Liberal Club and of the Authors' Club.

The 'dark and fantastic romance' was never written.

Normal was his nickname for Norman Cameron.

Roy Campbell, the South African poet, was one of Dylan's closest friends and favourite drinking companion at this time.

TO JOHN DAVENPORT

The Manor House,
South Leigh,
Witney,
Oxon.

September 24th, 1947

My dear John,

The above my permanent address, until they find us out. Do please forgive my not writing. I can only tap with one finger of my left hand on this decrepit engine. And sorry about no copy of my poem—tossed off in Florence one evening, between a Mass of Life and a little Crucifixion in oils—but found Roy Campbell had the last copy, which he was dragging around the thin puce belfries of the Third Programme. Roy had been the only person I had told, after lunch that day, that you were going to ask Redgrave if he, Redgrave, might think some time or another, of reading it if he liked it. Some of the words swirled into Roy's babble-box, a little of the highly hypothetical information strayed into that vague and thorny veldt, and the result must have been what Redgrave heard from the BBC : that he was quite definitely reading my poem. Do apologise to him for me, will you? I quite certainly had not misguided the BBC on purpose, nor mentioned R's name but in private maybe—in conversation. I shall be in town next Wednesday lunch: a week today. Could we meet? twelve or twelve-thirty? pub, Lib or Authors? I'd love to. Last time there were so many people, and I myself was just about an inch and a half above the ground: I mean, in the air, not sticking out.

I'm so glad you thought of getting a copy of my little egg from Normal.

I have rather a good film idea, which also might interest Redgrave: a dark and fantastic romance of the German 1830's. I'll try to type out a readable synopsis once I CAN USE TWO LEFT FINGERS AND HAVE A NEW RIBBON. Absolutely unexplained capitals!

Drop a line about Wednesday, can you?

Our Manor is a cottage, but only five minutes from Witney and exactly twenty five by train from Oxford. Do come down. Only one small single spare bed so far, but I think the new Davenport, that sveltie, could manage quite comfortably. One weekend snag is that the pub isn't open on Sundays, but others are only two miles off.

Do forgive me for not having written long before.

Love,
Dylan

MSS.: Texas

Robert Pocock was a B.B.C. producer and an old friend of Dylan's. He was apparently coming to stay with Dylan, and the George was a bar, with restaurant upstairs, much frequented by Dylan, in Oxford, at this time. Younger's Scotch, like Nicholson's, is a beer, not a whisky. Cordelia was the wife of Harry Locke—they too lived at South Leigh that summer. Phil was Philip Lindsay, the historical novelist.

TO ROBERT POCOCK

Manor House,
South Leigh,
Witney,
Oxon.
19th April 48

Dear Bob,

11.30 George this Saturday. Nicholson's XXXXX or Younger's Scotch. Lunch upstairs if greedy or faint. Cricket, Oxford v. Gloucester.

In the evening, in Witney, Cordelia and two odd friends, the Colgroves, will probably come with their van and take us to some country houses—public. My father & mother arrive to stay with us on Friday, which will imprison Caitlin, but she will be with us at least on Saturday morning. The landlord of the Fleece has nearly lost his eye, our dog Mable has eczema, our cat Satan had mange and is now dead, Caitlin has gone to London with Margaret Taylor & left me quite alone, the house beer has run out, I am 3 weeks behind with my filmscript, not having started it yet, my gas fire has just exploded, I have flooded the kitchen with boiling soup, I am broke. Caitlin has taken the cigarettes, I was suddenly sick in the middle of the night, Phil has just sent me his 25 shilling book about Hampton Court, rabbits have eaten the lettuce, and seven cows, who have opened the gate, are trying to get into the lavatory. There is no news.

Ever,
Dylan

By the summer of 1948 Dylan was anxious to return to Wales, and especially to Laugharne. Richard ('Diccon') and Frances Hughes had left their pretty pink house there, known as 'The Castle', which they had rented from a Mrs Starke.

This letter shows that Dylan was well aware that he was wasting both his time and his talent in England. Laugharne, now, assumed for him some of the qualities of that paradise lost for which he was ever searching.

TO FRANCES HUGHES

Manor House,
South Leigh,
Witney,
Oxfordshire

October 10 1948

Dear Frances,

Thank you for your letter.

I'm giving this to Margaret Taylor to give to you in Laugharne. Unfortunately, I can't get away myself; I'm trying to write a musical comedy film, and am weeks behindhand. Margaret Taylor has come to Laugharne to see if she can find out, for me, exactly how the Starke-Hughes-Castle case is going, and what chance there is of my getting the house for some years, and, if I did manage to, exactly what financial commitments I would be held to. Do, please, help her if you can.

I can't explain my 'longing' to have the castle any more clearly than I did in my letter to Diccon. I want very much to live in Laugharne because I know that there I can work well. Here, I am too near London; I undertake all sorts of little jobs, broadcasting etc., which hinder my own work. In Laugharne if I could live there, I would work half the year on my film-scripts, and half on my own poems and stories: cutting out all time-wasting broadcasts, articles, useless London visits.

I realise that there's a great difference between owning and renting a house, and that Mrs. Starke can be a querulous & annoying person to be tenant of. But, still, if anyone, not Mrs. Starke, is going to live in the castle, I'd like it to be Caitlin and me. So will you please, for both of us, let Margaret Taylor know how things stand? And if we could get the house, we'd like to buy, rent, or whatever, what furniture there still is in the Castle: that is, of course, if you are not going to take it away.

Anyway, we hope and we hope.

Caitlin's love,

Yours ever,

Dylan

MSS.: Richard Hughes, Esq.

The financial crisis remained chronic. Sydney B. is Sydney Box, the film producer, for whom Dylan was working at this time.

Picture Post was an illustrated magazine, not unlike *Life* but less glossy.

TO JOHN DAVENPORT

Manor House,
South Leigh,
Witney,
Oxon.
17 Nov. 1948

My dear John,

O God, what a pickle, and I'm entirely useless. If only I could raise ten pounds, ten mean little pounds, to help you whom I owe so much from the past. If only, just for our sake, I could raise a guarantee from someone else. But my lady-patron no longer plays, at least not in money, a night at the opera, yes, ballets and cocktails whenever, but not one more crisp crunchy note can I drag from her unloved breast.

My own foreign debt is pressing; the unanswered letters of the Italian lender grow briefer and less English. I have already borrowed in advance from my fee for my next unspecified filmscript in order to unfreeze my Bank account so that I can write little overdraft cheques to tradesmen and the publican. And, crowning all this, Brigit's, and Caitlin's mother and Brigit herself who is living with her have only this week written to say that they are penniless and that they must appeal to rich, cigary filmtycoon me.

I am so sorry, John, that my letter to you is as full of woes as yours to me. A wretched answer, I would to God I could send a better one. But I had to tell you how things are with me, if only they were one inch better, I could send some contribution. But all is stony here, and Christmas coming. Can Helen and Bill McAlpine do nothing? They are the only people I know who might help. Augustus? Oh, but you must have gone through all the possible names in your great unhappy head, my beamishless boy. And flippancy doesn't help. Would you care for a drink on Friday lunchtime? I'm in town to wheedle, Hennekey's downstairs 12.30 or 1? I'll ring and see anyway. I can at least buy some flat yellow pints, and we can whimper together. I'd love to see you. Why does your trouble coincide with mine? When I last saw you, at Brighton time, I was rolling in ready cash. Now I have to roll on credit. There's nothing here to sell. My soul's sold, my wits wander, my body wobbles, Aeronwy is too young, I won't let Caitlin, the only pictures on our walls are from Picture Post, our dog is a mongrel, our cat is half a mouse. Small cheer for the needy in the old Manor House. If you tackle the McAlpines, do so quickly: they leave London next weekend to take a cottage in this cowpad village.

I have not yet managed to see Sidney B about our working together. He is always out, or out to me, or showing his great teeth to Rank. But I may see him Thursday evening.

I will ring on Friday morning. I do hope we can meet.

All my apologies for so abysmally failing you.

Love,
Dylan

MSS.: Texas

In March of 1949 Dylan was invited to Prague by the Czecho-Slovak Writers' Union, who were staging an international congress. Dylan later remarked that he was the only person there who was not a Communist. The visit lasted less than a week.

Dylan was anxious to return to Wales, and Margaret Taylor had gone there to see if she could find a place for him and his family to live. The house called 'The Castle' at Laugharne was empty. Dylan had known it well both before and during the war, when Richard Hughes, the novelist, had lived there with his family. There now seemed to be some hope that Margaret Taylor might be able to rent it for Dylan. In fact this fell through, and a few months later she bought 'The Boat House', Laugharne, for him instead.

TO MARGARET TAYLOR

Spring 1949

Manor,

Thursday evening

My dear Margaret,

Your letter, just arrived by winged messenger, has set us dreamily grinning, hopelessly shaking our heads, then beaming and gabbling together again as we think of the great house at the end of the cherry-treed best street in the world, bang next to the Utrillo tower, with its wild gardens and owly ruins, the grey estuary, forever linked to me with poems done and to be, flat and fishy below with Tom Nero Rowlands, the one last fisherman, who hates the water, trudging through it like a flatfooted cat; saying to ourselves, 'No no no, do not dream of it, never for us too ugly too old', and then once more saying, not too loudly, 'Perhaps and perhaps, if we try, pray, whisper, fear the God, abjure drink and fighting, be humble, write poems, do not bite our nails, answer letters, collect the fallen apples for economical pulping into glass jars, do not throw her crutches at my mother, be good, be patient, sing, love one another, ask God for peace, perhaps and perhaps one day one day the owly castle and the noble house will be ours for some of the seven most heavenly years since pride fell.' Oh the kitchen for cooking & eating, for thinking Breughels! the room to the left as, praise be, you enter the house, that room for music and Caitlin dancing! the nursery for Aeronwy, that we must have more children to fill! the bedroom looking up at an unbalanced field, the field of infancy where even now we are all running so that, writing this in the rain, I can hear all our thin faraway children's voices glide over the plumtrees and through the ventilation skull-holes of this window! and the other bedroom looking out, happy as hell, at the clock of sweet Laugharne, the clock that tells the time backwards so that, soon, you walk about the town, from Browns to the gulls on the Strand, in the only Golden Age! the long cool once Dufy-hung living room: the only room in the world rightly described as one for living, and, at its end, the gravel path to the brass cannon pointing, as all cannons should point, uselessly out at the estuary air! the room, the velvet, padded room upstairs where poems are waiting like people one has always loved but never met, and O to sit there, lost, found, alone in the universe, at home, at last, the people all with their arms open! and then, but only through my tears, the hundreds of years of the colossal broken castle, owls asleep in the centuries, the same rooks talking as in Arthur's time which always goes on there as, unborn, you climb the stones to see river, sea, cormorants nesting like thin headstones, the cocklewomen webfoot, & the undead, round Pendine head, streaming like trippers up into seaside sky, making a noise like St Giles Fair, silent as all the electric chairs and bells of my nerves as I think, here, of the best town, the best house, the only castle, the mapped, measured, unhabited, drained, garaged, townhalled, pubbed and churched, shopped, gulled, and estuaried one state of happiness!

Shall I tell you what I think when we meet? I have plans and stratagems, dreams & details, a head herring'd with ideas, I am weak and ruthless and exultant about this. I would do anything. I will. To Caitlin, it is as adorable and as impossible to conceive as it is to me!

Oh, let's do what we can, I had to write this to you.

And we'd like to come out on Saturday.

Dylan

MSS.: Texas

In May 1949 they moved back to Laugharne, to 'The Boat House', which Margaret Taylor had bought for them. The following letter of thanks shows how grateful he was to her. This was to be Dylan's home for the remaining four years of his life. His parents he installed in a cottage called 'The Pelican', opposite Brown's Hotel.

Almost as soon as he arrived there he received a letter from John Malcolm Brinnin, inviting him to lecture in the United States. (For the background to this invitation the reader is referred to John Malcolm Brinnin's *Dylan Thomas in America*.) His reply was unequivocal.

TO MARGARET TAYLOR

Spring 1949

Boat House,
Tuesday

My dear Margaret,

I should have written. I have been meaning to write each day. I've been wanting to write, but have put it off and off. Oh, all those bells were cracked long ago! They ring like dustbins! But it's true that each day since coming to this place I love and where I want to live and where I can work and where I have started work (my own) already, I've been saying to my contemptible self, You must write to Margaret at once to say that this is it: the place, the house, the workroom, the time. I can never thank you enough for making this fresh beginning possible by all the trust you have put in me, by all the gifts you have made me, by all your labour & anxiety in face of callous & ungrateful behaviour. I know that the only way to express my deep deep gratitude is to be happy & to write. Here I am happy and writing. All I shall write in this water and tree room on the cliff, every word will be my thanks to you. I hope to God it will be good enough. I'll send you all I write. And ordinary letters too, full of trees & water & gossip & no news. This isn't that kind of letter. This is only the expression of the greatest gratitude in the world: you have given me a life. And now I am going to live it.

Dylan

MSS.: Texas

TO JOHN MALCOLM BRINNIN

The Boat House,
Laugharne,
Carmarthenshire,
Wales
May 28 1949

Dear John Malcolm Brinnin,

Let me first of all apologise for not having answered your letter long before this. Secondly, to thank you most sincerely for your letter.

And thirdly, to accept with great pleasure the invitation of the Poetry Center of your institution to come to the United States to give a reading of my poems.

About the first: I've been changing addresses, a lot, lately, and mail has been erratically forwarded. I had your letter only last week—but even then I should have answered it at once.

About the second: I feel extremely honoured to be the first poet to be invited from abroad, who was not already a visitor, and delighted too. I've wanted, for some time, to come to the States, and there couldn't be a pleasanter way of coming than this.

And about the third: I should like to come to New York to give my reading early in 1950, probably January or February. I should be only too glad to accept your sponsorship and to read in other places, including California.

Now about the financial side of it: I quite understand that you, as a non-profit-making organisation, must work on a modest budget, and, apart from transatlantic expenses, I should be prepared to accept, for my reading at your headquarters in New York, any fee that you yourselves think adequate. I must, however, point out that I have no private money, that I will arrive in New York with almost none and therefore must, by other arrangements made by you, make money immediately. I myself am very inefficient at arranging any financial details, but I am seeing my London literary agent next month & will ask him to get in touch with Ann Watkins Ltd of New York, with whom he is associated: she will then get in touch with you. I hope, also, that Ann Watkins will be able to fix up a few other jobs for me, outside of your sponsorship, so that I shall be able to bring back some money to England. I mention this—that I must bring back some money to England—because, in order to come to America, I shall, of course, have to refuse literary and broadcast commissions here for some months. And when I return to England, I shall be, more or less, starting off again, picking up scripts etc. here & there.

I hope I'm not writing confusedly: I've had influenza, and am full of injections.

I should like to stay in the States for about three months. Does that cover most of the points? I hope so. And I hope I'll hear from you soon again.

And, again, apologies for this overdue reply; & many many thanks for the honour you have paid me.

Yours sincerely,
Dylan Thomas

MSS.: John Malcolm Brinnin, Esq.

Almost all his letters written in the last quarter of 1949 are concerned with money troubles. He clung to his forthcoming American trip as the only hope of extricating himself and his family from these endless worries. (He now had three children, his youngest, Colm, having been born that summer.)

Jack Lindsay and Randall Swingler, who was still a Communist at that date, were co-editors of Rodney Philips's magazine *Arena*.

The B.B.C. was threatening to black-list Dylan altogether because of his failure to produce a script of *Peer Gynt* within the time specified by his contract. This threat, if carried out, would have deprived him of his principal source of income.

TO JOHN DAVENPORT

The Boat House,
Laugharne,
Carmarthenshire
13 October 1949

Dear John,

I've only now remembered that I addressed my yesterday's letter to you at Rossetti Mansions. It might not reach you. This, then, to make doubly sure, is to apologise for the fact that I haven't yet completed the promised poem for Arena, and to say that it will be ready for the next number and that the fee will be at least one crippling port, large, in the Savage or the Author's now that Kingsmill is dead and being cut by Dickens. And please do thank Jack and Randall for the telegram, and yourself, of course. Things are appalling here, which can only mean one thing. Bills and demand notes, at me like badgers, whoosh! up the manholes, or gathered, grinning and panting round my bed, odiously familiar, like the little hyenas in Paphnutius's cell. It is bad in a small community where everything is known, temporary insolvency goes the glad rounds as swift as a mis-carriage. I owe a quarter's rent on my mother's house, Llewelyn's school fees (for last term), much to each tradesman. Yesterday I broke a tooth on a minto. There are cats in the lavatory, tittering while you shit, and the official rat man comes every day to give them titbits before the kill. Unfortunately, for my peace of mind, the rat man has only one arm. I am three months behind with my filmscript, a year behind with Peer Gynt. I have the hot and cold rose-flush comings and goings after elderberry wine last night in a hamhooked kitchen with impossibly rich, and thunderingly mean, ferret-faced farmers, who dislike me so much they treat me like a brother. At last the National insurance has caught up with me who has never put a stamp on his card, having no card. If you see anyone likely, pinch his boots for me. I cannot come to London to hunt, for obvious reasons. Indeed, I dare not step out. This morning I had a toadstool for breakfast, and Caitlin called me a guttersnipe, though there seemed to be no connection. I'm sorry to write you such mournings.

See you at the barracudas.

Love,
Dylan

MSS.: Texas

James Laughlin IV, the owner of the publishing house, New Directions, was Dylan's American publisher.

Godfrey Winn is an English newspaper columnist with a tendency to gush that has made him extremely popular with the British public.

TO JAMES LAUGHLIN

The Boat House,
Laugharne,
Carmarthenshire,
Wales
October 13th 1949
(Thomas-hunting begins)

Dear Jay,

Have you heard that I'm supposed to be coming to the States in February 1950? I've been asked, by John Malcolm Brinnin—what's he like?—to read, grandly and solemnly, like a man with the Elgin marbles in his mouth, poems to the Y.M. & Y.W.H.A. at New York on, I think, February 23. Brinnin said that he could also fix up a few more readings in various parts, including California. Do you know of any people, places, institutions, etc. from whom or which, by reading aloud modern British poems and a few, as few as possible, of my own, I could get a handful of dollars? Ann Watkins is seeing to the Brinnin side: which, if his letters are any proof, is what he has. Perhaps, if anything occurred to you, you could have a word with, or drop a line to, her? I'd be very very grateful. I want to stay in the States for three months. And I want to be able to return to England with some money so that I won't, at once, have to chase again the hackjobs by which, dear Christ, I live, have at once to set into motion again the insignificant, wheezy little machines that sausage out crumbs and coppers for me, scriptlings, radio whinnies. I don't want to find myself in New York with only two or three scantily paying engagements in front of me, and to return as broke as when I arrived. We have a new, three months' old son. I would, naturally, have to support him, my other two children at school, and my wife, for the three months of my absence. I should like to be able to bring my wife with me. Would that be possible do you think? I don't want to load you with all my worries and apprehensions, but whom else do I load? The idea of the States puts the fear of Mammon in me, though I very much want to come. Briefly, can you help, in a practical way, to alleviate the worries of my visit? How, I don't know. But do write and tell me something soon, if you will. Maybe I should be writing like this to Brinnin, not to you. But you I know, all nine feet of you, as I remember, and me in my abbreviated coat, and Godfrey Winn. If I cannot bring my wife, then I must leave with her money enough for three English (or Welsh) enormously costly months? And how the hell am I to do that?

Here, we can nearly carry on by my drivelling for films & radio. Without me, the Boat House sinks, the cormorants have it. Indeed, I can hardly, now, walk up the main street of this sad, lovely town without the bowler-hatted shags at my throat and ankles.

So please do write. Suggest what you can. Say what you like.

I have a couple of poems and a few autobiographical sketches which, perhaps, you could try to place for me in the commercial magazines. I'll send them on when they are found, washed and typed.

There are, I suppose, no chances of a reading on the radio? Why should there be?

I want to enjoy my visit, and come back rustling, if wobbly.

Yours,
Dylan

MSS.: James Laughlin IV

The late Princess Caetani was an American lady who devoted a small part of her very large fortune to the publication, from Rome, of an avant-garde, international, literary magazine, *Botteghe Oscure,* called after the name of the street in which she had her palazzo.

TO PRINCESS CAETANI

The Boat House,
Laugharne,
Carmarthenshire
2nd November 1949

Dear Madame di Sermoneta,

I did enjoy, very much, meeting in London, though, to me, the meetings were all too brief and few. That, I feel, is entirely my fault. In London I am flustered, excited, unable to concentrate; I am so nervous, usually for no reason, that my nervousness too often turns to unintentional rudeness; I am stupid, shy, and garrulously arrogant in turn; all I seem to want to do is to get away from where I am and from what I am doing, however much I might like where I am and what I am doing; I can almost never say what I really mean to say; I am out of my world—though what that world may be, God knows—altogether. And it is for these reasons, and for many others, I am sure, which I am not, myself, perceptive enough to see, that our meetings were so brief, so very few.

So let me apologise, from this calm distance from London, for what must have appeared to be my vague and pointless behaviour and—what is worse—my ingratitude.

I wanted to talk to you about your magazine, and to hear you talk about it; I wanted to discuss with you several things in it that seemed to me to be of particular interest; I wanted to suggest to you the names of a few little-known English writers whose work I thought you might like to see.

And, instead of that, all I could do was to talk, disconcertedly, about myself, scatter you with ash, gollup your whisky-&-soda, make an inexact arrangement with you about a short story of my own, and then rush off into the London night I loathe.

But let me, anyway, and in writing, try to make exact the position of the story which I am to write for Botteghe. The next story I write is to be given to you immediately. In our conversation—if you can grace with that word a jumble of ineptitude from myself and some kind words from you—you gave me no time-limit by which the story should reach you. If you care to give me a rough time-limit, I shall abide by that. The story I will try to make as good as I can.

And you, do you remember, agreed to pay me, in advance, for that story, the sum of £100. And there is, of course, no further money than that due to me from Botteghe for that story.

You gave me a cheque for £50, and said that you could send on the remaining £50 very soon.

I hope I am right in my interpretation of our agreement.

And now, I come to the most shamefaced part of this shamefaced letter.

I need that other £50 so very desperately, so very quickly.

When I came home, thank God, from London, I found my wife ill, really ill, with worry over the summonses for debt that had been pouring into the house during my absence. The amount needed to clear them is, to us, enormous, insurmountable. But if I could possibly have that £50 straight, straight away, I could at least settle the most urgent and virulent debt of all.

I apologise for the horribly stilted manner in which I am writing to you. I, too, am too sick with money to feel, for a moment, free.

But all I mean is, I'm in a hell of a hole. I see no way of getting out of it. But that other money, if sent to me at once on the wings of the dove of the Air Mail from whatever country you are in, would help. (I was, of course, too careless, too conscienceless, to enquire from you where you were going when you left the Connaught Hotel. I can only hope this letter reaches you very soon.)

What self-pity I drench these pages in! How ghastly to read they must be! But all I can say, in any possible extenuation, is that, in all my moneyless days, I have never been more hopelessly engulfed in debt, that we can't sleep, and I can't work.

When I see you again, if ever, I can tell you, perhaps, what the hellish circumstances were. Now, however, there is no past tense: the hellish circumstances just are.

Thank you for your kindness in London.

Yours sincerely,
Dylan Thomas

MSS.: Texas

Ann Watkins was his American literary agent, but she had little to do with his visits to the United States.

TO JOHN MALCOLM BRINNIN

The Boat House,
Laugharne,
Carmarthenshire,
Wales
November 23 1949

Dear John Malcolm Brinnin,

First of all: many apologies for this month-long delay in answering your extremely nice and helpful letter. My lying cable said, 'Letter in mail'. And I did intend to write at once, but had to go away, felt suddenly ill, clean forgot, put it all off for a rainy day, was struck by lightning, any or all of these. And your cable about a second reading, my wife's mislaid, found only this morning in a mousenest handbag.

Thank you profoundly for your letter. I can't tell you how pleased I am that you should have suggested you look after my American readings. I can think of nothing more sensibly pleasant. What an abominable phrase! Nothing I have ever enjoyed has been sensibly pleasant. I mean, I can think of nothing better. I was very nervous about my visit: that is, about the arranging of readings to make some money. I should have made a mess of things. My life here, in the deep country, is incredibly complicated, but in a city, I spin like a top. And procrastination is an element in which I live. Thank you, very much indeed, for having, in the first place, made my visit possible, and for wishing to work with me. Naturally, I understand about the fee for expenses; I couldn't, anyway, allow you to work with me if you did not take a percentage. And the 15 per cent you mention is very, very moderate for all the troublesome work you'll have to do. I feel relieved now; and can face the whole undertaking with only quite minor paralysis.

It's very very good of you to lend me your New York apartment for my stay there. And the idea of a little rest cure in Saratoga Springs is also appealing: I think I shall need it.

As to the number of readings: you say that you will be able, you think, 'to arrange for, at least, fifteen engagements, and, very likely, considerably more'. How many jobs do you think I should do? I don't want to work my head off, but, on the other hand, I do want to return to England with some dollars in my pocket. And, of course, I want to get around the States a bit. I'll have to leave this to you. I have been asked to be one of the Kemball-lecturers-for-the-year at Mount Holyoke College, Massachusetts, at a fee of 150 dollars. I think I should accept this, don't you? And would it be possible to give a reading somewhere else near there— boring two birds with one stone? I should say, sometime in March for Holyoke. But you will know when to fit it in. I shall write today, to Holyoke, accepting, and saying that you will get in touch with them suggesting some dates, most possibly in March, which might be convenient for them. I enclose the Holyoke letter. Is that all right? Also: the Watkins agent has been writing to Robert Richman, of the Institute of Contemporary Art, about a reading at the library of Congress. I enclose Watkins' letter to Richman. Would you care to write to Watkins about this? and arrange what you think best—if anything. I must say Richman wants a hell of a lot of the profits. I hand the baby over, with bewildered gratitude.

I should, incidentally, like very much to go to California.

I hope, I do hope, that in most of the cases you will be able to arrange that travelling expenses be paid in addition to the fee. It seems very important. And that leads me to the trickiest, to my mind, problem of all: Treasury permission from here to go over to the States. And the money with which to travel. I've no idea how to approach the Treasury about this, or what U.S. Departments I must approach. No idea in the world. Can you help in this? It's a kind of bureaucratic nightmare: why are you going? who wants you to go? What will you do when you get there? Are you a Communist? Do you have clean thoughts? And the question of travelling money: I want, if possible, to go by plane, not liking the big dull sea except to look at. This costs in English money about £80. How many dollars that is, since the devaluation of the pound, I have no idea. I presume that the 500 dollars you offer me, through the Poetry Centre, includes my travelling expenses to America. Is it possible for you to let me have an advance cheque to pay for the plane journey? And soon! I say, 'soon', because I know I should book a plane trip well in advance. Whether you can or not, I've no way of telling—until you write. Do write quickly about this important point. And also about the Treasury etc. formalities, or what you know of them. I dare say my London Literary Agent can help a bit, but he's a stiff sod and frightens the life out of me: I believe he is always waiting for an Enormous Novel, which he won't get.

I do wish we could talk these things over a drink.

Lloyd Frankenberg has written to me, saying that he is to be in charge of a series of Poetry Readings at the Museum of Modern Art, & wanting me to give one. He said that, when he knew the dates & the fees, he would get in touch with the Watkins agents. I shall now write to him & tell him that, for my visit, you've very kindly undertaken to act as my agent etc. and will he arrange this through you.

About the readings themselves: Is there any strong reason why my readings should all be devoted to my own work? I most sincerely hope not. What I should like to do, more than anything else, is to read from a number of contemporary British poets, including myself. I far prefer reading other chaps' work to my own: I find it clearer. An hour of me aloud is hell, & produces large burning spots in front of the mind.

Will you be seeing Laughlin? He wrote to me about the same time you did, saying that 'to make any real money for you, things will have to be done hard and tough and business-like'. I hope you're an adamantine tartar. Laughlin also suggests that 'it might be well to get up a variant programme in which you would read the classic English poets'. What do you think? Personally, I shall be glad to read anything—& will certainly do my best to make it entertaining— except poems in dialect, hymns to Stalin, anything over 500 lines. Dare I, in my Welsh-English voice, read any American poets to American audiences? Over here, when I give broadcast readings, I quite often read some Ransome. But, whatever your opinion, I do very much want to read from other contemporary British poets. At the mere thought of reading only myself, I begin to feel hunted, invisible trolls shake hands with my Adam's apple.

There are so many urgent matters in this letter, I shan't now burden you with any more but will wait for your reply.

Very very many thanks again, for what you have done and will do, for the apartment, for all the friendliness.

I hope to see you a few days before the 23rd of February, in N. York.

Laughlin says there will be a party for me at the Gotham Book Mart as soon as I get there: I shall polish up my glass belly.

With best wishes,

Yours sincerely,

Dylan Thomas

Will you, anyway, get in touch with Jay Laughlin who, I'm sure, will be very helpful about lots of things. He said, in his last letter, that he'd be going into details with Watkins & seeing what, between them, they could cook up. Perhaps he can cook up something with you now. About MONEY, pretty money.

MSS.: John Malcolm Brinnin, Esq.

The novel he refers to is still *Adventures in The Skin Trade,* on which he had done no work for at least ten years.

The book of short stories and sketches is *Quite Early One Morning,* published after his death.

Ruthven Todd, the poet, was an old friend of Dylan's and was now living in New York.

TO JAMES LAUGHLIN

The Boat House,

Laugharne,

Carmarthenshire,

Wales

Nov. 23 1949

Dear J,

Thank you, a lot, for your nice letter. It's good to think I have a friend your side, helping to Cook Things Up.

Perhaps Brinnin has already got in touch with you, and told you that he's undertaken to act as my agent, for readings etc., for my three months' visit? It seems quite a wise move; he says he's capable of looking after all details, of getting jobs and collecting the dibs, which I'm certainly not. I do want to dig up a few lucrative readings, as well as to get around and, in my mazy way, enjoy myself. I've asked Brinnin to see you, & be a co-Cook.

My wife, incidentally, won't be coming over, or trying to come over, after all. Since the birth of our last son—4 loud months now—she's been most unwell. All she wants is a long and sun-soaked rest cure, which is hardly what she would get in New York in February. If I can possibly manage it—it is only the tiny problem of money—I'd like to send her, for 3 months, to Italy. She likes the little island of Elba, where she can live very well and cheaply. That would be nice. It is only money I have not got. (I have half a novel. Well, nearly half. The novel will not be more than 70–80,000 words. You wouldn't, I suppose, like to give me an advance on that? Well, I can but ask.)

I hope you won't have gone on your European trip before I arrive. I'll try to get to New York about February 20 that is, if Brinnin, on behalf of the Y.M. & Y.W.H.A. Poetry Centre, can advance me, from my 500 dollars for my first reading, enough for my plane fare. I don't want to, unless I have to, go by boat. I like it up in the air, having frequently lived there.

No, I haven't enough poems for a new book. Not for a year or more. I'll be publishing a collection of stories & sketches here in England, but several of the stories you've already printed, old ones, in The World I Breathe: J. M. Dent considered those particular stories to be, in parts, obscene. Now that I am better known here, they don't seem to mind so much. And the other stories & sketches that will make up the English book won't be enough to make a separate American one. I'll be sending some sketches to you for you to—as you very kindly suggested—bring across to Watkins to sell with aggression to the richer periodicals, I hope.

I'm having a tough time here at the moment. I want to write only poems, but that can't be. Never have I wanted to more. But debts are battering at me. I cannot sleep for them. Quite a moderate sum would clear them up & make the tradesmen twinkle. I wish I could sell my body to a rich widow; but it is fat now and trembles a little. I'm sick of being so damned & utterly broke, it spoils things. I want to build poems big & solid enough for people to be able to walk & sit about and eat & drink and make love in them. Now I have only the scaffoldings of poems, never being unbadgered enough to put up roofs & walls. My table's heaped with odd lines, single words, nothing completed. (And this letter did not, oddly enough, begin as a whine of my woes).

I hope Brinnin will keep you informed as to what arrangements he is making for me.

I look forward to my visit, to meeting you again. I like the idea of the Gotham Book party. I should like to go to New Orleans, but I suppose it is too far.

Is there anyone I should write to? Is there anything I should do? Oh, helpless baboon!

Thanks for Ruthven's address. Good old Ruthven, as you say. But I won't stay with him. Brinnin is lending me his apartment. Good old Brinnin too.

What else? I can't think. I'm cold, it's raining on the sea, the herons are going home, the cormorants have packed up, I must go and play darts in the cheerless bar, put my flat beer on the slate, listen to talk about swedes and bulldozers, Mrs. Griffith's ulcer, what Mr. Jenkins said to Mrs. Prothero who is no better than she ought to be, the date of Princess Margaret's birthday, the price of geese, Christmas coming—oh, horrid thought! No presents for the unfortunate, importunate, devilish, trusting children! No Scotch or puddings or mincepies or holly! Just cold bills on toast, boiled writs, summonses on the spit!—the deaths of neighbours, the infamy of relations, the stature of Churchill, the invasion of water voles!

If you can help Brinnin in any way, I know you will.

Yours ever,
Dylan

I'll send odd sketches along when typed.

MSS.: James Laughlin IV

Louis MacNeice did indeed go to Athens as British Council representative, but Dylan was not officially offered his old job with the B.B.C.

TO PRINCESS CAETANI

The Boat House,
Laugharne,
Carmarthenshire,
Wales
24th November 1949

Dear Madame di Sermoneta, (is that what I should call you? You have so many names)

Please forgive me for this long delay in answering your very pleasant letter and acknowledging, with a thousand thanks, your generous and most welcome cheque: I have been away, giving readings of poems (not my own) to various societies in Wales and haven't had time to write a word. The cheque helped, greatly. I can see now over the boiling edge of my debts. Thank you, for replying so graciously, and so soon, though you were ill in bed. I do indeed hope you are well again, and back in Rome.

I see that you are wanting the story by March the first. And March the first it will certainly be, if I am not, before then, popped into the cooler, peeled, pipped, and sliced. I have the skeleton of a story now, but so unpleasant that it should perhaps remain in the cupboard. I'll see. But a story, anyway, will come. And, later, a poem. I am glad you like Fern Hill best of my poems to date. I also used to like it, & think it was among the, say, half dozen of mine which came nearest to what I had in heart and mind and muscle when first I wished to write them. I do not, now, read any of my poems with much pleasure, because they tell me I should be writing other poems now; because, they say I should work on poems every day; because, when I see all their faults, I think that in the new poems I should be writing, those kind of faults, at least, would not occur again; because, falling so short of the heights I had wished them, they are cruel and not-to-be-gainsaid reminders of the fact that only through unceasingly devoted and patiently passionate work at the words of always new poems can I ever hope to gain even an inch or a hairslength. I do not like reading my old poems, because I am not working on new poems, because I must earn my living by bits and pieces of forced prose, by exhibitionist broadcasts, by journalistic snippits; because, nowadays, I can never spare the time to begin, work through, and complete a poem regardless of time; because my room is littered with beginnings, each staring me accusingly in the eyes.

Next year, in February, I go to the U.S.A. to give readings of poems and, I hope, to earn some dollars to bring, rustling, home. I shall spend 3 months there. Have you any friends there you would like me to see, or rather, whose addresses you would like to give me? I shall be going to, I believe, Washington, California, Massachusetts, as well as New York. But I know very few Americans.

And, when I return in the spring, I think I shall be offered quite a good job on the B.B.C., taking over Louis Macneice's job when he goes, as British Council representative, to Athens. This would entail only a few broadcast scripts for me to write, which I will enjoy, and those to be as imaginative & experimental as I like. So, perhaps, in the coming year my most horribly pressing problems will be solved. I now have only to live through the next few months, which include

Christmas. And how I am to do that, I've no idea in the whole world.

I am glad you will be spending some of the summer in England, and that we can meet then somewhere in the country. I shall look forward to that, very much.

So thank you again.

It's a fine life, if you don't weaken.

Your letter helped me.

In all friendship,

Yours sincerely,

Dylan Thomas

MSS.: Texas

The letter that follows is of course a parody.

TO JOHN DAVENPORT

Late 1949?

Boat House,

Laugharne

Dear Comrade,

I was sorry to miss you when I was up in the smoke last week, I was quite looking forward to a good chat about Arena in the 'local' but you know how it is, I got caught up with rewording a petition against decadent tendencies in the cultural field, I expect you'll agree with subsection 4, it was my idea, I had the hell of a job getting it past, I can tell you, they thought it was a bit individualist, but that's them all over. Bert and I had a regular square-up, but he came over to my way of thinking once we got down the old Coal Hole. I had him almost laughing in the end. 'You poets will be the death of me,' was all he could say. There's more to Bert than meets the eye, I happen to know, as a matter of fact, he often listens to the third but, for Christ's sake, don't let on I told you, he's as sensitive as a kid about being tough and anti-pansy—remember when he threw his beer all over that chap with long hair in that boozer, near Kew Gardens? Mind, I don't say he didn't deserve it, but it's his own hair, I said, remember, he can do what he likes with it so far as I am concerned. But here I am rambling on, and there's work to be done. I've got a little meeting in the back room of Brown's tonight, Ivy Williams is going to be chairman, you wouldn't think she was with us, would you? She's hot, I can tell you. We're trying to organise a left library in the snooker room, I know it sounds small beer, but by God, you don't know this burg or do you? It's true bloody blue to the core, even the workers vote Liberal and as for listening to a word against dear Winston—a chap almost knocked me down last week for saying this was a slave state, and he was only a lorry driver too earning four quid odd, it's uphill work down here I can tell you, and there's hardly any time left to get on with the old poetry. But still I've got a new one ticking over, it's going to be something pretty big, I hope, a kind of colloquial lycidas set in the Rhonndda valley.

I'll be painting London red again—and do I mean it—on Jan. second. See you then.

Dyl.

MSS.: Texas

The late Lawrence Gilliam was head of the B.B.C.'s Features Department.

TO DAVID HIGHAM

The Boat House,
Laugharne,
Carmarthenshire
December 1 1949

Dear David,

America:

I'm intent on going now, and had better straightaway acquaint you with what has been happening.

John Malcolm Brinnin has written to me at length, suggesting that he, as a wellknown lecturer, literary journalist, etc., in the States, and as Director of the Poetry Centre of the Y.M. & Y.W.H.A. of New York, should become my secretary and agent for my stay there. He offered me, as well as his own peculiar knowledge of the American literary scene (if you'll excuse me), with particular reference to its poetry, a flat, or apartment, in the centre of N. York and a country cottage some little distance out in which to relax (or recuperate). He said that the Lecture Agencies, which prefer novelists anyway, have nowhere near his own acquaintanceship with the institutions etc. which like poets, and would take, for their services, anything up to

40% of what I might make on my appearances as a reader and lecturer. I cabled back & agreed, realising that Ann Watkins Inc are primarily literary agents, and believing that Brinnin will really do a good job for me. (I hear extremely well of him from Laughlin.) Brinnin wrote to me today, saying that he had already 'Committed me to, or penultimately arranged, visits to (beyond the initial two Poetry Centre readings) Harvard, Library of Congress, Bryn Mawr, Vassar, Amherst College, University of Chicago, Iowa State University, University of Michigan, Wayne University, Detroit, Smith College, Holyoke College, Massachusetts, etc.' And he says he can arrange as many readings elsewhere as I am prepared to give. These alone, on top of the reading (or readings) for the Museum of Modern Art, as mentioned in Lloyd Frankenberg's letter make, for me, the prospect of my visit extremely worth while.

I wrote to Brinnin, before his letter arrived today, asking him to let me know, as soon as possible, what were the Treasury, Passport, etc. formalities through which I would have to go. And I expect to hear from him soon. But I should also like to have a clear word with you about all this. I understand nothing of it. Nothing at all. But surely a letter from Brinnin, acting as my secretary & Lecture-Agent, and detailing all the arrangements he has made with such eminently respectable & excellent-sounding institutions such as Harvard, Vassar, Bryn Mawr, Museum of Art, Library of Congress, would mean something to the Treasury & to all the bureaucrats concerned? I shall be in London at 4.30 p.m. on the 11th of December, and will stay on the 12th, 13th, & 14th, rehearsing for a broadcast play of MacNeice's. So could I, either on the 11th, or at some lunchtime on any of those other days, meet you so that I can get some of my most pressing problems ('Who do I go to?' 'What do I have to say?' etc.) straight, or straighter? I must, I suppose, hurry everything up, as visas, travel-tickets, etc., cannot be too easy to procure.

Incidentally, MacNeice has written me a private, off-the-cuff letter, though on behalf of Laurence Gilliam, asking me whether I would like to take his (MacNeice's, of course) job over, on the BBC staff, when he leaves to be British Council representative in Athens some time in the New Year. I replied, enthusiastically, yes. MacNeice said I would get the same salary as himself, would not be expected to produce the scripts I write (so long as I do produce them) and could do most of my work in Wales. It sounds, doesn't it, ideal. It will be imaginative scripts, of my own, that will, on the whole, be required. I am only hoping that the job will be open for me until I return from the States at, probably, the end of May.

Let me know what you think of my firm decision to go to America. And when you can see me to advise me, if you will, about all the technicalities of Treasury & travel.

I enclose, signed, the 4 Exemption Certificates you sent.

Yours,
Dylan

MSS.: David Higham Associates

Dylan had been asked to propose the toast, and make a speech, at the annual dinner of the British Medical Association, Swansea branch. He failed to turn up for the dinner.

TO MR CELLAN-JONES

The Boat House,
Laugharne,
Carmarthenshire
10 January 1950

Dear Mr. Cellan-Jones,

I owe you so many apologies I don't know where to begin, but as I must begin somewhere let me please say, shaggy forehead to ground and tail wagging in a desperate effort at propitiation, how very very sorry I was not to have been able to answer at once your kind and charming, censorious and forgiving, letter—which I did not deserve a bit but which I was deeply delighted to have. (Looking back, for a second, at what I've written, I see that an unfriendly eye—a Swansea doctor's eye, for instance—could interpret me as meaning that I think I did not deserve your censoriousness. That is far from the case. Indeed, I thought that your remark about having wished, on October 20th, to murder me in cold blood to be little short, or shorn, of lamb-like. I should have wished upon myself the Death of a Thousand Cuts; and especially if I were a Surgeon.) But I'm apologising now, in the first place, for what must have seemed to you the final rudeness, the last straw, if you'll forgive me, that breaks the Cellan's back: I mean, the fact that I did not acknowledge straightaway your incredibly lenient letter of nearly a month ago. I plead that the collected will of the Members of the Swansea Branch of the British Medical Association, working by a clinically white magic known only to their profession, drove me, soon after my inexcusable non-appearance at their Annual

342

Dinner, into a bag of sickness and a cropper of accidents from which I have not yet fully recovered. The first effect of this malevolent mass medical bedevilment I experienced a week after the Dinner when stopping, heavily disguised, at Swansea in order to try to learn how really execrated I was in the surgeries and theatres, the bolus-rooms and Celtic lazarets, of a town I can approach now only in the deepest dark and where certain areas, particularly around the hospital, are forever taboo to me. I felt sudden and excruciating pains, and when I whimpered about them to a friend he said 'Whatever you do, don't get ill in Swansea, it's more than your life is worth. Go in with a cough and they'll circumcise you'. So I knew what the position was, and I took my pains home. But even at home, word of my unworthiness had reached the doctor's ears, and I was treated like a leper (fortunately, a wrong diagnosis). Ever since then I have felt unwell. A little later I had an attack of gout—undoubtedly the result of some Swansea specialist sticking a pin into a wax toe—and a little later still was set upon by invisible opponents in the bogled Laugharne dark and fell down and cracked my ribs. So that when your very nice letter was forwarded to me—needing medical attention, naturally I could not spend Christmas in Wales whose every doctor loathed my every rib— I was in bed, in London, feeling like hell, unable to write a word, unable even to answer you, to thank you for your forgiveness and for all you said about my part in 'Swansea and the Arts'. I want to thank you now, belatedly but most gratefully, for that letter. And I do hope you understand why I did not acknowledge it long, long before.

This leads me to try to make an apology for a far more serious breach of courtesy and good faith, and one of which I am profoundly ashamed. I felt, and knew, it to be a great honour when I was invited to be your chief guest and to propose the British Medical Association at your Annual Dinner. I looked forward a very great deal to that evening, though not without much knocking at the knees, and wrote a long, but not, I hope, too ponderous, address, and demothed my monkey-suit, and borrowed some proper shoes, which hurt, and went up to London a few days before, on a radio job, with all the good intentions in the world. The evening of the 19th, when about to set out for Paddington, an acquaintance of mine said 'I have a new, a very fast, sportscar, a present from my Mother'—who should know better— 'and I will drive you down to Wales like winking. We will spend the night at Bristol'. The car was very fast, he did drive like winking, and we did spend the night at Bristol. Just outside Bristol, he drove his car into a telegraph post and buckled it, which I hope drove his Mother mad. And we spent the night, sick and shaken, in a hotel that frowned

343

at our bruises and blood; and when I crawled out of bed on the afternoon of the 20th, I could not find my acquaintance—the police, I was told, had called to see him—nor his buckled car in which I had left my bag in which I had left my strenuously worked-upon address, my suit, my borrowed hurting shoes. I looked round several garages; it wasn't there. And I was far too timid to dare to enquire at the police-station the whereabouts of car, acquaintance, bag, suit, address, or shoes. And, anyway, by now it was too late to catch a train which would get me to Swansea in time to deliver, in the suit I hadn't got, the address I couldn't find.

I should, I know, have informed you of this sad, sordid story the very next day. But I put such a confession off and off and off until it seemed too late to matter: by this time, I realised, I was among the doomed.

Written down cold, months after, it does, I agree, sound a thin tall story. The unfortunate fact is that I am one of those people to whom these stories really do happen.

I do hope you will be able, somehow, to accept this preposterous excuse, although it is so very lately given. And I hope you will be able to convey my most heartfelt apologies to your colleagues for all the inconvenience, and worse, caused by my failure to attend their Dinner.

And I hope, last of all, that because one Welsh writer has proved himself unworthy of the honour they were so generous to bestow upon him by their invitation, they will not, in future, think that no Welsh writer can be trusted. No Welsh writer can.

Thank you, again, for your letter and for the very kind things you said: I hope, one day, that I shall deserve them.

Yours very sincerely,
Dylan Thomas

MSS.: The B.M.A., Swansea Branch

I do not know what the story is of which he claims to have written half. I suspect that it was one of his old pre-war stories, perhaps 'In the Direction of the Beginning'. It is possible that it may have been the story which he called quite simply, 'A Story', though I doubt this, for that piece of prose was scarcely suitable for *Botteghe Oscure*. It may not have existed at all.

TO PRINCESS CAETANI

The Boat House,
Laugharne,
Carmarthenshire
12 January 1950

Dear Madame Caetani,

How extremely nice of you! Madame Subercaseaux sent us that lovely New Year's 'token'—and what an insufficient word that is—some time last week, and it arrived, not out of the blue, but of the pouring black. It arrived just at the very moment that the darling Bank wrote to me and said I must cash no more cheques, for however tiny amounts, until an overdraft (quite insurmountable) is paid. It arrived when I hadn't sufficient enough to buy cigarettes—what Lawrence called 'those tubular white ants'—and without these I feel naked and lost. It arrived when It was welcomer than the sun—and what a way to talk about money! Thank you, most really, for your goodness. We are trying to live on that 'token' now—and that alone —until my raked and weather-sloshed, leaking, creaking, bit of a boat limps home. Thank you again, and for your sweet letter.

And thank you for promising me to send me letters to your sisters in New York & Washington. I shall be in New York on or about the 20th of February, and in Washington sometime in March, when I read poems at the Library of Congress. And I will certainly, with your letters and your permission, look them both up. And I will try not to be arrogant and awkward and unpleasant, as I was with you— but these apologies are over now, and next time we meet I shall, I hope, and since your recent letters, be at my ease with you, & therefore simple and natural. I shall like to meet your sisters. Are they like you? And, yes, I shall be going to Harvard; and so perhaps I can meet your friends there? I'm not sure if I go to Princeton, but I shall know when I reach New York, and then, if I may, I shall write to you.

My story for you is only ½ completed. I have been worrying so much lately, about all the usual things with one or two miserable additions, that I've found it hard to sit down every day in peace (as

I must, if I'm to do my best) and write, without the little, prodding devils of responsibility at work behind my eyes. One of my newest worries is: how my wife is to live while I am away. This is a lonely place, & she has no-one to help with the children. I should like her to take a holiday somewhere, in the sun. She would like to go to Elba, which we love, but that is impossible. Somehow, I must claw up enough money just to keep her here—our house is warm & comfortable, and at the water's edge—until I return maybe with dollars enough so that, for some months, I need do nothing but write my own poems & stories.

It's a flat, dull day, with grey rain oozing like self-pity: in fact, a day like this letter. No more of it.

I will try, very hard, to finish the story before leaving—though indeed, I cannot leave until my wife is provided for. But something will happen. It always does. And often it is nasty. (I said, 'No more of it'. And here the pity again is galloning down the drab sky.)

Please don't forget—I know you won't—your letters to your sisters.

I have about 40 readings to do in the States, which will keep me tearing busy.

Yes, I am frightened of drink too. But it is not so bad as, perhaps, you think: the fear, I mean. It is only frightening when I am whirlingly perplexed, when my ordinary troubles are magnified into monsters and I fall weak down before them, when I do not know what to do or where to turn. When I am here, or anywhere I like, and am busy, then drink's no fear at all and I'm well, terribly well, and gay, and unafraid and full of other nicer nonsenses, and altogether a dull, happy fellow only wanting to put into words, never into useless, haphazard, ugly, unhappy action, the ordered turbulence, the ubiquitous and rinsing grief, the unreasonable glory, of the world I know and don't know.

Write soon, when you can; and forgive, if you can, the agitation of my letters, which is caused only by the superficial worries of mouth-to-mouth living & day after day; and thank you, with all my heart, for your New Year's gift and for the affection of your letter.

Yours sincerely,

Dylan Thomas

MSS.: Texas

Dylan was already, and very rapidly, acquiring in America the reputation of the rip-roaring drunkard. He was playing the part which some of his American audiences wished to see. When writing to his parents, on the other hand, he acted the son that they wished him to be. A comparison of this letter with John Malcolm Brinnin's description of Dylan's first few days in America is illuminating.

TO MR AND MRS D. J. THOMAS

Midston House,
22 East 38th Street,
New York 16
Sunday, 26th February 1950

My dear Mother & Dad,

How are you both? How are you keeping, Dad? Get stronger every day, please, so that when I come home to Laugharne, you'll be up and about and able to join me for one at Phil's. And Mother, too, by that time, must be spry enough to be able to run, like a goat, down the Boat House path. I was very sad to leave you at such a moment, with Dad so weak & with Mother not fit to do all the little things for him that must be done. I was very sad, driving away that morning, leaving you & Laugharne, but it had, God help me, to be done.

Caitlin's told you, I suppose, about our London visit and Margaret's house and party at which such a lot of old—& some new—friends turned up, so I won't add anything to that. Helen & Bill, by the way, send their fondest regards to you both.

The plane trip was ghastly. It seemed to go on forever, and all my fellow passengers seemed either actively unpleasant or moronic. The plane was stiflingly hot, & there wasn't any of the usual slight plane ventilation because of the height we travelled: in the stratosphere. We couldn't put down at the airport in Newfoundland because of icy weather conditions, so had to land somewhere in Canada. We got out for an hour: the cold was unbelievable, all the airport ground crew dressed up like Hudson Bay trappers and beating their great grizzly-bear-gloved hands together & stamping on the snow. And when we did, after several stifling eternities spent high as the moon, arrive in New York, it was to find it one of the coldest days there for years: when we got off the plane, it was four above zero. Luckily I'd rather the cold than the heat, and my old duffle-coat was very helpful. John Brinnin, my agent, a terribly nice man, met me at the airport—about an hour from the centre of the city—& drove me to my hotel: right in Manhattan, among the unreal, shooting skyscrapers, and my room was on the thirtieth floor. Then we drove around the city, me gawping, like the country cousin I am, at this titanic dream world, soaring Babylon, everything monstrously rich and strange. That evening, I went to a party, given in my honour by the Professor of English at Columbia University: pack full of American dons, critics, writers, poets, all of the older & more respectable kind. Then home to the 30th floor, to hear, all night, the roaring of heavy lorries, the hooting of ships from the East River—I could see the Queen Mary, or Elizabeth, from my window—& the banshee-screaming of police and ambulance sirens, just as on the films. There seems, at first sight, to be no reality at all in the life here: it is all an enormous façade of speed & efficiency & power behind which millions of little individuals are wrestling, in vain, with their own anxieties. The next day, Brinnin took me touring over half of this mad city: Broadway, Harlem, the Wall Street area, the East Side (where the Dead End Kids come from). I drank huge icy milkshakes in the drugstores, and iced lager beer in the Third Avenue saloons almost every one of which is kept by an Irishman. I ate fried shrimps, fried chicken, a T-bone steak the size of a month's ration for an English family. I went to the top of the Empire State Building, the tallest skyscraper in the world, had one look at the nightmare city, & came down quickly. That night I went to a party given for me by some of the younger writers. The next day Brinnin & I did little but peruse my itinerary, which seems to take me to every state in the U.S.A., & that evening I made my first public appearance before an audience of 800 people. The reading seemed to go very well. After that, a reception, so-called, in the flat of a young man whose name I didn't catch: flats are called apartments here, but this one had 20 rooms. The next day all over the city again, meeting many people, mostly again writers, painters, or actors. And yesterday, Saturday, my second appearance in the same hall as the first: 800 again, the full seating capacity. Today, Sunday, I go to the country, with Brinnin, until Tuesday, when I make my way to Yale University & from there to Harvard, Boston. After that, I've got about 10 readings in 20 days. Don't you worry about me, now. I'm feeling tiptop. By the way, the first people to come along to the stage-door after my first reading were three people from Llanelly, utter strangers, now living in N. York. I'll write again next week. Tell me everything. And get stronger. My forwarding address is c/o John Brinnin, Valley Road, Westport, Connecticut. All my love to you both. I think of you. Give my regards to Billy & Mrs. Thomas.

D.

MSS.: Dylan Thomas Estate

In Washington he had stayed with Mr and Mrs Francis Biddle.

Although earning, by English standards, a great deal of money in America, he was spending it almost as fast as he made it.

TO MR AND MRS JOHN NIMS

17th July 1950

The Boat House,

Laugharne,

Carmarthenshire

My dear Bonnie and John,

Remember me? Round, red, robustly raddled, a bulging Apple among poets, hard as nails made of cream cheese, gap-toothed, balding, noisome, a great collector of dust and a magnet for moths, mad for beer, frightened of priests, women, Chicago, writers, distance, time, children, geese, death, in love, frightened of love, liable to drip.

I never managed to come back, although I so much wanted to. I never answered your nice letters, nor acknowledged the hollyhocks. My only damp excuse is that animal-trainer Brinnin ('Bring 'em back half alive') whipped me all over the wilds after I reluctantly left you, from British Columbia to Florida; I hardly ever knew where I was; I lost the ability to form words on paper; I ranted through my one-night stands like a ruined, sonorous mule; I spent one liquid, libidinous fortnight in New York and was wheelbarrowed on to the Queen Elizabeth by some resident firemen, a psychoanalyst's insane wife, Oscar Williams and his wife, whip-cracking Brinnin, a hosier from the Bronx, an eminent playwright (if anonymous), three unidentified men who came either from the Museum of Modern Art or from McSorley's Saloon, a lifelong friend of half an hour, a glossy woman who had made some mistake, and hairy people. Lots of hairy people, all sighing with relief. I shared a cabin with an inventor of a new kind of concrete, called, so far as I could gather, Urine—the inventor, not the concrete—and spent my days with salesmen at the bar. As a result, I have never felt physically better in my life, and go for long walks, healthy as a briar pipe, and sing in the bath (which does not exist), and have clear eyes and a new front tooth—which must have grown, for I have no memory of going to the dentist—and a spring in my step and a song in my gut and poems to write and no need to hurry to write them. I must ruin my health again: I feel so preposterously well.

But I do wish I had been able to return to Niles and Schmoo myself

349

to sleep and meet your friends again. Not coming back was one of the things, in all my silly panting around, I most regret. But, if Caitlin and Colm and I come to the States next year—though how we shall achieve this, I don't know yet—may we stay for some days?

And if ever you manage to visit this country, beds, couches, cots, playpens, fish, cockles and mussels, flat warm Welsh bitter beer, affection, a dog as balanced and gifted as yours, sea and river, are all yours in this arsehole of the universe, this hymnal blob, this pretty sick, fond sad Wales.

Have you, John, a book of your poems to send me? I shall be giving some radio readings of American poetry, and want very much to read you and Lowell. In return I can send you an old bicycle or a new poem or a picture of Laugharne or any book you want.

Is there any news of the vague project you said you would work on for Caitlin and me and the hornless fiend who is playing at my feet with a scissors?

When you have time, will you write anyway & let me know how you are?

Love,
Dylan

MSS.: John Nims, Esq.

Dylan's American mistress came to England in the summer of 1950. Soon enough the usual kind friend told Caitlin all about it. She was, understandably, furious and threatened to leave Dylan. Their marriage was in danger, and Dylan was very frightened.

Meanwhile he had joined the Savage Club, in London, of which John Davenport was a member.

TO JOHN DAVENPORT

The Savage Club,
1 Carlton House Ter.
London, S.W.1
19.12.50

Dear Brother Savage John Davenport,

It is a time-honoured custom of the Club to which we both have the honour to belong, to address one another fraternally thus. If this were not so, the appellation I should, in all honesty, be compelled to attach to your name would be one singularly lacking in cameraderie.

Your cherished illusion is, I must suppose, that your fellow members remain in a state of ignorance as to the real purpose for which you joined the Club. May I point out to you that one member, at least, is under no illusion as to that purpose, which is to purloin from the smoking room the only copies of The Stage and The New Yorker?

If, as is obvious, you have no respect for other members who might wish to peruse those periodicals, have you none for Literature? This, as you well know, is a club which regularly wines and dines such notable practitioners of that Art as Reginald Arkell, Alec Waugh, Tschiffeley, Louis Golding, Dale Collins, and L. I. F. Brimble. Are you not letting down their good name, and the good name of all your fellow-scribblers—under which heading I humbly class myself—when you stoop so low as utterly and wantonly to disregard the injunction, Not To Be Taken Away, which is stamped upon every periodical in the Smoking Room?

Yours sincerely,

Dylan Thomas, F.R.S.L.

Early in 1951 he went to Persia with Ralph ('Bunny') Keene to make a documentary film about oil for the Anglo-Iranian Oil Company. Bunny Keene was to be the director, Dylan the script-writer. The film was never made, for almost immediately after their return to England Mossadeq seized Anglo-Iranian's assets and installations.

As these letters show, Caitlin had not yet forgiven him for his infidelity. The Princess is Princess Caetani.

TO AN AMERICAN FRIEND

January or February 1951

Abadan

XXXXXXX:

I am writing this in a tasty, stifflipped, liverish, British Guest House in puking Abadan on, as you bloody well know, the foul blue boiling Persian buggering Gulf. And lost, God blast, I gasp between gassed vodkas, all crude and cruel fuel oil, all petroleum under frying heaven, benzola bitumen, bunkers and tankers, pipes and refineries, wells and derricks, gushers and super-fractionators and shaft-el-Arab and all. Today I was taken to see a great new black-towered hissing and coiling monster, just erected in the middle of the refinery. It cost eight million pounds. It is called a Cat-Cracker.

Abadan is inhibited almost entirely by British—or so it seems.

There are thousands of young Britishers in the bachelor quarters, all quietly seething. Many snap in the heat of their ingrowing sex and the sun, and are sent back, baying, to Britain. Immediately, their places are taken by fresh recruits: young wellgroomed pups with fair moustaches and briar pipes, who, in the soaking summer, soon age, go bristled about, chainsmoke damp hanging fags, scream blue on arak, toss themselves trembly all sleepless night in the toss-trembling bachelors' quarters, answer the three-knock knock at the midnight door, see before them in the hot moonlight wetmouthed Persian girls from the bazaar who ask, by custom, for a glass of water, invite the girls in, blush, stammer, grope, are lost. These old-young men are shipped back also, packed full with shame and penicillin. And the more cautious stay on, boozed, shrill, hunted, remembering gay wonderful London so white-skinned and willing.

I visited oil-fields in the mountains last week. By night, the noise of frustrated geologists howled louder than the jackals outside my tent. Utterly damned, the dishonourable, craven, knowledgeable, self-pitying jackals screamed and wailed in the abysses of their guilt and the stinking garbage pails. 'Rosemary', 'Jennifer', 'Margery', cried the nearmale unsleepers in their near-sleep. And the hyenas laughed like billyho deep down in their dark diseased throats. O evergreen, gardened, cypressed, cinema'd, oil-tanked, boulevarded, incense-and-armpit cradle of Persian culture, rock me soft before lorn hotel-bedtime, I have nostalgia and gout. . . . My toe pulses like a painful cucumber in the arraky bar. O city of Haffiz and Sad'i and Mrs. Wiltshire the Consul's wife, tickle me till my balloon toe dies. . . . A lonely country. And so is stricken Persia, mosque and blindness, fountains and mudhuts, Cadillac and running sore, pomegranate and Cat-Cracker. Beer in an hotel bar costs ten shillings a bottle; whiskey, one pound a nip. There is no nightlife. Shiraz sleeps at nine. Then, through the dark, the low camel bells ring; jackals confess their unworthiness to live in an ignoble fury of siren howls and utter their base and gutter-breathed gratitude to the night that hides their abominable faces; insomniac dogs rumpus in the mountain villages; the Egyptian deputy-Minister of Education, who has the next hotel room, drunkenly gallumphs with a thin, hairy secretary; dervishes plead under my bed; there are wolves not far away. There is no night life here: the moon does what she does, vermin persist, camels sail, dogs defy, frogs gloat, snow-leopards drift, ibex do what they do, moufflon are peculiar, gazelles are lonely, donkeys are Christian, bears in the high hills hug. . . .

Dylan

MSS.: The recipient

The poem here referred to is 'Lament', published in *Botteghe Oscure* in November 1951.

TO PRINCESS CAETANI

The Boat House,
Laugharne,
Carmarthenshire
March 20 1951

Dear Marguerite Caetani,

I have been ill, with almost everything from gastric influenza to ingrowing misery. And only now my wife Caitlin has given me a letter that Davenport had forwarded from you nearly six weeks ago: She didn't know who the letter came from, and had half-mislaid and half-forgotten it in the general hell of sickness, children, excruciating worry, the eternal yellow grey drizzle outside and her own slowly accumulated loathing for the place in which we live. I was distressed that you should have no letter from me after yours of December 14th. I wrote, at length and wildly, my thanks and affection and small mouse-on-a-treadmill news, at once to your Paris address. I suppose I put the wrong address. I am sorry that you should, through my apparent carelessness, have come to think of me as mannerlessly ungrateful—as I am sure you must have come to think for that long, hateful silence of mine, though unpremeditated, was the nastiest answer in the world to your great kindness to us and to the fond, nice way you are so kind. I have a poem nearly finished, which will be about 50 or 60 lines long and is coarse and violent: I will send it as soon as it is done—when I can, if I can, shake off this nervous hag that rides me, biting and scratching into insomnia, nightmare, and the long anxious daylight. But I won't mind a bit if you do not want to use it (of course, I shall mind a bit, but only in a hidden, unimportant way). I want to write poems so much—oh, the old pariah cry!—but I worry too much: I'm at my worries all day & night with a hundred crochet hooks. Will you forgive me for worrying you with my limp but edgy letters? And will you forgive me for the silence before this whimper? I did not mean it. Thank you again, and the poem will come: the crotchety poem not quite clean, but worked at, between the willies, very hard.

I wish I knew what to do. I wish I could get a job. I wish I wish I wish. And I wish you a happy Easter, with all my heart. The sun came out this morning, took one look at wet Wales, and shot back.

Yours affectionately,
Dylan

MSS.: Texas

353

The late Gene Derwood, herself a poet, was Oscar Williams's wife.

TO OSCAR WILLIAMS

Boat House,
Laugharne,
Carmarthenshire
Wales
25th March 1951

My dear Gene and Oscar,

Ten months, nearly, since I saw you last, and longer, much, since I wrote. I meant and I meant and I meant, but somehow I never did write, although there was so very much to thank you for, fondness, beer, cheques, poems, paintings, a tooth. And books as well. I never thanked you for the new Modern Poetry which I recently took for a ride to Persia and read lots of in Bahrein and Shiraz and all the oily places. The Anglo-Iranian Oil Company sent me out to write a filmscript to show how beautiful Persia is and how little as a mouse and how gentle is the influence there of that Company: my job was to help pour water on troubled oil. I got out just before martial law—a friend of marshall plan's—and perhaps disguised, will be sent back to write a script to show, now, suddenly, how beastly Persia is and how grandly irreplaceable is that thundering Company. Incidentally the biggest thing in the Oil Refinery at Abadan is costing eight million pounds to put up, and is called a Cat-Cracker. I'd crack a lot of cats for that. Thank you, a great deal, for selling that piece of cheese for such a splendid sum. I'm enclosing the 2 Exemption Certificates, & hope I've filled them in correctly. I have a couple of poems but can't find them; when I do, I'll send them on. I saw John Malcolm Brinnin in London last summer, for a few revolving days. When I send the poems on, I'll write a longer letter with what grey and drizzly news I have. It has been raining in Wales since last June. I hope to come, with Caitlin, to the States next year: if there are any and if there is one. How are you both? Before a long letter, goodbye for a bit. And love, always, to you both.

Dylan

MSS.: Harvard

Mags is Margaret Taylor, and Mary Keene is Bunny Keene's ex-wife.

TO JOHN DAVENPORT

Laugharne,
12 April 1951

Dear John,

Sorry to have missed you on my last London visit. What a word visit is for my kind of occasional agitated bumbling in frowsy streets, unkind pubs, deleterious afternoon boozers, snoring cinemas, wet beds! I stayed all the time in the McAlpines', Bill frenziedly protecting his period furniture as though I were going to lay an egg on it, Helen singing Irish ballads to West Indians, and everyday I was chasing money and jobs. I have found a job, and a very fishy one too. I will tell you about it when we meet over flat beer in some chill emporium, but no money yet. And this job may make me stay in London for a long time, in which case Caitlin will have to be with me too, and of course her cockalorum. That is presumably what Mad Mags meant when she told you about our giving the Boat House up. She's wrong again, I've no intention of giving it up. But we probably will want a flat or house in London, and M said she had found half a house in Cheyne Walk by the Chimneys which she was enquiring about. Also, she has bought a cottage in Laugharne, in the downtown square or Grist, for her and her horrors in the holidays. So has Mary Keene bought a cottage there. We have reasons for leaving. It's like seeing a new wing built, for obstreperous incurables, on to a quiet bin one has got used to.

I should be up next week, and will get in touch. And I'd love to meet Canetti. I'll look out for Richard Jones's letter.

A pile of poems from Douglas Phillips—remember?—arrived a few days ago. I haven't read them properly yet, but think they've got a lot. All about masturbation, sin, violent death, decay, wet dreams, impermanent love, hatred of Carmarthen, and O looking, at random, at the words of one poem—festering sea-shores, wet vulva lips, gaseous virgins, putrid flame, lewd men, raving swordfish, sensual whips, tortured women rending wedding-gowns, charred mates, smiling cream over lip's soft brim, lascivious farmers, shaven thighs, childhood captured in rubber sheaths, love's limpets sucking oval stones, rubber wives ripping blubbered membrane veils, plasmal fruit, burst plackets, fishes' bladders, bloated pelvis, vulpine fur, etcetera.

But every now and then there are good bursting bits.

Stop press: M comes down on the midnight train tonight to discuss 'The Cheyne Walk Project'. If it comes off, I shall have a town house and a country house, and I have just borrowed 5/– from Ivy Williams to run them both.

Love,
Dylan

MSS.: Texas

For a description of Dylan and Brinnin in London, see the latter's *Dylan Thomas in America*, the title notwithstanding.

The B.B.C.'s comic radio programme never came off, or at least Dylan never wrote for it.

TO JOHN MALCOLM BRINNIN

Boat House,
Laugharne,
Carmarthenshire,
Wales
12 April 1951

Dear John,

How nice, nice, nice! Oh, my conscience, I had feared that you left London breathing—no, I can't possibly mean that—had left London saying: 'No more of that coarsened booby and his backstairs drizzling town. Foul enough in my America, feebly lascivious in his pigsty in the Earle, puking in Philadelphia, burgling the Biddles, blackmailing psychiatrists' mistakes for radiosets and trousers, fanging through the lesbians, hounding poor Oscar, but there! there in that English sink, intolerable, dribbly, lost. And, oh, his so-called friends! toadying slaves of the licensing laws, rats on a drinking ship'—or didn't we meet any friends? I can't remember, I remember I liked, very much, our being together, though you were in that Royal (was it?) jail and I in my false bonhomous Club. I remember meeting you at the station, and that was fine. And the London frowsty Casino, a momento of which I enclose: who are those perhaps-men, one bluebottle bloated, one villainously simpering, with floral and yachting ties, so untrust-worthily neat and prosperous with their flat champagne? I remember the Thames and old Pearl—whom I saw something of later but who, I imagine, left London, as I imagined you had done, rasping to herself: 'No more of that beer-cheapened hoddy-noddy snoring, paunched, his corn, his sick, his fibs, I'm off to Taormina where you know where

356

you are: oh, his sodden bounce, his mis-theatrical-demeanour, the boastful tuppence!' I haven't heard from her since she went away.

Now, for your letter. First: Next time I am in London I shall see what boys I know in the back rooms of the BBC and tell them that you are coming to London in July and that, if pressed in a vice bribed heavily and dined, you might just possibly think of reading, on the Third Programme, your poems, the poems of America, or of assessing the contemporary literary situation in Massachusetts, Virginia, and the Whaler Bar. I'll do my very best. You couldn't, I suppose, persuade your publishers to send me the shiny anthology and the new book of poems? I'd like them, a lot, anyway. And I will talk to the Institute of Contemporary Arts. I am so glad, indeed, that you will be here in July; and I shall be less revolting than last time, whatever the sacrifice. And let us meet the tiny great for tea, and go to Oxford where I know a human being. Caitlin will be in London in July, which will not make things any quieter. We both will probably be living there for some time: I am about to take on a new job; co-writing, with the best gagman in England—he is an Irishman from New Zealand—a new comic series for the radio. I have already thought of two jokes, both quite unusable. And may I come to Edith's party for you? Her parties are always brilliant opportunities for self-disgrace.

Give my love, if ever you see them or believe it, to Pearl, Lloyd & Loren, Marion & Cummings, Stanley Moss, Jean Garrigue, Gene Baroff, Jeanne Gordon, David Luege, Howard, the one I crossed out, Patrick Boland, and any ugly stranger in the street. Have a thousand boilermakers for me, and send me your stomach: I'll put it under my pillow.

I have written three new poems, one alright, which I will, if you like, send you when I can find them.

I have no news at all. I am broke and in debt. And that reminds me to thank you very much for sending to my, my, my! Chartered Accountants that quite legendary-looking account of my howl-for-my-supper earnings. The Accounts tell me I shall probably not have to pay any Income Tax on anything earned in the U.S.A. except:

(1) The amounts remitted by myself or by my Agent to this country: i.e. remittances made to my wife, bank, or any other person.

(2) The amount brought in by me when I arrived back in this Country.

Can you help? I think, through you, I sent about three small sums to Caitlin. Can you remember? And I came home, I think, with about 200 dollars.

If you can remember what amounts of money I sent to Caitlin

with your knowledge, would you be so kind as to write to Leslie Andrews and Co., 10 North Street, Horsham, Sussex, England, and let them know? And then that will really be the end of your agental duties until next time.

Now, next time: I would very much like (I'd adore it), to be imported to the States next year, 1952. The Poetry Centre paying my passage and the first fee. I would bring Caitlin with me, if by that time I have made, as I intend to do, much money from my ha ha scripts. And would you, could you, act as Agent or Christ knows what for me again? I do not think I would wish to go through the Middle West, excepting Chicago, again, but anywhere, everywhere, else, unless I have quite ruined myself in all those places where you were not with me. Could you put out feelers, spin wheels, grow wings for me? I am so deadly sick of it here. I would bring great packages of new poems to read, and much more pre-written prose to pad them in. I would be much better than I was: I mean, sick less often. I mean, I would so much like to come. Could you write to any friends or acquaintances I might have made and see if they would help? Would you, now?

No, Persia wasn't all depressing. Beautiful Isfahan & Shiraz. Wicked, pompous, oily British. Nervous, cunning, corrupt and delightful Persian bloody bastards. Opium no good. Persian vodka, made of beetroot, like stimulating sockjuice, very enjoyable. Beer full of glycerine and pips. Women veiled, or unveiled ugly, or beautiful and entirely inaccessible, or hungry. The lovely camels who sit on their necks and smile. I shan't go there again.

No news. Still broke and in debt. I spent all the Persian money on beetroot vodka, glycerine beer, unveiled ugly women, and as you conjectured, the camels, the camels, the camels are coming.

Yes, I do want to come to the States early next year. But I shall see you before then, & will do all I can to make you a very little money on the BBC. But naturally don't count on that. You will be here during the Festival of Britain, though nobody here has any idea of what we have to be festive about. And, mostly, I suppose, the BBC will be plugging homegrown poetry. However, I know some unpatriotic people on the Third Programme, and they owe me something for the pleasure they've got in my not being on the Third Programme recently.

I'm sick of Laugharne. It has rained here since last June.
Write soon.

Love to you,
Dylan

MSS.: John Malcolm Brinnin, Esq.

The short poem referred to is 'Do Not Go Gentle Into That Good Night', published in *Botteghe Oscure*, November 1951.

TO MADAME CAETANI

The Boat House,
Laugharne,
Carmarthenshire,
Wales
28th May 1951

My dear Madame Caetani,

I hope you've had, by this time, my brief, troubled letter and my rough, untroubled poem.

I have just finished the short poem I enclose. If you like the other one, the 'Lament', well enough to print, I think this little one might very well be printed with it as a contrast.

In spite of all the things that go with selling-up home, I am still trying to work. (Indeed, I am still trying to sell up home, which has to be, and quick.) And I hope to finish soon a longish play, as yet untitled, in verse and prose which I have been thinking of for a long time. I will send it to you soon. I do hope you will publish it—unless, of course, it is too long (or too bad)—as I am, at the moment of working on it, pleased & excited with it. It is gay, & sad and sentimental and a bit barmy. So am I. I'm looking forward to hearing from you.

Affectionately,
Dylan

The only person I can't show the little enclosed poem to is, of course, my father, who doesn't know he's dying.

MSS.: Texas

The poem here referred to is 'In The White Giant's Thigh', one of the four poems that together were to have been 'In Country Heaven'. Three were written, but the fourth, the title poem, was not.

TO OSCAR WILLIAMS

Boat House,
Laugharne,
Carmarthenshire,
Wales
28th May 1951

Dear Oscar,

I'm afraid I'm sending you only one poem—and that only the first section of a poem, though nobody need know that. I mentioned the title and idea of this poem over a year ago, in pretty New York, but scrapped all of it I had written on my return. I have only recently finished this version. The other poems I found since last writing to you, I have sent to Botteghe Oscure. This means, I get paid by them well, first, & then can sell the poems (well again, I hope) in the States. If I publish the poems first in the States, Botteghe Oscure doesn't want them. So, when they're printed in Italy, I'll send them along. I've no spare copies now. And my newest poems aren't yet finished. Sorry I couldn't type this one out. A few words, on looking through it, seem hard to read. The first word on line 7 is PLEADING. The fourth word in the third line from the end of page one is LANES. On page 3, in the third line, the word is ROISTER. In the 7th line of page 3, the word GAMBO means a farm-cart. In the last line but one from the end of page 3, it is THEY with the Simple Jacks. On page 4, line 7, RAIN and WRING are 2 separate words. I am sure this complicates matters. It's a conventionally romantic poem & perhaps you won't like it at all. But could you sell it for me for a LOT of money? I'm desperately in need of it. If you can get a cheque sent soon, will you see that it is made out on a London bank. Your last two lovely cheques took about 6 weeks to clear. I'm in such a state of debt & brokeness, I'm having to sell up my house as soon as I can & move to London which I hate. The house—what I own of it—will all go towards debts—& then not all of them, by a hell of a long way. I hope to keep my books. Oh, oh, oh! Misery me. Do what you can about this lush poem. And please excuse rushed writing & no news.

Love,
Dylan

MSS.: Harvard

360

Reggie Smith is a producer on the staff of the B.B.C.

Bill is Professor Bill Read, a close friend of Brinnin's. He is the author of a book entitled *The Days of Dylan Thomas* (1965).

TO JOHN MALCOLM BRINNIN

Boat House,
Laugharne,
Carmarthenshire,
Wales
August 31 1951

Dear John,

A very brief note of apology and affection. Your letter, waiting for me in John Davenport's, I mislaid, and now don't know where you'll be or when, for a moment, you may come to London. (I've written to Reggie Smith, who's on holiday, but couldn't give him a date, except that I thought it to be early in September. I know he will fix a recording if he can: probably of verse.) But from your little letter I see you will call at the American Express, Paris, around Sept 1–4. I do hope this will find you then. And I am so sorry I couldn't get up to London after you left Laugharne, & that I lost your letter, & that I haven't written. I've been in a mess about money, and, in London, about trying to fix a film-job for the winter. Caitlin has mumps, badly, and Oh! oh! oh!—I'm vague & distressed about me and poems and Laugharne & London—and the States. But, of course, I'll be there for the Columbia date on January 30. I hope, very much, we can meet in London before your return: I want to ask you about these dates, about what sort of poetry you think I should read, what kind of prose I should write for the several occasions. Also, I should like very much to see you again, before next January.

I hope you didn't have too muddled a time down here. Regards to Bill.

Please write soon, if ever you get this, and I'll write back fully.

Try to make London.

Caitlin sends you her love. And I send mine.

Dylan

MSS.: John Malcolm Brinnin, Esq.

Dylan had gone with Donald Taylor, John Davenport and other friends to watch the cricket at Lord's cricket ground, and to patronize the Tavern there, which serves drinks all afternoon. Later John Davenport had given a small party for certain American friends.

The 'plotless radio play' can only be the beginning of *Under Milk Wood*.

TO DONALD TAYLOR

31 August 1951
Boat House,
Laugharne

Dear Donald,

I had a foggy feeling, after our Lordly day and the evening with the afflicted Americans, that you and I had fixed a date to meet, but, for the death of me, I couldn't remember if or no, if, when and where. I hope I was mistaken, and that we hadn't arranged to meet, which sounds, maybe, discourteous, but you know what I mean. I tried to get in touch with Higham, but his nose was being scraped. If we did have a date, and I didn't (as was obvious) keep it, please forgive me. And, if we didn't, let's make another soon. I've such a lot to talk about, and that day (for me, at least) wasn't half long enough and was interrupted too much by bad cricket, indifferent drink, and women and fat men.

We come to London to live at the end of September, money willing and Caitlin's mumps gone (she's moaning now, like a sad football). But, before I make that complicated move, I want to have, fixed as firmly as possible, if even only in the mind, a programme of work to keep me in creditless London. Have your plans moved any, and do they still, after a day in which I am sure I spoke very little sense, include me? (It was very good to see you, and I make no apologies for my senselessness: I was quite happy.) I must know as soon as possible—though I realise that nothing happens quickly, except disaster, in your and my world.

I told you about my American commitments. Today—one reason I am writing this—I heard from America the very final dates they have fixed for me. My first lecture is at Columbia on January 30th, and my last in the Museum of Modern Art in the last week of February. Therefore, my whole trip would take, at the maximum, six weeks. I must reply, in the next few days, to my American sponsors and say, quite definitely, Yes or No. Suppose—and, Lord, I hope so—you and I are working, soon, fully together; could I, then, take six weeks off from January, say, 20th on? Could you let me know how you feel about this? You know that, above everything, I want to work with you, again, on films, and exclusively, if possible, on feature films this time. And you know, as I told you at probably incoherent length in the Insipid Writers' Club, that I must have a regular job this winter. If six American weeks interfere with these two things—and I do so hope that both things are the same, i.e. that the regular job is to write scripts for and with you—then I'll cancel the lectures. But I must say Yes or No to Columbia University etc. straightabloodyway.

A pity we can't meet again very soon. I could come up to London; but I wish you could come to Wales. Our house is almost childless now, and the weather, for the moment, windily good.

Have you any stories in mind which, perhaps, I could read or think about? Anyway, do please write quickly about these points. I saw T.V. people a few days after seeing you. They're full of work to do, but offer lamentable pay. And, help us, we all do need so much these once-longed-for but execrable days.

I am writing a plotless radio play, first thought of as a film.

Two acquaintances of mine have committed suicide within the last fortnight; one of them was a painter, Ralph Banbury: do you remember him? A tall, languid man, friend and pupil of Cedric Morris, with a Chinese grandmother.

Love,
Dylan

MSS.: Lockwood Memorial Library, Buffalo

Llareggub, which can also be read backwards, was the original title of *Under Milk Wood*, half of which was published, with the original title, in *Botteghe Oscure*.

Margaret Taylor was talking of selling 'The Boat House', but never in fact did so during Dylan's lifetime. It was she who had now provided him with a basement flat in Delancey Street, Camden Town, London.

TO MADAME CAETANI

Boat House,
Laugharne,
Carmarthenshire,
Wales
October 1951

My dear Madame Caetani,

Thank you for your telegram from Paris. And I hope my letter, addressed to Brown's Hotel, was forwarded to you.

This is a difficult letter to write, because I am asking a great request of you.

But let me first explain. The enclosed manuscript is called, as you will see, 'Llareggub. A Piece for Radio Perhaps', though the title is most provisional. And it is the first half of something I am delighting in doing and which I shall complete very shortly. Only very special circumstances—and I'll tell you of them in a moment, if I may—are preventing me from carrying on with it every minute of the working day.

I told you, as you may remember, that I was working on a play, mostly in verse. This, I have reluctantly, and, I hope, only temporarily, abandoned; the language was altogether swamping the subject: the comedy, for that was what it was originally intended to be, was lost in the complicated violence of the words: I found I was labouring at each line as though I were making some savage and devious meta-physical lyric and not a play at all. So I set the hotchpotch aside, and am prepared to wait.

But out of my working, however vainly, on it, came the idea of 'Llareggub'. (Please ignore it as a final title.) Out of it came the idea that I write a piece, a play, an impression for voices, an entertainment out of the darkness, of the town I live in, and to write it simply and warmly & comically with lots of movement and varieties of moods, so that, at many levels, through sight and speech, description & dialogue, evocation and parody, you come to know the town as an inhabitant of it. That is an awkward & highfalutin way of speaking: I only wanted to make the town alive through a raw medium: and that, again, is wrong: I seem hardly able to write today, or, at least, to write about Llareggub: all I want to do is write the damned thing itself.

Reading (as I hope you will) the first half of this piece as it stands, you'll see that I have established the town up to a certain moment of the morning. And the effect you will find, probably, rather jerky and confusing, with far too many characters and changes of pitch and temper. But the piece will develop from this, through all the activities of the morning town—seen from a number of eyes, heard from a number of voices—through the long lazy lyrical afternoon, through the multifariously busy little town evening of meals & drinks and loves & quarrels and dreams and wishes, into the night and the slowing-down lull again and the repetition of the first word: Silence. And by that time, I hope to make you utterly familiar with the places and the people; the pieces of the town will fit together; the reasons for all these behaviours (so far but hinted at) will be made apparent; & there the town will be laid alive before you. And only you will know it.

Let me particularise, & at random. As the piece goes on two voices will be predominant: that of the preacher, who talks only in verse, and that of the anonymous exhibitor and chronicler called, simply, 1st Voice. And the 1st Voice is really a kind of conscience, a guardian angel. Through him you will learn about Mr. Edwards, the draper, and Miss Price, the sempstress, & their odd and, once it is made clear, most natural love: every day of the week they write love letters to each other, he from the top, she from the bottom, of the town: all their lives they have known of each other's existence, and of their mutual love: they have seen each other a thousand times, & never spoken: easily they could have been together, married, had children: but that is not the life for them: their passionate love, at just this distance, is all they need. And Dai Bread, the baker, who has two wives: one is loving & mothering, sacklike & jolly; the other is gypsy slatternly and, all in love, hating: all three enjoy it. And Mrs. Ogmore-Pritchard who, although a boarding house keeper, will keep no boarders because they cannot live up to the scrupulous & godlike tidiness of her house and because death can be the only boarder good enough for her in the end. And Mr. Pugh, the schoolmaster, who is always nagged by his wife and who is always plotting her murder. This is wellknown to the town, and to Mrs. Pugh. She likes nagging; she likes his plotting, in supposed secrecy, against her. He would always like plotting, whoever he lived with; she would always like nagging, whoever she lived with. How lucky they are to be married. And Polly Garter has many illegitimate babies because she loves babies but does not want only one man's. And Cherry Owen the soak, who likes getting drunk every night; & his wife who likes living with two men, one sober in the day, one drunk at night. And the cobbler who thinks the town is the wickedest place to live in the world, but who can never leave it while there is a hope of reforming it; and, oh, the savour his cries of Gomorrah add to the pleasures of the little wicked town. And the old woman who every morning shouts her age to the heavens; she believes the town is the chosen land, & the little river Dewi the River of Jordan; she is not all mad: she merely believes in heaven on earth. And so will all of them, all the eccentrics whose eccentricities, in these first pages, are but briefly & impressionistically noted: all, by their own rights, are ordinary & good; & the 1st Voice, & the poet preacher, never judge nor condemn but explain and make strangely simple & simply strange.

I daren't look back over what I have written: I wrote it v. quickly, & most probably it reads like nonsense. But I terribly want to finish the piece. And it will be good (of its own kind). And this is where my great request of you at last comes in.

Can you pay me—and, I am sorry, <u>at once</u>—for this half of

'Llareggub' just as though it were finished? For without being paid well and at once, I cannot finish it.

In the middle of next week, we finally leave Laugharne for London. I mean, we have to leave: the house is sold. But still, I cannot leave without paying the whole of the debts I owe to this town. And they amount to about a £100. If I can pay this, we can leave for London, where I have borrowed a flat, and I can get on, at once, with the rest of 'Llareggub'. Oh, I want to so much. I can finish it in two weeks. But only if I can settle all up here.

I know the amount I am sending you of Llareggub (and, of course, quite possibly the quality: you may loathe the thing) is not worth a £100. But what I want is to be paid now for the whole piece in advance. Is that possible? I am pinning every bit of faith on that.

Can you cable me your answer?

Wouldn't it be awful if you thought the whole thing bunk. My head is full of it, I must go on.

Please forgive this letter.

Ever,

Dylan

MSS.: Texas

The reference to 'the shirtless Biddles' is explained by the fact that on his previous visit to America Dylan had purloined several of Mr Francis Biddle's shirts.

Sidney G. is Sidney Goodsir-Smith, the Lallans poet; Kathleen Raine and David Gascoyne are English poets.

TO JOHN MALCOLM BRINNIN

54 Delancey Street,

Camden Town,

London, N.W.1

3.12.51

Dear John,

Your letter just forwarded from Laugharne to our new London house or horror on bus and nightlorry route and opposite railway bridge and shunting station. No herons here.

Your letter, just read, has scared the lights out of me. First date in N.Y. January 23rd? I'll have to look lively. I'll also have to look like hell for money (£100) to keep girl & family here while Caitlin and I are junketing abroad.

Questions & answers:

(1) How long do we plan to stay? Between two & three months.

(2) Do we want to confine our movements to east & middle west or do we also want to go to the west coast? We certainly want to go to California, after the other dates you have arranged. Ruth Witt-Diamant, of San Francisco, (address: 1520 Willard St. S.F.) has recently written asking us the same question, or roughly the same. She says she will, given due warning, be able to arrange some S. Francisco readings. I am sure that Hunter Lewis, of B.C. University, Vancouver, would also invite me again. He said so in a letter this year.

(3) I don't think Florida for a month. A Californian month (or less) for us after New York. And then New York at the end again. I would, incidentally, like to go to Washington. Would that club like me again? The shirtless Biddles have invited Caitlin & me to stay with them there.

(4) Yes, yes, yes. I do want you please to be my little guide & agent.

On to other things. Oscar Williams, in his last letter to me, said that a group of mid-Western Universities were getting together to invite me for a jolly week with them at a figure like one thousand dollars. He did mention mid-February, but I see that that now conflicts with my pre-arranged New York commitments. I shall write to him today; but do you think you could, as little agent, also get in touch with him and find out if the date—if it is a real date—can be moved to end of February or first of March. Then we could go on to S. Francisco in March sometime. I could leave Caitlin there while I went anywhere else on Pacific Coast where I was invited.

The Socialist Party in New York City—address 303 Fourth Avenue, N. York 10, tel. Gramercy 5-6621—have written to me to ask me for a poetry reading. They say they're a small body (like me) & can't pay much at all, but I would like to do it for them if you can arrange it. Oh, the chairman of the Finance Cte of the S. Party is, if you didn't know, a Jane Browne.

Next things you want to know: (1) Visa. I haven't got one yet. My passport is left in Laugharne, & I will try to go down & get it at the end of this week. Before I get the visa, I am almost certain to need— as before—papers from you, as my agent, explaining the purpose of my visit to the States and instancing some of my more worthy-looking engagements. Perhaps if easily & quickly obtained by you, a letter from Columbia to you about me, from the Center, and from anywhere important else, would considerably help. Anyway, let me have some official papers of confirmation to show the scared baiters in power here.

(1) I have made no ship reservations for Cat and me, not knowing when I was due in N. York! I'll try to do this this week early, following your instructions about getting the steamship line to have their N. York office contact you at once at Poetry Center for payment.

(2) Caitlin will be coming with me, but not the baby.

(3) It's okay to say to the New School I'll do them a second programme of dramatic readings.

Now to my questions. What sort of poetry would, d'you think, most of my sponsors like me to read? Modern? including modern American, or is that presumptuous? Blake, Keats, Donne, Hopkins, Owen? And what about 'dramatic excerpts'? Marlowe, Shakespeare, Webster, Tourneur, Beddoes? Do tell me what, from your previous experience of 'my audiences', they most would like from me. I don't want to read too much of my own, except for a few recent ones. Laughlin, by the way, is bringing out a pamphlet of new poems for my visit.

How are you? How goes Sidney G.? He was moaning for weeks about his companions, Raine & Gascoyne. 'Och, there'll be wee orgies with those two sparocks.'

I'll get this off straightaway, without any news or affection; and will see about steamer bookings & visas very quickly.

Please you write quickly too; & do let me know your suggestions as to the contents of my programmes. And do do something about West Coast. That's what Caitlin wants most.

Love,
Dylan

PS. Mebbe, after all, a bit of Florida would be good, if possible. Miami? Gainsville first, & then Miami?

PSS. A very important point I forgot. If we're to spend one whole month in N. York, in an hotel, we'll be desperately broke. Is there anyone who would put us up for, say, a week while we look around for someone else to put us up for the next week, and so on? It really's important. The money I earn we want for the sights, not for board. Can you delicately hint around?

PSSS. I'm writing today to Ruth Witt-Diamant, but perhaps you could write as well—her address is on page one—to see what, if anything, she has done?

D.

MSS.: John Malcolm Brinnin, Esq.

Charles Fry, a partner in the now defunct publishing house of Wingate, had commissioned a book of American Impressions from Dylan. During this trip Caitlin was making notes for such a book, but it was never written.

Helen Strauss at this time ran the literary side of the William Morris Agency.

TO DAVID HIGHAM

HOTEL CHELSEA,
West 23rd Street,
7th Avenue,
New York 11, N.Y.
26th Feb. 1952

Dear David,

Caitlin & I are getting very anxious—to put it mildly. Today we heard from Dolly Long, 49 Orchard Park Estate, Laugharne, Carmarthenshire, the girl who is looking after our baby; she told us she had received no money from you in spite of my cable & Caitlin's letter. Do you remember, we arranged together that you would pay Dolly Long £3 a week for three months (or, if necessary, longer) out of the three monthly cheques for £50 each delivered you by Charles Fry? I realised that I owed Pearn & Pollinger & Higham £50, so perhaps you have taken the February Fry £50 for that debt. If this is so, WILL YOU VERY MUCH PLEASE send to Dolly Long—I repeat the address, 49 Orchard Park Estate, Laugharne, Carmarthenshire—the WHOLE of the March Fry of £50? And can you, please CABLE me at the above address. If Dolly isn't paid—the main reason I arranged to write a book for Fry, a book which is shaping well, though roughly—then we shall have to return to England somehow rightaway, breaking all my university lectures etc., as Dolly Long is poor & cannot look after a child for nothing.

So, PLEASE: Send her the whole (minus, of course, ten per cent) of Fry's forthcoming March cheque. This is most urgent, Caitlin's breaking her heart about the baby. AND DO PLEASE CABLE TO RELIEVE OUR DEEP ANXIETY.

I've seen Helen Strauss, by the way, & Mike Watkins. Mike wanted me to stay on with him, but, of course, I've followed your advice & instructions & told Helen Strauss that, along with your other writers, I have moved over to her. She is now in the process of settling some gramophone record contract for me.

I'll write again when there is news. My lectures—readings rather—

369

are going extremely well. We start for the middle west in the middle of March.

But the main purpose of this very worried letter is:

Please pay Dolly Long the whole March Fry £50. AND <u>PLEASE</u> CABLE us you're doing so.

I'm sick with anxiety.

Yours,

Dylan

MSS.: David Higham Associates

Dylan wrote few letters during this, his second, American trip. While staying with the Max Ernsts in Arizona he did write a number of postcards, of which this one is characteristic.

Dan Jones's children were christened Dylan and Catherine.

TO DANIEL JONES

Arizona, 21st March 1952

Caitlin & I are buried in the Tuzigoot stone
on the other side of this card.
We were killed in action, Manhattan Island, Spring, 1952,
in a gallant battle against American generosity.
An American called Double Rye shot Caitlin to death.
I was scalped by a Bourbon.
Posthumous love to you & Irene & Dylan & Catherine from

Caitlin & Dylan

MSS.: Dr Daniel Jones

This second trip was at least as gruelling as the first. Nor did Dylan and Caitlin manage to save money.

TO JOHN MALCOLM BRINNIN

4th April 1952
c/o Witt-Diamant,
1520 Willard Street,
San Francisco,
California

Dear John,

Three letters lie—I don't, of course, mean that—before me dated March 20, March 26, & April 1st. Here's a brief, but none the less stupid, reply to them all.

I'm awfully sorry, re March 20, that you've been sick. And not of us? A mysterious illness: probably test-tubing out from M.I.T.—to whose English students, & professor of English named maybe Fudge O'Dell, I owe a forever unwritten apology for never turning up. But I'm very glad you're better (April 1st) now, & on such a good day.

Thank you for the damnably urgent & answerable letter from Higham. I'm supposed, as perhaps you read, to write an introduction to the English forthcoming edition of my Collected Poems, which, I suppose, entails my reading them all. Daft I may be. . . .

Now, re March 26th, those 'ridiculous mishaps' that caused you to miss my wire from Sedoma proved agonising to us. Caitlin was frightfully ill all the way from New York to Pennsylvania State College and on the night-train to Chicago. During the Chicago journey, my bottled up bottle illness also grew severe; indeed, we were both so near to undignified death that, on reaching Chicago, we just could not go straight across the city to catch our next train to Arizona but had to lie down, dying, in an unrocking bed. (Incidentally, a roomette is only for one traveller, & Christ help him. We had to change to a bedroom. Dearer.) So we went to a cosy little hovel of an hotel & wept & sweated there until next day. The hotel was fabulously expensive; the Pullman reservation for Tuesday, the 18th, fell out of date. I had to buy a new one & so we arrived at Flagstaff with less than a dollar. The Ernsts were lovely, charming, & hospitable, but had no ready money & none to lend. We stayed there, absolutely penniless, for 8 days, being unable to buy our own cigarettes, to post a letter, or stand with a beer at Sedoma's cowboy bar, or even wire you again. We stayed there, saying 'Beastly' John Brinnin until help came from San Francisco. Arriving at San Francisco, we found your letters, & 2 cheques, & also a letter from the headmaster of Llewellyn's school saying he would be thrown out unless a £100 were paid by April 5th. I then wired you again. You sent a cheque for 200 dollars. And so, I had 400 dollars altogether. 300 dollars I wired to Llewelyn's school. The other 100 I spent on a Vancouver ticket. So (again) HELP.

(On top of this, Caitlin had carefully arranged for some laundry to be sent on from New York to San Francisco. This cost 40 dollars.)

I can just manage to get to Vancouver, & I'll leave Caitlin the fee for my S.F. State College reading which is tonight & which will be only 50 dollars.

About other engagements! Is the date, on April 26, at the University of Chicago the same as that, on April 24, at the Northwestern University, Chicago? Or can't I read?

It's summer here, not spring. Over 80. At Easter we go to Carmel & on to see Miller at Big Sur. We are both well.

Please, write very soon, with any news, some love & a Bit of Money. Caitlin sends her love. And as always, so do I.

Love,

Dylan

MSS.: John Malcolm Brinnin, Esq.

Dylan and Caitlin returned to England in May of 1952.

E. F. Bozman was chief editor with Dent's, who were then preparing Dylan's *Collected Poems* for publication.

Dent's also wished to publish Dylan's film script, *The Doctor and the Devils*. There were copyright problems involved in this, for Dylan had written it while on the payroll of Donald Taylor's company, Gryphon Films, to whom it rightly belonged. Gryphon had been wound up, and the property sold to another company. However, Donald Taylor did manage to sort this out, and although he too had contributed to the script—the original outline had been his—he arranged that Dylan receive the royalties.

Terence Kilmartin is literary editor of the Sunday newspaper, the *Observer*.

P. H. Newby, the novelist, was at this time head of the B.B.C.'s Third Programme.

TO DAVID HIGHAM

28th June 1952

The Boat House,

Laugharne,

Carmarthenshire

Dear David,

Thousands of apologies. That's so easy to write, but I mean every one. Though small, I must be one of your most infuriating thorns.

When in London, I spent a lot of time at Lord's—(where lazy thorns go, when they're pricking their agents)—bareheaded and balding in the sun. I developed what I thought to be sunstroke, and by kind, daft friends, was put, moaning, into a sleeper and trained home. But it wasn't sunstroke. I had pleurisy, and I'm only just recovered. Not serious pleurisy, except to me whom the States have taught an obsessive, and intriguing, hypochondria. But serious or not, I couldn't write. Now I'm resuming what I imagine to be work.

1) I saw Bozman, and got fresh proofs from him. I promised him the preface in a week, but illness supervened. And now I have to confess that I can't write an ordinary prose-preface at all, having no interest whatsoever in it. What I am doing, and doing quickly, is writing a Prologue in verse, but (fairly) straightforward and colloquial, addressed to the (may be) readers of the Collected Poems, and full (I hope) of references to my methods of work, my aims, and the kind of poetry I want to write. I hope it will be interesting; I know I'm interested in writing it. It will be about 160 to 200 short lines of verse, of which I have written about 80 so far.

2) I saw Donald Taylor. But far from my charming him out of his attitude, he, with his airy-fairy lackadaisical blarney charmed me into a kind of acquiescent and doped silence—'Just leave everything to me. Everything will be all right. I'll see or write to Higham and Bozman. Just don't you worry. I'll do what's best for us both', is, I dreamily believe, what he told me. Have you heard? Should I drop him a line? I can be much more definite with written words than I can in pleasant, lulling, and responsibility-procrastinating company. The script work he has for me is still vague, though he is, of course, most optimistic.

3) I didn't see Fry. I rang him up to put off our luncheon date till the evening; and by the evening, was, as I thought then, struck dumb and giddy by the sun. I'm writing to him this week-end, however, with explanation, to give him an idea of how I intend to do the book.

4) A letter came to me from Kilmartin, so I didn't need to see him. He was keen on having articles on America for the Observer. These articles, however, cannot now be chunks of the Wingate book, as that will be mostly of a fantastic nature and quite unsuitable for a newspaper. But I hope to be able to write, for Kilmartin, separate, straight pieces.

5) I've written to P. H. Newby about 'Personal Anthology' & will finish the anthology (of American Modern Poetry) as soon as a couple of books I am waiting for arrive from London. This is a quick job.

6) I couldn't of course take part in the MacNeice programme, which took place while I was ill.

I shall be in London for the Newby recording in the middle of July, & will ring you then. I have bought a panama hat for Lord's, to keep off the pleurisy. Hope to hear from you soon about Laughlin.

And all my sincere apologies again. Don't despair of me.

Yours,

Dylan

PS. By the way I forgot to give you my home phone number. It is: LAUGHARNE (pronounced Larne) 68.

MSS.: David Higham Associates

Dylan's hideous money worries—for which his own recklessness was in some ways to blame—were now aggravated by demands for back income tax, which he had never paid. Leslie Andrews was the tax accountant whom David Higham had found to help Dylan. From now until his death a substantial portion of Dylan's highly irregular income was held back at source to pay the demands of the Inland Revenue. These demands greatly increased his nervous unhappiness and this contributed, directly, to his early death.

On top of those demands there now came an additional bureaucratic horror.

TO DAVID HIGHAM

The Boat House,
Laugharne,
Carmarthenshire
21 July 1952

Dear David,

I had a nice letter from Fry, and an enthusiastic one from Bozman about the verse prologue to the Collected Poems. I posted, today, a short note to Donald Taylor, telling him I'd be in London this week— for a recording of American Poems—and want, very much, to see him about Hedgerley Films (whatever they might be) and, in view of Bozman's final refusal to print it unless it bears my name alone, about the ill-fated Doctor & the Devils.

Now the verse prologue should have been finished by this time, and would have been hadn't a London visit and two Welsh University lectures cropped up. The London visit was for various recordings for the 3rd Programme, and was interrupted by an urgent call to return to Carmarthen to meet the Income Tax Commissioners along with Leslie Andrews, who was contesting their right to tax me, for my 1950 visit to the States, on £1,907. Andrews was defeated, & now it's up to me & him to plug in lots more expenses. Whatever happens, there's going to be a lot deducted from this coming winter's earnings. And the university lectures, in North Wales, an area harder to get to from S. Wales than Ireland would be, took up a lot of time; I had to do them, though, as they made a few necessary pounds. I have to come to London again this week, to continue the recordings that were interrupted by the Income Tax trolls; but, immediately on my return at the end of the week, will hurry up & finish the prologue for Dent.

Which leads me to a very urgent matter: Last week, right after the

375

horror of the Tax Tribunal, an inspector called here from the Ministry of National Insurance. I'd filled up only one of my insurance cards since the scheme began, and had put off and forgotten, in about equal parts, the whole thing until this Inspector came. And now I have to pay £50. 12. 6d at once—last day tomorrow, Tuesday, 22nd July—or they will prosecute me & Make a Warning of me. So can you please, please, pay £50 into my bank—Lloyds Bank Ltd., 164 Kings Road, Chelsea, S.W.3.—tomorrow, the 22nd. That is, can you, please, advance me £50 on the strength of the Dent Collected Poems & on the various BBC jobs I'm now doing? There is nowhere else to approach in such a terrible hurry as this, & you've always been wonderfully good to me (better than I deserve) in the past.

If you could ring me up here, at Laugharne 68, when you have received this letter, and say that you can do this for me & that the £50 is on its way to my Chelsea bank, then I can write a cheque for that amount and take it in to the National Insurance office that day. That very Tuesday, the 22—or I am done for. The Inspector, otherwise, will prosecute from that moment. Please David.

And once the verse prologue is finished, I can get down, fast & properly, to the American fantasia.

Yours,
Dylan

I'll wait in all morning for your prayed-for call.

MSS.: David Higham Associates

The 'Prologue' to *Collected Poems* was the last poem he was to complete. 'Paper and Sticks' was omitted from that volume.

TO E. F. BOZMAN

Boat House,
Laugharne,
Carmarthenshire
10 September 1952

Dear Bozman,

More apologies than there's paper, for this crippling delay.

I intended, as you know, to write a more-or-less straight-forward & intimate prose preface, and then funked it. And then I began to write a prologue in verse, which has taken the devil of a time to finish. Here it is, only a hundred & two lines, and pathetically little, in size & quality, to warrant the two months, & more, I've taken over it. To begin with, I set myself, foolishly perhaps, a most difficult technical task: The Prologue is in two verses—in my manuscript, a verse to a page—of 51 lines each. And the second verse rhymes backward with the first. The first & last lines of the poem rhyme; the second and the last but one; & so on & so on. Why I acrosticked myself like this, don't ask me.

I hope the Prologue does read as a Prologue, & not as just another poem. I think—though I am too near to it now to be any judge—that it does do what it sets out to do: addresses the readers, the 'strangers', with a flourish, and fanfare, and makes clear, or tries to make clear, the position of one writer in a world 'at poor peace'. I will have a proof of this, won't I?

I'm writing to Higham, to say that the Prologue and the proofs are at last in your hands. And I'm begging him to have my contract with you settled as quickly as possible. Though the result does little to show it, I've spent two months at this poem, working hard at it every day and doing no other work-for-money at all. And consequently I've got very badly into debt, am faced with summonses, and cannot even now buy myself a beer and cigarettes. And daily it gets worse. So, please, do do all you can to let me have my advance royalties on the Collected Poems really quickly. It's very urgent. I'm in quite a desperate position, even to a few pounds, for day-to-day wants & needs.

You asked me, in a previous letter, about possible interviews with the press when the book comes out. Of course, I'd be pleased & will do whatever you can arrange.

All my apologies again.

Yours,

Dylan Thomas

PS. I shd, if possible, like a dedication: just

To Caitlin.

Proofreading the Collected Poems, I have the horrors of 'Paper & Sticks' on page 116. It's awful. I suppose it's quite impossible to cut it out? I shd so like it, somehow, to be omitted.

D.T.

MSS.: Messrs Dent

The Inland Revenue had ordered that David Higham deduct a percentage of his income to pay back taxes. For the rest, this letter is self-explanatory. Theodore Roethke had become a close friend. He was probably the American poet, of Dylan's generation, whom Dylan admired most.

TO OSCAR WILLIAMS

Boat House,
Laugharne,
Carmarthenshire,
Wales
October 8 1952

Dear Oscar,

How are you and bless you, you Little Treasure. Our love from us, looking over wet sand at nothing with some birds on it, to you eagled there looking out at the Statue of—what's its name? I think it has something to do with what Our Side gives to people after it has napalmed them. If anyone in any uniform said to me, 'Now we're going to make you free', I'd cut my throat with a blunt cunt. How are you, you label-less red hot red potato you, I salute you from this bronchial heronry.

Thank you, very, very, very much, for the two letters and the two cheques, they arrived in the old nick of time when every lane was mantrapped for me and grocers were armed to their sandy fangs and I couldn't even afford to go to the brewers' annual picnic, which, everyone assured me afterwards, was the best for years, chaos, blood, disaster, singing, from beginning to end.

Thank you, very much, for working so hard to get me some of that money, damn and blast it with a great big kiss. And I'm terribly glad you think you might be able to send along, from Miss Gardner (whom God wing!) the balance in full of a hundred and fifty dollars this month. I'm very poor now, I've been working on a poem, and it takes so long, and I've no time, then, to do any other jobs for our bread, marge, and gristle, so the money'll be wonderfully welcome. I'm sorry not to have written long before: I've had pneumonia etcetera and the etcetera was worse. But it's not through not thinking of you, cock, and that's a cockney expression and doesn't mean balls.

I saw John Brinnin and Howard Moss off on their backbound train, Howard being kissed goodbye by an adolescent boil with simper and spindles attached. I see Gene Baroff in London, who is so anglicized, who cossets and straitjackets his vowels so cruelly, he faints. I'm giving a reading on the BBC 3rd Programme of Roethke this week, and of Robert Lowell next week. Half an hour each. I'm trying to arrange a Williams (not WC). Good news about Poetry. (I mean, of course, Poetry Chicago.) What could good news about poetry be? (Bishop Eliot defrocked?) Oh, yes, and I'm introducing & arranging a half hour of Spoon River, and also a Personal Anthology —the B.B.C. has been running a feature called this for about six months now—devoted to Masters, Lindsay, Robinson & Sandberg, a fine old four for a programme and a boozeup. But going back to Karl and Poetry Chicago: Thank you—this is thank you today, and about bloody time—for suggesting and making possible that number you talked about. I'm sorry that I can't send on my new poem, myself, for that number, but my agent here, David Higham, will be doing so, direct to Karl. You see, the poem is a 'Prologue' to my Collected Poems, due to be published any moment now, and, had, therefore, to go through Higham's hands. I told him that Poetry Chicago wanted a poem, so perhaps Higham has already sent it along. (The Prologue, by the way, is a complete poem by itself, not just something written especially for a collected volume.) Any money coming from that Prologue will have to go through Higham, of course; but any other money from Karl—for the printing of the manuscript pages, for the possible prize you hinted at—can come, thank God, direct to me. And do I need it! And do I need it now! We are entirely without money, & want some more urgently, if that is possible, than ever before. Here, as you know, we are not as we are in the States, where we don't think or care about what we spend. Here, we have nothing to spend, and think and care about it all the time. So please, cock. (I've asked for a copy of Collected Poems to be sent to you.) I've another vast wodge of working-sheets for the Prologue Poem: want them, for sale? I'm enclosing a copy of that poem, too, for you yourself: on fine, thick paper it can take the place of a window pane, can be a very small tablecloth, or you can race cockroaches on it. How is Gene? Caitlin's & my love to her and you, always.

Dylan

The copied-out poem is really in 2 verses. I forgot, & have drawn in a line. Unnecessarily, & with great trouble, I have, as you might notice, rhymed all the way back from line 51 to line 1.

MSS.: Indiana

By now he would spend days, or even weeks, drafting such letters as this. The play of course is *Under Milk Wood*, of which *Botteghe Oscure* had published approximately half in April 1952.

TO MADAME CAETANI

The Boat House,
Laugharne,
Carmarthenshire,
Wales
6 November 1952

My Dear Marguerite Caetani,

It was beautiful to have your letter, and it made me feel a hundred times more ashamed, if that were possible, of my wretched, long, dark silence. Your letter was so warm, and good, as though I had never been barbarously bad to you at all, and as though, almost, I was forgiven for the breaking of promises, the filthy discourtesy incomprehensible to me also, even the whole dead year's dumb insult itself. It was beautiful to hear from you. I don't deserve one warm word but only bashing on the head and then forgetting cold as ice. I don't understand why I never wrote, why I never wrote if only to <u>explain</u>, to explain why I could not, at that time, in spite of my promises, finish the second half of my piece for you. Many times I began a letter, and then put it aside because the piece was not finished. And the drafts of letters piled up, and time lapped on and thickened, putting on skins of distance, and daily, and even more so nightly, I grew more ashamed of my silence and more angry with my procrastination until, at last, I couldn't write at all. I buried my head in the sands of America: flew over America like a damp, ranting bird; boomed and fiddled while home was burning; carried with me, all the time, my unfinished letters, my dying explanations and self-accusations, my lonely half of a loony maybe-play, in a heavy, hurtful bunch. These ostrich griefs were always with me, and whispered loudest in the late night when, indeed, I was all sand. 'Put it off, put it off', 'It's too late now', 'You can never be forgiven', 'The past is as dead as you'll be', 'Burn the daft drafts, unwind the half-play in your head so that nothing's left', 'Forget, you damned Welshcake, for doom'll nibble you down to the last crumb', 'Strangle your litter of wits in a sack, and splash!'—these agenbite-deadeners did their long-night worst, but the little voice in the dark, oh, throb, throb it went across Kansas and in all the ovens of the hotel bedrooms. (These pages, I think, are wilting in the grey nearly permanent drizzle that sighs down on to this town and through the birdscratched matchboard roof into my wordsplashed hut. It isn't rain, it must be remorse. The whole fishy bay is soaked in guilt like the bad bits of poems-not-to-be oozing to the marrow on the match-sticked floor, and the half-letters curling and whining in the warped drawers. I'm writing this guilty noise in a cold pool, on a November afternoon, in mists of depression. Forgive me even for this, if you can. I find my pitiful wallow in the drizzle of regret an indulgence I can't pity. This weather gets me like poverty: it blurs and then blinds, creeps chalky and crippling into the bones, shrouds me in wet self, rains away the world.)

I can't explain why I didn't write to explain why I couldn't finish the piece. (No, I can't explain. When I try to explain my fear, the confused symbols grow leaden and a woolly rust creeps over the words. How can I say it? I can't. I can say: One instinct of fear is to try to make oneself as little, as unnoticeable, as possible, to cower, as one thinks, unseen and anonymous until the hunt is past. My fearful instinct is to bloat myself like a frog, to magnify my unimportance, to ring a bell for a name, so that, as I bluster and loom twice my size, the hunt, seeing me monstrous, bays by after different & humbler prey. But that is not what I mean: the symbols have wet-brain, the words have swallowed their tongues.)

All that I can't explain. But why I didn't finish the piece there and then, as I said I would, is another matter. I was, as you know, leaving home—though, am, miraculously, home again now in this tumbling house whose every broken pane and wind-whipped-off slate, child-scrawled wall, rain-stain, mousehole, knobble and ricket, man, man-booby-and-rat-trap, I know in my sleep. I was leaving for ever, it seemed, had nowhere to go, nothing to go with, and, after you had wonderfully helped me to pay off some of my many debts here, I went to London, which to me is nowhere, and lived by odd reviews—and they were odd too—odder broadcasts, pretending to women's clubs, putting off, putting off, all the nasty time, and one thing I wanted to do: finish my piece for you, and make my peace. But nothing could happen. Then I went to the States with my luggage of dismays and was loudly lost for months, peddling and bawling to adolescents the romantic agonies of the dead. I made money, and it went, and I returned with none; and once more, with the unfinished letters, poems and play weighing much more heavily now on a mind nearly out of its mind with its little, mountainous anxieties and aches, reviewed, begged, lectured, broadcast, waited, with no hope, for the time when I could come back here and write truly again. I waited, and I put off, full of fear and wishes.

It is all a very inadequate explanation, and it cannot call itself an excuse, and indeed my fears are inexcusable, though very real to me in their mean, mad way. And my talk, though terribly but weakly true, of 'putting off' all the time, is terribly putting off, I know.

These are the reasons, however—and expressed in depression and with little hope of them being believed or thought worthy—for my silence and my broken promises. About John Davenport and René Char, I had heard nothing until your letter; and, even if I had heard, how could that, in any way in the world, affect you and me: your goodness to me, your faith in me, and my affection and gratitude kept, so it would appear, so obstinately secret?

I'm trying to work again now, and faithfully promise you the rest of the thing, and whatever other work I have, by, at the latest, the first of February. I won't fail you. Or have I joined forever the folds of the snarling and letting-down black once-friendly sheep? Oh, I do hope not.

It is so difficult for me to live and keep my family alive. There are many petty jobs which would make me just not enough money for tradesmen and rent, for clothes and school, for parents, shoes, and cigarettes, but these petty jobs, by their nature and by the time they claim, stop me writing as I would wish to write. But how, without these jobs, am I to live, to write, at all? These problems keep me treadmilling small nightmares all the waking nights.

About another visit to the States, I don't know. Though I can only play a poet there, and not make poetry, yet there I can, if only for a few months, live and send money home. I may have to go again. I cannot go on thinking all the time of butchers and bakers and grocers and cobblers and rates and rents until I bleed. After I have finished what I am now working on, I may have to give up writing altogether. (My need—as I imagine it—to write, may be all conceit. The bellows that fan the little flicker is nothing but wind, after all. And writing is certainly not one of the ancient secrets of the head-shrinking tribes. Ach, my endless bleating of private woes because I am not 'allowed' to write, as though the trees would grow inward, like toenails, if I renounced this passion for self-glorification. 'Peace, let me write. Gag the tradesmen, I must write. Alms, for the love of writing.' Perhaps I should be better off pulling teeth. But even this momentary disgust I blame upon the weather. And even this disgust is 'material for writing' just as trees, and toenails, and glorification, and teeth.) I think it's time to stop this. I wanted, at first, only to say that I am profoundly ashamed of my silence and of my broken promises, and that I will not fail you again, and that I do, with all the bloody muscle of my heart, ask for your forgiveness. But the letter got caught up with my despairs, though, always, I want, one day, to write you a happy letter. Because I am very often happy, and not always, here by the sea, without cause.

Please forgive me, and try to trust me again.

The old, cold pool of the day is a little warmer now.

Yours ever,

Dylan

MSS.: Texas

Collected Poems was published on 10th November 1952, just one year less one day before his death. It was received with almost unanimous praise by the critics, of whom Mr Prys-Jones was one, and also by the public, who bought some ten thousand copies during the last year of Dylan's life.

TO A. G. PRYS-JONES

Boat House,

Laugharne,

Carmarthenshire

21st November 1952

Dear A. G. Prys-Jones,

First of all, do please forgive me for not answering your dizzyingly kind letter long before this, and for not acknowledging the typescript of the review—a review I am quite dumb before. I've been away in London, no letters were forwarded from Laugharne, and in that ghastly city I caught so much cold I'm still croaking and snuffling about the house like an old, slippered crow.

It was extremely good of you to send on the full copy of the review —but in face of its staggering praise of my poems, what can I say? Cold 'thank you', even, could sound damnably immodest, as though perhaps I were thanking you for something which I expected, something I thought my due, which is light years from the case. I was amazed at the praise; honoured by the constructive work and care which had gone into the appreciation of these often absurdly difficult poems: and, of course, delighted by the fact that you understood, so deeply, the underlying purpose and direction of the stuff itself—even though some of the poems, and many of the passages and lines, I had,

I know, made impenetrable to others by my own tortuous ignorance of the particular dark in which I was trying to move.

Yes, amazed, honoured, and delighted, that's all I can say, and thank you, too. (But I could have written so much more freely if you had damned the book to little wild bits.)

I'm hoping to have a Collected Stories, including some new ones and many that have appeared only in small forgotten magazines, at the end of next year. My next book will be pretty awful; a film-scenario I wrote some years ago, which no-one would film, and which Dents seem to think is worth printing, as a story in itself, I just don't know: it's a long time ago and all over to me. It will be called 'The Doctor and the Devils'. And I'm hoping also to bring out an extravagant play, as yet unfinished and maybe the radio will do it first, about a day's life in a small town in a never-never Wales. It sounds very ordinary, but it isn't that anyway, it's odd as anything, and I'm enjoying writing it. No title yet, only an unprintable one.

Once again, but never finally, all my thanks and regards.

Very sincerely yours,

Dylan Thomas

MSS.: Texas

Despite the success of *Collected Poems,* his money worries got worse and worse, and once again, as so often in the past, he turned to Stephen Spender for help.

Edith is Edith Sitwell. Natasha is Natasha Litvin, the pianist and wife of Stephen Spender. John Raymond, the literary critic, was at this time literary editor of the *New Statesman*.

TO STEPHEN SPENDER

Boat House,
Laugharne,
Carmarthenshire
22nd November 1952

Dear Stephen,

Were you at Edith's on Monday? I couldn't turn up, I was sick and wretched though I wanted very much to see you and Natasha again and to say goodbye to Edith, and now that I'm more or less home again I'm wretcheder than ever. I seem to be finally caught and tangled.

I knew, when I was in London helping to raise Cain, that I had left scores of unsettled debts behind me and that there were several summonses on the way. Then, on Monday morning, more dreadful letters were forwarded. I got back here to more bills, and to hear that the bailiffs will be moving in unless I pay what I can never pay because I have no money at all, even for bread or cigarettes but have to borrow the shillings for these. The bailiffs will be moving in because I can't pay enough, on account, of the income-tax I owe on money I earned, and spent, in America in 1950. And I have nothing to go on with day to day. There's no need to write a hideously long list of all I owe and all I must pay at once at once because I'm not asking you for anything but—Do you know anyone who could help me now? I don't know anybody. I can't write properly. I can't write anything anyway, I can't work or sleep because of this. From all I earn, anyway, the Income Tax, for that damned American trip, take 75 per cent & will now take everything. Of course I've no savings, and this house isn't mine to sell. Only immediate help can save me from I don't know and I can't say because I have never been so full of despair nor Caitlin neither. Do you know anyone you can ask? I can provide that anyone with a real long row of my debts so that he can see that it isn't for me to spend. I can't go on like this. I'm used to living up and down and mostly down, but this is over the edge and the end. I've been helped before, in the past, & that was wonderful. But I've never needed it as I need it now. I'm sorry that my first letter for so long to you should be like this, but I don't know who to turn to and perhaps you know someone. Surely there is someone—though I'm sure I don't know why. It's nice, I suppose, to be overpraised, as I've been recently, but it makes this despair much worse, if that were possible, and I suppose it always is, to know that those overwords were about somebody quite else, somebody I don't know at all, and not about who I am and what I am and the hating, unwanting where-I-am, and all the misery because I haven't a couple of hundred pounds or so and never bloody will. (Here they are, and I did want to keep them out, near-hysteria and rage and selfpity.) Please help if you can. And surely, surely there's someone somewhere, I'll keep on saying to myself till I hear from you.

Love to you and Natasha,
Dylan

I'm sending this to John Raymond at the New Statesman to send on to you.

MS.: Harvard

Stephen Spender, reviewing *Collected Poems* in the *Spectator*, had said that Dylan was influenced by Welsh bardic poetry.

TO STEPHEN SPENDER

Boat House,
Laugharne,
Carmarthenshire
9th December 1952

My dear Stephen,

This isn't about the same miserable subject as my earlier letter—though .he situation is, if that were possible, worse than it was then, and it certainly looks as though it's going to be worms and water for Christmas—but only to thank you, very much indeed, for your notice, of my Collected Poems, in the Spectator. You were, as you know, the very first person ever to write to me about a poem of mine; and this is now the clearest, most considered and sympathetic, and, in my opinion, truest, review that I have ever seen of my writing. I mean, that your statement of understanding of my aim and method seems to me to be altogether true; and no critic has attempted, in writing about my most uneven and unsatisfactory work, to set out, plainly, the difference between the writing of poetry from words and the writing of poetry towards words—though that's, of course, oversimplification. No writer before you; and I do want, please, to thank you again very much.

I do hope, by the way, that my first, almost despairing letter wasn't a dreadful nuisance to you, and didn't seem an impertinence. I had, & have, no-one to turn to, and felt sure you would understand my present, beastly difficulties.

Please thank Natasha for her telegram. I will write her separately, if or if not this wretchedness is somehow lifted or even eased.

Oh, & I forgot. I'm not influenced by Welsh bardic poetry. I can't read Welsh.

Yours,
Dylan

MS.: Harvard

J. Alexander Rolph was at this time compiling his *Dylan Thomas: a Bibliography*, which was published in 1956. I print this letter as an example of how courteous—and helpful—Dylan could be.

TO ALEXANDER ROLPH

Boat House,
Laugharne,
Carmarthenshire
11 December 1952

Dear Alexander Rolph,

So very sorry not to have written long before. Thank you, a lot, for your letters, and your awfully kind offer to try to get hold of any difficult-to-get items for me should I need them: I won't forget that. You said you were moving to Weybridge in the New Year. When? I don't think I'll be in London until about the 12th or 13th of January: about that date I'm helping to raise Cain again, or his Shadow rather, this time without Edith S. and at the Albert Hall. If you haven't moved by that time, do let's fix up to meet for some drinks one evening round then.

I'm afraid I'm going to be nearly no good at all to you in answer to these questions about when & where etc. My memory's bad, I keep no files or old numbers of periodicals. New English Weekly. Yes, perhaps I did contribute to it after 1935, though I'm not sure. I seem to remember 2 poems and another prose piece, then 'After the Fair'. And a regular novel review in, about, 36, 37, or 38.

Of the periodicals you mention, all, I think, are finished. And 'Caravel' was the only one I believe to be not British. If you like I could put you in touch with Ruthven Todd, in New York, whose knowledge of these fly-by-night magazines used to be enormous.

Do you know my American selection of poems & stories called 'The World I Breathe', brought out by New Directions in 1939? There are 4 stories in that that don't appear in 'Map of Love'. Of these, one, 'A Prospect of the Sea', was, I think, printed in a Penguin of Modern Welsh Stories. Again, I don't know if it was reprinted from a periodical: I rather think I sent, on request, the manuscript to the editor. 'The Burning Baby', also in 'The World I Breathe', was published in Roger Roughton's 'Contemporary Prose & Verse', just before the war.

A London magazine called 'Janus' published a story of mine called 'The Horse's Ha', which hasn't been in book form yet. And another little magazine, called 'Yellow Jacket', edited by Constantine Fitz-Gibbon (who's brought out a couple of novels fairly recently) printed 2 stories, called, as far as I remember, 'The Vest' and 'The True Story'.

Robert Herring's 'Life & Letters ToDay' printed, I think, 2 or 3 stories, including one called 'The Lemon', which also has not yet been in a book.

The Booster was edited by Henry Miller in Paris before the war: I'm afraid I don't know when. (Miller's address is, I think, quite simply Big Sur, California.) There were certainly very few numbers of it brought out under Miller. It was, I think, originally a little 'organ' run by, or for, American business-men visiting Paris, full of rotation-like gossip. Miller, as an American exile living in Paris, somehow got temporary hold of this bit of hail-fellowry, & immediately printed Alfred Perles, Lawrence Durrell, very odd drawings, himself, & one contribution by me—all to the surprise of the subscribers.

The Map of Love. My memory's almost gone here. Some of the stories, I believe, were printed in periodicals. One of them at least, I am sure, appeared in 'New Stories', a brown magazine, & was later re-printed in one of E. J. O'Brien's Best Stories of the Year, or whatever he called it. 'The Orchards' was, I think, published in Elizabeth Bowen's 'Modern Short Stories', which was an early Penguin, though whether she reprinted it from the 'Map of Love' or from a magazine I can't remember.

And I feel pretty certain 'The Tree' was published somewhere. Maybe in the N. E. Weekly.

Any other things I can remember about poems or stories—especially about stories in the Map of Love—I'll send you.

Oh, I do remember: 'The Mouse & The Woman', in 'The Map of Love', was, I'm fairly sure, published in 'Transition' just before the war. Enough to go on with?

Let me know about the date of your going to Weybridge, & whether we can meet in London round about Jan. 13.

Yours,

Dylan Thomas

PS. Some prose was printed by Keidrych Rhys in his 'Wales', now also defunct. 'Prologue To An Adventure', printed in 'The World I Breathe' appeared in one of the New Directions yearly anthologies—& also somewhere, forgotten, else. 'The Holy Six' & 'The School for Witches', in the same 'W. I Breathe', haven't been published in periodicals.

MSS.: Texas

Ellen Borden Stevenson had at one time been married to Adlai Stevenson, who had been defeated when he ran for President in 1952. She was then living in Chicago and was much involved in the cultural life of that city. She had been helpful and kind to Dylan during his American trips. It is odd that he did not know how to spell her name.

TO OSCAR WILLIAMS

Boat House,
Laugharne,
Carmarthenshire,
Wales
Jan 5 1953

Dear Oscar,

Love to you & Gene from Cat & me, always.

This is only a little note, because Christmas here has been so confused that I'm still ½ daft with it. My father, in great pain, & blind, died a few days before Christmas, & I had a lot of sad business to attend to: I'm the only one left if you exclude, as well you may, a sister in Bombay. The children have been ill. Caitlin's pregnant again. The water pipes have burst & the house is flooded, etc. etc. And the etceteras are almost worse than the rest. So this, before a real letter, is only to say: Thank you, thank you, for the cheque for 150 dollars, previously unacknowledged, and for the last, December 8, cheque for 100 dollars. Oh, Mrs. Stephenson, would you were the first lady of the land * * * And, please, I would like straightaway, the balance due to me on that piece of Chicagoanery, of 200 dollars. Without those cheques you've been whistling across the water, we couldn't have lived through these foul months.

New York I am supposed to come to end of April; alone, maybe, at first, to be joined by Cat in the early summer.

I return, signed, the Golden Treasury slip. You do me over-proud. The 'Prologue' sheets I shall send this week, along with a short story. Also, I received the Skin-Trade 198 dollars, praise be.

(And I am longing for the last Stephenson 200 dollars.)

No news now; just thank yous, please send, & all love.

Doctor & Devil is a bad book: an old commissioned filmscript, Let's all forget it.

What Guggenheim news?

Again,
Yours,
Dylan

MSS.: Harvard

The death of his father in December, 1952, had upset Dylan greatly.

TO ALFRED JANES

Boat House,
Laugharne,
Carmarthenshire
Jan 5 1953

Dear Fred,

Thank you, very very much indeed, for writing on my father's death. Poor old boy, he was in awful pain at the end and nearly blind. The day before he died, he wanted to get out of bed & go into the kitchen where his mother was making onion soup for him. Then, a few hours afterwards, he suddenly remembered everything, & where he was, & he said, 'It's full circle now'.

My mother is very good and brave about it; and she wants to thank you very much, as well, & to wish you a good New Year.

I do hope to see you soon.

Ever,
Dylan

MSS.: Alfred Janes, Esq.

This is the genesis of the book which appeared posthumously with the title *Quite Early One Morning*. The British edition did not finally include the early, 'poetic' stories, which were also published posthumously in *A Prospect of the Sea*.

TO E. F. BOZMAN

Boat House,
Laugharne,
Carmarthenshire
6th January 1953

Dear E. F. Bozman,

Thank you for your last letter of the 2nd of January, in which you mentioned one possibility of an autobiography, especially in relation to my early years. Well, of course, I have produced a more-or-less autobiography in my 'Portrait of the Artist as A Young Dog'. And I really haven't enough desire, or material, to try to write another. And the childhood broadcast you mentioned—I'm afraid I don't know which one it was—is one of only six similar broadcasts: not nearly enough for even the smallest book. These six were, incidentally: Two on *Memories of Christmas*, one on *Memories of August Bank Holiday*, one called just *Memories of Childhood* and the other *Early One Morning*, and the other, in dramatic radio form, called *Return to Swansea*.

I have also a recent short story, about the adolescent period, called *The Followers*.

In an American book of mine, published by New Directions, called 'The World I Breathe'—a book of verse and prose—there are five stories which haven't appeared in an English book: 2 of them haven't appeared in any periodical. These five are:

> The Holy Six
> A Prospect of the Sea
> The Burning Baby
> Prologue to An Adventure
> The School for Witches

and are all very young and violent and romantic.

There are also, in periodicals, 4 stories of a similar kind:

> The Lemon
> The Horse's Ha
> The Vest
> The True Story.

I think that the broadcast reminiscences, all fairly riotously innocent, together with the death and blood other group typified by the Burning Baby, would make an interesting volume: especially if somehow through a longish introduction, through an introductory story, or through some as-yet-unthought-of prose-links, I could explain their origins and bring them closer together.

If you would be interested in this, I could have the five stories from 'The World I Breathe' typed out, write to a friend on the B.B.C. to gather together the reminiscent broadcasts, of which, unfortunately, I have no copy, and ask John Alexander Rolph, my bibliographist-to-be, to find the four stories in the old, fled periodicals. Perhaps we could discuss this on the 20th or 21st.

Yours sincerely,
Dylan Thomas

This would, I realize, be a hotchpotch of a book, but the separate items could be introduced, in some way, so as to make them cohere into a kind of oblique autobiography: a growing-up, (a) in stories written while growing up and (b) in memories of childhood written when grown up.

MSS.: Messrs Dent

Charles Fry, who had commissioned the book of American impressions, was losing patience at Dylan's failure to deliver this book. He was even talking of taking legal action to recover the advance which Dylan had received more than a year before.

TO CHARLES FRY

The Boat House,
Laugharne,
Carmarthenshire
16th February 1953

Dear Charles,

First of all, a tremendous number of apologies, profound, very very nervous, terribly late, too late perhaps. These apologies, we both know, are childsplay to make and we're not children (though I feel, sometimes, even now, as useless as a fat child in a flood) and contracts and the writing of books aren't playing. And what perhaps kills trust between persons most, is silence: that dead, muffling, insistent, insolent silence of which I've been guilty for so very long. All I can say at the beginning of this inadequate, breathless, and honest-as-I-can-be letter is: my apologies come from my head and my heart. And the silence, which I hate, came from no intended insolent carelessness or any desire to dishonour a promise I was longing to keep, but from one tortuous cause alone, which I will try to explain: a cause that, aggravated by guilt and grief and illness, became daily more intolerable to me until now, at this most urgent moment, I can still hardly write at all.

Let me straightaway apologise, please, for never having had the courtesy to answer a letter, or the courage to write directly to you and try to explain my one real problem which has, for a year now, nagged and savaged me and made me lose nearly every shivering ounce of faith in myself. The reasons I didn't answer, I couldn't answer, your kind and justifiably firm letter of December were, mostly, all circumstantial ones, though magnified and distorted, no doubt, by my small, deep hell of the last year. These 'circumstantial' reasons were: my father died that month, blind, of cancer, and everything that had to be done was done by me: this included the care of my mother, who is a permanent invalid, and her maintenance, for the pension she and my father existed on died with him. The children got sick, and I had no money. Early this year, my best friend in the world, a woman of my own age, died of drink and drugs. And I've been ill too. So far, so very obviously bad, a mock Russian Whine or drab borrowed slice of Gissing. Perhaps these recent happenings could just about pardon my not writing letters. But they have, of course, nothing to do with your chief worry and mine: why the book I promised, and so very much want to write, is not yet written. These happenings can't pardon that, and my detailing of them is not intended to. The 'nagging, savaging, destroying' problem, the real reason why the book is as yet unwritten, that is what you want explained. And how can I write that reason down? That is the thing itself: for a whole year I have been able to write nothing, nothing, nothing at all but one tangled, sentimental poem as preface to a collection of poems written years ago.

Perhaps it doesn't sound and seem—that phrase, 'I have been able to write nothing'—the throttling bloody hell it's been to me for this whole waste of a twisted year. And this letter is sure to be silly and pretentious enough without my griping on about words being the light and reason of my life etcetera. I went to America, as you know, about this time last year, and kept a jungle of a diary which I felt quite certain I could, on my return to this wet idyllic tomb on the coast, shape and order into a book neither you nor I would be ashamed of: and I was excited, as I still am, at the thought of wheedling and hacking a proper work out of the chaos of places and people I'd scrawled in planes and trains and bedrooms-like-boilers. I went on all over the States, ranting poems to enthusiastic audiences that, the week before, had been equally enthusiastic about lectures on Railway Development or the Modern Turkish Essay; and gradually I began to feel nervous about the job in front of me, the job of writing, making things in words, by myself again. The more I used words, the more frightened I became of using them in my own work once more. Endless booming of poems didn't sour or stale words for me, but made me more conscious of my obsessive interest in them and my horror that I would never again be innocent enough to touch and use them. I came home fearful and jangled. There was my hut on a cliff, full of pencil and paper, things to stare at, room to breathe and feel and think. But I couldn't write a word. I tried then to write a poem, dreading it beforehand, a few obscure lines every dumb day, and the printed result shook and battered me in any faith in myself and workman's pride left to me. I couldn't write a word after that. These are the most words I have written for a year.

And then, because I wouldn't write at all, I got broke—I'd brought little or no money back from the States—and kept the wolf just a hairy inch from my door and my sleep by croaking poems, and such, on the air: an appalling retrogression to an American habit that had gone bad on me. I didn't croak enough to keep me going, and lectured, then, to English women: less intimidating, maybe, but less profitable, too, than American. And all the time I couldn't, I really couldn't do the one thing I had to do: write words, my own words, down on paper.

Now I can understand that one ordinary, I suppose, reaction would be to this endless jumbled dull confession: Here's somebody who read aloud and lectured too much too often and too long in a too-hospitable place and who became sated with public words and with his own exhibitionism. On his return, he couldn't get down to work; he missed the willing audience, the easy, but killing, money; as time went on, he became frightened of his failure to meet his literary commitments and now, groaning as though all disinterested heaven were lurching on to his head, conjures up, to a squeal of Welsh bag-pipes, some vague psychological hoo ha to account for his timidity and sloth.

I know it goes deeper than that. I've lived with it a long time, or so it seems, and know it horridly well, and can't explain it. I haven't been able to write a word, of anything. Behind me, all the time, I heard, And you'll never be able to write a word again. I thought it would break me up into little self-pitying bits.

But an odd thing's happened, and only now. Or perhaps it isn't odd, and time alone has done it. Whatever the reason, since the disasters, big and midget, I mentioned some time ago, on page 93 of this letter, I've got unknotted. Now for God's sake I can't explain that; but there it is. And Higham is going to get lots of other difficulties straightened out, so that I can get down to those ogre words again without night-mares of doubt and debt, and my dear diabolic family shall be protected for a time. And I'll write that American book, or die.

I'm coming to London Monday next. Higham, I hope, has fixed up a time to meet you; (For me to meet you, I mean).

I daren't read back over these pages, in case I scream with denial & embarrassment.

It must be time alone that's done its work.

Please try to firgive me for my mean, tortured silence; and for his letter.

Yours ever,
Dylan

MSS.: Texas, from the Dylan Thomas Collection of George J. Firmage

He was now preparing for his third visit to America.

TO OSCAR WILLIAMS

Boat House,
Laugharne,
Carmarthenshire,
Wales
27 February 1953

Sending work-sheets
separately
D.

Dear Oscar,

One New American Library cheque has just arrived. I cannot take my sticky eyes from it, and I remember that great line: 'the heal's wide spendthrift gaze towards paradise'. Thank you, so very much, for the bother and speed & business of it. And forgive me, please, for the asthmatic brevity of this. I'm about to catch a bus to catch a train to catch a film-man and, almost certainly, to miss the bus. I'm so fat now I can't hurry; I have elephantiasis: a huge trunk and a teeny mind. It's full-moon time, & the town is baying. And I'm awfully worried about my scheduled visit to the States. I have to write a book by June, & haven't begun it. We're being thrown out of this house—though only we would live in it, over-run by rats: us and the house. I hardly dare write to Brinnin to say it is all too difficult, but must do so quickly or he will need a hundred new kinds of pills all big as roc eggs. Perhaps if Caitlin were settled in some new warren, I could fly over for a few dates: but we're moving to Christ knows where by the sea. I want very much to meet the mogul you mentioned & to find out about that 4000 a year each etc: it sounds wonderful: we could go anywhere on that, except Laughlin's heart and ski-run. But I don't know how I'm going to see you at all this year, with the commissioned book yapping at me, the house being pinched, and all my depression at the thought of ever moving again except into my long and dirty home. I'll write you again when I hear from John Malcolm once he has heard from me in a re-balding letter.

395

I enclose the signed note for the Prologue poem; also the work-sheets. I do hope you can sell them for an impossible sum. My agent here has said he will help me with my debts but allow me no money: so I must have some of the stuff on the side. You must take some money yourself from whatever you can get for these messy sheets—poems won't change the sheets for their guests—so that we can both celebrate. Please.

The trivial story I can't find but will. It was published in World Review.

The bus is getting up steam. Love to you & Gene from us all, and thank you deeply.

I look forward to a letter.

Yours ever,
Dylan

I'll be doing a broadcast of your poems some time this spring. Will let you know when. The BBC doesn't much like doing American copyright poems: they hate spending dollars. I <u>may</u> have to put some English poems in the same programme: if I have to, I'll choose very good ones.

MSS.: Indiana

Dylan Thomas had won the William Foyle Poetry Prize, worth £250, for the best book of poems published in the past year.

By the end of Dylan's life David Higham was doing far more for him than is customary on the part of an author's agent. As this letter shows, Dylan had become almost totally irresponsible about money, simply cashing cheques until the bank returned them. He would then ask David Higham to pay the most pressing bills.

Dylan's elder son, Llewelyn, was still at Magdalen College School, Oxford.

TO DAVID HIGHAM

Boat House,
Laugharne,
Carmarthenshire
17th March 1953

Dear David,

I do hope you got my last letter, written just after we met in London. I've been expecting an answer, and am worried about it. I hope you aren't ill; or that anything in my letter or at our lunch offended you: I'm awfully sorry if it did.

If you got that letter you'll remember I enclosed with it a bill from our local Brown's Hotel, mostly for the letting of a house, for £190. Now that—though it must, of course, be paid, eventually however slowly—is not, at this moment, nearly as urgent as other quite small ones which have cropped up in the town and which I really must pay at once. (Friendly Brown's can wait. These tradesmen and rates-men can't.) And the most urgently pressing bill is one for £35 to Magdalen College School, Oxford. As soon as I won that Foyle's award, the very first cheque I wrote was to the school, for that amount; but they kept the cheque without presenting it for so long that when they did present it, it was returned by the bank, the Foyle's money being by that time finished. This is really distressingly important for me to pay now.

I don't know how my account stands with you, but you should have received from the BBC over £100 for four personal anthologies I recorded in the Swansea studios several weeks ago and which have been broadcast on the Welsh Region, week by week. Also, I recorded a childhood Reminiscences sketch for the Welsh Region, from Swansea last week, for £20 and this coming Friday am to record two more, at, I believe, the same fee. So that there should be £100 in the kitty and £60 coming. The £100 should certainly be there by now. Can you therefore, let me have the money for Magdalen College School, or arrange to pay it, at once? And can you please pay into my bank all you possibly can, at once as well. I need £50 for various small bills here which simply must be paid this week. I have no money at all. I'll ring you at your office in the morning, hoping that you will have read this by that time and that you will be able to let me have £50 directly in the bank and enough to pay the school. The Income Tax must, this time, wait for its share.

And also, when I ring I do hope I'll find that you aren't ill or offended.

Yours ever,
Dylan

MSS.: David Higham Associates

His third American trip began on 21st April 1953—the date of his arrival in New York on board the *United States*—and ended on 3rd June when he flew back to London.

It will be recalled that Henry Treece had called the poetic movement of which Treece formed part 'The Apocalypse'.

TO JOHN MALCOLM BRINNIN

I shall be applying for
a visa next week: in
Cardiff, this time.   I
do not think they are
quite so screening-strict
there as in London.   URGENT,
& just remembered: Let me have,
at once, a formal and official
Poetry Center letter Dear Mr.
Thomas-ing me and saying what
cultural & important engagements
you have fixed up for me.

Boat House,
Laugharne,
Carmarthenshire,
Wales
18th March 1953

Dear John,

After all sorts of upheavals, evasions, promises, procrastinations, I write, very fondly, and fawning slightly, a short inaccurate summary of those events which caused my never writing a word before this. In the beginning, as Treece said in one of his apocalapses, was the bird; and this came from Caitlin, who said, and repeated it only last night after our Boston-Laugharne babble, 'You want to go to the States again only for flattery, idleness, and infidelity'. This hurt me terribly. The right words were: appreciation, dramatic work, and friends. Therefore I didn't write until I knew for certain that I could come to the States for a visit and then return to a body and hearth not irremediably split from navel to firedog. Of course, I'm far from certain now, but I'm coming. This unfair charge—flattery, idleness, etcetera—kept me seething quiet for quite a bit. Then my father died, and my mother relied on me to look after her and to stay, writing like fury, pen in paw, a literary mole, at home. Then a woman—you never met her—who promised me a real lot of money for oh so little in return died of an overdose of sleeping drug and left no will, and her son, the heir, could hardly be expected to fulfil that kind of unwritten agreement. Then a publisher's firm, which had advanced me money for an American-Impressions book of which I never wrote a word, turned, justly, nasty, and said I had to do the book by June 1953 or they would set the law on me. Then Caitlin was going to have another baby and didn't want it. Then Margaret Taylor said that she was going to sell the rickety house we wrestled in, over our heads and live bodies. So this was the position I was in, so far as my American visit was concerned: Caitlin was completely against it, and was going to have a baby; my mother was against it, because I should be near her and working hard to keep the lot of us; and I was reluctantly against it, because I was without money, owing to an unexpected suicide, and I could not, naturally, leave a mother and pregnant wife and three children penniless at home while I leered and tubthumped in Liberty Land; and the publishers were legally against it, because I had to write a book for them quickly; and on top of all that, the final reason for my knowing I could not come out this spring was the prospect of the rapid unhousing of dame, dam, chick-to-be, and the well-loved rest. (I write like a cad. I should whip myself to death on the steps of my Club for all this.) Well anyway; I won a prize, for the book of the year, of £250 (pounds). And a brother-in-law in Bombay said he would look, from a distance, after my Mother's welfare. And Margaret Taylor has, temporarily, relented. And I think I can give the demanding publishers the script of 'Under Milk Wood' (when finished) instead of, for instance, 'A Bard's-Eye View of the U.S.A.' And Caitlin's hatred of my projected visit can be calmed only by this: that after no more than 6 weeks' larricking around I return from New York with enough money to take Colm, her and me for three winter months to Portugal where all, I hear, is cheap and sunny. Or, alternatively, that I find, in a month, a house for us, in your country, and can send for Caitlin to join me in the early summer and keep us going, through summer and autumn, by work which is not cross-continental reading and raving. Of the alternatives she would prefer the first. So do you think it possible? Do you think I can earn a lot in six weeks: enough, that is, for a Portuguese winter? I do not care, in those six weeks, how much I read, or how many times, or where. I think, for economy, it would be best for me to stay in a New York hotel—the Chelsea, I trust— for only a little time and then to move in, manias and all, on to friends. I am hoping that perhaps my old friend Len Lye, who lives in Greenwich Village, near Ruthven Todd, will put me up: I am only small, after all, and alone, though loud. I haven't his address, but will get in touch with him once in Chelsea'd New York. So, friend and agent, as much as I can do in six weeks please is perhaps best for us all.

I have put down, in more or less true detail, all the above little hells to show why I have been unable, till now, to write and say, 'It is fine. Go ahead.'

About 'Under Milk Wood'. I shall not have the complete manuscript ready until the week of my sailing. I have, anyway, some doubts as to the performance of it by by myself and a professional cast. Some kind of an approximation to a Welsh accent is required throughout, and I think I could make an hour's entertainment out of this myself. Shall we discuss it later? I shall have the m.s. with me, embarking from the liner, and if you still think, after reading it, it needs other and professional voices, then I don't believe it would need all that 'careful preparation' you mention. I should be very glad, by the way, to hear from you, as soon as possible about any ideas you might have as to what I shd read aloud in my general verse-reading programmes. What poets, and of what centuries? I'd like a wide repetoire. Caitlin sends her love to your mother.

Yours always, dear John.
Dylan

MSS.: *John Malcolm Brinnin, Esq.*

Theodore Roethke had now become one of Dylan's closest friends in America.

TO THEODORE ROETHKE

Boat House,
Laugharne,
Carmarthenshire,
Wales
31 March 1953

Dear Ted,

Sorry not to have written before to thank you for sending the Dancing Poems. I think they're wonderfully good. I kept putting off writing until I knew when I'd be in the States, so that I could say, See you, I hope, in the so-and-so. Now so-and-so is April 21st, and I'll be in and around New York until June 5. Any chance of seeing you for a few hours, evenings, days? A line to me c/o Brinnin, saying Yes, or even, Yes, perhaps, would be fine to look forward to.

I asked the BBC, officially, about getting hold of a copy, for you, of the recording I made of the three poems of yours, but the BBC

said, we never, we never, we never. Which is not true. Now I'm
climbing into the BBC by the back door, and falling over the slimy
accents, and hope to get a copy soon. I'm glad and proud you want
one: I hope I haven't boomily buggered the poems up. The recording
got several letters: 'terrific poems', 'gibberish', etc, and one or two
simple serious & passionate ones from people I didn't know of that
did show how disturbed they were by the strange things that had
happened to them across the air. You still have a grotesquely small
audience here, but very fierce.

Had your wedding card. Congratulations. Best wishes, & sympathy,
to your wife. Hope you had a nice, loud, elbowy, dancing time and
fell on some guests.

I haven't seen a copy of Poetry Chicago yet with your piece about
my book.

Are you writing poems? I want very very much to see them. And
do try to meet, New York or Chicago. Or anywhere.

Yours,
Dylan

MSS.: Theodore Roethke Estate

TO E. F. BOZMAN

Boat House,
Laugharne,
Carmarthenshire
31 March 1953

Dear E. F. Bozman,

I hope that by this time the first quite big chunk of material for the
new book has reached you, & also the accompanying letter. I don't
remember, however, if I indicated, in my letter, what material exactly
was to be typed (& it was extremely kind of you to suggest that you
might get it typed for me). In case I didn't, the list is:

The Followers (World Review)
Holiday Memories
Quite Early One Morning (typescript)
Adventure (Seven)
The Vest
The True Story (Yellowjacket)
The Horse's Ha (Janus)
The School For Witches

The Holy Six   (This World I
The Burning Baby   Breathe)
Prologue To An Adventure
A Prospect of The Sea

I've heard today from friends of mine who've helped me collect the above that I can expect to have nearly all the rest next week. This will include 'Return Journey', a long piece, 'Memories of Childhood', and 'Memories of Christmas', all originally broadcast: that is, written to be spoken aloud but also, very much, to be read. 'The Crumbs of One Man's Year', that was broadcast one New Year's Day & is, I hope, quite a good piece. A short story of the fantastic kind, called 'The Lemon'. Another Christmas piece. And a little very early story called 'After The Fair', which appeared in the New English Weekly many years ago. My bibliographer-to-be, John Rolph, has tracked this last down to the files of a public library but is not allowed to take the copy out and, having no shorthand, cannot easily copy it. I shall have to think how to get hold of this as—whatever its literary merits; I can't remember a thing about it now—I should like to include it: it's the earliest story of mine & will take its place next to some little piece describing the author just about that time of his life.

I'll write again; & I do hope we can hurry a contract up. I'm going to the States, for 6 weeks lecturing, on April 16th, and must have some money to keep my family going while I am away and to settle some outstanding debts before I leave. I'm desperately broke.

Yours,

Dylan Thomas

MSS.: Messrs Dent

At this time Higham was withholding approximately half Dylan's earnings for the Inland Revenue. And his bank account was heavily overdrawn. Subterfuges had to be devised.

TO DAVID HIGHAM

16th April 1953
(as from) The Boat House,
Laugharne,
Carmarthenshire

Dear David,

Thanks for everything you're doing. This is just to give you my American address: c/o J. M. Brinnin, 100 Memorial Drive, Cambridge,

Mass. And to say: will you, for the next five weeks—i.e. until I come back from the States—send whatever moneys come in to me (I mean the 50% of them) direct to Caitlin at Laugharne, and not to my bank? Please.

Yours ever,
Dylan

MSS.: David Higham Associates

It was not an enjoyable crossing.
The proposed trip to Ireland never took place.

TO THEODORE ROETHKE

Telephone: Laugharne (pronounced Larne) 68.

Boat House,
Laugharne,
Carmarthenshire,
Wales
15th June 1953

Dear Ted,

I missed, very much, seeing you in America, heard you were with your wife, you normal old thing, at Wystan's in Ischia, and hoped, a lot, I'd be back in time to see you hereabouts. I returned, on June the third, just missing the crowning horror, with a broken arm and rhubarb eyes and feeling like the Island of Bourbon—which, according to the Encyclopaedia Britannica of 1810, the only work of reference in Laugharne, has fpiders of the fize of a pigeon's egg, moft enormous bats, and a burning mountain which throws out vaft quantities of bitumen, fulphur, and other combuftible materials and makes all about ufelefs. And I got somehow back to our very small house in the grey perpetual rain with a party of Liverpool-Irishmen who insisted on carrying my crippled and fear-dumb mother (who lives nearby), down the dangerous cliff-path, dropping her every now and then with cries of 'Watch out, Ma', and who all fell asleep on the floor and then, fully clothed, went riding the childrens' rubber animals and birds on the rough sea: none was drowned, but one very nearly, and the village's opinion of him was, 'He wasn't fit to be on a swan'.

I had a good bad enough time in New York and in Cambridge too where I met some old and fond friends of yours whose names I never caught, suffered in Syracuse and Carolina, made them suffer in

Amherst, was called a Red in Washington but so was Mr. Taft, felt curiously thwarted in Bennington which talks of you with a reverent terror, Winterset, and signed an excellent paper-back book contract—copies in every drugstore, with a suggestive cover—for the story you read a bit of in New World Writing. That story is what I'm about to work on now. I haven't tried to write poetry since last October. Your new poems—written in Europe? not, I suppose, that it matters where —I think are beautiful. I'd like to hear you read them, and to go through them very carefully with you. Perhaps we can learn a little from each other, and anyway it will be very enjoyable if we learn and know nothing and only blunder loud about. I'll find out what I can about publishers in England for the Waking Poems, and we'll see Louis MacNeice together, a very good chap, about a rant at the BBC. And so: when can we meet? I shall be in London, taking up the revised version of the kind-of-play to the publishers, at the very beginning of July, and then have to come back, on July 6, to Llangollen in North Wales to report, for the Welsh BBC, on an International Eisteddfod there, which lasts until the 11th. I have a suggestion for after that. You said you were going on to Ireland after London. Caitlin, who comes from County Clare, and I want to go to Ireland, too. So, if I can raise enough money, shall we all go together? Laugharne is only about 30 miles from Fishguard from where the boats cross to Rosslare. And from Rosslare we could go into County Cork by train, eat and drink a bit in the West, and wind up in Dublin. Perhaps you and your nameless wife—my very best to her—would spend a day or two here on the way from London to Fishguard, before all setting off. Can we talk about this in London—if you can be in London anytime from July 1 to 5 or 6. If you can't, do write please. Ireland together would be wonderful, I hope.

Here—for any news & nonsense I have can keep until London, Laugharne, or/and Ireland—are two songs from the play, to fill up the page.

1st Song

Johnnie Crack and Flossie Snail
Kept their baby in a milking pail
Flossie Snail and Johnnie Crack
One would pull it out and one would put it back
O it's my turn now said Flossie Snail
To take the baby from the milking pail
And it's my turn now said Johnnie Crack
To smack it on the head and put it back

Johnnie Crack and Flossie Snail
Kept their baby in a milking pail
One would put it back and one would pull it out
And all it had to drink was ale and stout
For Johnnie Crack and Flossie Snail
Always used to say that stout and ale
Was good for a baby in a milking pail.

.   .   .   .

2nd Song

I loved a man whose name was Tom
He was strong as a bear and two yards long
I loved a man whose name was Dick
He was big as a barrel and three feet thick
And I loved a man whose name was Harry
Six feet tall and sweet as a cherry
But the one I loved most awake or asleep
Was little Willie Wee and he's six feet deep

Oh Tom Dick & Harry were three fine men
And I'll never have such loving again
But little Willy Wee was the man for me.

Now men from every parish round
Run after me and roll me on the ground
But whenever I love another man back
Johnnie from the hill or Sailing Jack
I always think as they do what they please
Of Tom Dick & Harry who were tall as trees
And most I think when I'm by their side
Of little Willie Wee who downed and died.

Oh, Tom Dick & Harry were three fine men
And I'll never have such loving again
But little Willy Wee who took me on his knee
Little Willy Weazel was the man for me.

Now when farmers' boys on the first fair day
Come down from the hills to drink and be gay
Before the sun sinks I'll lie there in their arms
For they're good bad boys from the lonely farms
But I always think as we tumble into bed
Of little Willy Wee who is dead dead dead.

405

Oh, Tom Dick & Harry were three fine men
And I'll never have such loving again
But little Willy Wee who took me on his knee
Little Willy Weazel was the man for me.

. . . .

From us both to you both,
Dylan

MSS.: Theodore Roethke Estate

Dylan broke his arm in America. 'Old Captain Oscar Cohen' is Oscar Williams who was, in fact, of Russo-Jewish origin.

TO JOHN MALCOLM BRINNIN

Laugharne,
16 June 1953

My dear John,

Just arrived back here, fractured and barmy, to torpor and rain and Ivy's dungeon, and I've nothing to tell you except a thousand thank-yous and how much I miss you. In spite of Milk fever, bonebreak, some nausea, Carolina and Richman, old Captain Oscar Cohen, I enjoyed myself an awful lot, especially in Cambridge & Boston. And hank your mother too for every kindness.

I haven't heard yet from Sarah Caldwell about the opera, and wrote to Stravinsky today, so I don't know yet any autumn plans. But there's an International Literary Spenderless Conference at Pittsburgh in October, to which I've been invited, and, though to hell with Conferences, I shall quite likely go there on the way (I hope) to California via (somehow) Memorial Drive: and with Caitlin too.

I'm going to start work tomorrow and shall revise Milk Wood for publication and broadcasting here. I'll also be seeing David Higham soon, and will get Milk Wood copyrighted as a play for public performance. Could you, then d'you think, do something, with Tom Brockway and with the woman of Wolfe & influence, whose name I've forgotten, about getting it done across the States? And then, after finishing 'In the Skin Trade', I want to begin on a new, and, in one sense, proper-er, play. About this I'll tell you in—is it?—August. Do

406

write to me, however briefly, though please not shortly; and could you let me know Sarah Caldwell's address at Boston University? The very best to Joe.

Ever,

Dylan

MSS.: John Malcolm Brinnin, Esq.

Dylan was excited and pleased, though also somewhat frightened, at the idea of writing a libretto for Igor Stravinsky.

Sarah Caldwell ran the Music Center, of Boston University, which was originally prepared to finance the writing of this opera, but which later withdrew their offer.

TO IGOR STRAVINSKY

The Boat House,

Laugharne,

Carmarthenshire,

Wales

16th June 1953

Dear Mr. Stravinsky,

I was so very glad to meet you for a little time, in Boston; and you and Mrs. Stravinsky couldn't have been kinder to me. I hope you get well very soon.

I haven't heard anything yet from Sarah Caldwell, but I've been thinking a lot about the opera and have a number of ideas—good, bad, and chaotic. As soon as I can get something down on paper, I should, if I may, love to send it to you. I broke my arm just before leaving New York the week before last, and can't write properly yet. It was only a little break, they tell me, but it cracked like a gun.

I should very much like—if you think you would still like me to work with you; and I'd be enormously honoured and excited to do that—to come to California in late September or early October. Would that be convenient? I hope so. And by that time, I hope too, to have some clearer ideas about a libretto.

Thank you again. And please give my regards to your wife and to Mr. Craft.

Yours sincerely,

Dylan Thomas

MSS.: Dr Igor Stravinsky

'The Hairies' was his nickname for the women who ran Caedmon, the record company that was making discs of Dylan reading his own and other poets' poems.

TO OSCAR WILLIAMS

Boat House,
Laugharne,
Carmarthenshire,
Wales
June 22 1953

Dear Oscar, Little dear Honourable Treasurer of mine, how are you? Did you discover Columbus well? and, give my best to Long Don Drummond the Potent Man? I missed you a lot my last days, and was Lizzed away to the plane alone. I almost liked the plane-ride, though; it was stormy and dangerous, and only my iron will kept the big bird up; lightning looked wonderful through the little eyeholes in its underbelly; the bar was open all the way from Newfoundland; and the woman next to me was stonedeaf so I spoke to her all the way, more wildly and more wildly as the plane lurched on through dark and lion-thunder and the fire-water yelled through my blood like Sioux, and she unheard all my delirium with a smile; and then the Red Indians scalped me; and then it was London, and my iron will brought the bird down, safely, with only one spine-cracking jar. And, queasy, purple, maggoty, scalped, I weak-wormed through festoons, bunting, flags, great roses, sad spangles, paste and tinsel, the million cardboard simpers and ogrish plaster statuettes of the nincompoop queen, I crawled as early as sin in the chilly weeping morning through the city's hushed hangover and all those miles of cock-deep orange-peel, nibbled sandwiches, broken bottles, discarded vests, vomit and condoms, lollipops, senile fish, blood, lips, old towels, teeth, turds, soiled blowing newspapers by the unread mountain, all the spatter and bloody gravy and giant mousemess that go to show how a loyal and phlegmatic people—'London can break it!'—enjoyed themselves like hell the day before. And, my God, wouldn't I have enjoyed it too! In the house where I stay in London, a party was still going on, at half-past seven in the wet, beige morning, that had started two nights before. Full of my news, of the latest American gossip from the intellectual underworld, of tall goings-on, of tiny victories and disasters, aching to gabble I found myself in a company of amiable, wrestling, maudlin, beatle-skulled men, semi-men, and many kinds of woman, who did not know or care I had been so far and wildly away but seemed to think I had been in the party all the whooping time. Sober, airsick, pancaked flat, I saw these intelligent old friends as a warren full of blockish stinkers, and sulked all morning over my warm beer as they clamoured and hiccupped, rolled rodgering down, fell gaily through windows, sang and splintered. And in the afternoon, I stood—I was the only one who could—alone and disillusioned among the snorers and the dead. They grunted all around me, or went soughing and green to their Maker. As the little murdered moles in the Scotch poem, like sma' Assyrians they lay. I was close to crying there, in the chaotic middle of anticlimax. It was all too sordid, Oh how I hated these recumbent Bohemians! Slowly, I went upstairs to bath. There was a man asleep in the bath. And tears ran down my cheeks. Two creatures stretched dead in my bed. And, now, the rain was boo-hooing too all over London.

P.S. I am sorry to add to this that by the end of the day I was happy as a pig in shit myself, and conducted the singing of hymns with my broken arm, and chased people and was caught, and wound up snug as a bugger in Rugby. Oh, my immortal soul, and oh, my tissues!

I returned to Laugharne ten days later; and now, in my left mind again, I shall begin to go on with the Adventures In the Skin-Trade. It is still raining here, just as when I left, but the sun hops in and out between the drizzles and fish skip in the sea and the old people are dying off like moths and our murderer goes around with an axe hanging by a string from his belt and white owls wheeze in the castle and there was a fight in the churchyard last night and I can hear now the cries of the village idiot being tortured by children in the Square and Aeron my daughter rides the waves proud on a rubber swan and Colm on a red duck and Ted Roethke is coming down in three weeks and we're going to Ireland together and Caitlin's brown as a berry from the bits of the sun through the West rain and I've revised 'Under Milk Wood' for an English publisher, adding many pages, and here comes the sun again and things, all said and done, all dead and gone, are just about liveable, praise bloody be!

I could find no silver belt, but, before leaving, commissioned some-one to search for and buy one and I know she will; so any day now, Gene will have it, with my love. I hope she is well again.

Thank you very much for the photographs of you, Cecil Scott, and me: we all look like vampires full of breakfast.

Did I see you before I recorded for the Hairies? I took your advice, and read only my poems on both sides of the disc. The Yeats I had no time to do—my own recording lasted all night long—but I will record when I return. I may be returning—though my Californian plans are still cloudy—in October. Another performance of Milk Wood has tentatively been dated for October 6 or 7, and I've been invited to an International Literary Conference at Pittsburgh a few days later. So I may see you quite soon, with Caitlin too, and see more of you, and clearer, than this last muddled time.

I am giving some radio readings of American poets in August, but cannot find the copy you gave me of your book of American Poetry. Could the publishers send me one, do you think? I do hope so: it is a fine book, and I should like it very much, and it will be useful.

And I would, a lot, appreciate Mrs. beautiful Adlai's last hundred dollars (minus expenses) as there are hundreds of debts to settle here. Could you, quickly?

The Murder of the Rosenbergs should make all men sick and mad.

Yours always.

Dylan

Caitlin sends her love.

Thank you everything you did for me, Oscar, during my stay, before & after, for the Mentor contract & countless kindnesses, and for being in New York and for being at all.

MSS.: Harvard

The McAlpines, with whom Dylan usually stayed when in London, had left some time before for Japan, where Bill McAlpine had a job with the British Council. The party described in a previous letter was, incidentally, not held in their house.

TO THEODORE ROETHKE

Telephone: Laugharne (pronounced Larne) 68.

Boat House,
Laugharne,
Carmarthenshire
17 July 1953

Dear Ted,

Thank you for your letter & enclosures. I liked the revision of the fine poem, and the other two poems, Squeeze & Dinky, are better, or nicer anyway, than Goethe.

I don't think damn it I'll be able to raise enough lovely to get to Ireland in the very near future—bills suddenly stormed in, and the Eisteddfod cost a tiny fortune and my health—but I'll try. I'll try all right.

I'm coming to London on Monday the 20th. I don't know where I'm staying yet, as where I stay isn't any more, but will you please leave a message at the Savage Club, 1, Carlton House Terrace, London, S.W.3.—the number's in the telephone book.

If you haven't found one yet, a pretty good hotel is the Royal Court, Sloane Square, Chelsea—but just a little stuffy.

The BBC Third Programme is longing for you—the word is the word of the old fat friend, John Davenport, I got hold of on the BBC —& we'll see him when we meet & fix up a torrential recording.

Hope this reaches you at the American Express.

I'm glad your wife was Beatrice O'Connell & is now Roethke. My wife was Caitlin Macnamara and is now unfortunate.

All the best to you both from both of us,

Dylan

MSS.: Theodore Roethke Estate

Ralph Wishart ('Ralph-the-Books') was a Swansea bookseller and one of Dylan's oldest friends.

'Dan' is Dr Daniel Jones, another very old friend.

TO RALPH WISHART

Boat House,
July 28 1953
Laugharne,
Carmarthenshire

Dear Ralph,

I'm really terribly sorry about the misunderstanding and you've every right to think I'm a dirty dog. Well, I am, if you like, a middle-aged dog with a dirty mind, but of course I was coming to see you, and still am, and always will, and the reason for my not coming in on Monday or afterwards is very simple. I was driven up from Laugharne on the day of that broadcast, arriving in good time—good time, that is, for a quick one in the King's Head—about seven o'clock in the evening. You were, of course, shut. After the broadcast was, to the relief of thousands, over, I was driven straight back to Laugharne— if you can call it straight, stopping about thirty times—and I haven't been to Swansea since.

I didn't write to explain, as perhaps I should, because I knew I was coming up to Swansea any time to call on the B.B.C. and I would be meeting you then. Now I'm coming up, for the first time since I saw you after my Llangollen visit, tomorrow, Thursday, to see D. J. T. V. Thomas. I'll drop in after lunch—with, I hope to God, a cheque.

How's Dan? I'll be seeing him too, I hope. Thanks for everything, & sorry again.

All the best,
Dylan

MSS.: Ralph Wishart, Esq.

John Ormond Thomas is a poet and journalist. Stewart Thomas is a Swansea solicitor who was looking after Dylan's legal affairs. D. J. Thomas ran the Swansea television studio. None was any relation of Dylan's.

TO DANIEL JONES

Laugharne,
Monday,
August 24 1953

Dear Dan,

Will you be in Swansea this week? John Ormond came down here, warbling and nut-fed, a few days ago, and said you were in Cardiff. If you aren't, and are home again, will you let me know quickly? I don't want to come to adanabandoned Swansea.

I owe you some money, and hope to give it to you when I see you.

I have to see T. V. D. J. Thomas in Swansea, and Aneirin, but will get that over quickly and then—Oh, to bask unasked in a Bass cask, etc!

Isn't life awful? Last week I hit Caitlin with a plate of beetroot, and I'm still bleeding. I can't finish a poem, or begin a story, I chew my nails down to my shoulders, pick three-legged horses with beautiful names, take my feet for grey walks, moulder in Brown's, go to bed as though to an office, read with envy of old lonely women who swig disinfectant by the pint, think about money, dismiss it as dirt, think about dirt.

Do write a postcard, if you're at home, or telephone Laugharne 68.

Ever,

Dylan

MSS.: Dr Daniel Jones

As the end approached it became necessary, in Dylan's mind, not only to circumvent his bank manager, but also David Higham as well.

TO E. F. BOZMAN

Boat House,

Laugharne,

Carmarthenshire

11th September 1953

Laugharne 68

Dear E. F. Bozman,

I was sorry I wasn't able to see you when I came to London last: I'd a very short time there—just for a little broadcast, and to see about my daughter's new school—and David Higham told me that, so far as he knew, there was nothing very urgent to discuss. I wanted to meet you anyway; and I do hope now we'll be able to lunch together before I go to the States early in October.

Well before I leave, I'll have finished the final corrections and amplifications of 'Under Milk Wood'. I think it's much better now— (it sounds as though it had been ill). One of the reasons I'm going to America is to take part in three public readings of it, with a professional cast, at the Poetry Center, New York. (The other, and main, reason is to go to California to begin work with Stravinsky on a new opera.) And, when I return some time in December, I hope that it can be given one or more reading-performances, most likely on a Sunday night, in London; with any luck, I'll be able to get firstrate Welsh actors to read it. Higham, in the meantime, and as soon as he has my complete version, will see to it that someone like Sherek has a chance of reading it with this in mind. 'Under Milk Wood' will also be broadcast next year, in full, and it should be possible to arrange this broadcast to happen about the same time as publication. I myself have good hopes altogether of the success of Milk Wood; and I'm <u>very very</u> grateful to you for taking it over.

About the <u>Book of Stories</u>—I suggest, tentatively, the title of 'Early One Morning', the title of one of the stories—I have reckoned out that there are now eleven of these, including a very recent one that will, I think, be appearing in next week's 'Listener'. And I want to write two or three more, still on a childhood theme, to complete the book. In spite of what you very rightly say about the 'rawness' of the other, and earlier, stories I sent you some time ago, I still think that one, and one alone, of these '<u>A Prospect of The Sea</u>' could well take its place in the volume. Perhaps, when you have the rest of the stories together, you would consider this again? (Though I may very well be completely wrong about it.) And, thinking back, <u>yes</u>, 'Early One Morning' does seem to me to be a good title.

Higham told me that you were prepared to consider again the short novel, '<u>Adventures In the Skin Trade</u>'. I'm so glad. When I come back from America, I intend to settle down & finish it. And, after that, another 'Play for Voices', using the same form as in Milk Wood.

Now to a much more difficult part of this letter. Straightaway, I just <u>must</u> say that I'm in money trouble again, and this time quite seriously again. And I'm wondering, and hoping terribly much, that somehow you can help me. I really do need help at this **very** moment. As perhaps you know, David Higham has taken over what I suppose I must call my 'financial affairs' in a very expert way. As well as seeing to my eldest children's school-fees—my daughter will be beginning boarding-school next week—he also keeps money aside for income-tax and allows me a sum per month for personal expenses. But I'm afraid that that sum isn't enough to pay tradesmen's accounts etc. and now I'm being pressed to pay at once some most urgent debts I have simply had to incur over recent months. I cannot ask Higham to help me with these: he is doing all he possibly can with the money at his disposal. And I do not know what on earth to do. I'm trying to put this down as simply and flatly as I can; but, really, I'm <u>sick</u> with anxiety, and find it terribly hard to work. What's particularly infuriating is, that I'm about to make quite a lot of money in the States. The Stravinsky libretto is, in itself, an assurance of that. (I hope one day you'll publish the libretto.) And I'm going to give a short series of very well paid commercial lectures—(I mean, by that, not to universities, as on my previous visits, but in townhalls & to large unacademic paying audiences. The lectures, incidentally, won't be lectures, but readings of poetry.) There money is, a lot of it, so near;

and here I am in the most awful position, owing to everyone here and the debts mounting every day nightmarishly. I can't say 'Stravinsky' to tradesmen, insurance, etc. etc. Oh Lord, I am in a mess.

Can you help? I don't know how. And really, I need help without Higham's—no, I can't say 'knowledge', that sounds like working behind his back; perhaps I mean his friendly superintendence. He thinks me extravagant, as perhaps I am. But my debts are all for unextravagant country living, & they've mounted up horribly. Have you any suggestions? Could Dent advance me any good sum on 'Milk Wood', or on 'Early One Morning'? Or could I somehow borrow money & pay it back from my American earnings in October & November? It's so hard for me to think. We haven't, now, even enough to take Aeronwy & Llewelyn to their schools next week; & it seems so silly; but the silliness is frightening in this remote place. Or in any place, I suppose, except that here nearly everyone is very poor: certainly, all my friends. Now I am beginning to gabble.

Can you write me, or ring me?

When I rang this afternoon, I felt too awkward to say anything. I couldn't even ask for your private address, which is what I had rung for. Forgive me. And for this letter.

I just realised: in one breath I talk of going to the States in a very few weeks, probably three weeks or less, & in the next breath say we cannot afford the trains to London. This sounds absurd. My American ticket is, of course, paid for by the Poetry Center, New York. But before I go, I have to clear up everything here & leave it (almost) sweet & smiling.

Yours,

Dylan Thomas

And I daren't look back over the last part of this letter in case I cross it all out in horrified embarrassment.

MSS.: Messrs Dent

This letter is undated and probably unfinished. It may have been written in 1952 or even 1951.

TO MADAME CAETANI

1953?

Dear Marguerite Caetani,

What can I say?

Why do I bind myself always into these imbecile grief-knots, blindfold my eyes with lies, wind my brass music around me, sew myself in a sack, weight it with guilt and pig-iron, then pitch me squealing to sea, so that time and time again I must wrestle out and unravel in a panic, like a seaslugged windy Houdini, and ooze and eel up wheezily, babbling and blowing black bubbles, from all the claws and bars and breasts of the mantrapping seabed?

Deep dark down there, where I chuck the sad sack of myself, in the slimy squid-rows of the sea there's such a weed-drift and clamour of old plankton drinkers, such a mockturtle gabble of wrecked convivial hydrographers tangled with polyps and blind prawns, such a riffraff of seabums in the spongy dives, so many jellyfish soakers jolly & joking in the smoke-blue basements, so many salty sea-damaged daughters stuffing their wounds with fishes, so many lightning midnight makers in the luminous noon of the abysmal sea, and such fond despair there, always there, that time and time again I cry to myself as I kick clear of the cling of my stuntman's sacking. 'Oh, one time the last time will come and I'll never struggle, I'll sway down here forever handcuffed and blindfold, sliding my woundaround music, my sack trailed in the slime, with all the rest of the self-destroyed escapologists in their cages, drowned in the sorrows they drown and in my piercing own, alone and one with the coarse and cosy damned seahorsey dead, weeping my tons.'

What can I tell you? Why did I bray my brassy nought to you from this boygreen briny dark? I see myself down and out on the sea's ape-blue bottom: a manacled rhetorician with a wet trombone, up to his blower in crabs.

Why must I parable my senseless silence? my one long trick? my last dumb flourish? It is enough that, by the wish I abominate, I savagely contrive to sink lashed and bandaged in a blind bag to those lewd affectionate raucous stinking cellars: no, I must blare my engulfment in pomp and fog, spout a nuisance of fountains like a bedwetting what in a blanket, and harangue all land-walkers as though it were their shame that I sought the sucking sea and cast myself out of their

416

sight to blast down to the dark. It is not enough to presume that once again I shall weave up pardoned, my wound din around me rusty, and waddle and gush along the land on my webbed sealegs as musical and wan and smug as an orpheus of the storm: no, I must first defeat any hope I might have if forgiveness by resubmerging the little arisen original monster in a porridge boiling of wrong words and make a song and dance and a mockpoem of all his fishy excuses.

The hell with him.

MSS.: Texas

No letter written during his last visit to America, where he arrived in New York on 20th October 1953, is known to me. It is probable that he wrote none, and that this cable to Mrs Stevenson is his last communication in writing.

CABLE TO MRS ELLEN STEVENSON

25th October 1953

DEAR ELLEN OSCAR WILLIAMS HAS TOLD ME THAT YOU WOULD LIKE ME TO PRESENT MY PLAY ENTITLED 'UNDER MILKWOOD' IN CHICAGO I SHALL BE DELIGHT-ED TO DO SO WITH OR WITHOUT CAST BUT NOT WITHOUT CASH SOME TIME BETWEEN NOVEMBER 12TH AND NOVEMBER 15TH ON MY WAY TO HOLLYWOOD WOULD YOU KINDLY GET IN TOUCH WITH MY MANAGER JOHN BRINNIN 100 MEMORIAL DRIVE FOR FULL DETAILS THANK YOU VERY MUCH LOOK FOR-WARD TO SEEING YOU WITH WARM REGARDS

DYLAN THOMAS

MSS.: Texas

He lapsed into a coma on the night of 4th–5th November and died on 9th November without ever regaining consciousness. His body was taken back from New York to Laugharne, and he is buried in Wales.

Index of Letters